# Point Lookout, Maryland

## The Largest Civil War Prison

Robert E. Crickenberger Jr.

Savas Beatie
California

First edition, first printing

Library of Congress Cataloging-in-Publication Data

Names: Crickenberger, Robert E., Jr., 1952- author
Title: Point Lookout, Maryland : The Largest Civil War Prison / by Robert E. Crickenberger, Jr.
Other titles: Largest Civil War prison
Description: El Dorado Hills, CA : Savas Beatie, [2025] | Includes bibliographical references and index. | Summary: "The name Point Lookout conjures images of suffering and despair, a notorious Federal prison camp where thousands of Confederate captives endured unimaginable hardships. Crickenberger reexamines Point Lookout with fresh eyes, peeling back layers of myth to reveal a more nuanced truth. He draws on extensive, previously unpublished research to explore the complex experiences of both guard and prisoner. From the camp's daily realities to its broader impact on the prisoner-of-war system, Crickenberger's scholarship, based on extensive primary accounts, illuminates Point Lookout's critical role in shaping not only the Civil War but also the future of American incarceration. A vital resource for historians and casual readers alike, this book uncovers an overlooked chapter of history with clarity, depth, and unflinching honesty"-- Provided by publisher.
Identifiers: LCCN 2025022662 | ISBN 9781611217551 hardcover | ISBN 9781611217568 ebook
Subjects: LCSH: Point Lookout Prison Camp for Confederates | Maryland--History--Civil War, 1861-1865--Prisoners and prisons | United States--History--Civil War, 1861-1865--Prisoners and prisons | Prisoners of war--Maryland--Point Lookout--History--19th century | Prisoners of war--Confederate States of America | Prisoners of war--United States--History--19th century
Classification: LCC E616.L8 C75 2025
LC record available at https://lccn.loc.gov/2025022662

SB
Savas Beatie
989 Governor Drive, Suite 101
El Dorado Hills, CA 95762
916-941-6896 / sales@savasbeatie.com / www.savasbeatie.com

All of our titles are available at special discount rates for bulk purchases in the United States. Contact us for information.

To my parents, Bob and Celeste

and

Daniel D. Harlan Crickenberger
Sergeant, Company G, 10th Virginia, Prisoner of War
Point Lookout, MD: May 14–July 28, 1864
Elmira, NY: July 31, 1864–June 21, 1865

# TABLE OF CONTENTS

# LIST OF MAPS



*Photos have been placed throughout the text for the convenience of the reader.*

# Acknowledgments

No work of this size and depth is done alone. Writing this book has been a journey that has taken over forty years. It was a challenge to undertake something that I wasn't certain I had the courage to do, but I felt it had to be done. I knew through personal experience that there was more to Point Lookout than what was currently being presented.

It has been an interesting story that has taken me to different states investigating many leads and conducting research in many collections and archives. This also afforded opportunities to cross paths with many interesting people whose ancestors experienced life at Point Lookout, both Blue and Gray. Several shared their collections of artifacts and personal archives that were invaluable in my research.

I was told many times that research is never ending. This has proven true. It continues today with meeting descendants of both prisoners and guards and the discovery of new materials that describe the horrors of prison life as experienced by those who were there. Fortunately, this is not the end. I had the honor of meeting with academics who share the same depth of interest in the Civil War as I do. I gained a great deal from their experiences as well as their invaluable advice. I was fortunate to meet others who were as ardent about Civil War research as I am. Many of them helped me to see prisoner stories in new and innovative ways.

First of all, I want to recognize and thank retired Maryland Park Service rangers Gerald R. Sword and Donnie Hammett, both of whom were influential during my many early visits to Point Lookout in 1977. With their encouragement and support, I began working with them as a volunteer in early 1978. Little did any of us know what seed they had planted and to what lengths our enthusiasm for the preservation of Point Lookout would lead. I will be eternally grateful for our first visit.

I would also like to express gratitude to Mr. Ross Kimmel, supervisor of Cultural Resources Management, Maryland Park Service (retired). His friendship and support over many years in every project that I have undertaken at Point Lookout, including this book, would not have come to fruition without his encouragement. Ross has been a champion of historical preservation and interpretation within the Maryland Park Service and has been a great supporter of the Friends of Point Lookout in our preservation efforts at Point Lookout over many years.

This project would never have gotten off the ground without the help and encouragement of a very long list of friends who wanted to see this project completed as much as I. I want to single out one particular supporter, critic, and one who refused to let me put this project aside when the task seemed overwhelming. I am most grateful to have had the honor and pleasure to work with as friend, historian, and mentor, Kendall Mattern. As I wavered at times and felt that I was not capable of such a task, he did not let me falter and stayed the course. The rewrites were many but I will always be grateful for his support and allowing me the benefit of his knowledge. I want to thank my niece, Melissa Murray, for her encouragement, endless patience, and editing skills. Deep thanks also to one of the most accomplished and tenacious researchers that I have ever had the pleasure to meet and work with, Kimberly Thompson, who always welcomed the challenge to dive into the subregions of the National Archives and the Library of Congress.

Over the years, I have been blessed to have had the opportunity to work with the greatest group of friends and colleagues at Point Lookout. Many have been supportive of this project during its production and have taken the time to read parts of the manuscript, offering suggestions and worthy criticisms. Not only have they been supportive in this work, but they have been most dedicated to Point Lookout in the interpretation and preservation of the historic site. I offer my profound thanks to: Kathy Kleiman, Patrick Harrington, David Ferraro, Ronald Sweeney, Duane Whitlock, James Abels, Lawrence Sangi, James Madden, Tim Martin, Kendall Mattern Sr., and the many other dedicated individuals who make up the Friends of Point Lookout. A special thanks is given to author and friend Marc Storch, for sharing his research and vast knowledge of Wisconsin in the Civil War as well.

Gratitude and recognition should also be given to the dedicated Maryland Park Service staff (both past and present) at Point Lookout, particularly Maryland Park rangers Jonas Williams, Samuel Behrens, and George Kahl, who not only gave of their time to read the manuscript, but who also walked the swamps and fields of Point Lookout with me, seeking sites and locations referred to in the many works of the era's participants. Their input and suggestions have been most helpful and appreciated in the completion of this book.

You never know to whom research will lead. I had the utmost pleasure to meet some of the greatest scholars of Civil War history, beginning with Dr. Allen C. Guelzo. Professor of Humanities, The Hamilton School of Classical and Civic Education, University of Florida; Mr. Josh Grosek, Math Professor, College of Southern Maryland; Dr. John M. Coski, Historian, The American Civil War Museum, Richmond, Virginia; and Robert Zeller, President, Center for Civil War Photography.

I am also grateful for the assistance of Mr. Brian Cheesboro formerly of the National Archives and Records Administration in Washington, D.C.; McKenzie Lemhouse and Todd Hoppcock, Library Specialists, South Caroliniana Library, University of South Carolina; the Staff of the Charleston Historical Society, Charleston, South Carolina; the Staff of the William H. Owens Museum, University of South Dakota; Mr. Eric Barnes, Environmental Systems Operator, Maryland Environmental Service; Mr. Frank "Frankie" Tippett and fellow staff of the St. Mary's County Historical Society (where I spent many hours poring over records and files with Mr. Tippett. We'll miss you, Frankie); Terry Reimer, Director of Research, National Museum of Civil War Medicine; Mr. Jordon Steele, Hodson Curator of the University Archives, Sheridan Libraries, Johns Hopkins University, Baltimore, Maryland; and the most helpful staff at the University of Maryland, University Libraries, Archival Collection, Manuscript Collection, Special Collections and University Archives section.

I am ever grateful for the chance meeting with Mr. and Mrs. Donald Blaus at Point Lookout, who shared the letters of their ancestor, Lt. Erastus W. Everson, 20th Veteran Reserve Corps, who spent over a year at Point Lookout during the war. The information they offered was most helpful in telling the story from the perspective of the Union guards during one of the most pivotal periods of Point Lookout prison.

I would be remiss if I did not recognize those who made this project a reality. I am most grateful to Mr. Theodore P. Savas of Savas Beatie Publishing for recognizing the importance of this work and providing the opportunity for its publication. His guidance and insight were invaluable and always appreciated by this author. Deep thanks are also due to Veronica Kane, Sarah Closson, and Sarah Keeney of Savas Beatie for their assistance throughout the publishing process. Veronica, a very patient and understanding production manager, guided this novice writer through the many stages of production to completion. I cannot thank her enough. I also wish to express my gratitude to editor Dave Snyder, whose professional and insightful editing produced a concise and professional manuscript; to cartographer Edward Alexander, who transformed my crude, hand-drawn sketches into polished maps of Point Lookout; and to Derrick Lindow, who took on the tedious task of indexing the book. I remain deeply indebted to all of them for their dedication to this unique work.

As I give thanks and credit to so many for their support and encouragement, I must also give the utmost recognition and gratitude to my parents, and to my wife and children, not only for their love and understanding over the many years I have spent in this work, but for tolerating my obsession with Point Lookout for what seems to have been an eternity. It has taken a great deal of dedication to the subject, including several years of research and road trips to write this book, but without them and their support, none of this would have been accomplished.

# Foreword

I first met Bob Crickenberger at a living history event held at the Spangler's Spring area of Gettysburg National Battlefield Park in the spring of 2000. At that time, I was looking for a new progressive Civil War group to join, one that combined the authentic portrayal of Union soldiers with an in-depth history of the units we were representing on any given Civil War battlefield. Waking up on the hard ground at Spangler's Spring on the Sunday morning of that weekend and following a busy day of demos we presented all day Saturday, I heard Bob call, "It's time for 'Sunday Services boys!" Only partially awake, I followed the rest of the unit of "Company C" halfway up Culp's Hill and deposited myself on the ground, along with the rest of the men by one of the many unit monuments found on Culp's. Bob proceeded to pull book after book from his camp sack, and read from unit memoirs and secondary sources, providing us all with a deep dive into the combat proceedings for the men whom we were portraying that weekend. Right then and there I was hooked. I knew I had found a unit that took its history very seriously, led by a man who understood what history was all about.

Since that event, now more than twenty years ago, Bob and I have developed a deep and abiding friendship. Along the way I have accompanied him on many more living history weekends throughout the Eastern Theater of the war, on many private trips to various museums and battlefields, and spent countless hours just "talking history." I taught a Civil War elective to seniors in high school for many years, and I had come to know and understand a great deal about those calamitous years. But what Bob knows and understands about the events of 1861–1865 is on a level of depth and sophistication that I will never attain. There has never been a conversation between us over all these years when Bob has not taught me something new regarding the Civil War, especially when it comes to Point Lookout prison camp in southern Maryland. Other than all of the time Bob has spent with his family "up the road" at Chesapeake Beach, Bob has "lived" at Point Lookout. Bob truly lives, eats, and sleeps history.

When we first met, I knew that Bob wanted to write a definitive history of the prisoner-of-war camp at the Point, and I have watched with admiration for how conscientious and relentless he has been in seeking out materials in support of his book. Bob's research is both complete and impeccably balanced, taking into consideration the firsthand records and views of both the North and the South. As a result, Bob has produced the definitive history of Point Lookout prisoner-of-war camp that will stand the test of time.

Congratulations, my friend,

Kendall Mattern

# Preface

Prisoners of war expect humane treatment by their captors while waiting for exchange. Ideal as this may sound, seldom has this ever been the case. In earlier wars, priority was placed on the exchange of prisoners, but they could be further subjected to ransom, enlistment into the army of their enemy, parole, or even suffer some form of retaliation. According to Emmerich de Vattel's internationally recognized *Law of Nations*, acts of war committed by the members of the armed forces of belligerents are not considered criminal acts. Therefore, soldiers that are captured are not liable to be tried as criminals for committing recognized acts of war. Instead, they become prisoners of war. Receiving prisoner of war status, they expect to receive *non-punitive* detention and protection.[1]

More Americans experienced internment as a prisoner of war in the Civil War until World War II. The American experience had been that policies and regulations that governed the treatment of prisoners and their care continued to remain flexible, tenuous, and non-binding from the time of the American Revolution until the first shots were fired upon Fort Sumter. With the advent of the Civil War, it was evident that neither belligerent had learned the lessons of the previous three wars when it came to the care and treatment of prisoners of war.[2]

The *United States Army Regulations of 1861 (revised in 1863)* addressed the subject of the prisoner of war in three diminutive articles that stated that prisoners would be disarmed, receive subsistence, then sent to the rear to be paroled and

1 Stephen C. Neff, *Justice in Blue and Gray: A Legal History of the Civil War* (Cambridge, MA, 2010), 20–24.

2 Alan Marsh, "POWs in American History: A Synopsis," National Park Service, https://www.nps.gov/ande/learn/historyculture/pow_synopsis.htm; Charles W. Sanders, *While in the Hands of the Enemy: Military Prisons of the Civil War* (Baton Rouge, LA, 2017), 25–26.

exchanged based on the orders (if any) of the "General commanding-in-chief, under the instructions of the government." From the outset, the caring for prisoners was seldom a priority of either government. The obvious action to take was to exchange prisoners as soon as possible. It would take a degree of recognition of the legitimacy of the Southern belligerent by the Lincoln administration to be governed by the *Law of Nations* regarding prisoners. Was it a war between belligerents, a territorial war, or a rebellion of states against the national government? Initially, neither regarded the conflict as a civil war.[3]

The eventual Dix-Hill Exchange cartel of 1862 (named for its first exchange commissioners, Union Gen. John Dix, and Confederate Gen. Daniel H. Hill) stated that prisoners were to be paroled if not exchanged within ten days of their capture. Due to the initial success of the cartel, those prisons in operation were basically void of prisoners by mid-1862. However, by mid-1863, the cartel began to have its problems with prisoner exchange because of captured Black Union soldiers. This would cause a major slowdown to any further exchanges. It became evident that neither government had anticipated the possibility of a breakdown of negotiations and a resulting accumulation of prisoners by both sides. As a result of the breakdown of the cartel arrangement, prison populations began rapidly to increase. Neither government was prepared to supply care, protection, and security for so many prisoners for such a prolonged period. Unprecedented hardships and suffering in both prison systems resulted.[4]

Due to the failure of negotiations, prisoners began languishing in camps for extended periods. They suffered from conditions that resulted from acts of retaliation and the politics of government officials, much like American prisoners had during the Revolutionary War and the War of 1812. The Federal government reinstated the position of commissary general of prisoners in 1861. The United States Army Regulations of that year contained nine articles outlining the duties of the commissary general of prisoners. Along with these guidelines, the appointed officer was expected to conduct business as directed by the administration. As the Civil War developed into a prolonged conflict, the need for clearly defined regulations governing the treatment of prisoners of war became paramount.[5]

3 Revised United State Army Regulations of 1861, Fed. Reg. (1863); Neff, *Justice in Blue and Gray*, 29.

4 United States War Department, *War of the Rebellion: Official Records of the Union and Confederate Armies* (Washington, D.C.: United States Department of War, 1880), Series 2 vol. 5:306–307. Hereafter cited as "*OR.*"

5 United States Department of the Army, "Article IV," in *Revised United State Army Regulations of 1861. With an Appendix Containing the Changes and Laws Affecting Army Regulations and Articles of War to June 25, 1863* (Washington D.C., 1863), 11–12.

Lincoln, of course, refused to recognize the legitimacy of the so-called Confederate states. There was some discussion within Lincoln's cabinet at the beginning of the war (especially at the prompting of Secretary of the Treasury Salmon Chase) as to whether granting prisoner-of-war status to captured Confederate was tantamount to legal recognition. Eventually, the Lincoln administration agreed to grant prisoner-of-war status, but as a matter of concession rather than as a legal right. Lincoln's continued refusal to recognize any aspect of the rebellious Confederacy would remain unchanged throughout the remainder of the war.[6]

As the Lincoln administration soon discovered, the acknowledgment of the status of prisoners of war would be one more hurdle to overcome, along with what to do with the mounting prisoner of war population. Issues concerning their treatment remained unresolved as hundreds of prisoners quickly grew into thousands. Without specific regulations, their treatment continued to remain open to interpretation between the two governments, influenced by conditions not specifically addressed by antiquated international laws.

During the mid-1800's, no new progressive or modern code emerged to provide answers or fill in the gaps left by earlier customs regarding prisoner treatment. Even though the Federal government claimed to be guided by the internationally recognized *Law of Nations* in the conduct of war, Lincoln considered these laws invalid, in some cases, specifically when it involved the treatment of prisoners (even though he would quote the same laws to justify later legislative actions). In April 1863, Maj. Gen. Henry Halleck (then general-in-chief of the armies of the United States) recognized the necessity to produce a succinct, yet precise, updated version of the laws of war to be followed by U.S. armies in the field.[7]

To accomplish this, Halleck renewed his acquaintance with renowned German international lawyer and professor, Franz Lieber. Lieber, assisted by an appointed committee of military and government officials, was commissioned by the president to create and publish regulations that were issued to the U.S. services, in the form of General Order Number 100, (otherwise known as the *Lieber Code*). John F. Witt stated that Lieber "aimed to write a distillation for the laws of war for the age of democratic nations and mass armies" that covered a wide assemblage of previously unanswered questions and procedures regarding the conduct of war. Even though Lieber's code was issued as a general order to the Union Army, it was

6 Dr. Allen C. Guelzo, e-mail interview by Robert E. Crickenberger, Jr., Chesapeake Beach, MD, June 26, 2021.

7 Emer de Vattel, Bela Kapossy, and Richard Whatmore, *The Law of Nations, Or, Principles of the Law of Nature, Applied to the Conduct and Affairs of Nations and Sovereigns, with Three Early Essays on the Origin and Nature of Natural Law and on Luxury* (1758; repr. Indianapolis, IN, 2008); Doris Kearns Goodwin, *Team of Rivals: The Political Genius of Abraham Lincoln* (New York, 2005), 550.

basically regarded as a set of guidelines and referred to as a "moral cloak" for how the Union would wage war for the duration. Prison camp commanders would regard the *Lieber Code* in this same way.[8]

The 33 articles of Section III of the *Lieber Code* specify the basic principles pertaining to the treatment of prisoners of war. The foundations of these articles are rooted within the law of war and the *Law of Nations* as they were influenced by the earlier European conflicts of the 18th century. The more advanced *Lieber Code* continued where the earlier customs left off. Even though the *Lieber Code* specifically states that a prisoner is due wholesome food and attention to medical needs, other factors needed for prisoner maintenance, such as security, shelter, and clothing, are not mentioned. These items were assumed and expected to be automatically provided to enlisted prisoners based on the *Law of Nations*. In accordance with these customs, the War Department reactivated the post of commissary general of prisoners in 1861 to administer prisons and maintain Rebel prisoners of war.[9]

The significance of the *Lieber Code*, particularly in the eyes of the global powers, was that the Lincoln administration would be the first government to issue such advanced regulations to its armies while at war and active in the field. Since the *Lieber Code* was considered a restatement of existing laws of war rather than new legislation, Congressional approval was not necessary, and the code immediately went into effect upon approval by the president.[10]

The accumulation of prisoners created several challenges for both Union and Confederate officials. Due to the suspension of the Dix-Hill Cartel and the further lack of cooperation by either government regarding exchanges, government-owned facilities such as forts, penitentiaries, and training camps rapidly filled. Fort Lafayette, in New York harbor, had its casemates filled with prisoners, practically rendering the fort defenseless. Prisoner housing became such a problem in early 1862 that Federal authorities resorted to housing Confederate prisoners in prison ships anchored in the Mississippi River in St. Louis, Missouri. As these available sites became exhausted, the need for additional new prisoner camps became apparent. Faced with the limited number of facilities available for prisons in 1863, the War Department ordered the creation of additional prison camps, beginning

8 *OR* 3:3/148–164; John Fabian Witt, *Lincoln's Code: The Laws of War in American History* (New York, 2013), 231–232, 252.

9 T. Cole Jones, *Captives of Liberty: Prisoners of War and the Politics of Vengeance in the American Revolution* (Philadelphia, 2020), 16.

10 Thomas Erskine Holland, *The Laws of War on Land* (London, 1908), 71; Neff, *Justice in Blue and Gray*, 57.

with Point Lookout. These new prison camps were expeditiously established and became part of a second wave of camps created to answer the growing need. The massive camps at Rock Island, Illinois (December 1863) and Elmira, New York (July 1864), then others, would soon follow.[11]

The prison camp at Point Lookout, Maryland (named Camp Hoffman by the prison administration, but commonly referred to as Point Lookout), was designated, initially, to hold 5,000 prisoners with the capability to expand by an additional 5,000. It was a vast, open field that would become a 30-acre prison camp surrounded by a 12-foot wooden stockade wall, crowned with a catwalk for guards. Its composition featured 10 divisional streets, nine mess halls, a sutler shop, and a post office, in addition to other support offices. Due to the eventual overcrowding of the stockade, the footprint of the prison would change twice to accommodate the ever-expanding population, forcing an enlargement of the prison within three months. Later, the prison would expand from the original 38 acres to 45 with the inclusion of the adjacent seven-acre officer's stockade and parole camp, making Point Lookout the largest prisoner of war camp during the war. (The prisons constructed at Point Lookout; Hart's Island, New York; Camp Butler, Newport News, Virginia; Johnsons' Island, Ohio; and Rock Island, Illinois, were the few prisons constructed whose sole purpose was to incarcerate prisoners of war).

Over 214,000 Southerners were confined in prisons and camps during the Civil War. The prison population at Point Lookout would exceed its designated population of 10,000 inmates in a matter of a few months after opening. Its peak population would surpass 22,000 prisoners during April 1865. The final accounting submitted in August 1865 would reveal that over 52,000 prisoners had passed through the prison gate during its two-year existence. Each state of the Confederacy was represented not only by the soldiery, but by members of the Confederate States Navy and over 190 civilians (a number which included seven women) and several Black men. These numbers also included citizens of several countries including England, Canada, Ireland, Scotland, and Germany.[12]

Almost two years to the month after Point Lookout was opened, it was shut down and its books closed. By 1867, most of the government buildings and materials that were not sold at public auction were dismantled by the Quartermaster Department and returned to the inventory of its departmental depots in

11 *OR* 3/2:291–292, 327–328.

12 William B. Hesseltine, *Civil War Prisons* (Kent, OH, 1962), 1; DeAnne Blanton and Lauren M. Cook, *They Fought like Demons: Women Soldiers in the American Civil War* (New York, 2003), 76, 86.

Washington and Baltimore. Hammond General Hospital at Point Lookout would flourish for another year as an asylum for wounded and sick soldiers and sailors.

Point Lookout's remote location, however, did not prevent its inclusion in newly created, innovative, policies and legislation designed to accelerate the Northern war effort. One of the most important pieces of legislation, passed in early 1863, permitted the recruitment of Black males, both Freedmen and former slaves, into the Union Army. As a result, Federal forces received thousands of Black males into their ranks that were soon seeing combat during Grant's Overland campaign.

This was followed by the creation of the Invalid Corps (Veteran Reserve Corps) a new branch consisting of men no longer fit to serve as frontline soldiers but who could still serve in noncombatant roles such as prison guards. This was followed by the creation of the U.S. Volunteers whose soldiers were once prisoners of war held at Point Lookout (two regiments would be mustered from Point Lookout). Once these new policies and organizations reached southern Maryland, they would impact the everyday lives of both the Southern prisoners and Union guards at Point Lookout.

Another new program would find its way to Point Lookout called the National Reburial Program. The precursor to this program was in progress during the late war but was formerly established by war's end and would continue for another couple of years. This program would recover and identify the various cemeteries at Point Lookout, further affecting the status of Point Lookout during the postwar years of Reconstruction.

Fortunately for the latter-day researcher and students of the Civil War, thousands of those imprisoned at Point Lookout produced a litany of personal records of their lives as prisoners. These accounts provide searing eye-witness descriptions of prisoner experience, survival, and death. Their memories of prison life add an essential human component to a history that too often focuses on battles, campaigns, tactics, and the outsized personalities of high officials.

My family lineage includes my ancestor, Johann Frederick Kruckeberg, who was a Hessian soldier captured on December 26, 1776, at the battle of Trenton. Fortunately, he remained in the United States. Since that time, several Crickenberger's have served, including during the War of 1812 and in the Civil War for the Confederate Army. My paternal grandfather served in the U.S. Army during World War I. My father served in the U.S. Navy during World War II and in the U.S. Marine Corps during the Korean and Vietnam wars. I served in the navy during the Vietnam War, where our family service ends.

My personal interest in Point Lookout began in January 1978 after discovering that Sgt. Daniel D. Crickenberger, Company G, 10th Virginia, had been held there as a prisoner of war. Daniel was one of 11 related Crickenberger's who fought for the Confederacy. Daniel was captured on May 12, 1864, at the battle of Spotsylvania Courthouse, arriving at Point Lookout on May 14 by way of Belle Plain, Virginia (a massive holding area for captured Confederate soldiers during the war). He would remain at Point Lookout for approximately three months after which he was transferred in July 1864 to Elmira, New York, remaining there until his release in July 1865. It did not take long for a review of existing histories regarding Point Lookout, along with my research, to determine that a new study of Point Lookout was justified. Existing studies of this southern Maryland prisoner of war camp have relied upon too many postwar memoirs and diaries which often contain significant biases and faded memories, distorting the debate over responsibility for the conditions suffered by the prisoners at Point Lookout.

The primary purpose of this book is to clarify the record by the inclusion of newly uncovered information pertaining to what took place at Point Lookout, revealing the significant role that the camp played in the prisoner of war system. I wrote this book in the hopes that it would spark increased interest in the subject of Civil War prisons for the specialist and the general reader both. This book is the result of years of research and dedication to the preservation of Point Lookout and its memory. I am further indebted to the historians who preceded me with their research into this endlessly fascinating prison site. They provided me with the foundation for this study of how and why the prison camp evolved, and how it impacted the lives of so many thousands of Confederate prisoners, Federal guards, civilians, prison administrators, and family members.

# Chapter 1

# The Prison Camp at Point Lookout

Before the bombardment of Fort Sumter in April 1861, properties and stations manned by United States forces in the South were either surrendered to, or captured by, the newly organized Confederate government. These seizures produced the first prisoners of war even before the first land battles had been fought between the United States and the Confederacy. Over the course of the war, approximately 409,608 soldiers—about one out of every seven who served—surrendered themselves or were captured in battle. Most non-combatants were incarcerated for engaging in covert operations or for political reasons.

Prisoners of war could be held for weeks, months, or in some cases more than a year. Thousands suffered in debilitating conditions, and many continued to experience lasting effects in the post-war years. Of those captured, more than 214,000 were Confederates, of whom approximately 26,000 died while imprisoned. The number who later died because of the lasting effects of imprisonment cannot be calculated. From the outset of the war, the care of prisoners and the establishment of adequate facilities were not considered critical by either government as contributing to victory. In the early months, captives expected to be treated humanely under the assumption that they would be paroled and exchanged quickly, since many believed the war would be short-lived. Neither government was prepared for the large number of prisoners produced by extended campaigns.[1]

After hostilities commenced in mid-1861, Federal authorities acknowledged the possibility that the conflict might last longer than first anticipated.

1 Charles W. Sanders Jr., *While in the Hands of the Enemy: Military Prisons of the Civil War* (Baton Rouge, 2015), 1.

Quartermaster General Montgomery Meigs
*Library of Congress*

Quartermaster General Montgomery C. Meigs advised Secretary of War Simon Cameron to appoint an officer as commissary general of prisoners to manage the growing number of captives. The post was reactivated on October 7, 1861, with the officer designated, according to U. S. Army regulations, to serve directly under the quartermaster general. Cameron selected Lt. Col. William Hoffman of the 8th U.S. Infantry, who at the time had recently been paroled and was awaiting exchange (he was formally exchanged on August 27, 1862). With Cameron's approval, Meigs ordered Hoffman to fill the post.[2]

Hoffman was displeased with his appointment to a noncombatant position about which he knew very little. He soon lodged a protest, side-stepping Meigs, by writing directly to the secretary of war to express his dissatisfaction. Despite Hoffman's objections, Meigs secured him for the post. Meigs formalized the appointment with Special Order No. 284 on October 23, 1861, assigning Hoffman to the office and placing him directly under the quartermaster general in accordance with regulations.[3]

On January 13, 1862, Edwin Stanton replaced Simon Cameron as secretary of war. Stanton insisted that Hoffman report directly to him rather than to Meigs. On June 17, 1862, the adjutant general issued General Order No. 67 announcing Hoffman's appointment and outlining his authority, duties, and responsibilities as commissary general of prisoners, answerable only to the secretary of war. Hoffman established uniformity in the department regarding the management of prisons, reports, and inspections. He soon discovered, however, that his rules and regulations were often interpreted at the discretion of prison commanding officers. This issue was rectified with General Order No. 190, issued May 3,

2 Leslie Gene Hunter, "Warden for the Union: General William Hoffman (1807–1884)" (PhD diss., University of Arizona, 1971), 2.

3 Sanders, *While in the Hands*, 68–69; *OR* 3/2:121.

Colonel William Hoffman,
Commissary General of Prisoners
*Library of Congress*

1864, by Secretary of War Stanton. The order expanded Hoffman's authority over prison camps and their commanding officers in all matters. It further stipulated that Hoffman served under the direction of the secretary of war and answered directly to him, which meant that any order from Hoffman carried the authority of Stanton.[4]

Meigs and Hoffman were part of the antebellum United States Army, which in 1861 numbered approximately 16,000 men in 198 companies stationed throughout the United States and its territories. It was an army that operated on a spartan budget, forcing officers to restrict expenditures and employ creative means to provide equipment and supplies for their men. They functioned within a strict accounting system under the constant threat of fraud investigation. As a result, officers discovered that by converting a portion of the funds allotted for rations, they could generate a budgetary surplus, which allowed them to purchase and substitute other needed items. Even after the commencement of hostilities, this frugal budgeting remained a part of U.S. military culture, and Hoffman both used and encouraged this method among his subordinates as commissary general of prisoners. He was eventually responsible for 32 active prison camps and several parole camps for exchanged Union prisoners.[5]

Hoffman's abstemious spending proved to be more extensive and effective than Meigs had anticipated. Their prewar habits of frugality remained evident in

4 *OR* 4/2:4, 30; Revised United State Army Regulations of 1861, Fed. Reg. (1863), Articles 121, 253; *OR* 7/2:105–108

5 Curtis S. King, William Glenn Robertson, and Steven E. Clay, *Staff Ride Handbook for the Overland Campaign, Virginia, 4 May to 15 June 1864: A Study in Operational-level Command* (Fort Leavenworth, KS, 2006), 1; Hunter, "Warden for the Union," 231.

the establishment, command organization, and daily operations of prisons and prison sites.[6]

## The Rising Number of Prisoners and the Establishment of Point Lookout

By mid-1863, the Lincoln administration determined that the war was no closer to conclusion than it had been during the previous two years of fighting. Lincoln soon transformed his administration's conduct of the conflict, abandoning what he described as the "rose-water approach" taken by his generals for a more aggressive strategy. The results of this shift did not become evident until early 1864, when the newly promoted army commander, Lt. Gen. Ulysses S. Grant, began conducting vigorous campaigns on multiple fronts. Grant's aggressive battlefield offensives strained Confederate resources beyond their capacity to reinforce armies, slowly exhausting the Confederacy's limited manpower. In doing so, the sustained northern pressure produced an unprecedented number of prisoners.[7]

Prior to Grant's assumption of command, the prisoner exchange system known as the Dix-Hill Cartel, the prisoner exchange agreement negotiated between the two governments, began to collapse over the legitimate status of captured Black soldiers, who were then being recruited into the U.S. Army and Navy. The resulting suspension of exchanges created an influx of prisoners for both sides, with camps quickly reaching their intended capacities. The Lincoln administration recognized that halting the prisoner exchanges would deprive the South of much-needed manpower. Thus, prisoner populations in northern facilities continued to grow. This situation worsened after the simultaneous Union victories at Vicksburg and Gettysburg in July 1863, which added an even greater number of captives.

It soon became clear that prisoners of war constituted something like a parallel army that each government was responsible to maintain. The care and upkeep of prisoners-imposed burdens on both governments, especially as additional resources became necessary. This strain was particularly severe for the Confederacy, which struggled to provide for its forces in the field. Denying care to prisoners was politically fraught for both governments, but especially for the South as it sought foreign recognition and legitimacy. According to the provisions of the *Lieber Code* (General Orders No. 100) issued by the United States in April

6 Sanders, *While in the Hands*, 70–71, 90.

7 John Fabian Witt, *Lincoln's Code: The Laws of War in American History* (New York, 2012), 2.

1863, prisoners of war were to be protected by their captors and were entitled to wholesome food and medical attention when needed.[8]

Prison sites were seldom suitable for confining human beings for extended periods. Facilities were hastily organized and insufficiently planned by both governments. The prevailing assumption was that sites would be used only for short-term confinement, with little consideration given to the possibility of a prolonged war. Locations were selected primarily for convenience and expediency, less for long-term feasibility as prisons. Often, the buildings chosen were vacant and had previously served industrial or commercial purposes. By the end of the war, approximately 180 locations and structures were used as prisons (98 Union and 83 Confederate), of which 32 Union and 34 Confederate camps were designated major prisons in the North and South, respectively.[9]

The rapidly growing prisoner population created significant challenges for both the Union and Confederate administrations. Due to increasing battlefield captures and the absence of cooperation between the governments in exchanging prisoners, numbers began to exceed what Union officials had originally anticipated. Existing government-owned facilities such as masonry forts, penitentiaries, and former training camps found themselves rapidly filling to capacity.

As existing prison sites became fully occupied, the need for additional camps grew urgent. In response, the War Department issued orders in 1863 for the expedited establishment of new prison facilities designed to accommodate the growing number of prisoners. Within General Order No. 190, dated May 3, 1864—which also established the authority of the commissary general of prisoners—seven prisons were designated principal prison camps. Point Lookout was named first among these principal prisons, reflecting its status as the largest and most significant Union prison camp. (Point Lookout was also referred to as a "depot," or "station", meaning that imprisonment was intended to be temporary, with the expectation of transferring prisoners farther north.)[10]

## Point Lookout (Camp Hoffman)

In the summer of 1857, William Cost Johnson had purchased 400 acres at Point Lookout from William Taylor with the intention of establishing a seaside resort. For a few years Johnson operated the resort, which included more than 100

8 *OR* 3/3:156–157, (Art. 76/79.)

9 Lonnie R. Speer, *Portals to Hell: Military Prisons of the Civil War* (Mechanicsburg, PA, 1997), 323–339.

10 *OR* 7/2:106.

cottages leased to subscribers under 20-year renewable agreements and a small multi-story hotel. With the onset of war, business at the resort declined sharply. To recoup his losses, Johnson sold the property to William Allen, an architect and builder from Baltimore. During the war, much of the land was leased by the Federal government for military purposes, including the establishment of Hammond General Hospital and Camp Hoffman, a prisoner of war camp.[11]

By June 1862, Allen faced financial difficulties similar to those of his predecessor. To recoup his losses, Allen offered the land to the federal government for use as a U.S. Army hospital. Point Lookout was well suited for military purposes because of its convenient water access, which made it an excellent base of supply for the army and a suitable site to care for sick and wounded soldiers. A preliminary inspection of the location and its cottages by a "reliable army surgeon of experience," seconded by Surgeon General William A. Hammond, recommended to Meigs that he accept Allen's negotiations to rent the site for the hospital and begin construction immediately.

Although inspectors found Point Lookout to be flat, sandy, barren, and producing little fresh, potable water, Hammond's request was granted. At the time, the Point Lookout site was considered healthy for its occupants, though it possessed few natural advantages other than access to the Potomac River and the Chesapeake Bay. The transportation advantages meant that the hospital site soon grew to encompass a supply depot, and then began to serve as a key location for receiving and transferring prisoners of war. But the health complications remained. In 1870, Medical Inspector John Wilson stated during one inspection that he "regretted that so fine a hospital, with so good an outfit, had been there constructed."[12]

On July 4, 1862, Hammond ordered Surgeon Clinton Wagner to Point Lookout to take command and establish a hospital there. Hammond further directed him to bring sufficient bedding, furniture, and other supplies necessary to begin operations. He was also instructed to take rations for 1,000 men for 20 days. At the time, the site was occupied by a guard sent by Maj. Gen. John Dix,

11 "Historical Overview," Point Lookout Lighthouse, https://www.ptlookoutlighthouse.com/overview.shtml; Edwin W. Beitzell, *Point Lookout Prison Camp for Confederates* (St. Mary's County Historical Society, 1972), 2, 19.

12 Beitzell, 19; Abby Hopper Gibbons, *Life of Abby Hopper Gibbons: Told Chiefly through Her Correspondence*, ed. Sarah Hopper Emerson (New York, , 1897), 1:370; United States Surgeon General's Office, *The Medical and Surgical History of the War of the Rebellion (1861–65)*, comp. Joseph K. Barnes, et al. (Washington D.C., 1888), 1.3:59, 942, https://catalog.nlm.nih.gov/permalink/01NLM_INST/1o1phhn/alma991888583406676.

Surgeon General William Hammond,
United States Army
*Library of Congress*

who had been ordered to secure the location before Wagner's arrival.[13]

On July 9, 1862, Meigs sent Acting Assistant Quartermaster Capt. Abraham Edwards to Point Lookout to begin construction of the Army hospital. In August 1862, Edwards contracted with the former owner, William Allen, for its construction. Among other requirements, Edwards was to provide Allen with transportation for his workers to and from Point Lookout. He estimated construction costs for the hospital at approximately $51,000. Rations were also to be supplied along with construction materials. In return, Allen was required to complete the work to Edwards's satisfaction. Men from Companies A and G of the 8th New York State Militia (Engineers) were detached from Annapolis to Point Lookout to serve as mechanics and laborers, along with other civilian contract workers, in the hospital's construction and support facilities.[14]

Designed by Surgeon General Hammond, the hospital was considered unique for its wheel-and-spoke layout. Its location provided a general hospital closer to the front for the thousands of casualties in need of medical care. Major cities such as Washington, D.C. and Baltimore, as well as what would become key battlefields, were easily accessed, with a steady flow of waterborne traffic to and from its wharf. The hospital was one of 192 general hospitals operated by the U.S. government during the Civil War. It later became one of 25 hospitals included in

13 Surgeon General William Hammond to Asst. Surgeon General R. C. Woode, "The Letters of Surgeon Clinton Wagner," Nov. 7, 1862, Record Group 29, Entry 576, Box 57, National Archives and Records Administration, Washington, D.C. (hereafter "NARA").

14 Capt. Abraham Edwards to Gen. William Hammond, "The Letters of Surgeon Clinton Wagner," Nov. 7, 1862, Record Group 92, Entry 576, Box 57, NARA, Washington, D.C., Gerald J. Sword, "Hammond General Hospital, Point Lookout, Maryland," *St. Mary's Monthly Bulletin of the St. Mary's County Historical Society*, Feb. 1983; Capt. Abraham Edwards, Record Ledger Sheets from the Assistant Quartermaster's Department (unpublished manuscript, 1862).

the Department of Washington, one of the largest military departments among the 16 created during the war. The facility would be designated Hammond General Hospital, sharing the site with a lighthouse at the southern tip of the peninsula.[15]

The foundation of the hospital rested on pilings that raised the structure two to three feet above the ground. It covered nearly all the land between the bay and the river, measuring more than 500 feet in diameter. Extending in all directions of the compass, the hospital was built in the pavilion style using the balloon construction method of the period.[16]

Medical staff, both military and civilian, along with supplies and materials, were sent to Point Lookout as it began receiving sick and wounded from the army. As construction progressed, Captain Edwards used the numerous summer cottages included in the rental agreement, as well as the Fenwick Hotel, as hospital wards and quarters. The cottages were generally two stories and contained three to four rooms. Once the cottages and hotel were filled, Edwards erected 80 additional hospital tents to accommodate about 700 patients, with capacity for more incoming casualties.[17]

In correspondence dated July 11, 1863, Assistant Adjutant General Brig. Gen. Edward R. S. Canby expressed concern to Secretary of War Stanton about where the wounded Confederate prisoners from the recent battle of Gettysburg should be housed. Commissary General of Prisoners Hoffman recommended that several Federal hospitals within the Middle Department, headquartered in Baltimore and commanded by Maj. Gen. Robert C. Schenck of the VIII Corps, be used. This included Hammond Hospital, then still under construction. The decision to use the Hammond Hospital complex for wounded Confederate prisoners was overturned at Schenck's request, based on the advice of his medical director. Schenck later suggested to Canby that the wounded Confederates should be sent farther north to other hospitals, rather than placing them in southern Maryland. Despite these recommendations, the secretary of war would soon assign another purpose to Point Lookout.[18]

15 Ira Spar, *Civil War Hospital Newspapers: Histories and Excerpts of Nine Union Publications* (Jefferson, NC, 2017), 1, 6.

16 Scott Sidler, "How to Tell If You Have a Balloon House," *The Craftsman Blog*, Aug. 10, 2015, accessed Feb. 20, 2025, https://thecraftsmanblog.com/how-to-tell-if-you-have-a-balloon-frame-house/.

17 George Everett, *Point Lookout, Md. View of Hammond Genl. Hospital and U.S. Genl. Deport for Prisoners of War*, map (Baltimore, MD, 1864).

18 "Hammond General Hospital," *National Republican* (Washington, D.C.), Feb. 14, 1863, second edition, Local Affairs, accessed Feb. 20, 2025, https://chroniclingamerica.loc.gov/lccn/sn86053570/1863-02-14/ed-1/seq-2/; *OR* 6/2:98-99, 102, 132.

By the outbreak of the war, the construction of prisons was not yet regarded as a priority by the War Department, as existing buildings and forts were readily used. Only when prisoner numbers began to exceed the capacity of these facilities did the government seek additional locations and begin construction at other sites. No formal guidelines or requirements had been established for the new prisons. Each differed in construction, maintenance, and capacity. Time constraints and active campaigning prevented committees from carefully considering prison locations or conducting site studies before construction. The government's primary criteria at this stage consisted of practical concerns including space, capacity, acreage, and accessibility.

Point Lookout was no exception. The prison stockade resembled many other prisons constructed in both the North and South during the war. The unused farmland located north of the Army hospital made the site practical for selection by Secretary of War Stanton.

At the time the Quartermaster Department inspected Point Lookout in 1862, two small working farms occupied a portion of the 250 acres of the future prison complex. This land was included in the initial acreage arrangement, and much of it had been cleared of corn and livestock. Because the land was already in use as farmland, the task of clearing the acreage for the prison stockade was simplified. Army correspondence suggests that the decision to establish a prison without an onsite inspection was essentially an overnight decision by officials in Washington. The urgency of securing the site, combined with the availability of open fields and water transportation, weighed heavily in favor of selecting the location for military purposes.[19]

A year later, the secretary of war and the commissary general of prisoners decided to open Point Lookout as a prisoner of war camp. The acreage was already under federal contract and only partially occupied by the hospital complex. No further negotiation was required to use the remaining land for the proposed prison site, which satisfied both Meigs and Hoffman. Once the decision was made, Stanton ordered Maj. Gen. Henry W. Halleck to formalize the selection of the site through the proper chain of command. In accordance with Stanton's order, on July 20, 1863, Meigs informed Assistant Quartermaster General Daniel H. Rucker of the acquisition. Rucker then began the process of establishing Point Lookout as a prisoner of war camp.[20]

19 William Child, *Letters from a Civil War Surgeon: The Letters of Dr. William Child of the Fifth New Hampshire Volunteers* (Solon, ME, 2001), 183.

20 *OR* 6/2:132.

On July 23, 1863, the establishment of the new prison camp at Point Lookout advanced rapidly with the issuance of General Order No. 226 by Assistant Adjutant General Ethan D. Townsend. This order detached St. Mary's County, Maryland, from the Middle Department, officially creating the District of St. Mary's. The prison officially designated Camp Hoffman in honor of the Commissary general of prisoners, was more commonly referred to as Point Lookout. As the large hospital neared completion almost a year later, the first guards and prisoners began arriving at the new prison. Construction of a stockade had not yet begun, the result of the hasty decision to establish a camp there. Meanwhile, a large number of prisoners from Gettysburg were already destined for Point Lookout, with no facility in place to house them.[21]

Lieutenant Erastus W. Everson of the 20th Veteran Reserve Corps offered a tongue-in-cheek description of Point Lookout. "It was a saying of the soldiers who guarded the Confederate prisoners of war at Point Lookout, Maryland," Everson wrote in a letter home, "that when the world was created, there remained a surplus of sand which was dumped at the confluence of the Potomac River and Chesapeake Bay, as being entirely out of the way." Everson further described this "bastille" as a "treeless and otherwise barren locality . . . the discomforts of the burning sands were nearly unbearable and the reflection of the sun's rays ruinous to the eyesight, while in winter the bleak winds had an unobstructed sweep across a vast stretch of water—the bay on one side and the river on the other."[22]

Confederate prisoner Capt. Randolph Shotwell, 8th Virginia, described the effects of the white sand that covered a significant portion of the Point Lookout area. He wrote that the sand proved just as debilitating as any other adverse condition there:

> Great clouds of dry sand began their tireless whirling . . . no pen nor tongue can portray the plague of this fine sand eternally filling the air, inflaming the eyes, penetrating the air, the beard, the ears, nose, and clothing; covering blankets, towels, paper, etc., with a thick coat of grit within an hour's time after brushing them off; and filtering through the canvas so that at morn each sleeper seems peppered with white powder.[23]

21 John H. Eicher, David J. Eicher, and John Y. Simon, *Civil War High Commands* (Stanford, CA, 2001), 59–60, accessed April 17, 2011, https://books.google.com/books.

22 Erastus Watson Everson, "Narrative and Personal Notes," unpublished manuscript, South Carolina Historical Society, Charleston, SC, n.d., 1–2.

23 Randolph Abbott Shotwell, *The Papers of Randolph Abbott Shotwell*, ed. Rebecca Cameron and Joseph Gregoire de Roulhoc Hamilton (North Carolina Historical Commission, Raleigh, N.C. 1929), 1:120-121, digital file.

1st Lieutenant Erastus W. Everson, 20th Veteran Reserve Corps
*The Donald Thompson Collection*

South of the prison camp on the Chesapeake Bay side was an area commonly known as "the grove." The grove was primarily composed of pine trees, like it is today, and located along the shoreline of the Chesapeake Bay side of the Point. The commanding officer and his staff chose cottages within this grove—the only stand of trees along the waterfront—for their residences. Many cottages dotted the shoreline and were protected from wind and sun by the grove's pine trees. The next area of significant forest was located north, beyond the boundaries of the Point Lookout military complex.

From a practical point of view, Point Lookout was an ideal location for a prisoner of war camp. The acreage north of Hammond Hospital was open, flat, and devoid of forestation. This land required no clearing to construct the extensive prison stockade. The existing network of roads was clear and accessible, although waterborne transportation remained more efficient.

From a military perspective, Point Lookout could be easily defended by a small force. The land approach from the north involved crossing two narrow peninsulas or "spits" separated by Point Lookout Creek (now Lake Conoy), creating natural choke points that were easily defensible. Attacking forces would have encountered armed earthen works, small log stockades, and palisade walls pierced for both artillery and musketry. These defensive works were completed rapidly, with one positioned on the Potomac River side and another on the Chesapeake Bay side to defend the approaches.

The location of Point Lookout provided vital support for supplying the hospital and garrison with rations, clothing, transportation, and livestock. The six-pier wharf near the hospital and lighthouse facilitated ready access for waterborne traffic to both the Potomac River and Chesapeake Bay. Point Lookout was approximately 70 nautical miles (7–8 hours by vessel) from departmental command headquarters at Fortress Monroe, Virginia; 85 nautical miles (8–9 hours) from Fort McHenry in Baltimore; and about 70 nautical miles (7–8 hours) from Washington, D.C. Until the telegraph line was constructed in early 1864, communication and reinforcement relied on ship (steam or sail), which could be completed within a few hours when necessary, enabling the expedient transportation of supplies, guards, and prisoners.[24]

The assistant quartermasters assigned to Point Lookout began constructing the prison in early August 1863. Once the tall stockade walls were completed, the refreshing bay breezes largely disappeared. The height of the walls restricted the flow of fresh air and allowed odors, smoke, and stagnant, suffocating air to dominate the enclosure. Prisoners endured scorching heat and oppressive humidity during the summer months in southern Maryland, which turned refuse, human waste, and rotting garbage from thousands of inmates into a miasmic haze within the prison.

The number of guards rarely kept pace with the prison population, which increased beyond the available force. Although they enjoyed the relative quiet of Point Lookout, the veterans of the Army of the Potomac soon discovered that their service as prison guards was neither simple nor easy.

24 National Oceanographic, "AA Navigational Charts," map, 2016, Series 1–7.

# Chapter 2

# The Guard Force at Point Lookout

The campaign-weary men of the 2nd and 12th New Hampshire Volunteer Regiments viewed their new assignment with relief, hoping they were finally about to receive a well-deserved rest. They had been assigned guard duty at the new prison at Point Lookout, and looked forward to light days after their strenuous combat exertions. However, immediately upon their arrival on July 31, 1863, they realized they were required not only to guard the prison, but also the hospital complex, the adjacent wharf, the storehouses, and their own camps, in addition to escorting prisoners transferring to and from other prisons.[1]

They also had to guard prisoners assigned to work details both within and outside Point Lookout, while other comrades were ordered to construct barricades and artillery positions for the defensive works protecting the post. Their assignments seemed endless, too few men for too many roles, many of which were also physically taxing. Far from providing a rest, the new assignment would strain the ranks of the two New Hampshire regiments, which together barely mustered 300 men. Several months would pass before they received new recruits or additional units to reinforce the guard force.

Prior to the arrival of the prison's newly assigned commandant, Gen. Gilman Marston, and his brigade of New Hampshire men, the task of patrolling pro-secessionist St. Mary's County and protecting Hammond General Hospital had fallen to assorted contingents of federal infantry and cavalry stationed at Point Lookout. Many had been there as early as a year before Marston's arrival in 1863.

1 William F. Fox, *Regimental Losses in the American Civil War, 1861–1865, a Treatise on the Extent and Nature of the Mortuary Losses in the Union Regiments, with Full and Exhaustive Statistics Compiled from the Official Records on File in the State Military Bureaus and at Washington* (Albany, NY, 1889), 137, 139, 144.

Brigadier General Gilman Marston
*Library of Congress*

Marston was ordered to supply 20 men as mounted patrols to replace the departing units. These detachments ensured that St. Mary's County and southern Maryland would not become a back door to Washington, D.C., for a Confederate invasion or a haven for pro-secessionist activities such as recruitment, support for the Confederate Army, disloyalty to the Union, and blockade running.

Although the actions of the previous Federal patrols had come under legal scrutiny by authorities in Washington, pro-Southern activities were reduced by their presence. At that time, many of those captured or arrested were detained at Hammond Hospital because of the lack of a dedicated prison facility. Eventually, this 20-man detail was reinforced by detachments from the 2nd and 5th U.S. Cavalry.

The New Hampshire men revealed the strain associated with their insufficient guard force. Their letters home included detailed descriptions of extended duty hours, endless guard rotations, grueling details, and the gradual increase of duty posts as the prisoner population grew. Their correspondence also described the few moments of recreation they enjoyed, as well as their rations, camp life, and the weather of southern Maryland. Now that these New Hampshire regiments were in the rear echelon of the army at Point Lookout, the assignment kept them out of harm's way and away from the rigors of active campaigning. Despite this, they continued to endure death, disease, pestilence, and bad water, as well as the constant fear of being outnumbered by thousands of prisoners of war. The possibility of a mass breakout, given the overwhelming number of prisoners, remained a constant, terrifying threat. This fear, in particular, kept them in a state of constant vigilance until the closing of Point Lookout as a prison.

For a brief period, the guard force at Point Lookout numbered about 2,500 men. This figure was seldom matched or surpassed because of the demands of Grant's Overland campaign in the spring of 1864. As Grant gathered many inactive units from rear-echelon areas, the veteran New Hampshire men were soon ordered to return to the front. Their departure required the transfer of a newly created reserve force to Point Lookout to replace them. As the prison population steadily increased in the months following the opening of Point Lookout, the too-small guard force remained under continual strain.

## The Opening of Point Lookout Prison Camp

On July 23, 1863, Halleck issued orders to Marston to report immediately to Gen. George G. Meade, commanding the Army of the Potomac, to "receive a guard of about 300 men for the prison camp at Point Lookout."[2] On the same day, Halleck ordered Meade to assign Marston a guard force drawn from the 2nd, 5th, and 12th New Hampshire regiments (approximately 450 men), and if additional troops were needed, to take them from other New Hampshire regiments. Meade was also instructed to turn over any prisoners of war he had in his custody so they could be taken with him to Point Lookout. These prisoners of war were to be the first to arrive at the new prison.[3]

From Meade's headquarters, Marston was ordered to proceed to Washington, D.C., with his prisoners and guards and to apply for transportation to Point Lookout. "Tents, lumber for kitchens, cooking apparatus, etc. had already been ordered to that place by the quartermaster department." The camp was intended to accommodate approximately 10,000 Confederate prisoners of war. He was also instructed to requisition 20 horses and sufficient equipment to mount that number of men for patrols operating throughout St. Mary's County.[4]

Marston was officially placed in command of the district by General Order No. 236, dated July 23, 1863. Located on the lower Potomac, the new command was designated the District of St. Mary's, which encompassed the entirety of St. Mary's County, Maryland. The assignment created a brigade of New Hampshire soldiers, who were also, incidentally, represented by Republican Congressman Marston who had retained his congressional seat throughout the war.

According to Capt. Asa Bartlett of the 12th New Hampshire, it was rumored that the decision to assign Marston and the New Hampshire troops to Point Lookout may have been influenced by Governor Nathaniel S. Berry of New Hampshire, a staunch Republican, ally and friend of President Lincoln. Prior to the war, Marston had served as a Republican congressman representing the First

2 *OR* 6/2:141.

3 *OR* 27/1:1:98.

4 *OR* 6/2:141.

District of New Hampshire. When hostilities began, he enlisted in the 2nd New Hampshire Volunteer Regiment.[5]

### The Guards—Arrival, Relief, and the First Orders

During the days following the battle of Gettysburg, elements of the Army of the Potomac marched through Warrenton, Virginia, in pursuit of the retreating Confederate army. On July 26, 1863, the survivors of the veteran 2nd New Hampshire Volunteer Regiment filed through the town and hailed their former commanding officer, the recently promoted General Marston, who was standing in the doorway of a house along their route of march. He acknowledged their cheers as the combat-weary and footsore men slogged past.[6]

Marston announced that his new mission was to have the three regiments (2nd, 5th, and 12th New Hampshire) detached from the Army of the Potomac to form a brigade under his command, stationed on the Lower Potomac. After their next halt, the rest of the brigade marched on, leaving the 2nd and 12th New Hampshire resting and awaiting orders. The 5th New Hampshire departed for Washington, D.C., on August 1 under orders to return home and fill their ranks with recruits. They would arrive at Point Lookout in mid-November 1863.[7]

On the evening of July 30, 1863, Marston and the shattered remnants of the 2nd and 12th New Hampshire boarded the steamer *John Brooks* in Washington and began making their way south down the Potomac toward their new assignment. They arrived at Point Lookout wharf at approximately nine o'clock the following morning. With them traveled a small force of about 136 Confederate prisoners of war, the first to be incarcerated at Point Lookout. As preparations for the prison continued, Marston formally assumed command on August 1, 1863, becoming the first of five officers to command Point Lookout and its prison.[8]

From the outset, Marston had little choice but to operate the prison as if it were already at full capacity. This placed a considerable strain on his fatigued

5 Ibid., 140; *OR* 29/1:2:571; Asa W. Bartlett, *History of the Twelfth Regiment New Hampshire Volunteers in the War of the Rebellion* (Concord, NH, 1897), 145.

6 *OR* 27/1:3:152.

7 Child, *Letters from a Civil War Surgeon*, 234.

8 Martin A. Haynes, *A History of the Second Regiment New Hampshire Volunteer Infantry, in the War of the Rebellion* (1896; repr. Lakeport, NH, 1996), 198–199; War Department office of the commissary general of prisoners, *Morning Report of Prisoners of War, Point Lookout, MD*, report no. 241 (1863); Letter by Gilman Marston, "Letters Received by the Office of the Adjt. Gen. Main Series 1861-1870 Marston," August 3, 1863, accessed March 18, 2025, https://www.fold3.com/publication/822/us-letters-received-by-the-adjutant-general-1861-1870/.

soldiers. Acting assistant quartermasters, captains Abraham Edwards and Nelson Plato, along with Surgeon Augustus M. Clark, acting medical inspector of prisoners of war, were instrumental with the rapid castrametation and organization of the prison.

On August 15, 1863, construction of the prison stockade fence was still underway as prisoners set up their tents in the camp area. In a communication to Commissary General of Prisoners, Col. William Hoffman, Marston stated that he was prepared to receive an additional 1,000 prisoners and that he could care for them with ease and safety, even though the stockade was not yet completed. Hoffman granted Marston's request by sending 800 additional prisoners, followed later that month by another 400 to 500.[9]

That same month, Private Martin Haynes wrote home that the camp had quickly expanded in size but that the number of guards had remained the same. The arrival of additional prisoners brought the total to more than 1,800, guarded by approximately 300 Union soldiers. By the beginning of September, Maj. Gen. Ethan A. Hitchcock, commissioner for the exchange of prisoners, reported that 1,800 (actually, 1,837) prisoners were recorded on site at Point Lookout. With the eventual arrival of the 5th New Hampshire in November, the guard force increased by 750 much-needed men.[10]

Originally, guard duty rotated each week between the 2nd New Hampshire and the 12th. Because there were too few guards, the men had to form two reliefs of twelve hours each out of every twenty-four, on alternating days. Fortunately for them, Marston suspended other camp duties and regimental and company drill. During September 1863, as the prisoner population increased and additional guard posts were established, prison authorities created a third guard shift. Matters worsened for the 2nd New Hampshire in particular, as the unit was about to lose men it could not spare from already depleted ranks. In mid-July, the remaining men of the 17th New Hampshire, whose enlistments had not yet expired, had been ordered to fill the ranks of the 2nd. However, those enlistments were due to expire within days, and they would soon be going home, once again reducing the strength of the guard force.[11]

The site selected for the prison camp was an expansive farmer's field. To deter escape attempts or the possibility that prisoners might overpower the guards while the stockade was under construction, two Dahlgren boat howitzers were

9 *OR* 6/2:214.

10 Ibid., 243; Martin A. Haynes, *A Soldier Boy's Letters to "The Girl I Left Behind Me": 1861–1864* (1916; repr. Lakeport, NH, n.d.), 134.

11 Ibid., 129.

positioned in crossfire over the open area until the enclosure was completed. By late October, the stockade fence surrounding the prison was nearly finished. Only adjustments to the catwalks and gates remained, along with the construction of several cookhouses and mess halls for the prisoners.

As the stockade neared completion, the guard forces began to enjoy some relief since, up to that point, they had been guarding open ground. The finished stockade reduced the number of men required and enabled the force to operate three shifts instead of the overly burdensome two. In November, in addition to the numerous guard posts around the prison, authorities added a corporal's guard of about eight men to the main entrance gate and at the newly built guardhouse just outside the gate. These additional posts once more increased the number of men required to man them.[12]

On November 9, a week before the arrival of the 5th New Hampshire, Hoffman informed Marston that another 1,800 prisoners were on their way to Point Lookout from Washington. He also advised Marston that he could retain the guards escorting this group of prisoners until additional permanent guards could be provided. As it turned out, this practice of retaining escort guards occurred on several occasions during the prison's existence. Hoffman also sent another 3,000 tents for the additional prisoners and guards.

In mid-December (and again in February 1864), a rumor circulated about a planned mass breakout by the prisoners. In response, Major General Benjamin F. Butler directed Battery F, 1st Rhode Island Artillery commanded by Capt. James Belger, to report immediately to Point Lookout.[13] Battery F arrived on December 24 from Yorktown, Virginia, and remained on station until it was relieved by the 2nd Independent Battery, Wisconsin Light Artillery. The 2nd Wisconsin Artillery arrived on January 20, 1864, and camped "in park" alongside Battery F until the Rhode Island battery was reassigned and departed a few days later, on January 23. The 2nd Wisconsin remained at this post until the closing of Point Lookout in July 1865.[14]

In April 1864, Brig. Gen. Edward W. Hinks arrived to take command of Point Lookout, relieving Marston. Before assuming this post, Hinks had been assigned to court-martial and recruiting duties. He remained in command of Point Lookout through April 1864, after which he was transferred to lead a

12 Ibid., 130, 133, 144.

13 *OR* 6/2:489, 745.

14 Philip Steven Chase, *Battery F, First Regiment Rhode Island Light Artillery, in the Civil War 1861–1865* (Providence, RI, 1892), 114–116; William De Loss Love, *Wisconsin in the War of the Rebellion; A History of All Regiments and Batteries* (Chicago, IL, 1866), 1019–1020.

Brigadier General Edward W. Hinks
*Author Collection*

new division in the XVIII Corps at Yorktown, Virginia.[15]

At the start of his command, the security and well-being of both the guard force and the prisoners of war constituted Hinks's central priority. Shortly after his arrival, on April 18, 1864, Hinks ordered Surgeon Anthony Heger (chief surgeon of the District of St. Mary's at Hammond Hospital) to establish a guard from among those under his care who were judged physically fit for duty. This order reflected Hinks's efforts to supplement his main guard and reduce the number of posts manned by the diminished force of available soldiers. This newly formed guard force was directed to connect with the general guard on the beach to the right of headquarters, located on the bay side, and continue south around the Point, covering the lighthouse and linking with the provost marshal guard at the wharf area on the Potomac River side. Guard beats were ordered to extend 100 yards in length, and these additional guards were placed under the same general orders governing the permanent garrison as issued from Hinks's headquarters.[16]

Between February and April 1864, the guard force at Point Lookout underwent a significant transition. After its arrival, the primary duty of the 2nd Wisconsin Artillery was to man not only its own guns but also the many additional pieces dispersed throughout the Point. By late 1864, approximately 16 artillery pieces had been posted around Point Lookout to defend against outside attack and deter a prisoner breakout. These included the field pieces eventually emplaced within two of the three redoubts constructed later that year.

To help man the additional field pieces, soldiers from the guard force—including the 11th and 20th Veteran Reserve Corps and men from various

15 Eicher, Eicher, and Simon, *Civil War High*, 298, 723.

16 *Book No. 253*, Vol. 1, District of St. Mary's, *Press Copies of Letter and Telegrams Sent* (Washington, D.C., n.d.), 81.

United States Colored Troops (U.S.C.T.) units—were detailed and trained by the Wisconsin artillerymen to supplement the gun positions at Point Lookout. Although these additions significantly strengthened the post's defenses, the reassignment of these men further reduced the already strained number of guards.

## United States Colored Troops Arrive

Point Lookout guard reinforcements, like U.S. Army troop reinforcements generally, was made possible by the enlistment of thousands of free and formerly enslaved Black men. Though controversial, the idea of organizing and arming formerly enslaved men in the military services of the United States was not new. Black men had served in both the army and the navy since the American Revolution. Strategically, the recruitment of former slaves provided access to an untapped manpower source, which increased the number of men in the field against Confederate forces. The effective recruitment of former slaves also reduced the bonded labor compelled to work on Confederate fortifications, thereby keeping fewer Southern White soldiers free for frontline service.[17]

Emancipation and the arming of former slaves were not, in many cases, welcomed by everyone in the North or its army. Captain Charles Francis Adams Jr. of the 1st Massachusetts Cavalry stated in a letter home his low opinion of former slaves as combat soldiers, writing that they were better suited for fatigue parties and could not be depended upon as soldiers. He doubted that they could be "made to stand before their old masters." Ironically, Adams was later appointed commanding officer of the 5th Massachusetts (Colored) Cavalry while it was stationed at Point Lookout. Once in command, Adams, the young Boston aristocrat, wrote to his father from Point Lookout in 1864, revising his earlier attitude toward his new charges. He conceded that they could make good soldiers but still had a long way to go before being equal to their White counterparts. In short order, the former slave and the freedman showed their worth once given the opportunity to demonstrate themselves in combat.[18]

To supplement the guard force at Point Lookout, General Butler requested the transfer of the 36th U.S.C.T. to the post. The 36th (formerly the 2nd North Carolina) landed at the wharves of Point Lookout in February 1864 and was assigned guard duty. After debarking from transports, the regiment marched

17 James K. Bryant, *The 36th Infantry United States Colored Troops in the Civil War: A History and Roster* (Jefferson, NC, 2012), 40.

18 Charles Francis Adams Jr., *A Cycle of Adams Letters 1861–1865*, ed. Worthington Chauncey Ford (Boston, MA, 1920), 1:171, 2:194–195.

Major General Benjamin F. Butler
Commanding Officer, Department of Virginia and North Carolina
*Library of Congress*

in column to its new camp to the sound of the regimental band as it moved north along the country road from the lighthouse. The camp was situated near a brick house beyond the main entry bridge, outside the protection of the palisade walls and artillery batteries, and across from the smallpox hospital. Why Marston chose to establish the 36th's camp north of the garrison remains speculative. Perhaps it was a defensive measure on his part, but its placement also effectively segregated the regiment from the rest of the guard camps. The 36th U.S.C.T. remained in this camp until its transfer to the Army of the James on June 30, 1864.[19]

The 1,000 men of the 36th U.S.C.T. significantly expanded the number of guards available for duty. At this point, more than 8,600 prisoners were present, with more arriving weekly. Their growing numbers made it necessary to add guard posts to protect Point Lookout, further stretching the approximately 2,000-man guard force. By this time, there was a buffer of four to five lines of guard posts, which lessened the chances of escape.

## Change of Command

Private Martin Hayes of the 2nd New Hampshire wrote home in January 1864 that Marston periodically interrupted the boredom of camp life by conducting raids with a select armed force into neighboring counties of Virginia across from Point Lookout. Marston considered these "expeditions" necessary to forage for firewood and to seize other items classified as contraband of war, such as horses, cattle, and other supplies. These expeditions—the practice would be continued by commanding officers Hinks and Col. Alonzo Draper—consisted

19 Bryant, *The 36th*, 80; *Book No. 253*, 64.

of 150 cavalrymen and detachments of 150 men from the 2nd and 12th New Hampshire, who "came home loaded with every conceivable kind of plunder." Among the contraband they captured were "quite a number of prisoners—soldiers on furlough, conscript officers."[20]

In April, General Hinks was relieved of the command of Point Lookout and transferred to Yorktown, assigned to command the Third Division, XVIII Corps, Army of the James. As the senior officer present, Col. Alonzo G. Draper, commanding officer of the 36th United States Colored Troops, relieved Hinks and assumed command of Point Lookout.

April and May 1864 were active at Point Lookout, with Federal troops coming and going. In mid-April, the 2nd and 12th New Hampshire Regiments were ordered to report to the commanding officer of the XVIII Corps at Yorktown, Virginia. To supplement the reduced guard force after the departure of the two veteran New Hampshire regiments, the 4th U.S.C.T. arrived from Baltimore on or about April 11, 1864. The 4th moved into the recently vacated camp of the 12th New Hampshire on the Potomac River side of the Point. Lieutenant Samuel W. Van Nuys of the 4th claimed that the combined guard force of the 4th, 5th New Hampshire, and 36th remained to stand guard over 7,000 prisoners, with their guard rotation occurring every third day and requiring more than 300 men and officers per rotation.[21]

The 837 men of the 4th U.S.C.T. spent only a short tenure at Point Lookout, departing on April 25 to join the XVIII Corps at Old Point Comfort near Fortress Monroe. They were soon followed by the 750 men of the 5th New Hampshire on May 15, when the regiment transferred to Yorktown to take its former place in the II Corps. Prior to the transfer of the 4th U.S.C.T. and the 5th New Hampshire, the 450 men of the 4th Rhode Island arrived on April 1 to fill the void created by the departure of the two regiments. The 4th Rhode Island occupied the former campground of the 12th New Hampshire along the shore of the Potomac River. Corporal George H. Allen of the 4th Rhode Island described the extent of his guard duty after his arrival in April 1864, noting that "there were forty-four posts along the line of guard besides patrol and supernumeraries. Consequently, it required nearly the whole regiment to form three reliefs."[22]

20 *OR* 33/1:268–269 and 37/1:71–73, 163–167; Haynes, *A Soldier Boy's Letters*, 158.

21 Elba L. Branigin, *History of Johnson County Indiana* (Indianapolis, IN, 1913), 469.

22 Edward G. Longacre, *A Regiment of Slaves: The 4th United States Colored Infantry, 1863–1866* (Lincoln, NE, 2003), 67; George H. Allen, *Forty-Six Months with the Fourth Rhode Island Volunteers, in the War of 1861 to 1865, History of Its Marches, Battles, and Camp Life* (Providence, RI, 1887), 259; Allen, 264.

## The Veteran Reserve Corps

Another innovative force created by the U.S. War Department was the Veteran Reserve Corps (V.R.C.). The V.R.C. was organized to employ soldiers no longer able to endure the hardships and rigors of campaigning but still physically capable of performing non-combat duties such as guarding prisons and escorting prisoners. At Butler's request, the 11th V.R.C. (organized at Elmira, New York, on October 10, 1863), First Battalion, arrived on April 24, 1864. They served as prison guards, mounted patrols, scouts, and escorts for prisoners transferred between prisons. While at Point Lookout, the 11th V.R.C. was credited with capturing 50 blockade-running boats and their crews, 50 smugglers, two officers and one soldier of Mosby's command, and many Federal deserters. The regiment mustered out of service by detachments at Point Lookout between June 29 and November 23, 1865.[23]

Not long after the arrival of the 11th V.R.C., the 20th V.R.C. (organized in Baltimore on January 12, 1864) reported for duty with 321 men in May 1864. The men of the 20th V.R.C. performed the same duties as those of the 11th. So diverse was the makeup of the V.R.C. units that the 11th and 20th included men representing nearly every state of the Union. Arriving with the 20th V.R.C. were the last in the line of provost marshals and their assistants: Maj. Allen G. Brady and Capt. John W. Barnes, formerly of the 17th Connecticut and 90th Pennsylvania, respectively. Both officers of the 20th V.R.C. served in these posts until the closing of the prison camp. Like the 11th V.R.C., the 20th mustered out of service by detachments from Point Lookout between late June and November 23, 1865.

Eighty-man details operated as mounted patrols and scouts, while 43 men were placed on other detached services. Forty others were detailed as artillerymen for Redoubts No. 1 and No. 2, and 140 more were assigned to serve as provost or police guards for the prison. On June 28, 1864, Companies A and C of the 10th V.R.C. (organized in New York on October 19, 1863) arrived for the purpose of escorting prisoners. The men of this 1st Battalion unit were not present at Point Lookout as long as the other two Veteran Reserve Corps units, being transferred after only a few months.[24]

Many soldiers considered the V.R.C. program a dodge for those seeking to shirk their responsibilities as soldiers. Corporal George Allen of the 4th Rhode

23 *OR* 5/3:562; Frederick H. Dyer, *A Compendium of the War of the Rebellion* (Des Moines, IA, 1908), 1741.

24 *Book No. 253*, 365; Erastus Watson Everson, unpublished manuscript, 21, Papers No. 28/710/22, South Carolina Historical Society, Charleston, SC.

Island, quoted in his regimental history, claimed that the men of the V.R.C. played the game of disability to secure a transfer from active units into the "Invalid" or "Diarrhea Corps." Allen described them as having only "shell fever" and a "heavy appetite for rations." He stated that the V.R.C. units at Point Lookout mustered about 700 to 800 men and were organized into three reliefs for guard duty. However, when the second relief was ordered to fall in "at 10 o'clock, scarcely a score of them could be found. Thus, we were forced to do double duty on account of these [dead] beats."[25]

## The Lack of Guards and Another Change of Command

The rear echelon of the Union army began to feel the drain of manpower as Grant continued reinforcing his massive force for the spring campaign season, and Point Lookout was not excepted. On May 20, 1864, Hoffman reported to Secretary of War Stanton that, considering all troops present at the Point, there were approximately 1,654 men and officers to guard 11,000 prisoners (563 officers, 10,192 enlisted men, and 192 citizens, totaling 10,947 prisoners). Hoffman further stated in his report that the number of men present was sufficient to guard the prisoners, but not sufficient to continue fulfilling auxiliary duties such as those of artillerymen and mounted guards.

Hoffman further recommended to Draper that he relocate the camp of the 36th U.S.C.T. closer to the other guard camps and the prison, to better position the regiment in the event of a mass breakout attempt. He also requested of Stanton that a "regiment of disciplined troops or two regiments of militia be added to the guard." In Hoffman's opinion, the guard force needed to be strong enough both to control prisoners and to defend against any possible enemy attempt to liberate the camp.

On May 29, Hoffman sent correspondence to Draper cautioning him of the necessity of having his command and his officers "be perfectly prepared to meet any emergency that may arise either from an external attack with a view to the release of the prisoners of war or from any effort on their own part to this end." The message to Draper indicates that Hoffman had by then considered the possibility of both an attack on Point Lookout and a mass breakout. Butler intervened on Draper's behalf by requesting additional U.S.C.T. regiments or regiments of the V.R.C. to fill the immediate void created by the transferred units. Hoffman informed Draper he was sending one or two new regiments to his command and further cautioned him, when employing prisoners for fatigue duty,

25 Allen, *Forty-Six Months*, 268.

to use only those who had expressed loyal sentiments and applied to take the oath of allegiance.[26]

By June 22, 1864, the District of St. Mary's was no longer part of the Department of Virginia and North Carolina. It was placed under the command of the XXII Corps, commanded by Maj. Gen. Christopher C. Augur, headquartered in Washington, D.C. This change folded Point Lookout and St. Mary's County into the defensive perimeter of the nation's capital. Augur ordered Draper to "relieve the 36th U.S. Colored Troops with the 5th Massachusetts Dismounted Cavalry . . . [due to arrive at Point Lookout] . . . and send the former regiment to Gen. Butler [now in Yorktown, Virginia]." Draper was further instructed to "remain in command at Point Lookout until the arrival of Gen. Barnes who will relieve you." Brigadier General James Barnes arrived on July 4 to officially assume command of Point Lookout, relieving Colonel Draper, who was ordered to rejoin the 36th U.S.C.T.[27]

In early July 1864, the arrival of the men of the 5th Massachusetts (Colored) Cavalry compensated for the loss caused by the transfer of the 1,000 men of the 36th U.S.C.T. Segregated from the other Union guard camps, the 5th Massachusetts Cavalry established its camp slightly farther north than where the 36th had been stationed, in the area known as Scotland Beach along the Chesapeake Bay shoreline. The main road leading to Point Lookout passed through this area, making the 5th Massachusetts camp strategically important for regulating incoming traffic and serving as an advanced defensive post. However, the camp's distance from the Point itself limited its ability to provide effective support in the event of an emergency.

The 5th Massachusetts (Colored) Cavalry mustered approximately 1,000 men, about 200 short of the full complement for a U.S. cavalry regiment. In July 1864, when the external threat intensified, prison authorities relocated the camp of the 5th farther down the Point, behind the south side of the palisade walls. The fact that the 36th and the 5th together mustered more than 2,000 men and officers demonstrates that neither experienced much difficulty recruiting at this stage of the war.

It was rumored that the 5th Massachusetts (Colored) Cavalry had been sent to Point Lookout because of accusations of cowardice stemming from the unit's conduct at the battle of Baylor's Farm (Second Petersburg) in June 1864. Although unfounded, these accusations resulted in the regiment's demotion to dismounted

26 *OR* 7/2:154, 166–167, 177.

27 *OR* 40/1:2. 582.

status, which required relinquishing all cavalry accoutrements and equipment. Now on foot and armed as infantry with Enfield rifles and standard infantry gear, the 5th reported to Point Lookout in early July 1864.

The regiment served as guards and scouts there until its transfer to the Army of the James in late March 1865. Before leaving Point Lookout, the 5th regained its mounted status, along with its horses and equipment. Ironically, the regiment then came under the command of General Hinks who had been transferred from Point Lookout a year earlier. The 5th Massachusetts (Colored) Cavalry would earn the distinction of being the first Black cavalry regiment to march into the recently captured Confederate capital of Richmond, Virginia.[28]

Barnes reported to the War Department on July 15, 1864, that the departure of the 36th U.S.C.T. in late June had greatly reduced his effective guard force and that replacements were urgently needed. Despite the arrival of the 11th and 20th Veteran Reserve Corps regiments, two companies of the 10th Veteran Reserve Corps, and the 5th Massachusetts (Colored) Cavalry in early July, the effective guard force could muster only about 2,500 men. This may appear to be a substantial guard force for a prison, but in order to watch over a rapidly increasing prison population of more than 15,000 inmates, a much larger guard contingent was required—essentially a ratio of six prisoners to one guard.[29]

For a brief period in July, the 139th Ohio Volunteer Infantry, a hundred-day regiment scheduled for discharge the following August, was transferred to Point Lookout. The small addition of the 139th's men made little difference. In August 1864, Capt. Charles Bowditch of the 5th Massachusetts (Colored) Cavalry noted that, "guard duty generally consisted of up to one-hundred sixty men on twelve hour shifts manning guard posts, besides patrols, and supernumeraries that generally formed three reliefs."[30]

In a communication dated August 1, 1864, to General Barnes, Lt. Col. George H. Washburn, commanding officer of the 20th V.R.C., reported that his men were breaking down under the rigorous demands of fatigue details, drill, and mounted patrols, while also being assigned to the Grand Guard, which was the designation of the overall guard of Point Lookout, two out of every three days. They were often detailed to duty the morning after being relieved from guard,

28 Steven M. LaBarre, *The Fifth Massachusetts Colored Cavalry in the Civil War* (Jefferson, NC, 2016), 79–92, 104–105, 130–132; *OR* 46/1:3:83.

29 *District of St. Mary's, Press Copies of Letter and Telegrams Sent*, Vol. 2, *Book No. 254* (Washington, D.C., n.d.), 1; Allen, *Forty-Six Months*, 266.

30 Charles P. Bowditch. War Letters. Unpublished manuscript, Aug. 7, 1864, Family Papers Massachusetts Historical Society.

leaving little time for rest. At this time, the understrength force was responsible for guarding approximately 16,000 prisoners. This burden taxed the men of the 20th V.R.C., as well as the rest of the garrison, almost beyond endurance, with barely enough numbers to cover the many tasks and posts required to secure and defend Point Lookout. The relentless daily regimen pushed these men nearly to the breaking point.[31]

Private George P. Risdon of Company F, 20th V.R.C., was assigned to the mounted detail that scouted and patrolled St. Mary's County instead of performing guard duty at the prison. In a letter home, Risdon wrote that his patrols covered much of lower St. Mary's County, including Leonardtown, Piney Point, and Great Mills. He also estimated the prison population at approximately 17,000 upon his arrival at Point Lookout. "This is a rather rough place here. The duty is hard."[32]

Everson wrote home describing the daily routine, politics, and other matters of interest during his time stationed at Point Lookout. He echoed the complaints of both Washburn and Risdon, characterizing their assignment there as "onerous because of the large and constantly increasing number of prisoners . . . all able-bodied men had been sent to the front" and not expecting any relief.[33]

On September 15, 1864, Barnes informed the Secretary of War that his guard force had once again been reduced to 2,161 men on post, having lost 5 officers and 185 men to detached duty within the district, followed by another 6 officers and 96 men absent as prisoner escorts. Frequent complaints from post commanding officers charged that Federal authorities failed to provide a sufficient guard force, compelling the guards to endure a rotation of three exhausting shifts protecting the prisoners and maintaining prison security, in addition to auxiliary duties. Still, Grant's front maintained the priority for reinforcements.

During the early months of 1865 more prisoners arrived from the battlefields around Richmond and Petersburg than were being released or transferred to prisons farther north. By April and May, the situation worsened as the guard force at Point Lookout was reduced by orders transferring troops west to Louisiana or Texas, or home for eventual discharge, at a faster rate than prisoners were leaving. To counter this steady reduction, prison authorities devised an unorthodox plan

31 *District of St. Mary's, Press Copies of Letter and Telegrams Sent,* Vol. 1, *Book No. 258* (Washington, D.C., n.d.), 37.

32 George P. Risdon, "Letters of Charles P. Risdon, Private. Company F, Twentieth Veteran Reserve Corps," *Chronicles of St. Mary's,* June 1983.

33 Everson, Narrative and Personal Notes, 31.

to replace the departing guards. They established a "trustee" system, assigning selected prisoners to guard duty in exchange for extra rations.

Prisoner Sam Pickens of the 5th Alabama recorded on May 30, 1865, that

> The negro guards within the Camp have been taken out & Rebels substituted. A Co. of 40 or 50 [prisoners] has been formed with [Alonzo] Morgan . . . as Captain. . . . The[y] are unarmed but I suppose the men will willingly obey them rather than have "Old Cuffy" [reference to the men of the U.S.C.T.] in here. These men doing Guard duty get extra rations, Sugar, Coffee & tobacco.[34]

In the closing months of the war, the guard force consisted of the 11th and 20th V.R.C. regiments, the 2nd Wisconsin Independent Light Artillery, five companies of the 10th U.S.C.T., three companies of the 20th U.S.C.T., the 24th and 28th U.S.C.T. regiments, and the 29th Connecticut (Colored). Along with guard duty, elements of the 28th U.S.C.T. manned the guns of Fort Stanton (Redoubt No. 1). One company of the 24th U.S.C.T. was ordered to remain during Point Lookout's closing days to secure federal property in August 1865. Many of these men departed between June and August 1865. Prison authorities reported that, prior to the final release of prisoners later that June, the guard force had been reduced to a mere 650 men guarding 18,000 prisoners—a ratio of one guard for every 28 prisoners.

## Guard Life at Point Lookout

The 2nd and 12th regiments were the first in a succession of guard regiments that would enjoy the recreation aspects of Point Lookout. Private Haynes wrote, "This will be an agreeable change from the past few weeks —to be in a settled camp, no more long marches, mail and rations regular, a chance to bathe, fish, and have a good time on the water." By the time their replacement regiments arrived, these enjoyed pleasures became restricted and almost non-existent due to their increased duties and extended hours guarding thousands of prisoners.[35]

Captain Asa Bartlett of the 12th New Hampshire wrote that after the arrival of the 2nd and 12th Regiments, the men were marched to their designated campgrounds. Once dismissed from the ranks, they rushed to the Potomac River to drown the vermin and lice, more commonly referred to as "gray backs," the

34 G. Ward Hubbs, *Voices from Company D: Diaries by the Greensboro Guards, Fifth Alabama Infantry Regiment, Army of Northern Virginia* (Athens, GA, 2003), 384–385.

35 Haynes, *A Soldier Boy's Letters*, 124.

ever-present companions of both armies. The following day, the men burned their filthy, worn-out uniforms in bonfires. "Coats, pants, vests, shirts, socks, shoes and caps" were quickly consumed by the flames, after which the quartermaster department issued complete replacements of uniforms. With the battlefield behind them, now in clean uniforms, shaven, hair trimmed, the men's morale began to improve.[36]

Haynes reported that the men camped on level ground in A-frame, or "common," tents, conveniently near the shore of the Potomac River, so close that, "The first thing this morning, when reveille was blown, nearly every man in the regiment made a dash for the water for a plunge and a swim." The next morning began with a dress parade of all troops, during which "General Order No. 1, Commanding Officer, Point Lookout," was read to the assembled soldiers. The order announced that Gen. Gilman Marston had assumed command of the "District of Saint Mary's," after which the reading of General Order No. 2 followed, establishing the daily routine for the Union soldiers. Shortly afterward, Special Order No. 2 was issued, detailing twenty men from both regiments to serve as mounted scouts under the orders of General Halleck.[37]

Guard rations at this time consisted of baked beans, coffee, beefsteak, potatoes, boiled pork, boiled fresh beef, boiled salt beef, and parsley greens. A loaf of soft bread was included, and occasionally a ration of molasses. The designated cook in Haynes's company (Company I), along with the cook from another company, was permitted to construct a small two-chambered brick oven at the end of the company street to prepare beans, meat, and bread. "Clay is used for mortar and where the bricks come from is one of the company secrets." Other companies followed suit and built a number of these small utility ovens themselves.

Haynes recounted the tactics the men used to supplement their rations, which included the bounty provided by Point Lookout Creek, the Potomac River, and the Chesapeake Bay. He described the abundance of seafood in all three. The men especially enjoyed harvesting oysters from the enormous beds less than a stone's throw from shore, using improvised rakes to work them. Fishing was another favored pastime. "The boys catch some nice fish here, among which are sea trout," Haynes described. "We were in the seventh heaven of the soldier's paradise."[38]

36 Bartlett, *History of the Twelfth*,145–146.

37 Haynes, *A Soldier Boy's Letters*, 126; Martin A. Haynes, *History of the Second Regiment New Hampshire Volunteers Its Camps, Marches and Battles Martin A. Haynes* (1865; repr. Manchester, NH, 2021), 155; *District of St. Mary's, Press Copies of Letter and Telegrams Sent*, Vol. 4, *Book No. 251* (Washington, D.C., 1863).

38 Haynes, *History of the Second*, 128, 135, 157.

Following the issue of new uniforms, the men established regimental camps on the Potomac River side of the Point. The 12th located its campground just south of Point Lookout Creek (present-day Lake Conoy), with the 2nd New Hampshire settling immediately to its south. The company officers (captains and first and second lieutenants) resided in proper relation to their companies, with their quarters constructed along the shore of the Potomac River. The field and staff officers resided "in the tenements" on what was dubbed "Chesapeake Avenue," closer to command headquarters on the bay side of the Point. Eventually, Marston ordered them to relocate their quarters in proximity to their regiments. Before the end of 1863, the New Hampshire men also received the new "Model 1863" Springfield rifle.[39]

The area north of the prison pen on the shore of the Chesapeake Bay later became the camp of the 5th New Hampshire, established upon its arrival in November. The camp was named "Camp Cross" in honor of their former colonel, Edward E. Cross, killed in action at the Wheatfield during the battle of Gettysburg.

The artillery batteries that arrived the following February occupied the ground south and west of the prison along the Potomac River shoreline. The infantry camps bordered the prison on the north and west, with the Chesapeake Bay forming a natural barrier on the east until construction of the fourth side of the prison stockade completed the enclosure.

During August, Haynes described the men beginning to "stockade" their tents by using vertically installed lumber that elevated them at least four feet, with a wedge tent placed on top as the roof. He also noted the construction of a defensive palisade wall near their camps, and that the "sinks" (latrines) over the river had been started. An 80-foot flagstaff had been raised "on the parade ground in front of the regiment" for dress parades and guard mount. The flagpole also served as an instrument of punishment. At least 20 new replacement soldiers or "substitutes," were apprehended for desertion had been tied to the flagpole as a punitive measure, in addition to being "bucked and gagged or otherwise disciplined."[40]

Thanks to its new location, the garrison enjoyed consistent mail service. Once they were encamped at Point Lookout, mail began to catch up to the New Hampshire men. A post office was already in operation prior to their arrival, permitting delivery to the Point, which now included the Union garrison. Haynes was made mail clerk for the 2nd New Hampshire.

39 Haynes, *A Soldier Boy's Letters*, 130, 138.

40 Haynes. *A History*, 131, 133, 135, 142, 152.

Shelters for the Union guard soon improved. Haynes noted in January 1864 that the wedge, or common, tents in which they were then quartered were replaced by the much larger circular Sibley tents. Their wedge tents were sent to the prison to house the ever-increasing number of prisoners. Haynes and his company continued to stockade their Sibleys in the same fashion, using cut logs to extend the height of their new quarters by at least four feet. Each tent was intended to hold at least 10 men rather than the usual four to which they had been accustomed.[41]

Marston allowed a wide range of privileges within the limits of military rules and discipline. Passes were issued to officers and men permitting visits to the villages of nearby Leonardtown and "The Pines" (the present-day town of Ridge.) The Pines was located approximately seven miles north of Point Lookout. According to Capt. Thomas Livermore of the 5th New Hampshire, The Pines was also the name of a tavern frequented by officers and enlisted men.[42]

After adjusting to the sudden arrival of several hundred Union men, local civilians soon recognized the benefits of the additional business brought by the northern soldiers. The influx provided an immediate boost to the local economy, particularly at the local tavern known as, "The Pines." Captain Bartlett stated that the local tavern was a short pleasure trip into the country and that it was a place to "have a home-reminding chat with the girls, and to get a wee sip of 'apple jack' as an appetizer." Bartlett also observed that the relationship between officers and enlisted men was somewhat relaxed, as "camp guard had long been a thing of the past." As there was no immediate threat, the men, for the time being, were exempt from camp guard, but not that of the peninsula and the prison. Enlisted men were permitted to come and go as they pleased so long as they reported for roll call on time and were present for their turn at guard and other regimental duties.[43]

Soon after the camps and daily routines were established, the 2nd New Hampshire began construction of a Masonic Hall. Diary entries indicate that the Masonic Order thrived among both the Federal guard and the prison population during the war. Masonic intervention was called upon on more than one occasion while Point Lookout was in operation. Lodges were built by both the 2nd and 5th New Hampshire regiments and served a dual purpose as hospitals. Fraternal organizations also included an ad hoc society known as "the Bummer's Club" ("bummer" was a term used to describe a loafer or an idle person). This inclusive

41 Ibid., 150.

42 Thomas L. Livermore, *Dates and Events 1860–1866* (Boston, MA, 1920), 317.

43 Bartlett, *History of the Twelfth*, 155.

organization was composed of officers from various guard units as well as camp doctors, chaired by the chief surgeon of Hammond Hospital.[44]

Another pastime enjoyed by both men and officers was sailing. They collected boats from the coast above the garrison, and soon the nearby shoreline was crowded with them. The men became so skilled at sailing on the river that they ventured around the point even in the roughest weather. Their numbers grew so large that Marston found it necessary to take control of the many boats used by both military and civilian occupants, placing the "canoes and boats . . . whether captured or abandoned . . . in the custody of Capt. A[braham] Edwards A.A.Q.M . . . Edwards will grant written permits for their use."[45]

The arrangement of the guard camps included the essential features required for organization and sanitation. Latrines, referred to as sinks, were crucial both for maintaining sanitary conditions and for the comfort of the men. These sinks were shallow trenches typically placed at a distance from the camps to reduce the risk of contaminating water sources and spreading disease. At Point Lookout, however, this practice could not be followed. The site lies only one to two feet above sea level, leaving the groundwater table extremely high. As a result, any significant digging quickly caused holes and ditches to fill with water.

The new camp latrines were designed to match those used by the prisoners in the pen. While permanent facilities were under construction, Marston ordered that temporary latrines for the Union men be of the trench type commonly employed while on campaign. However, because of the high-water table, the trenches quickly filled with water and soon became unhealthy, miasmic bogs infested with flies and mosquitoes. General Hinks, then the commanding officer, ordered the sinks to be filled with clean gravel and buried. Eventually, offshore piers and platforms were completed with privies positioned over the river rather than on land. Haynes wrote on August 10, 1863, "I watched the operations of a pile driver. We are to have a sink way out over the river and the piles for its support are being driven into the sand." As at Hammond Hospital, latrines, or sinks, were constructed over the river, providing a practical solution for both prisoners and guards, as the tide carried away the waste. This proved a better alternative than the continual digging of ditches for latrines.[46]

As the camps were bordered by the bay, river, marshes, and swamps, mosquitoes and flies plagued the men without distinction. In August, Haynes

44 Haynes, *A History*, 208, 211; Everson, Papers No. 28/710/22, 28–29.

45 *Book No. 251*, General Order 15.

46 Haynes, *A Soldier Boy's Letters*, 130.

wrote home describing his struggle against the swarms of flies that he and his tentmate endured. "Dan and I have just risen in our wrath and put an end to—well I won't try to tell how many millions of flies. By the judicious application of a couple of towels we wiped cartloads of them from the face of the earth."[47]

In June 1864, Lt. Erastus Everson recalled plagues of mosquitoes. "Another pest was the mosquito, or rather the myriads of them that occasionally seemed to come in clouds from across the water. They clung to and covered everything." Only the odorous, soot-producing smudge pots could drive them away and provide relief.[48]

In addition to manning the numerous guard posts around the Point, soldiers performed the usual camp duties essential to the functioning of a regiment. These included fatigue or work details, inspections of troops and camps, dress parade, and the police guard necessary to secure an army in the field. With the arrival of new recruits, drill exercises were ordered: a minimum of two hours in the morning and two hours in the afternoon for all those not assigned guard duty. "We usually drilled by companies two hours in the forenoon and by regiment two hours in the afternoon," Capt. Thomas Livermore of the 5th New Hampshire described. "The company officers attended a school in tactics and regulations in the evening held by a field officer."[49]

The procedure for the off-going guard was to discharge their weapons before returning to camp. Some men of the 2nd New Hampshire found amusement in firing their rifles at the mortar boat U.S.S. *William Bacon*—as well as other nearby vessels—anchored just off their camp on the Potomac River. This mischief not only angered Marston but also greatly disturbed the crews of the ships. Marston ordered that such "target practice" cease and that the relieved guard henceforth discharge their rifles on the bay side of the Point.[50]

Several sutlers' stores operated throughout Point Lookout. One primary location was Hammond Hospital, while each of the guard regimental camps also accommodated a sutler. Despite regulations set by the commissary general of prisoners and the post commanding officer, sutlers at Point Lookout were still

47 Ibid., 135.

48 Erastus Watson Everson, Papers No. 28/710/22, 32.

49 Child, *Letters from a Civil War Surgeon*, 239; Livermore, *Dates and Events*, 314.

50 *Book No. 255*, Vol. 3, *District of St. Mary's, Press Copies of Letter and Telegrams Sent* (Washington, D.C., 1865), 6; *District of St. Mary's, Book 251,* General Order No. 2.

often accused of operating unscrupulously. Commandants tended to encourage them to self-regulate or face consequences imposed by the regiment.[51]

## Racial Friction Within the Guard Force

Even though they wore the same uniform, relations between the Black and White soldiers of the guard were not harmonious. While the men of the White guard units welcomed the relief provided by the arrival of Black soldiers, many resented efforts to treat them as equals. This resentment led to further rancor and discrimination against the men of the U.S.C.T. from White soldiers, both officers and enlisted.

Despite the Emancipation Proclamation and the repeal of the Militia Act of 1792, more than two centuries of enslavement and its horrors were not suddenly erased. The men of the White regiments, for the most part, refused integration with the Black units, and in some cases the feeling was mutual. White guards expressed as much contempt and animosity toward U.S.C.T. soldiers as did the Confederate prisoners. Tensions between prisoners and guards escalated further once the U.S.C.T. men began staffing posts.

Lieutenant Everson reasoned that both the geographical origins of Black recruits and their former stations in life most likely influenced their military bearing. He further surmised from his own experience that he was "convinced . . . that colored men enlisted in cities and large towns in the North . . . were much more difficult to manage than those who had recently been slaves. The first named had learned all the evil ways of their localities; to obey with the last-named class was natural."[52]

In June 1864, Everson was involved in an incident that underscored the ongoing animosity between White and Black troops. The case resulted in the arrest and eventual court-martial of one of Everson's sergeants in the 20th V.R.C., who had refused to serve with a squad of Black soldiers. The outcome of the court-martial set a precedent for the future integration of Black and White troops. After District Commanding Officer Gen. Christopher C. Augur and Secretary of War Stanton reviewed the case, Stanton sent a strongly worded telegram to Gen.

51 "Civil War Prison Scenes Preserved in Cartoons," *The San Francisco Call* (San Francisco, CA), May 28, 1911, 5, accessed March 4, 2025, https://chroniclingamerica.loc.gov/lccn/sn85066387/1911-05-28/ed-1/seq-5/.

52 Everson, Papers No. 28/710/22, 107; Everson, Narrative and Personal Notes, 33.

James Barnes that included an order "forbidding a repetition of the act of placing colored non-commissioned officers over White ones."[53]

Throughout the operation of Point Lookout prison, incidents of racial friction persisted between the rank and file of both White and Black troops. Prisoner Lt. John Blue of the 11th Virginia Cavalry recorded that men of one V.R.C. unit, "or some of them at least had assured us that they would not interfere if we would manage to drown every negro on the Point." Several prisoners likewise stated that "the white troops were incensed against them [U.S.C.T. guards] and often 'rocked' them while walking their posts."[54]

The act of "rocking" referred to the indiscriminate throwing of stones at the U.S.C.T. guards who patrolled the catwalk and other guard posts of the prison and camps. Several prisoner witnesses reported that both prisoners and White guards engaged in such actions. Private James Huffman of the 10th Virginia recalled, "They [U.S.C.T. guards] became so obnoxious, hateful, and mean that we stoned them of nights . . . We would gather a pocketful of rocks and on dark nights stone them like fury and run to our tents and go to sleep instantly, if not sooner." The U.S.C.T. guards, in turn, retaliated against the prisoners regardless of the source of the thrown stones.[55]

Post commanders also had to address complaints lodged by local citizens against soldiers of the Black units. Susan Welch, a farmer from the nearby town of Ridge, reported that a detachment of the 5th Massachusetts Cavalry destroyed 76 rails of her farm fence. A more serious matter arose in February 1865 when two cavalry troopers of the 5th Massachusetts—Privates William Underhill and George Butler of Companies E and D, respectively—were court-martialed for offenses committed against a family in St. Mary's County. Underhill was acquitted but fined six months' pay for indecent and disorderly conduct. Butler, however, was found guilty and sentenced to twenty years in prison.[56]

These incidents frequently tested the patience of post commanders, often forcing them to issue revised general orders. After losing patience with the men of the 5th Massachusetts Cavalry because of their disciplinary problems, an exasperated Barnes was reported to have remarked that there were "just two

53 Letter by Erastus Watson Everson, "Letters," n.d., South Carolina Historical Society, Charleston, SC, note 3, 34.

54 *Book No. 258*, 40; John Blue, *Hanging Rock Rebel: Lt. John Blue's War in West Virginia and the Shenandoah Valley*, ed. Daniel P. Oates (Shippensburg, PA, 1994), 277; Letter by James T. Wells, James T. Wells Papers, n.d., Smith and Wells Papers, South Caroliniana Library.

55 James Huffman, *Ups and Downs of a Confederate Soldier* (New York, 1940), 91–92.

56 *Book No.258*, 42; LaBarre, *The Fifth*, 111–112.

places where they [Black soldiers] were unfit for duty—one of them is in the field and the other out of it."[57]

## Remedy or Pandora's Box?

A supposed solution was found to counter the foul, contaminated water pumped from the wells, but it proved more of a curse than a remedy for the post's commanding officers. The time-honored substitute for bad water, whiskey, soon became available thanks to the additional rations allowed to the hospital, in addition to routine rations allowed the garrison and support staff. Although Hoffman outlawed its use by prisoners except for medicinal purposes, whiskey inevitably found its way into the prison population. For the guard and hospital staff, whiskey became the preferred additive that made the water at Point Lookout tolerable. Yet smuggled whiskey led to a host of headaches for the post's commanders.[58]

Alcohol consumption had become widespread throughout the garrison, to the point that Marston halted deliveries of alcohol to the post sutler in an attempt to curb its availability to his troops. On March 16, 1864, Marston issued General Order No. 3, prohibiting the sale of alcohol by "stores, traders, taverns and others" to any government or military personnel without a license to sell spirits within the Military District of St. Mary's. Physicians and surgeons were exempt from this order, provided that "spirituous liquors and wine were used in the practice of their profession." His efforts, however, proved futile, as the avenues for acquiring and consuming alcohol in various forms and quantities were nearly impossible to control. Drunkenness and alcoholism among both officers and enlisted men continued to plague Point Lookout for the duration of the prison's existence.[59]

The distribution and acquisition of alcohol continued through official channels despite the efforts of successive commanding officers at Point Lookout to control its abuse. Surviving records reveal that the commissary department was permitted to issue whiskey by requisition to the garrison and that it was also supplied regularly to various other personnel at the post. This likely explains why so many officers and men were arrested for drunkenness, both on and off duty.

57 Everson, Narrative and Personal Notes, 6–7.

58 Everson, Letter, August 7, 1864; W. J. Rorabaugh, *The Alcoholic Republic: An American Tradition* (New York, 1979), 5.

59 "General Orders No. 3," *Hammond Gazette*, March 23, 1864, 2, accessed March 8, 2025, https://www.loc.gov/resource/sn82002197/1864-03-23/ed-1/?sp=2&st=image&r=-0.116,0.371,1.233,0.742,0; Nathan A. Mazoli, "Not the Soldiers We Need," *Army History* (Fall 2022), 49, accessed March 8, 2025, https://ky.ng.mil/Portals/59/Army%20History%20Magazine/Issues%20by%20PDF/Army_History_Magazine_125.pdf?ver=6rXuMtNQvbyQ4CGbR7ei0g%3D%3D.

To regulate the whiskey ration and curb rampant drinking, General Barnes issued General Order No. 33, District of St. Mary's, which restricted the whiskey ration for officers to one gallon per month—a measure that still seems generous. Officers generally retained much for personal use but also rationed portions to the men of their commands.[60]

Surgeons from the hospitals at Point Lookout requested whiskey in varying quantities, usually ranging from a gallon to a canteen (one quart). Requisitions also came from the inspector general and his staff, the harbor masters, telegraph operators, post printers, and the officers and staff of the quartermaster and commissary departments. In addition, the provost marshal was authorized to issue a whiskey ration to Confederate prisoners as compensation for labor performed or as an incentive to volunteer.

Requisitions also included those from naval officers for their mess and for the crews of visiting ships and boats. Civilians employed by the federal authorities at the Point were permitted a ration, including the lighthouse keeper, Pamelia Edwards. Orders were further issued to the regimental commanding officers of the guard force to requisition whiskey for their men to celebrate holidays. From mid-May 1864 to July 1, 1865, more than 600 gallons of whiskey were issued by the post commissariat to those who requisitioned it. This figure accounts only for whiskey that was "officially" requisitioned and issued.[61]

Whiskey was not the only proposed replacement for the bad water. In May 1864, Lt. Col. Gilbert Jennings, commanding officer of the 11th V.R.C., requested permission from Barnes "that the sutler of his regiment be allowed to sell ale in limited quantities, to the enlisted men of his regiment." His justification was that the Assistant Surgeon of the regiment "recommends it on account of the water obliged to be used." Jennings's request was quickly returned by General Barnes, marked "disapproved."[62]

## Draftees and Substitutes

Arriving with the 5th New Hampshire were the new men brought in through the draft and substitute programs of the Enrollment Act. The Enrollment Act, also known as the Conscription Act, became law on March 3, 1863. Its purpose was to replenish the depleted ranks of the Federal army. It was hoped

60 *Book No. 255*, 486.

61 *Book No. 251,* General Order Aug. 1863–Aug. 1865; Ibid., Special Orders Aug. 1863–Aug.1865.

62 *Book No. 258*, 36.

that the arrival of new men would ease the burden of guard duty for the Point's beleaguered regiments. The additional numbers were welcomed, but meaningful relief was another matter. Haynes observed on November 14, 1863, that, "750 . . . mostly substitutes . . . have not come to help us on guard duty, but to be drilled preparatory to going to the front."[63] The inexperience and low morale of many of those that were assigned to the Point often added to the manpower woes, as they required greater command vigilance to prevent desertion. This responsibility further strained the already meager guard force at Point Lookout.[64] Illness also continued to sap the ranks of the available guard forces.

By the end of the year, recreational activities previously enjoyed by the soldiers came to an abrupt end. Passes, once available to veteran soldiers, became almost nonexistent except for requests involving extended leave. Marston's sudden change in policy followed the arrival of 800 men of the 5th New Hampshire on November 14, 1863. According to Capt. Thomas Livermore, most of these soldiers were "drafted men, who for the most part had sold themselves without patriotism or a desire to do their duty as soldiers." Captain Asa Bartlett wrote of his disdain for the new men, noting that their ranks were being reinforced with the "bounty-jumping class of recruits" whom he described as "the lowest class of almost every nationality." According to Bartlett, the new men engaged in "every scheme and effort to evade duty or desert the service," concluding that "they were not worth the trouble of keeping."[65]

Haynes agreed with the captain, writing that their first allotment of drafted men were "foreigners watching for an opportunity to desert." He further complained that they "never had a guard around our camp until today, but now it is to be a fixture." Some of the new recruits drowned while attempting to escape to Virginia, including one who used a coffin taken from the Point as a boat. One deserter was executed by order of court-martial, a sentence intended to discourage further desertions among these men. By mid-December, the 2nd received an additional 350 conscripts.[66]

The new substitutes and draftees created additional headaches for the veteran New Hampshire troops and for General Marston. The old members of the brigade quickly learned that these men were not cut from the same cloth as the "Boys of

63 Haynes, *A Soldier Boy's Letters*, 142–143, 148.

64 United States Congress, "An Act for Enrolling and Calling out the National Forces, and for Other Purposes," in *The Statutes at Large, Treaties, and Proclamations*, ed. George P. Sanger (Boston, 1863), 12:763.

65 Livermore, *Dates and Events*, 313; Bartlett, *History of the Twelfth*, 151, 153–154.

66 Haynes, *A History*, 206; Haynes, *A Soldier Boy's Letters*, 152–153.

'61" and could not be depended upon. To prevent desertion, many of the enlistees were transported under guard to ensure their arrival. Despite these measures, some slipped past the guards and were never seen again.

The new draftees' continual attempts to desert led to the enforcement of mandatory roll calls three times a day, one more than required for prisoners, for the men guarding Point Lookout. Chaplain John W. Adams, assigned to the 2nd New Hampshire, wrote that,

> some of these ex-prison convicts would step behind a soldier in his own tent, throw his overcoat cape over his head and face, and clasping it with both arms, an accomplice would rob his pockets and escape before he could be seen. I was told that Col. Bailey [commanding officer of the 2nd New Hampshire], never trusted himself alone with these men without his hands upon his side arms.[67]

The veterans resented having their privileges curtailed and regulations enforced because of the actions of the new men. In addition to guarding them, they were also burdened with forcing the recruits to perform the duties of a soldier. The officers and NCOs of the garrison employed several prescribed methods of punishment to enforce compliance and discipline among those who refused to obey orders.

## Punishment and an Execution

Punishment for minor infractions of rules and regulations came in various forms. Authorities meted out justice by administering corporal punishment to those found guilty of minor transgressions. These punishments could include hanging by the thumbs, confinement, extra duty, or other non-lethal measures devised by commanders. By the time of the Civil War, however, flogging—whipping an offender—had been outlawed by both the United States Army and Navy. Army regulations stipulated that more serious offenses, such as desertion, murder, sleeping while on guard, and aiding the enemy, warranted capital punishment or "such other punishment as shall be inflicted by the sentence of a court martial."[68]

Private Henry A. Burnham of Company E, 5th New Hampshire, was found guilty by court-martial of the charge of desertion while at Point Lookout. He had also illegally collected four enlistment bounties. Burnham deserted, was captured, tried by court-martial, and placed in the guardhouse. While awaiting sentencing,

67 John W. Adams, *My Experiences as Army Chaplain* (Westbrook, ME, n.d.), 5.

68 Bartlett, *History of the Twelfth*, 155–156; U.S. Department of the Army, *Revised United*, 493.

he broke confinement and fled a second time with fellow deserters. During this attempt, Burnham and his companions tried to escape by boat across the bay. Their guards quickly discovered the escape, and Burnham and the others were recaptured and returned to the guardhouse. Because of these repeated desertion attempts, the members of the court-martial again found Burnham guilty of desertion and sentenced him to execution by firing squad.[69]

On the morning of May 9, 1864, in accordance with General Orders No. 15, the troops of the command were marched to an open field across from what was then known as "the grove." This area, consisting mostly of pine trees, remains much the same today and was located on the Chesapeake Bay side of the Point. The field used for the execution lay on the Potomac River side, across Route 5 near the present-day picnic pavilion. The command formed three sides of a hollow square, and a detachment of 12 men from the provost guard placed Burnham before the firing squad. After delivering his final words, he was ordered to bend to one knee, after which the command to fire was given.[70]

The execution of Burnham was intended to serve as a warning to potential deserters and to demonstrate the gravity of his offense, with the expectation that future offenders would be dealt with in the same manner. After the departure of the 2nd New Hampshire in April 1864, two privates from the regiment were also found guilty of desertion while at Point Lookout, but they were not executed until the unit reached Yorktown, Virginia, on April 19, 1864.

Some deserters caught by guards at Point Lookout received summary punishment immediately during their escape attempts, eliminating the necessity of a court-martial. In one incident, a substitute was captured one night while attempting to desert. After his arrest, he verbally abused his captors beyond their tolerance. The deserter was returned to camp "silent and submissive and buried the next day." Joint escape attempts by Confederate prisoners with Union soldiers usually resulted in both being shot by the guard. On more than one occasion, Confederate prisoners reported hearing rifle fire at night and later saw the bodies of both Union and Confederate soldiers lying dead on the bay-side beach.[71]

During one of the surprise camp inspections conducted by company officers, it was discovered that several substitutes were constructing a boat in preparation for escape. Captain Edwin Bedee, of the 12th New Hampshire, determined that they should not be denied a boat ride after expending all that effort building the

69 Mazoli, "Not the Soldiers," 38.

70 Child, *Letters from a Civil War Surgeon*, 242.

71 Bartlett, *History of the Twelfth*, 154.

craft. As punishment, Bedee ordered four of the would-be escapees to carry the boat on their shoulders—two on each end—while two more sat inside and plied the oars as if rowing for their lives. To ensure fairness, Bedee rotated the positions after each circuit of the camp so that all of them could enjoy the sights of their trip equally.[72]

Other forms of punishment were devised by regimental commanders to stem the tide of desertion. Watching these punishments being carried out provided a measure of amusement and satisfaction to the veteran soldiers of the garrison. Harsh as some measures may have seemed, they failed to diminish the determination of these "subs" to desert or to commit other crimes. Still, despite the lower quality of men appearing in the ranks, not all the new recruits were undesirable. Adjutant Elias H. Marston stated that approximately 86 of these new men from Concord, New Hampshire, would prove themselves to be good soldiers, bringing the number up to 800 men for duty in the 5th New Hampshire.[73]

The prison camp was soon expanded, which doubled the number of posts. This further strained resources, often requiring twice as many men for guard duty. Marston ordered that every man, regardless of his usual assignment, "shall take a gun" and stand guard. This order included officers' servants, company cooks, hospital "bummers," and other auxiliary personnel until reinforcements arrived.

## Sanctuary

Confederate authorities feared that the flight of enslaved people, often with their families, would drastically weaken the Southern war effort, since they were the primary source of agricultural and military labor. The departure of male slaves between the ages of 16 and 26 was of particular concern, as this group represented the peak of labor productivity. Their escape not only promised to strengthen eventual recruitment into United States forces but also to undermine the Southern economy. Federal authorities at Point Lookout recognized these realities at the local level and were quick to exploit them.

In mid-1862, construction began on Hammond Hospital. Former slaves fleeing north sought sanctuary at Point Lookout, which appeared safe after the Federal army occupied the site. They were given the opportunity to assist in building the hospital and to work for the government within the complex, taking advantage of a safe refuge before continuing farther north. At Point Lookout, abolition activists also concealed them from former masters who sought to reclaim

72 Ibid., 156.

73 Child, *Letters from a Civil War Surgeon*, 240.

their runaway property. The Act Prohibiting the Return of Slaves required Union officers to protect fugitive slaves from their owners, under penalty of dismissal from the service if found guilty of refusal. This provision continued to provide sanctuary to the formerly enslaved.

Eyewitness accounts from hospital attendants reported that local slaveholders arrived several times to reclaim their runaway slaves, citing their rights in affidavits under the Confiscation Act. Some abolitionist supporters at the hospital considered the affidavits to be ruses to regain their alleged "property." Despite abolitionist protests, local slaveholders continued to petition the commanding officer at Point Lookout for the return of their chattel. Abolitionists continued to shelter those seeking freedom as they could.

In February 1863, the new commanding officer of Point Lookout and Southern Maryland, Brigadier General Henry H. Lockwood, arrived to assume command of the newly created First Separate Brigade posted in that region. Because Lockwood was from the border state of Delaware, his loyalty came under suspicion by the abolitionist faction at Point Lookout. Citing the conditions of the Act, he surrendered runaway slaves harbored in the hospital area to their owners, once proof of their oath-taking had been provided. With the issuance of the Emancipation Proclamation on January 1, 1863, Lockwood modified his policy and totally refused to return enslaved people. He was eventually transferred in June 1863 to command a brigade in the XII Corps of the Army of the Potomac.[74]

By late 1863, the influx of formerly enslaved people seeking asylum at Point Lookout presented an additional challenge for Federal authorities. As their numbers grew, a camp for contrabands—or at least a designated area for them—became necessary. Guards, already overburdened with protecting thousands of prisoners and their camps, were now assigned the additional responsibility of safeguarding the many formerly enslaved people and their families at Point Lookout as they pursued their freedom.

Once legislation was passed in mid-1863 permitting the recruitment of formerly enslaved men as soldiers for the United States Army and Navy, many from the contraband camp enlisted in the United States Colored Troops. When the 36th U.S.C.T. and the 5th Massachusetts (Colored) Cavalry arrived at Point Lookout, additional men from the camp enlisted, as did others into the 38th U.S.C.T. being recruited in St. Mary's County. Recruitment reduced the camp's population slightly. Nevertheless, hundreds of women and children remained, and many more continued to arrive.

74 *OR* 3/3:153.

Private Haynes described the desperate measures some enslaved families were taking, now that the sanctuary they sought was being granted under the protection of United States forces at Point Lookout. "A slave family . . . came over last night from Virginia. There were a man and his wife and three children, they traveled all day, on foot to reach the river . . . although the water was very rough, they all packed into a little dugout canoe and got safely across the 6 or 8 miles of tossing waters that to them was a highway to liberty." Haynes later recorded that "seven boatloads of negroes have come in from Virginia . . . there were 32 men, women, and children with all their household truck, packed into one boat."[75]

The camp established for the formerly enslaved—referred to as "Camp Contraband"—enabled prison authorities to better provide for and protect the many who arrived each week. This designated area was situated just south of the prison stockade and directly across from the stable and livery area. The main road that ran through Point Lookout bordered the camp, giving its inhabitants the opportunity to welcome newly arriving Confederate prisoners and bid farewell to those departing. Private James Franklin of the 4th Alabama commented on October 21, 1863, that after they arrived, prisoners were marched to the stockade along the country road at Point Lookout. They were escorted by some of the formerly enslaved who lined the route. The prisoners marched "past a camp of contrabands who all turned out to greet us . . . Cuffee appears to be having a regular holyday here."[76]

In correspondence dated April 7, 1864, the commanding officer, Gen. Edward Hinks, requested instructions or "views" from his superior, Gen. Butler, regarding the "proper disposition of the contrabands" gathering at Point Lookout. At that time, more than 400 formerly enslaved people were residing at the Point in deplorable conditions. Their shelters consisted of shacks and discarded army tents—similar to those used by the prisoners—or, in some cases, holes in the ground covered with whatever materials could be found. "Humanity and decency," Hinks explained, "demand some immediate action in their behalf."[77]

Due to the severe overcrowding of the camp, many of the formerly enslaved were transported north to work as laborers. Others found employment at Point Lookout as servants for army officers, while some were hired by the government as teamsters, loading and unloading supply ships, cutting firewood, digging ditches,

75 Haynes, *A Soldier Boy's Letters*, 138, 145, 155.

76 Bartlett, *History of the Twelfth*, 164; James Franklin, Diary of James Franklin, unpublished manuscript, n.d., 25, Virginia Historical Society, Richmond.

77 *Book No. 253*, 13–14.

and even digging graves. Some of these workers received pay for their labor, while many others were compensated with shelter and food provided by the government.

As the number of contrabands increased, Col. Alonzo Draper of the 36th U.S.C.T., who succeeded Hinks, ordered Assistant Quartermaster Capt. Hollister E. Goodwin to provide an additional 48 shelter halves (referred to as "dog" tents) to Sergeant A. C. Potter, who oversaw the contraband camp, in order to house the growing number of refugees arriving at Point Lookout. Less than a month later, Potter was ordered by the new commanding officer, General Barnes, to "turn over all contrabands under your charge to the Superintendent of Government Farms on the Patuxent River," thus relieving him of this assignment.[78]

Another solution to the overcrowding of the contraband camp came in the form of agricultural labor for the Federal government. Both Colonel Draper and General Hinks, in separate correspondence as early as April 1864, suggested to Butler that they be permitted to confiscate certain deserted farms and plantations in St. Mary's County for the purpose of employing the hundreds of contraband men, women, and children to work the land for the government. This policy amounted to the seizure of vast tracts of real estate, along with personal property and assets abandoned by the original owners within the District of St. Mary's County.[79]

Plantations and farms previously owned by known Southern sympathizers and abandoned once Federal authority was established were targeted for confiscation. Among the first seized was "The Plains," owned by Col. John H. Sothoron, along with two adjoining plantations, "Sandgates" and "Cole's Creek," both abandoned by their owner, Capt. Joseph Forrest, then serving in the Confederate army. Eventually, one of the four manors owned by the Thomas family, known as "Mattapany" plantation—whose owner had three sons in Confederate service—was also confiscated. All four plantations afforded direct access to the Patuxent River, facilitating the transport of troops, crops, and supplies. In total, federal authorities seized approximately 7,000 acres. These were not the only properties taken, as at least four additional plantations came under scrutiny by Point Lookout authorities in the Great Mills and Ridge/St. Inigoes areas.[80]

The former plantations were occupied and worked by hundreds of contrabands transferred from Point Lookout. These "government farms," as they were called,

78 *Book No. 255*, 148, 169.

79 *Book No. 253*, 32–34; *OR* 3/3:152.

80 William A. Dobak, *Freedom by the Sword: The U.S. Colored Troops, 1862–1867* (Washington, D.C., 2011), 316–317; Rick Richter, *Three Cheers for the Chesapeake! History of the 4th Maryland Light Artillery Battery in the Civil War* (Atglen, PA, 2017), 173; *District of St. Mary's Book No. 253* Vol.1, 119, 408; *Book No. 255*, 136.

were guarded by Union troops from Point Lookout and, for a time, by soldiers from the recruiting depot at Camp Stanton in nearby Benedict, Maryland. Temporary hospitals were also established, including the Cole House on the Cole's Creek plantation, which was used as a hospital for contrabands. They were staffed and supported by assistant surgeons and stewards from Point Lookout. Since the guards, surgeons, and other personnel were assigned from the Point, prison authorities provided them with rations and supplies, as well as supporting the farm workers.[81]

Situated along the Patuxent River, the farms offered a strategic location for transporting crops and supporting organizational needs. The former plantations were worked with farm tools and implements confiscated during raids in Virginia led by Draper and Hinks. Farm machinery from plantations in St. Mary's County was also seized for this purpose. This plan ultimately resolved the overcrowding of the contraband camp—leading to its closure—as the farm system became fully operational. The recruitment of Black men from the farms into United States service caused a minor reduction in production, but there was no shortage of others willing to take their place.

After the close of the war, property owners returning to reclaim their land were first required to swear an oath of allegiance to the United States. Once the conditions of ownership were met, property claims and requests for compensation could be submitted. John Sothoron and his son returned to the area in 1867 after having fled to Canada following a shooting incident on his farm involving a federal recruiting party. Sothoron's claims for losses of property were denied in 1868, though the land itself was eventually restored to him. Two of the Thomas sons—one of whom had been twice imprisoned at Point Lookout—also returned after the war, reclaiming possession of at least three of their manors: Mattapany, Deep Falls, and De La Brooke.[82]

The Freedmen's Bureau, established by the State of Maryland in November 1864, should not be confused with the Federal Bureau of Refugees, Freedmen, and Abandoned Lands, created by Congress in March 1865. The Federal bureau eventually replaced and assumed the responsibilities of the Maryland bureau once it was established. Until then, the Maryland bureau was tasked with overseeing the seizures of farms carried out under Draper and Hinks. The properties were administered by bureau agent Lt. Edward T. O'Brien, in keeping with the general

81 *Book No. 258*, 92.

82 Sothoron and his son, shot and killed Lieutenant Eben White while White was recruiting Sothoron's slaves for the Union army. Sothoron also wounded one of two U.S.C.T. soldiers accompanying Lt. White.

practice that all confiscated lands fell under the management of Federal army officers. Locally, Capt. Asa A. Lawrence commanded the bureau's branch office in nearby Leonardtown.[83]

Former slaves fleeing the South were not the only refugees seeking safe passage north. Dr. Emmon Walton, one of the federal physicians assigned to the prison, wrote anonymously for the *Baltimore American*. In several articles, he described White refugees crossing the Potomac River to Point Lookout as they fled a war-torn South devastated by armed conflict and economic hardship. In one account, Walton reported witnessing a group of Germans who had traveled from as far away as Georgia. They recounted journeys on foot before bribing train conductors in Richmond to secure passage as far north as possible, eventually crossing the river to Point Lookout.[84]

It was not long before the reality of the war began to overtake the New Hampshire men. No longer were they permitted to leave the post to visit the local tavern or enjoy the pleasures of the Potomac River at their ease. The liberties they enjoyed came to an end as the prisoner population increased, intensifying their duties and obligations to the security of the garrison. As each week passed, a steady flow of prisoners from distant battlefields arrived and without a stockade, heightened vigilance and augmented guard rotations were more important than ever.

83 Edwin W. Beitzell, "The Activities of the Freeman's Bureau in Southern Maryland, 1865–1870," *St. Mary's Monthly Bulletin of the St. Mary's County Historical Society* (February 1959), 282–289.

84 "Physic" clippings from the *Baltimore News American*, circa 1864, 1.1.3, Box 1, Folder 2, Point Lookout Civil War collection, 0372-MDHC, Special Collections and University Archives. University of Maryland, College Park, Maryland. Articles dated May 1, 1864 & July 6, 1864.

# Chapter 3

# Prisoner Arrivals and Organization

Federal authorities relied on the waterways bordering Point Lookout as the most expedient and secure route for transporting the wounded and sick of the Union army to Hammond Hospital. This system eventually carried thousands of prisoners, guards, civilians, and tons of supplies and livestock destined for Point Lookout.

Prisoners disembarked at the large wharf adjacent to Hammond Hospital on the Potomac River shore. From there, they were marched to an open area near the wharf and formed into lines for inspection by guards. Point Lookout officials preferred the security of the water route rather than risk marching thousands of prisoners through the secessionist areas of southern Maryland. Those arrested locally by Federal authorities were taken directly to the prison stockade. They were then registered and inspected in the same manner as military prisoners.

The first contingent of prisoners, under guard, arrived at Point Lookout with Marston and the 2nd and 12th New Hampshire regiments. Prisoner registration records show that those confined at Point Lookout came from every state of the Confederacy, including the four border states. Although enlisted men were detained in a stockade separate from the officers, all were treated the same.

A prisoner was permitted little on which to survive once inside the prison. Prison authorities considered depriving prisoners of personal items necessary to maintain order and control. Incoming prisoners underwent a thorough inspection by guards, who confiscated contraband articles that might provide comfort or aid an escape attempt. Prison life was miserable and survival within it a constant struggle.[1]

1 Emmerich De Vattel, "The Right to Weaken an Enemy by Every Justifiable Method," in *Of War*, Vol. 3, *The Law of Nations or the Principles of Natural Law in Four Books* (1758; repr. London, 2005), 344–345.

Prisoner accounts vary regarding how inspections were conducted by the guards. Inspections occurred both upon arrival and upon departure from Point Lookout to other destinations. Arrival inspections were largely procedural rather than regulatory and were regarded as harassment bordering on cruelty, though Federal authorities considered them necessary. Over time, inspection methods became more rigorous as prisoners grew increasingly adept at concealing items banned by the authorities.[2]

Prisoners were formed into a single row, or "rank," or at times into lines in open ranks at the wharf area. One account described how they were ordered to form a hollow square and instructed to drop all their gear on the ground in front of them, followed by the command to "unwrap, spread out and disgorge everything we had." Private George Q. Peyton of the 13th Virginia complained that the guards took all their tent flies and gum blankets, leaving them with nothing to protect themselves from the weather. He told one guard that he had nothing to cover himself with and was given an old gum blanket that "wasn't much good." The guards then ordered the prisoners to drop their knapsacks and everything else before marching them away.[3]

Prisoners were not permitted to possess items belonging to the U.S. Army, particularly anything marked or stenciled "U.S." Such items could be used to aid an escape. One prisoner recalled that after they were ordered to empty their pockets and drop their baggage on the ground, "federal sergeants kicked overcoats, blankets, oilcloths, canteens, and basically everything that had 'U.S.' on it into the Potomac River."[4]

To circumvent the guards and their inspections, prisoners sewed personal items into the lining of their clothes before arrival. Some inspectors went so far as to rip the lining out of hats and trousers after requiring prisoners to dump the contents of their pockets on the ground. It soon became standard procedure to have the men strip off all their clothing, leaving only "what was absolutely next to the skin" during inspections.

One prisoner wrote that some of his fellow inmates who possessed gold rings cut a plug from a piece of meat and concealed the rings in the cavity to prevent discovery by inspectors. Their efforts were futile, as guards soon found the rings.

2 McHenry Howard, *Recollections of a Maryland Confederate Soldier and Staff Officer under Johnston, Jackson and Lee* (Baltimore, 1914), 333.

3 George M. Neese, *Three Years in the Confederate Horse Artillery* (New York, 1911), 333; George Quintus Peyton, comp., *A Civil War Record for 1864–1865*, ed. Robert Allen Hodge (1981), 97.

4 Charles T. Loehr, "Point Lookout," in *Southern Historical Society Papers* 18, ed. R. A. Brock (Richmond, VA, 1890), 114–120.

However, the guards, as it turned out, offered them back to the prisoners. Another prisoner wrote that an inspecting officer told them that "if they didn't have a good shirt, they better appropriate one now [from the piles of contraband] as they may not have another opportunity soon to obtain another at their establishment."[5]

Confederate officers were subject to the same inspections and confiscations as enlisted men. Even so, exceptions occurred when officers surrendered under negotiated agreements that allowed them to retain personal items as part of the terms of their capitulation. Confederate Maj. T. B. R. Chinn of the 9th Louisiana, who surrendered after the Federal victory at Port Hudson, was sent to Point Lookout, arriving with all of his private luggage, which he retained until he was later exchanged. This included "two large trunks, one containing his wardrobe and bedding; the bedding consisted of a single hair mattress, pillow, sheets, blankets, etc. . . . and a chest containing his dining paraphernalia."[6]

Upon arrival, prisoners were instructed to surrender any items of value at the time of inspection. Their names were attached to the items, and they were given a receipt. The articles were then deposited in the provost marshal's office for safekeeping. These items would be returned upon presentation of the receipt when the prisoner was exchanged or released. Prisoners failing to comply forfeited any items "confiscated for all time to come."[7]

Prisoners often complained that their confiscated items were never returned when they departed Point Lookout. They usually discovered that their deposited belongings could not be found. Since most prisoners were more concerned with leaving Point Lookout, many did not press the issue for the return of their property. In contrast, one of the more fortunate exceptions was Pvt. Samuel Pickens of the 5th Alabama, who stated that upon his release on June 25, 1865, he "drew crackers & bacon then marched to the Pro[vost] Mars[hals] office where money, watches, etc., were returned to owners."[8]

According to an army circular of July 7, 1862, no prisoner was permitted to possess money. This regulation applied to all paper currency, gold or silver coinage of the United States or Confederate States, as well as that of any foreign government. The confiscation of valuables was intended to prevent prisoners, particularly those with currency or jewelry, from bribing guards to facilitate escape. Any money collected from prisoners during inspections, or sent to them

5 Peyton, *A Civil War Record for 1864–1865*, 97; Neese, *Three Years in the Confederate Horse Artillery*, 353.

6 Blue, *Hanging Rock Rebel*, 270–271.

7 Neese, *Three Years in the Confederate Horse Artillery*, 333–334.

8 Hubbs, *Voices from Company D*, 387.

by friends or relatives, was to be held and recorded at the provost marshal's office. Prisoners were given credit in the form of a checkbook, whose vouchers were redeemable for items sold by the prison sutler. Both the transactions and the books were monitored and regulated by the provost marshal.[9]

After the inspection was completed to the satisfaction of the officer in charge, the prisoners were formed into ranks of marching order. They were then marched to the prison stockade along the main or "country road," which ran north through the center of the Point from the wharf area. At the assistant provost marshal's office, located in front of the main gate of the prison, the prisoners were once again subjected to the ritual of roll call and inspection. Several prisoners recorded that they were greeted by fellow inmates with calls such as "grab your pocketbooks" as they approached the prison gate, "referring to the strict search to which all newcomers were subjected."[10]

Private E. H. Sutton of the 24th Georgia recorded that once inside the prison he was greeted with the call, "fresh fish!" as the gate of the pen closed behind them. "This call would quickly pass over the whole camp, and many of the boys would line up along the street to see if they knew them, hoping to hear news from the front or from home." Another prisoner recalled that this "saluted our ears," adding that those who greeted him "looked so starved . . . their faces were so lean and pinched . . . in course of time I looked as they did." New prisoners were then assigned to divisions and subsequently to companies within each division. After receiving their division assignments, they were turned into the pen to find their street and report to the senior Confederate sergeant of that division.[11]

## Prisoner Organization

As the first prisoners arrived on a warm day in July 1863, Marston ordered that their shelters be organized in accordance with U.S. Army regulations. On August 13, he issued General Order No. 3, establishing the necessary organizational assignments and ranks required to operate each division and company of prisoners, including daily roll calls, sick calls, and the assignment of camp duties. Since the prison stockade had not yet been constructed, the initial prison area was limited to no more than 10 open acres of tents. As the prison

9 L. Leon, *Diary of a Tar Heel Confederate Soldier* (Charlotte, NC, 1913), 66.

10 Child, *Letters from A Civil War Surgeon*, 237; Letter by Wells, "James T. Wells."

11 E. H. Sutton, *Civil War Stories* (Demores, GA, 1910), 60; B. T. Holliday, "Vain Efforts for Avoid Prison," 1920, in *Confederate Veteran* 28, ed. S. A. Cunningham, 10th ed. (Nashville, 1920), 382–385.

Prisoner artist depiction of the prison gate. *Point Lookout State Park Collection*

population grew in the following months, it became necessary to modify the organizational structure of the prison.[12]

Once construction of the prison stockade fence was completed in November 1863, the prison underwent another reorganization. Following Hoffman's army circular of July 1862, Marston organized the prison as if it were an army camp in the field, except that the streets were called divisions, and the divisions were subdivided into companies. Each division contained tents and other structures arranged on either side of the street, facing one another, with the streets running east to west within the compound. Each street included a ditch on either side for drainage. According to prisoner accounts, a divisional street was approximately "twenty feet in width, ran along the front of these houses and at right angles to this street were long rows of tents of all imaginable patterns and of no pattern at all."[13]

The prison camp administration began with the provost marshal and his assistant. Designated as the commanding officer of the prison camp and head of the police guard, the provost marshal's office was located near the commanding

12 *Book 251,* General Order 3.

13 A. M. Keiley, *In Vinculis: Or, the Prisoner of War, Being the Experience of a Rebel in Two Federal Pens, Interspersed with Reminiscences of the Late War, Anecdotes of Southern Generals, Etc.* (New York City, 1866), 59. Accessed March 12, 2025. http://catalog.hathitrust.org/Record/000773606.

officer's headquarters by the lighthouse. The assistant provost marshal's office was located outside the main gate of the prison. The provost marshal and his assistant were responsible for ensuring that all daily operations of the prison were carried out. The provost marshal established a hierarchy by assigning a Confederate sergeant to the position of sergeant-major of the camp, whose duty was to serve as liaison between the provost marshal, his assistant, and the prisoners. The camp sergeant-major was permitted to appoint positions such as camp postmaster and chief of police.

The divisional streets were numbered consecutively one through ten, beginning with the first division on the northern end of the pen and continuing south. The last street bordered the surplus area that contained the prison hospital. Each division was subdivided into 10 companies of one hundred men each. The companies were lettered alphabetically, beginning with company "A" and ending with "K" (the letter "J" was not officially used by either army). This organization made each division consist of 1,000 men, meeting the designated capacity of 10,000 prisoners for the prison.

A prisoner was assigned to the position of orderly or first sergeant within each company. His primary duty was to conduct roll calls within the company when required. These rolls were then verified by a Federal non-commissioned officer, who was placed in charge of the division, prior to the march to the mess halls and the issuing of rations. This system prevented prisoners from moving between divisions to obtain extra rations. The NCO was also responsible for assigning newly arrived prisoners to their quarters.[14]

Taking advantage of Southern physicians who had either been captured or had surrendered, prison authorities assigned a prisoner-physician to each division to conduct daily sick calls. They were assisted by company sick sergeants, who were responsible for maintaining records of each sick prisoner, ensuring that every sick man received his ration, administering ordered medicines, and monitoring the prisoner's status whether in camp or in the prison hospital.[15]

By mid-May 1864, the assignment of newly arrived prisoners to specific divisions had all but ceased due to overcrowding. In October 1864, Pvt. George Peyton of the 13th Virginia recalled that once he and his fellow prisoners arrived at the pen, they were separated and scattered throughout the prison to find their

14 *Book 251*, General Order 3; Neese, *Three Years in the Confederate Horse Artillery*, 337.

15 W. E. Doyle, "A Confederate Prisoner," 1926, in *Confederate Veteran* 34, ed. S. A. Cunningham, 51-52. 2nd ed. Vol. 34. Nashville: United Confederate Veterans, 1926. Accessed March 19, 2025. https://archive.org/details/confederateveter3419conf/page/50/mode/2up.

own quarters. Divisional streets were rapidly exceeding their one-thousand-man limit, as the camp began to exceed its intended ten-thousand-man capacity.[16]

The number of men living in a division within the pen could rise as high as 1,500 to nearly 2,000 per street, making living conditions cramped, unsanitary, and intolerable. Captain Randolph Shotwell of the 8th Virginia described his arrival at Point Lookout in June 1864: "And now we marched into the . . . [officer's] pen and told to 'Scratch into some hole or other!'—meaning to find shelter as best we could."[17]

## Barracks Versus Tents

As the first prisoners arrived at Point Lookout, Quartermaster General Montgomery Meigs ordered that old and worn tents be provided to the new prison for shelter. Tents of every configuration, condemned for field use by the Union army, were sent to Camp Hoffman to house the thousands arriving each month. Overcrowding in these shelters was a problem from the beginning and profoundly affected the health and well-being of thousands of prisoners.[18]

As the cold winter months approached, Marston sent a request to Hoffman on October 12, 1863, for the construction of barracks to shelter prisoners. Hoffman informed Marston that Stanton had inexplicably denied the request. As it turned out, Stanton's refusal to allow the construction of barracks at Point Lookout was never explained, nor was it his last rejection. No definitive reasons were ever given to satisfy the camp commanders as to why Stanton continued to deny repeated requests. Although the secretary of war rejected the building of prisoner barracks, he authorized the construction of mess halls, cookhouses, and a commissary building for the storage, preparation, and issuing of rations.[19]

Unlike captives held in prisons farther north, the prisoners at Point Lookout were relegated to threadbare, leaking canvas tents rather than the security of wooden barracks to shield them from the harsh weather of southern Maryland. Many of the tents that sheltered prisoners at Point Lookout were described as deteriorated and unfit for active field service by the Union army.[20]

16 Peyton, *A Civil War Record for 1864–1865*, 98.

17 Shotwell, *The Papers of Randolph Abbott Shotwell*, Vol. 1, 120.

18 *OR* 6/2:132.

19 Ibid., 368, 390.

20 *OR* 7/2:918–919.

Secretary of War, Edwin M. Stanton
*Library of Congress*

Prisoners were often assigned to tents already overcrowded, which further enhanced unhealthy living conditions. Tent capacities were based on prisoners lying on their sides like spoons in a case (hence the soldiers' term "spooning.") Several prisoners stated that it was like being packed like sardines in a box: "When we wanted to turn over in the night the signal was given, and all made to turn from necessity."[21]

The largest tent available, the Sibley or "bell" tent, was the most widely used at Point Lookout by both prisoners and the guard force. The larger tent accommodated more men than the other styles of tents issued. The Sibley had a different configuration from the square or rectangular tents, being circular once set up. Prisoner Robert Craddock of the 1st Virginia stated that as early as December 1863, 3,000 prisoners were assigned to wedge-style tents that housed an average of five men each. The remaining 6,000 were placed in Sibley tents, which held between 14 and 20 men, although originally constructed for 10. Overcrowded shelters created severe, and often deadly, conditions within the prison population. To improve health and sanitary conditions, each tent and shelter was ordered to be taken down at least once a week to allow the ground to air and dry.[22]

Prisoners assigned to Sibley tents suffered due to their unusual circular, conical shape. This design required men to sleep on their sides with their feet pointed toward the center, like the spokes of a wagon wheel. A fireplace, common to other structures, could not be used in this type of tent. Instead, prisoners were forced to build fires in shallow pits dug in the ground at the center, hoping that the smoke

21 Holliday, "Vain Efforts," in *Confederate Veteran* 28, 383. Accessed March 19, 2025. https://archive.org/details/confederateveter28conf/page/n7/mode/2up.

22 "Prison Life at Point Lookout (Conversation with Robert Craddock)," *The Daily Dispatch* [Richmond], Dec. 17, 1863, 1–2.

would drift upward and escape through the open apex. To worsen the situation, the firewood gathered by work details was unseasoned and often green, producing suffocating, eye-stinging smoke for the inhabitants whenever it burned.[23]

On May 20, 1864, Col. Alonzo Draper, then commanding officer of Point Lookout, complained to Hoffman that his request for new tents had been denied by the chief quartermaster at Fort Monroe, who in turn ordered Draper to surrender the Sibley tents then occupied by his guard force to supplement those needed for prisoners. The denial was explained as the result of a recent order issued by General Grant, giving priority to soldiers in active campaigns over troops in the rear echelon.[24]

The wedge or "common tent," which provided space for five to six men, was another type issued for prisoner use. On May 23, 1864, Hoffman requested from Chief Quartermaster Rucker additional Sibley tents for the increasing number of prisoners being sent to Point Lookout. In reply, Rucker ordered his assistant to send old common tents, rather than the higher-capacity Sibley tents Hoffman requested, noting they "could be supplied sooner than shanties could be put up by prisoners." Condemned common tents soon arrived to house the constantly expanding prisoner population of Point Lookout.[25]

Faring somewhat better than the enlisted men, Confederate officers in the adjacent stockade were billeted in the more spacious Sibley tents, which were floored with wooden planking and supplied with small stoves. Regardless of rank, they also experienced overcrowding. Lt. John Blue of the 11th Virginia Cavalry wrote that he and fellow officers were transferred from Hammond Hospital's holding area to the officers' pen. Blue recorded that they were "quartered in a double row of large tents with a street thirty yards in width running east and west between. Ten men were quartered in each tent."[26]

When tents were assigned, they were the same as those issued to the enlisted men, described as "a lot of condemned canvas, ruined by salt water and mildewed . . . there were so few that from seven to ten men were huddled in each tent." The secretary of war ordered that the Confederate officers be transferred from Point Lookout to Fort Delaware by June 24, 1864, after which their tents were added to the enlisted pen. Incoming Confederate officers were thereafter temporarily

23 Letter by Wells, "James T. Wells."

24 *Book No. 253*, 148.

25 *OR* 7/2:162.

26 Blue, *Hanging Rock Rebel*, 269–270.

housed in several cottages near Hammond Hospital until they were either exchanged or transferred north to another prison.[27]

As the prison population expanded, additional tents were issued to accommodate the increase. These replaced the tents that were torn or falling apart. In June, guard units at Point Lookout were ordered to exchange their new Sibley tents for common wedge tents, the former then being assigned to prisoner use. Despite this redistribution, the measure only temporarily addressed the continuing demand for additional tentage.[28]

An extensive inspection of the prison camp conducted in November 1863 by Sanitary Commission representative Dr. William F. Swalm reported, "Of their shelter there can be no possible complaint, for they all have good tents," noting that all forms of tents were provided and used by the prisoners. In some cases, however, the number of prisoners per tent, as Swalm recorded, was either at or above the prescribed capacity for that particular style. At the time of his inspection, overcrowding was already evident, as the population was fast approaching 10,000 prisoners incarcerated at Point Lookout.[29]

The crammed prisoners soon began to create more suitable accommodations by utilizing materials they smuggled into the prison. They constructed walls from wooden boards scrounged from the prison grounds to raise their shelters off the ground, increasing both space and headroom inside. Dirt removed from the drainage ditches in each divisional street was also piled along the perimeters of tents and shelters, elevating the structures several inches. Raising the shelters allowed more air to circulate, to the relief of their occupants.[30]

## "Cracker box houses" and "Shebangs"

Cracker box houses, also referred to as "shebangs," were shanties constructed by prisoners to provide more substantial shelter than deteriorating tents. The principal materials used in their construction were the shipping crates, or "cracker boxes," originally used for the distribution of hard crackers, also known as army bread. These crates were plentiful after ration issues and were made available for

27 Shotwell, *The Papers of Randolph Abbott Shotwell*, Vol. 1, 120–121; Henry Kyd Douglas, *I Rode with Stonewall, Being Chiefly the War Experiences of the Youngest Member of Jackson's Staff from the John Brown Raid to the Hanging of Mrs. Surratt* (Chapel Hill, NC, 1940), 256–257.

28 Allen, *Forty-Six Months with the Fourth Rhode Island Volunteers*, 265; *OR* 6/3:562.

29 *OR* 6/2:577.

30 J. William Flinn, "A Southern Soldier's Experience in a Northern Prison, 1894," Nov. 1893, South Caroliniana Library, Columbia, SC.

sale by the prison sutler or commissary department. Prisoners who could afford them purchased the crates at a price of 10 to 15 cents each.

Prisoners meticulously dismantled wooden crates to preserve the much-needed wood and to salvage the nails required for building their shacks. The accumulated boards were hidden to prevent theft until enough lumber had been accumulated to complete a shanty. These unusual shelters soon appeared throughout the prison. Permission to construct a shebang was first required from the assistant provost marshal.

Pvt. Anthony Keiley of the 12th Virginia described the interior of a typical cracker box house:

> A fireplace was made in the end of sun-dried bricks of home manufacture . . . having been raised four or five feet was surmounted by a flour barrel . . . the floor was spread with sand from the beach, a table and a couple of chairs were improvised, bunks constructed a name painted over the door; and the family moved in.[31]

Chimneys were generally built from homemade bricks fashioned and sold by prisoners, from barrels, or from a combination of both. Shelters either contained a stove, which could be purchased from the camp sutler, or a more rudimentary fireplace constructed by hand. Because nearly every shelter had some type of heating device, burnable firewood was a constant problem. Although many prisoners later claimed otherwise, federal inspectors and civilian reporters recorded that nearly all tents and shebangs had some form of heating during the colder months.[32]

The size of a shebang was usually determined by the tentage available and the space allotted for the structure. Shelter halves, common tents, and tent flies of various sizes were often used for roofing. Residing in Company B, Third Division of the prison, Private Woodhouse described his "cracker box house" as about "ten by thirteen feet, the sides & ends of which are built of the planks of cracker boxes & is hence called a cracker box house & also covered with canvas . . . We have quite a snug chimney to it . . . Seven including myself inhabit it."[33]

Cracker box houses were often works in progress, continually modified until they met the needs of their occupants. Packing-crate planks were also used for

31 Keiley, *In Vinculis*, 72.

32 Edward Spencer, "Point Lookout," *Overland Monthly and Out West Magazine*, May 1870, 418, https://name.umdl.umich.edu/ahj1472.1-04.005; *OR* 6/2:577.

33 Chandler Woodhouse Story-Dennis, ed., *My Beloved Wife, Be Hopeful: 1864–1865, Letters from Henry: Surviving Point Lookout Civil War Prison Camp* (Virginia Beach, VA, 2019), 103.

the construction of doors, bunks, and other furniture for these primitive shelters. Nearly any material that could be obtained was employed to create a sturdier structure than the thin, torn, and worn-out tents originally provided.

One division that contained many of these structures was dubbed "cracker box row" by the prisoners. Prisoners and visitors both noted that most of its inhabitants were, somewhat surprisingly, soldiers from Maryland. Their proximity to their home state gave them greater access to the funds needed to purchase construction materials. Eyewitnesses also referred to this division as "Baltimore Street" and the "cracker house brigade."[34]

Many of these houses were christened by their owners with names or titles that expressed personal sentiments, sarcasm, political opinions, or thoughts of home. Prisoners concocted a type of paint, made from a mixture of vinegar and soot, to create name boards that adorned the thresholds of their huts. Names such as "Churchman's Abode," "Lyon's Den," "Here's Your Mule," "The Alhambra," "Spotswood Hotel," "In for the War," "Dixie," and "Home Again" became familiar throughout the camp.[35]

As the number of prisoners steadily increased, hundreds of additional tents were added to the vast sea of canvas. These new tents greatly reduced the available space within the prison and constricted the prisoners' living area. The swelling population encouraged the spread of communicable diseases by intensifying the already unhealthy and suffocating miasmic atmosphere of the pen. It was not long before three additional divisional streets were created, bringing the camp to a total of thirteen by early 1865.[36]

The reasons why the secretary of war never permitted barracks for the prisoners at Point Lookout have remained speculative. Stanton's decision may have been influenced by location, cost-effectiveness, or the prison's status. Some have theorized it was retaliation for the mistreatment of northern prisoners, but no correspondence has surfaced to support this claim. It is difficult to understand why the severe winter conditions of southern Maryland were not taken into account. Hundreds, if not thousands, of prisoners suffered from exposure and inadequate shelter during the extreme cold, lacking sufficient protection from the elements.

34 Spencer, "Point Lookout," 418.

35 "From Point Lookout: The Rebel Prisoners, and How they are Treated How they Employ their Leisure—A Day at Point Lookout," *New York Times*, October 6, 1864.

36 Edwin L. Drake, ed., *The Annals of the Army of Tennessee and Early Western History: Including a Chronological Summary of Battles and Engagements in the Western Armies of the Confederacy*, Vol. 1 (Nashville, TN, 1878), 271.

The argument regarding construction expense is challenged by the costs incurred in building the massive sixteen-wing army hospital and its support buildings, as well as nine prison mess halls, the commissary building, and the seven-building prison hospital within the complex. Why were these structures approved but not the much-needed prison barracks?

## Life Goes On

After prisoners were inspected, registered, and assigned to their divisions, they settled into overcrowded shelters that would be their homes for weeks or months to come. They conformed to a daily routine prescribed by prison authorities, which was not strenuous but necessary to maintain discipline and sanitary conditions within the prison. Many recorded in their diaries and letters home descriptions of their living conditions: the frigid winter cold, the insufferable heat and humidity of southern Maryland summers, the lack of clean water, and the scarcity of rations. The sea of white canvas tents affected prisoners' eyesight on sunny days, and blowing sand filled their tents, eyes, and ears. They also documented observations of the guards, roll calls, inspections, work details, and the physical layout of what many referred to as the "town camp."

Prisoners required little time to complete the tasks demanded of them, leaving the rest of the day free for their own pursuits. The routine of prison life proved redundant and monotonous, offering ample idle time that fostered laziness, lethargy, thievery, and other mischief among prisoners. Conversely, it also encouraged ingenuity, creativity, and industrious activity, improving survivability within this harsh prison environment.

## Chapter 4

# The "Town Camp" of Point Lookout

Prisons in operation prior to Point Lookout enjoyed facilities that often had been constructed for other purposes. These locations required less retrofitting for prisoner housing. Sites such as Fort Delaware, Fort McHenry in Maryland, and the Old Capitol Prison in Washington, D.C., were readily accessible and required minimal modifications to accommodate incoming prisoners. This was not the case at Point Lookout.

The castrametation of Point Lookout began as soon as the prison guards and their charges stepped off the transport boat on July 31, 1863. The site for the new guard camps and future prison was personally selected by General Marston. Marston was acting on instinct, as none of his experience had thus far fitted him to run a prison camp; the same was true for most other prison commanding officers. No precedents or printed guidelines addressing the operation of a prisoner-of-war camp were available. It had been nearly 50 years since the need for any type of military prison camp had arisen.

Marston was aided by officers of the quartermaster department in selecting the only available ground that would permit the creation of the prison and its eventual expansion. The chosen area was located approximately one-half mile north of Hammond Hospital in a barren field now covered with dried cornstalks, wild onions, and marshy terrain.[1]

Marston did know that occupying the same ground for an extended period would cause the spread of disease among the prisoners, creating a serious problem.

1 William S. Humphries, "Escaped from Point Lookout Prison," 1911, in *Confederate Veteran*, ed. S. A. Cunningham, 7th ed. (Nashville, TN, 1911), 19:344.

It was evident that a steady flow of essential supplies would be required to feed and keep healthy the massive number of occupants living at Point Lookout.

Marston determined that fresh water would be supplied from hand-dug wells, but he soon found that the water from these wells was unpotable, even potentially deadly; a steady supply of suitable drinking water was already a problem for the administration of the army hospital. Massive amounts of firewood were required daily for cooking and heating during the cooler months. It was soon discovered that this vital resource was scarce on the bleak peninsula. A consistent supply would have to be sourced elsewhere—if the quartermaster department could not provide it—to adequately support, as expected, a population of thousands.

The vast, open parcel of ground was bordered on the north by Point Lookout Creek, on the east by the Chesapeake Bay, and on the west by the Potomac River. It could be easily defended by artillery and a determined guard force in the event of an attack or prisoner breakout. Marston skillfully employed the geography of Point Lookout as a defensive measure, to compensate for his lack of manpower.

General Meigs's order establishing Point Lookout listed the items immediately required for constructing the prison and its structures. He instructed that the prison be capable of incarcerating a total of 10,000 prisoners of war, with an initial order of necessary tentage. The required camp and garrison supplies were ordered, along with enough lumber to construct the stockade, prison kitchens, and storehouses. Standard cast-iron boilers for cooking in the prison cookhouses were also requisitioned.[2]

Meigs expressed his concerns to his assistant, General Rucker, saying there was no one on site experienced enough to organize or oversee the planning and construction of the new prison and support buildings. He suggested that "the general plans be prepared by a person of experience, and I know none who has had more in such constructions than Mr. Clark." Meigs was referring to Dr. Augustus M. Clark (surgeon and acting medical inspector of prisoners of war). He further indicated that Clark had previously visited Point Lookout and was familiar with the location. "The slightest sketch will enable us to begin the work on a system and increase it as may be necessary." Acting assistant quartermasters Captains Abraham Edwards and Nelson Plato, responsible for logistical support at Point Lookout, would supervise the construction of Hammond Hospital, Point Lookout prison, and all additional support buildings.[3]

2 *OR* 6/2:132–133.

3 Ibid.

Surgeon Augustus M. Clark, U.S.V. Acting Medical Inspector of Prisoners of War. *The Military Order of the Loyal Legion of the United States and Founding Forward*

## Confinement

Prior to the construction of the stockade, prisoners were confined to a designated area on the Chesapeake Bay side. Perimeter guards from the 2nd and 12th New Hampshire regiments were supported by a few mounted guards who patrolled the area north of the prison. The first prisoners were ordered to erect their tents on the bayside of the field. Simon Seward of the 13th Virginia Cavalry stated that "the prison was square, containing about a space of 10 or more acres, and at the time had no fence around it. The guards continually marched up and down on their beats."

Additional prisoners began to arrive while the prison camp was still in its initial phase of organization. Private Martin Haynes wrote on August 10 that the increasing number of prisoners "called for extra vigilance on our part . . . two Dahlgren boat howitzers were posted to command the rebel camp and are going to have four more . . . while the rebels are set to do their own work—to dig wells, build cookhouses, etc."[4]

There was little for prisoners to do beyond the usual mundane work details of the camp, anticipating their next meal, and planning their escape. Since the "prison" still lacked stockade walls, some daring souls made attempts to flee. To enforce prison rules and regulations, Capt. Joab N. Patterson was appointed the first of three provost marshals assigned to command the prison camp, with Capt. George E. Sides as his assistant; both officers were from the 2nd New Hampshire.[5]

4 Bartlett, *History of the Twelfth*, 146; Simon Seward, "Perilous Escape from Point Lookout," 1908, in *Confederate Veteran*, ed. S. A. Cunningham (Nashville, TN, 1911), 19:172; Haynes, *A Soldier Boy's Letters*, 133.

5 Ibid., 200.

Marston, who anticipated more prisoners arriving within weeks, needed a substantial prison stockade as soon as possible. By the end of August 1863, 1,800 prisoners were encamped on the bayside, guarded by fewer than 300 Union troops. Construction of a temporary prison pen began before the ordered lumber for the stockade arrived. This first version of the pen was built with pine logs readily available just north of the prison site.[6]

Captain Asa Bartlett of the 12th New Hampshire described the first attempt to build a stockade wall for the prisoners.

> No sooner were the regimental camps laid out, and tents erected than work was commenced on the stockade around the prisoner's quarters . . . consist[ing] of pine logs split in the middle and cut long enough to trench fast in the ground and leave ten or twelve feet above as the height of the pen. On the outside of this stockade, near the top, was built a staging about four feet wide for the sentinels to walk on . . . To thus circummure a space of ground big enough to accommodate several thousand men was no small undertaking and an invitation was given to the "johnnies" to assist [with construction].[7]

Prisoners continued to exploit the absence of a permanent barrier with repeated escape attempts. Fortunately for Marston, the requisitioned lumber arrived in September, allowing construction of a permanent prison enclosure with a stockade wall that encompassed the camp.

To accelerate construction of the massive prison stockade and its support buildings, federal authorities employed several civilian carpenters along with approximately 200 prisoners and formerly enslaved men. According to the *Lieber Code*, prisoners could be required to work "for the benefit of the captor's government," meaning they could be compelled to labor on the prison wall and other facilities.

Prison authorities offered compensation to encourage prisoner participation in the construction. Volunteers received extra rations and tobacco, both commodities highly valued among the prisoners. Observing the federal workforce labor on their new quarters, many prisoners eventually accepted the offer, motivated partly by boredom but more by the promise of additional rations.[8]

6 *OR* 6/2:243.

7 Bartlett, *History of the Twelfth*, 146.

8 *OR* 3/3:Article 17, 156; Letter by Wells, "James T. Wells."

Private Martin Haynes,
2nd New Hampshire
*Library of Congress*

Construction of the prison stockade began in mid-August 1863. Three sides of the stockade wall were completed by late September or early October 1863. The fourth side, which opened to the Chesapeake Bay waterfront, was closed by the end of October. The enlisted prisoners' stockade at Point Lookout resembled a five-sided enclosure, covering approximately 32 acres. The smaller, adjoining Confederate officers' stockade contained about eight acres to accommodate an expected 2,500 officers. A country road, or main thoroughfare, ran north from the lighthouse, traversing the peninsula in a southwest to northeast direction, forming the western boundary of both stockades. The eastern walls of the prisons were defined by the Chesapeake Bay shoreline.[9]

The stockade wall stood approximately 12 feet high. Along its exterior ran a platform or walkway for sentries, positioned four feet below the top of the wall and extending outward the same distance. These catwalks gave guards an elevated view of the prison interior, allowing them to monitor activities within the prison. Stairs at all three outside corners of the stockade provided access to the catwalks.[10]

The access gate to the prison stood at the southwest corner of the stockade. A log blockhouse was built outside the main gate to serve as both a guardhouse and a defensive position in case of attack or a mass breakout. The stockade was "pierced for musketry and mounting two howitzers" to cover the main gate. A

9 Quartermaster, "Drawings and Inventory List Point Lookout, MD," map, RG 92, Entry 576, Box 57, National Archives, Washington, D.C.; Henry Brewerton, "First and Third Sections of Rebel Prison at Point Lookout, MD," map, 1865, Drawer 135, Sheet 21, National Archives, College Park, MD; Letter by Gen. Gilman Marston, Jan. 18, 1864, 0047-MDHC, Maryland Manuscripts Collection, University of Maryland, College Park, MD.

10 M. Ludington to Montgomery Meigs, Oct. 25, 1865, Group 92, Entry 576, Box 57, Record of the Office of the Quartermaster General, National Archives, Washington, D.C.; Haynes, *History of the Second*, 157–158; Allen, *Forty-Six Months*, 259.

Prison camp entry gate. *Author*

second room functioned as a guardroom to confine both Confederate and Union violators of prison rules and army regulations.[11]

Major Charles S. Stewart of the United States Army Corps of Engineers was assigned to Point Lookout on July 9, 1864, by the chief of engineers, Gen. Richard Delafield, to assess the defensive strength of the existing fortifications and to select

11 Haynes, *A History of the Second*, 203–204.

locations for additional earthworks. The new defenses were designed both to repel external attacks and to discourage mass breakout attempts. Stewart evaluated the prison stockade, which he judged inadequate for its intended purpose:

> The prisoner pen is probably some 1900 yards in circuit & consists simply of a high board fence, perhaps, 13' in height . . . The whole seems to me a very insecure arrangement for the purpose contemplated when the relative number of the confined and the garrison are considered.[12]

A deadline was established inside the stockade perimeter. Its purpose was to create a barrier between guards and prisoners, serving as a warning that approaching the stockade wall without permission could be fatal. The deadline at first consisted of wooden stakes set about 15 feet from the inside base of the wall. This no-man's-land followed the prison's interior perimeter, encompassing the divisional streets of the town camp. The road running in front of the mess halls formed the western boundary of the deadline, which was secured by a line of guards to restrict access. In its final form, the deadline became a trench about a foot wide and a foot deep, replacing the stakes.[13]

Regulations required guards to warn violators first and then fire if the prisoner failed to comply. Prisoner accounts indicate that warnings were rarely given. Prisoners assigned to work details or to receive rations were permitted to cross the line with authorization. By October 1864, large lanterns were mounted inside the stockade near the wall to "throw a brilliant light along the wall and on both sides of the dead line at night," aiding the guards' night watch. Guards patrolling the catwalk were positioned about 25 to 30 paces apart.[14]

Sentinels pacing the prison catwalks were vulnerable to harsh weather. Although federal guards received seasonal clothing, they continued to suffer from the extreme conditions. By May 1864, prison authorities constructed small open-

12 Charles S. Stewart to Delafield, July 22, 1864, Records 77 File Number S-9225, DeGrange Index 1864–1865, National Archives, Washington D.C.

13 *OR* 7/2:165; Allen, *Forty-Six Months*, 260; Flinn, "A Southern Soldier's Experience in a Northern Prison."

14 Ross M. Kimmel and Michael P. Musick, comps., *I Am Busy Drawing Pictures: The Civil War Art and Letters of Private John Jacob Omenhausser*, illus. John Jacob Omenhausser (Maryland State Archives, 2014), Annapolis, Md., 92; Neese, *Three Years in the Confederate Horse Artillery*, 336–337; Sutton, *Civil War Stories*, microfiche, 48.

sided shelters on the catwalks. These sentry boxes provided limited protection from the Point's severe elements for the guards on duty.[15]

Three gates on the bayside of the prison provided access to the shoreline and to prisoner latrines during daylight hours. The latrines, or "sinks," were located on platforms reached by catwalks extending 30 to 40 yards over the bay. At sunset, all three gates were closed, preventing prisoner access to the beach and, most importantly, to their latrines. The latrines stood in the same restricted area where prisoners also washed laundry, swam, bathed, and fished. To reach the beach, prisoners crossed a series of boards that bridged the deadline to leave the prison and returned the same way. Any prisoner who strayed from the prescribed pathway was challenged by the guards for the transgression.[16]

The boundaries of the deadline were extended about 200 yards into the bay to permit prisoner access to the water. Pilings driven into the muddy bay bottom formed this extension of the deadline. The addition allowed prisoners to venture farther into the bay, away from the polluted waters near the latrines. Prisoners were permitted to sit on the pilings to fish and swim, provided they remained within the extended deadline. Eventually, some devised methods of escape from this area.[17]

The main street or "Grand Thoroughfare," as prisoners called it, ran north to south in front of the cookhouse and mess hall buildings and was bordered on both sides by deep drainage ditches. Prisoners were denied access to this area unless granted permission, typically as cooks, mess hall workers, or for other assigned details. A line of guards patrolled the thoroughfare to enforce its off-limits status. Running parallel on the east side of the road was a line of water pumps and wells that supplied water for prisoner use.[18]

A mixture of pea gravel, sand, and shells from the bayside beaches was used to construct the road as well as all the divisional streets. Confederate Sgt. James Wells noted that "each company street was well drained and made as hard and firm as pebble and sand could make it." A civilian visitor remarked that the streets were "as hard and smooth as an asphaltum road."[19]

Flooding was a persistent problem caused by the high-water table and flat terrain, which provided little opportunity for adequate drainage to either the bay

15 Bartlett, *History of the Twelfth*, 160; John R. King, *My Experience in the Confederate Army and in Northern Prisons* (Clarksburg, WV, 1917), 27.

16 Keiley, *In Vinculis*, 59; Peyton, *A Civil War Record for 1864–1865*, 98.

17 Kimmel and Musick, *I Am Busy Drawing Pictures*, 76–77.

18 Hubbs, *Voices from Company D*, 371.

19 Letter by Wells, "James T. Wells."

or the river. The drainage system in place was far from effective, leaving camp conditions deplorable for the prisoners. Storms and high tides made it necessary to dig a network of shallow ditches along both sides of the divisional streets. A main ditch ran north to south through the center of the camp, connecting with the east–west divisional street ditches.

Military protocol required the segregation of officers from enlisted men to prevent them from organizing escape attempts or schemes to overpower the guards. To enforce this separation, a separate stockade of about eight acres was constructed. It was divided from the main stockade by a wagon road roughly 20 feet wide, which also served as a guard beat. Entrance to this stockade was provided by a gate on the Potomac side and another on the bay side.[20]

## The Swalm Report and Town Camp Structures

As camp construction and reorganization proceeded, Dr. William F. Swalm of the United States Sanitary Commission arrived in November 1863 to inspect Point Lookout prison. His unsolicited visit was prompted by Confederate allegations that prisoners were suffering neglect and abuse in northern facilities. Swalm's report was sent to Colonel Hoffman, who then forwarded the findings to Marston. After inspecting prison living conditions, medical treatment, and other operations under Marston's supervision, Swalm concluded that there was little positive to report.

Marston received the report with indignation, viewing it as unwanted scrutiny by an uninvited civilian rather than an authorized military inspection. In his closing remarks refuting Swalm's report, Marston asserted that the prisoners in his charge were being "treated as prisoners of war ought to be by a civilized people." He further affirmed that they were provided "shelter, clothing, food, water, and given daily access to the waters of the [Chesapeake] Bay . . . the Government in this regard, as respects the well [healthy] men, is accomplished."[21]

As a follow-up, Frederick N. Knapp, Esq., representing the Sanitary Commission (which had originally sent Swalm), requested a permit from Hoffman to send another inspector, Dr. Alexander McDonald, to examine other prison camps in the system. Hoffman informed Frederick Knapp that army medical inspectors would carry out such examinations for the remainder of the war. Both Marston and Hoffman agreed that negative reports, in the wrong hands, would reinforce Confederate accusations—true or not—of prisoner mistreatment. On

20 Blue, *Hanging Rock Rebel*, 269.

21 *OR* 6/2:645.

Various prisoner shelters. *Author*

December 17, Surgeon Augustus Clark, acting inspector of prisoners of war, was ordered by Hoffman to Point Lookout to conduct a follow-up inspection.[22]

As the stockade walls neared completion, construction of the mess halls within the prison began. In his inspection, Swalm reported that six mess halls had been built and were serving prisoners, along with a smaller commissary building used to store rations and supplies. The cookhouses were located along the western wall of the prison stockade, running south and perpendicular to the wall.

The prison mess halls measured approximately 145 feet in length and 22 feet in width. The last 20 feet of each building, nearest the stockade fence, was partitioned off as the cookhouse, while the remaining space served as the dining room. The distance between the buildings was about 30 to 40 feet. Each hall contained three or four long dining tables and could feed 1,500 men per ration in three shifts of 500.[23]

22 *OR* 6/2:740.

23 *OR* 7/2:918–919; M. Ludington to Montgomery Meigs, "The Letters of Surgeon Clinton Wagner," Oct. 25, 1865, Record Group 92, Entry 576, Box 57, National Archives, Washington D.C.

The first five completed mess halls were opened to serve the prisoners. Until the remaining halls were finished, each of the five accommodated two divisional streets of prisoners. By October 1863, each cookhouse was equipped with four or five 40-gallon boiler pots, referred to as bean pots or farmer's boilers. Each pot fed about 400 men. By the time of Surgeon Clark's inspection in December, the camp had expanded to nine mess halls, six of which were in use as intended. Clark confirmed that each building contained five 40-gallon cauldrons with a combined daily capacity of roughly 9,600 pints of soup, and he noted that rations were inspected daily by the officer of the day.[24]

Each mess hall included an exterior side door at the rear for access to the cook room. A serving window was cut into the interior wall separating the cook room from the hall, allowing cooks to pass prepared rations through. Mess assistants then placed the rations at each place setting on the tables for the prisoners. The main entrance doors were located on the eastern, or front end of the building, which faced the Grand Thoroughfare and allowed easy entry and exit once prisoners were served. The buildings were constructed on pilings three to four feet off the ground to prevent flooding from storm tides. Each had six windows on either side for ventilation and a pitched roof covered with rolled felt paper.[25]

A 20-foot buffer separated the back of each mess hall from the stockade wall, preventing prisoners from scaling the buildings to climb over the prison fence. This space created a blind spot that required the establishment of an additional guard post.[26]

## "If it were not for hope, how could we live in a place like this?"[27]

Point Lookout was far from an ideal location for a prison camp. The site was desolate and unable to sustain the thousands of occupants it was intended to hold. Despite these clear shortcomings, plans proceeded with its establishment as a prison. During the first three months, a 12-foot-high wooden stockade was hastily erected, containing a row of mess halls and cookhouses to accommodate

24 *OR* 6/2:742.

25 Kimmel and Musick, *I Am Busy Drawing Pictures*, 51, 54.

26 J. B. Traywick, "Prison Life at Point Lookout," in *Southern Historical Society Papers*, ed. R. A. Brock (Richmond, VA, 1890), 18:433.

27 Charles T. Loehr, "Address before Pickett Camp Confederate Veterans," in *Southern Historical Papers*, ed. R. A. Brock (Richmond, VA, 1890), 18:113.

Prison interior as it appears today. *Author*

the rapidly growing prison population. The new stockade also included a hospital, sutler store, bulletin board, and post office.

Neither government entered the war intending to harm prisoners, nor were prison camps created as places of comfort or solace. For the most part, prisons became sites of misery, human deterioration, and, in many cases, slow and agonizing death. Life at Point Lookout was no different. A prisoner's survival depended on his ability to withstand the harsh elements, hostile guards, disease, and malnutrition. In addition, inmates often found themselves in deadly competition with other prisoners for what was deemed necessary to survive in a prison environment.

As the unceasing flow of new prisoners strained Point Lookout, it became clear that the site was more than a temporary prison. Within its walls of pine boards and under the watch of the guards, each prisoner had to eke out a means of survival among thousands of strangers. Dehumanization began the moment the gate of the newly constructed prison closed behind him. His survival depended on his individual will to endure. Thus began his existence as a prisoner of war at Point Lookout, Maryland.

## Chapter 5

# Prison Conditions and Daily Routine

As the sultry days of August passed, prisoners' daily routine began with reveille and roll call. Morning rations were issued, followed by the mandatory policing of the camp. Another roll call was held in the early afternoon, after which the day's final rations were distributed. These duties required no more than two to three hours, leaving prisoners to while away the remaining hours of a sweltering Maryland summer day. At sunset, taps and lights-out marked the close of daily activities.

These simple routines began to change as early as December 1863. As the prison population grew from the initial 136 inmates to more than 9,000, both the daily regimen and the camp itself expanded. The schedule soon included additional duties necessary to maintain order and security. The expanding camp also required ongoing maintenance of its structures. Each morning, details were formed to clean the camp and assist in the construction of the stockade and mess halls. Sick call was introduced, together with personnel and shelter inspections.

By May 1864, disease began to spread rapidly as the prison population swelled to more than 12,000. Smoke-filled air from countless fires and saturated ground from occasional storm tides made life difficult and uncomfortable. The high stockade fence blocked the refreshing bay breezes, leaving the air heavy and foul. Within the confines of the stockade, swarms of mosquitoes and flies thrived, while rats and lice infested the grounds. The prison offered no shade to shield prisoners from the scorching summer sun and provided little protection against the harsh winds and freezing rains of winter storms.

The harsh conditions at Point Lookout pushed inmates to the limits of endurance. As one prisoner observed, "In speaking of prisons, the word good should be left out, for there are none that are good . . . Grub was short, treatment rough and sometimes unhuman. [The guards] delighted in showing their authority . . ." Point Lookout was no exception.[1]

## The Tedium of Prison Life

The life of a prisoner was as regimented as that of a soldier in the field, with one notable exception: the absence of drill exercises essential to military discipline. For soldiers, drill occupied much of the day in preparation for battle, but this practice had no place in the life of a prisoner of war. Roll calls, ration issues, work details, and camp routine remained the same—yet here the similarity ended for the prisoner.

After the first ration issue was complete, orders were given for the morning detail, which primarily involved sweeping and repairing the prison's divisional streets and cleaning the many drainage ditches interlacing the camp. For sanitary reasons, filth was not permitted to accumulate anywhere within the prison. To aid in this work, "brooms, wheelbarrows, and shovels [were issued] to accomplish this detail. They were required to clean the streets end to end every day then to remove the trash outside the prison and dump it along the beach for the tide to take out."[2]

The morning detail also included emptying the mess hall "slop" or garbage barrels. Each barrel was "generally full of every imaginable filth . . . Four strong men could carry one when full with difficulty." The contents were dumped into the bay for the tide to carry away, after which the barrels were washed out and returned. Once the cleanup and policing details were finished, prisoners spent the rest of the day tending to their basic survival.[3]

## Inspections

Weekly inspections of the prisoners and their camp were conducted every Sunday by the provost marshal. Prisoners were ordered to appear outside their quarters with their possessions laid out for inspection. As the provost marshal and his staff passed down the divisional streets between the ranks of assembled prisoners, cleanliness, shelters, and clothing (or the lack thereof) were scrutinized

1 Huffman, *Ups and Downs of a Confederate Soldier*, 90.

2 *Book No. 251,* General Order Aug. 1863–Aug. 1865, Special Orders Aug. 1863–Aug.1865, Special Order No. 108 dated April 18,1864, 12–13; Neese, *Three Years in the Confederate Horse Artillery*, 340.

3 Inmate, "Point Lookout in 1865," *Saint Mary's Beacon* (Leonardtown, MD), May 7, 1896, 2.

to determine what was needed or what was excessive. Shelters were also searched for contraband, as well as evidence of tunnels, boats, or weapons.[4]

At times, prison authorities found it necessary to take a full accounting of the inmates by marching them through the gates leading to the beach. This allowed the provost marshal to obtain an accurate head count and to separate the sick and unhealthy from the general population. The maneuver also provided an opportunity to conduct a thorough inspection of the camp, during which items considered contraband were confiscated.[5]

Spontaneous inspections were carried out to catch prisoners off guard who might be in possession of contraband. Prisoner George Neese of Chew's Battery wrote of one inspection that involved what he considered a "barbarous deed." During a surprise inspection, Federal guards, under the pretense of issuing new blankets, ordered prisoners to form in line on their streets and "were told to be sure and have all our blankets on exhibition, good, bad, and indifferent . . . a Yankee squad passed along the line and, without much ceremony, took every blanket from us, save one to each man throughout the camp."[6]

In his inspection report of November 1863, Swalm noted that many prisoners were relieving themselves outside their quarters, day or night. This unsanitary practice created conditions ripe for the spread of disease and fouled the air within the prison confines. Swalm's account suggested that prisoners appeared careless in tending to their bodily needs, often using whatever spot was convenient, including the camp's drainage ditches. This situation was likely the result of severe overcrowding, which made access to latrines difficult, compounded by an overall shortage of facilities, restricted times of use, and the sundry illnesses prisoners suffered.[7]

Because of the high-water table at Point Lookout, latrines could not be dug deep enough for the proper disposal of human waste. The latrines available for prisoner use during the day were located outside the stockade on the bay side of the prison. This location, combined with the small number of "sinks" or "closets" (daytime latrines), forced prisoners to push through thousands of others to reach them and then compete for a turn at the limited facilities. According to prison regulations, the beach gates were closed at the last notes of "taps," ending all

4 Keiley, *In Vinculis*, 68–69.

5 G. W. D. Porter, "Nine Months in a Northern Prison," in *April–December, 1878*, ed. Edwin L. Drake, Vol. 1, *The Annals of the Army of Tennessee and Early Western History* (Nashville, TN, 1878), 330–334; Neese, *Three Years in the Confederate Horse Artillery*, 343.

6 Neese, *Three Years in the Confederate Horse Artillery*, 344.

7 *OR* 6/2:579.

activity within the prison. Prisoners were also ordered to remain inside their shelters throughout the night or face punishment. This made access to the latrines after sunset a challenge.

The alternative was the use of a limited number of "night boxes" or "tubs" designated for overnight use by the prisoners. The morning cleanup detail also included washing these soiled wooden boxes or crates, which were positioned at the eastern end of each divisional street. Once cleaned, the boxes were stored away until their nightly use was again required.

Regulations required prisoners to remain inside their shelters after taps and not to go outside for any reason. They were, however, permitted to use the night boxes without penalty, provided they returned to their shelters afterward. This placed men suffering from dysentery and diarrhea at an extreme disadvantage. Diarrhea and dysentery were among the leading causes of death at Point Lookout, with 20,474 reported cases and 2,050 deaths between September 1863 and July 1865. Prisoners using the night boxes ran the risk of being shot or harassed by the roving night patrols or by guards pacing the catwalks. As an alternative, some relieved themselves in the surrounding ditches.

According to the testimony of Sgt. William Laird, the Confederate sergeant major of the prison camp, a prisoner was shot by a roving guard as he attempted to use the night box located in front of Laird's tent. No warning was given, as Laird reported in his written statement of April 19, 1864. The inaccessibility of the latrines worsened the prisoners' suffering and contributed to unsanitary conditions within the camp, worsening already unbearable conditions.[8]

Prison commanding officer General Hinks addressed the unsanitary conditions in Special Order 108, which created a camp police force led by a Federal officer to oversee and enforce the newly established prison policing system. Despite Hinks's efforts to resolve the sanitation problems, such conditions persisted until the closing of Point Lookout.[9]

## The Relief of the Chesapeake Bay and Potomac River

The location of Point Lookout offered prisoners access to the natural resources of the Chesapeake Bay. The shoreline gave them periodic opportunity to leave the stockade and enjoy the water, sea breezes, and a change of scenery. It provided a convenient place to swim, fish, and crab, as well as to bathe and wash clothes. The

8 *Book No. 251*, 22; Barnes et al., *The Medical and Surgical History of the War of the Rebellion*, 1.3:46; *OR* 7/2:383.

9 *Book No. 251*, Special Order No. 108.

gates to the shoreline generally opened at sunrise, remained open for several hours during the day, and closed by sunset.

For security reasons, officers were allowed to bathe for two hours separately from the enlisted prisoners. One officer remarked that, out of necessity, they left one man behind to guard each tent. The officers marched the 50-yard distance to the bay in a column of fours between two lines of guards. They washed their clothes and bathed in saltwater, an experience unfamiliar to some of them.[10]

## Work Details

As early as November 1863, the strain on the small guard force was becoming apparent. Exhausted soldiers grew unable to perform many of the auxiliary details in addition to their primary duties. Prison authorities began considering the use of prisoners as a supplemental workforce to alleviate the manpower shortage. Prisoners were assigned to perform the work necessary to maintain the prison and the large army hospital.

In response to Marston's request to use prisoners, the ever-frugal Hoffman stated that no civilian workers were to be hired or perform work that could not be accomplished by the prisoners themselves. This policy saved the prison fund money that would otherwise have been spent on outside labor. Soon, the number of prisoner work details expanded to include unloading freight from numerous ships and barges as well as the construction of fortifications.[11]

Prisoners eagerly sought opportunities to work outside the confines of the prison. Time beyond the walls allowed them to forage for items they could sell, trade, or consume themselves. Food and scraps of wood were most desirable, provided they could be smuggled past the ever-watchful guard. Prisoners also brought in metal to make tools for construction or to aid in digging escape tunnels. Perhaps more importantly, any time spent beyond the stockade boosted morale by offering respite from the monotony of prison life and the unhealthy conditions of the camp.

In late July 1864, the secretary of war ordered additional fieldworks constructed at Point Lookout. This large construction project, consisting of three redoubts or forts, required the labor of more than 300 prisoners in addition to guards. Prison officials offered tobacco, whiskey, and an extra food ration as compensation for participation. Prisoners noted that this was the most desirable work detail.

10 Blue, *Hanging Rock Rebel*, 272.

11 Hunter, "Warden for the Union," 92.

Work detail announcements were posted daily on the camp bulletin board near the prison gate. These announcements generally stated how many men—usually 30 to 100—were required for various details. Prisoners monitored the bulletin board each day, with some checking almost hourly, for notices regarding details, prisoner exchanges, packages, and letters. Several hundred anxious men gathered at the main prison gate, awaiting selection based on the needs of each detail.[12]

Prisoners fortunate enough to be selected were usually mustered into a company, their names recorded, and marched outside to the site of their work. Those chosen were "usually compensated with an extra ration . . . when a requisition was made for a certain number of men to go outside a thousand would rush for the gate all eager to get extra rations for their work."[13]

Even though prisoners may have been comrades in cause and on the battlefield, this association often ended in prison. On one work detail, tempers reportedly flared between prisoners from Mississippi and North Carolina. The Mississippians accused the Tar Heels of being less supportive of secession, since their state was the last to leave the Union. This accusation did not sit well with the North Carolinians, who showed open hostility toward Mississippi.[14]

Prisoners were often, and sometimes humorously, inventive when smuggling items into the prison. Despite their ingenuity, the guards learned to foil their schemes and uncover their hiding places. Prisoners frequently helped themselves to anything belonging to the Federal government—items they could either trade or use for survival in prison. Food, coal, "or anything else we see not guarded" was considered fair game before returning to camp. Some enterprising prisoners sewed extra bags or pockets inside coats and trousers to conceal items in the hope of avoiding detection by vigilant guards.[15]

One of the more desirable details was unloading the many supply ships, boats, and barges that lined the piers and wharves at Point Lookout. Prisoner George Jones of the 24th Virginia Cavalry wrote,

> I was in a detail of 100 men to unload a large boat loaded with rations for the prisoners . . . prisoners took advantage of it by going into a cracker box or open a barrel of sugar and coffee and anything else they could . . . every rebel had his breeches and pockets full . . . However, when the work parties returned to

12 Keiley, *In Vinculis*, 114.

13 G. W. Jones, *In Prison at Point Lookout* (Martinsville, VA, n.d.), 4.

14 Haynes, *A Soldier Boy's Letter*, 131.

15 Peyton, *A Civil War Record for 1864–1865*, 102; S. N. Boseworth, "Escaped from Point Lookout Prison," in *Confederate Veteran*, ed. S. A. Cunningham, 10th ed. (Nashville, TN, 1910), 18:471–472.

> the prison, they were halted and then . . . they formed us in two-rank files and marched us up within twenty paces of the gate.

Unfortunately for work detail's such as Jones's, prisoners had one final "ceremony" to perform before reentering the prison. "[A Union officer] then gave the command to 'shake rags' . . . [meaning to] 'take off your trousers and disgorge,' which we proceeded to do . . . There was in one pile a mass of every article unloaded from the boat, making a heap as large as a hogshead, at which the boys looked wistfully and with many regrets."[16]

Unloading shipments of flour barrels for the bakery required thirty or more prisoners. The main bakery at Point Lookout was a substantial operation. A large staff of bakers and assistants drawn from the prison population performed the labor, while U.S. Army bakers and officers from the Subsistence Department supervised the work. The bakery contained five enormous brick ovens constructed with approximately 30,000 bricks, housed in a bakehouse measuring 30 feet wide by 120 feet long. Two wings, each 25 by 38 feet, flanked the structure, with a third wing measuring 20 by 46 feet. The bakery was an essential enterprise that operated 24 hours a day, seven days a week. It could produce up to 25,000 loaves of bread per day, feeding the thousands confined at Point Lookout. Prisoner details also removed the empty barrels for reuse.[17]

One prisoner tied the cuffs of his pant legs shut, then filled his trousers to near bursting with flour from the unloading. He could barely walk, but managed to reach the prison gate, only to have the guard cut the bindings. He was then trailed by a solid path of flour into camp, accompanied by the derisive laughter of both prisoners and guards.[18]

Stories of prisoner ingenuity like these fill the diaries and letters of both guards and prisoners. Although sometimes humorous, such accounts reveal the lengths to which human beings will go to survive.

The compensation provided to prisoners consisted of extra rations or equivalent credit on their prison sutler checkbooks. Initially, prisoners were paid wages in U.S. currency credited to their sutler checkbooks. However, Hoffman discontinued this form of compensation. A visiting correspondent from

16 Jones, *In Prison at Point Lookout*, 4–5.

17 "Public Sale of Government Property," *Daily National Republican* [Washington, D.C.], Jan. 1, 1866, Auction Sales, 2, accessed March 25, 2025, https://chroniclingamerica.loc.gov/lccn/sn86053570/1866-01-01/ed-1/seq-3/; Spar, *Civil War Hospital Newspapers*, 157.

18 W. R. Burwell, "Forbes Lost His Rations," in *Confederate Veteran*, ed. S. A. Cunningham, 12th ed. (Nashville, TN, 1903), 9:553.

*The New York Times* reported that "details of from two to three hundred prisoners . . . work upon the fortifications . . . [they] received as extra compensation for their labor five cents' worth of tobacco and one gill [four U.S. fluid ounces] of whisky per day—one half in the morning and one half at night—or the money value thereof was credited to their sutler accounts."[19]

Prisoners found ways to obtain more than their allotted whiskey from the work details. Some would double back to the end of the line and receive a second ration without being detected by the guards. One account recorded that a prisoner became "so drunk that he could not find the house when he got back to camp."[20]

Many prisoners who received whiskey devised ways to smuggle it into the prison. Before long, some began selling their rationed whiskey to fellow inmates at exorbitant prices or trading it for other goods. Prison authorities discovered that the whiskey was sometimes held in the mouth until it could be spat into bottles, creating what became known as "spit whiskey." Despite efforts to curb this smuggling, whiskey continued to circulate among the prison population. The practice was not only illegal but also unsanitary, carrying the potential to spread disease. In response, the provost marshal revised the rationing procedure: one guard issued the drink from a bucket while another held the recipient's nose to ensure he swallowed the whiskey. In this fashion, the ration was distributed to the men as they returned through the prison gate.

Assignments to various details eased the monotony of prison life for those fortunate enough to be selected. These prisoners found temporary relief in body and mind, as well as opportunities for profit through smuggling whatever they could obtain. Although abuses by guards persisted, some prisoners observed that certain guards displayed limited sympathy by occasionally turning a blind eye.

Prisoners documented many incidents that revealed their ingenuity in slipping items past the guards. Work details also created opportunities to hear the latest rumors regarding the progress of the war while they labored throughout the peninsula. In addition to the camp bulletin board, the prison sutler served as another gathering place where prisoners exchanged news, anticipated possible assignments, and bargained for something to supplement their meager rations.

## The Prison Sutler

Lieutenant Erastus W. Everson of the 20th V.R.C. remarked that it was "better to be sutler than President," and serving as the post sutler at Point Lookout was

19 *OR* 7/2:366-367; "From Point."

20 Peyton, *A Civil War Record for 1864–1865*, 111.

no exception. He also observed that the position of post sutler was highly coveted and not easily obtained without some "greasing of the way" by the candidate. Everson reflected that "the process of appointing a sutler and his retention would certainly be an interesting chapter to read. At a glance, the sutler could not fail of doing a thrifty business" at Point Lookout.[21]

Article 6 of Hoffman's July 1862 circular stated that a prison sutler was appointed by the War Department and placed under the authority of the post commanding officer, "who will see that he furnishes proper articles and at reasonable rates," while paying a tax based on sales. This tax was paid into the general or prison fund. The provost marshal, who controlled the prisoners' money held on account, paid the sutler weekly. Prisoners were not permitted to spend more than five dollars a day at the sutler's store unless the provost marshal granted special permission.[22]

At least once every two months, the commanding officer of Point Lookout convened a Post Council of Administration as required by U.S. Army regulations. The council consisted of the provost marshal, three regimental officers, the surgeon in charge of Hammond Hospital, the post quartermaster, and post sutlers. The council ensured that all sutlers complied with the Congressional Act of March 2, 1862, along with the various general orders and circulars that regulated their operations. Sutlers were required to provide a detailed list of items offered for sale and their prices.[23]

Cash or valuables confiscated from prisoners upon arrival at Point Lookout were recorded by the provost marshal, who applied the funds to each prisoner's account with the sutler. The sutler then issued a scrip or checkbook to the prisoner, which he used to charge purchases at the sutler's store. The checkbook also listed the rules and regulations governing transactions. If a balance remained, it was recorded on the first page of the checkbook.

If a prisoner was exchanged or released, any money remaining on record with the sutler was given to him in cash upon departure from Point Lookout. In the event of a prisoner's death, the money was transferred to the prison fund. The provost marshal's office was also responsible for reconciling prisoner account books.[24]

21 Letter by Everson, "Letters."

22 *OR* 4/2:152-153; Letter by Everson, "Letters"; Memorandum, "Sutler's Receipts," n.d., Box 107, Point Lookout Prison Camp, 1863–1865, University of Michigan William L Clements Library, Ann Arbor, MI.

23 *Revised United State Army Regulations of 1861, Fed. Reg. (1863)*, 34.

24 Keiley, *In Vinculis*, 78-79.

Prison wall showing prison sutler window. *Author*

Money received through the mail was applied to a prisoner's sutler account. Prisoners soon found ways to circumvent this rule. They discovered that if clothing could be received through the mail, money could be sent as well. Senders concealed currency by sewing it into the linings of garments, thereby evading the system. Some time passed before officials uncovered the ruse.

It was not the intention of Federal authorities to establish large prison sutler shops or to treat the sutler as a supplemental source of food for prisoners. According to regulations, the sutler was permitted to sell only those items approved by the secretary of war and the commissary general of prisoners. However, as prison populations increased, Hoffman revised his view of the sutler's role by issuing modifications to the prescribed list of allowable goods. The revised list included both edible and non-edible items for sale to prisoners to supplement their issued rations.[25]

The camp sutler at the town camp was located at the southern end of the prison stockade near the main gate. Business was conducted through a window or

25 Francis A. Lord, *Civil War Sutlers and Their Wares* (New York, 1969), 87.

slit cut into the stockade wall, with goods positioned immediately outside. This arrangement allowed transactions between the sutler and prisoners while limiting opportunities for theft or a sudden rush to seize the sutler's supplies. Atherton W. Quint of Manchester, New Hampshire, served as the first prison sutler.[26]

The sutler usually attracted more "spectators than customers," as very few prisoners had money to spend or goods to trade. Although allegedly regulated, sutlers were known, or at least suspected, of inflating prices based on supply and demand. Prisoners claimed that sutler prices were often inflated "two and three hundred per cent for his wares," a practice he could get away with since he knew that "the famishing prisoners would be forced to buy at any price," even "4 times its worth." Commodities such as "bread, meat, vegetables, coffee, sugar, fruit, writing materials, shoes, clothing, [and] blankets" were among the most purchased items. Prisoners alleged that some clothing offered by the sutler was property confiscated during their arrival inspection.[27]

In July 1864, the prison sutler announced that the sale of food items was suspended due to a rumor that sutlers in Southern prisons were prohibited from selling such goods to their northern counterparts. Prisoners suspected this was a "ruse concocted by the prison sutler to have a run on his shop to quickly sell his perishables before the warm, summer weather spoiled them." The stratagem apparently succeeded, as "the sutler's 'powerful' butter, game herrings, animated cheese and sour meal began to disappear with a celerity that must have been very satisfactory to him if not to the deluded Confederates, who were thus seduced into an unusual quantity of purchases." The claim proved false, as prisoners had suspected.[28]

In March 1864, Hoffman authorized an expanded list of sutler items for his prisons. The list included dry goods such as tobacco, paper, envelopes, penknives, postage stamps, clothing, towels and handkerchiefs, as well as white sugar, crackers, cheese, pickles, canned fish, matches, fruits, and vegetables. Tableware was also permitted, including crockery and tinware. Prisoners who could afford the luxury of having their photograph taken at one of the studios at Point Lookout paid for the service, along with any copies, through a voucher submitted by the photographer to the provost marshal.[29]

26 Shotwell, *The Papers of Randolph Abbott Shotwell*, 1:123; Haynes, *A Soldier Boy's Letter*, 155.

27 Spencer, "Point Lookout," 417; Flinn, "A Southern Soldier's Experience in a Northern Prison," 17, 21–22.

28 Keiley, *In Vinculis*, 111–113.

29 Memorandum, "Voucher to J. B. Spaulding," n.d., Box 112, Folder 3, Point Lookout Prison Camp, 1863–1865, University of Michigan William L Clements Library, Ann Arbor, MI.

Hoffman further stipulated that no sales to prisoners could be made before eight o'clock in the morning or after half an hour before sunset. Prison commanders were instructed to supervise the sutler to ensure that the privilege was not abused by either the sutler or the prisoners. They were also ordered to see that all transactions were settled using the funds held in each prisoner's individual account.[30]

Prisoners manufactured items in the stockade that were either sold or traded to the sutler for credit. The sutler in turn sold these goods to the many ship captains who arrived at Point Lookout, and the captains eventually resold them to customers in northern cities. Prisoners detailed to unload transport boats and ships often sold or traded items directly to captains and travelers, bypassing the camp sutler. The most common items sold by sutlers were prisoner-made rings, fans, and "ornaments or curiosities." One prisoner stated that "the sutler gave prisoners credit for items the prisoners made for the sutler to sell, not only to other prisoners, but to the guards and any visitor to the prison." The sutler then recorded the credit from such sales in the prisoner's scrip book.[31]

Sutlers also sold tools and materials necessary for manufacturing items, including "wood, boards, boxes, gutta percha [an early form of plastic], horsehair, old pieces of silver, and a few small tools such as what silversmiths and wood carvers would use." Prison visitors often purchased items directly from prisoners, paying them in cash. To the prisoners' delight, this provided hard money in their pockets. "If a prisoner received money from friends at home or elsewhere, he might buy . . . a blanket, an overcoat, etc."[32]

In December 1863, Hoffman announced, by direction of the secretary of war, that "all trade with the sutler by prisoners of war at Fort Delaware was prohibited." This order applied to all prisons. The directive, issued by Stanton, was an act of retribution in response to reports that Federal prisoners in Richmond were allegedly being denied relief packages sent from the North. It was later revealed that this claim was unfounded. By February 1864, business with the sutler resumed, along with the receipt of packages from family and friends—though not from the Confederate government or rebellious states.[33]

30 *OR* 6/2:1014–1015.

31 "The Rebel Prisoners at Point Lookout MD," *Evening Star* [Washington D.C.], Sept. 12, 1864, afternoon edition, 2, accessed March 26, 2025, https://chroniclingamerica.loc.gov/lccn/sn83045462/1864-09-12/ed-1/seq-2/; Jones, *In Prison at Point Lookout*, 7.

32 Flinn, "A Southern Soldier's Experience in a Northern Prison," 17–18.

33 *OR* 6/2:625.

Prisoners selling handmade fans to a Union officer. *Point Lookout State Park Collection*

In August 1864, Stanton again clamped down on outside deliveries, instructing Hoffman that "no supplies of any kind will be furnished to prisoners of war by their relatives or friends, except in cases of illness." In such cases, only close relatives could send "articles of food as may be approved by the surgeon in charge of the hospital." The same restriction applied to relatives sending clothing, and then only to "destitute prisoners." Hoffman issued Circular No. 4 on August 10, 1864, which incorporated these requirements and further reduced the list of items that the sutler could sell to prisoners. Food items were excluded from this list.[34]

## Gamblers, Tradesmen, and Shop Keepers

Prisoner Sidney Lanier of the Confederate Signal Corps offered a sociological portrait of the prisoners at Point Lookout. He described the aristocrats, who did no work; the artisans, who survived by labor; and the drones, who starved while doing nothing to help themselves. "Drones" there may have been, but most prisoners preferred not to remain idle waiting for the next roll call or ration issue. Those not assigned to work details divided their time between improving their shelters or engaging in other tasks within the prison that contributed to their comfort or survivability.[35]

Some of the more enterprising prisoners used their civilian skills and trades to provide goods and services to the prison population. Services included tailoring, haircutting, shaving, shoe repair, and laundry. Handcrafted items included dice and toothpicks fashioned from the animal bone salvaged from rations. Fans, small chains, doll furniture, and small lidded boxes materialized from scraps of wood. Lead bullets produced chess and checker pieces, along with fish sinkers. Prisoners fashioned hand saws from barrel hoops, while necklaces, breast pins, shirt buttons, and lockets were made of gutta-percha (a thermoplastic-like latex substance, often black in color), which was inlaid with gold, silver, or pearl. Rings were chiefly produced from animal bone, coat buttons, or gutta-percha.

One remarkable example of prisoner ingenuity was a working clock "made entirely of bone and placed inside a canteen [which] was exhibited to anyone who wished to see it for a cracker." Other craftsmen used whatever wood they could obtain to create items for sale to guards or fellow prisoners. Wooden ware such as noggins, tubs, buckets, piggins (a wooden ladle), and pails were crafted by skillful prisoners.

34 *OR* 7/2:576–574.

35 Sydney Lanier, *Tiger Lilies: A Novel* (New York, NY, 1867), 198.

One Georgia prisoner even constructed a crude steam engine that functioned as a lathe. "The first engine made in camp . . . The boiler was made from an old camp kettle, the mouth of which was plugged with wood. The pistons and connecting rods were of wood, and the valves and piston heads were contrived from old mustard boxes." The steam-driven wonder was "turning lathes from which the pen handles, bodkins, etc., were turned out . . . there were seven of them in different parts of the camp, and they would whistle every morning." Another account described a prisoner-made violin, noting that "the most surprising sample of mere mechanical ingenuity which I saw was a violin made of a cracker-box, wherein all the curves and undulations of that preternaturally twisted instrument were reproduced with the utmost fidelity."[36]

There were a few sketch artists among the prisoners, such as Pvt. John J. Omenhausser of the 46th Virginia, who depicted daily life at the prison. Omenhausser later became well known for his series of watercolor books created at Point Lookout. These artists often sold or traded their work to guards or to others who could pay cash. Several of Omenhausser's watercolor collections survive in institutions today.

Prisoners who manufactured watch fobs out of horsehair either purchased material from the sutler or gathered it while on work details. Another method of acquiring horsehair was to wait for an inspecting official to ride into the prison camp and then ambush the unsuspecting animal from behind, pulling out as much hair as possible. Prisoners became so brazen in these attempts that a guard detail was eventually ordered to escort visitors and their horses while inside the prison.[37]

Prisoners were known to construct makeshift "restaurants", usually arranged on benches, planks, or blankets in front of their shelters. Their displays featured goods they had produced or acquired for sale, often announced with a homemade sign offering a place to sit and eat. Those seeking a wider clientele carried their products around the camp, positioning themselves along the divisional streets and calling out their offerings to starving prisoners. Malnourished inmates provided a ready customer base and were usually willing to pay the asking price. Variations of lemonade, soups, and coffee were sold, along with such delicacies as pies and pancakes, all priced at a hardtack cracker or two, or a chew of tobacco. Union currency, of course, was never refused.

Prisoners recalled that "you would find gingerbread and molasses-candy of domestic manufacture for sale, and, strangely enough, one or two regular eating-

36 Letter by Wells, "James T. Wells"; Keiley, *In Vinculis*, 76.

37 Everson, Narrative and Personal Notes, 41.

Private John J. Omenhausser, 46th Virginia and his sketchbook.
*Ross Kimmel; Point Lookout State Park Collection*

houses, where a very respectable dinner could be obtained for fifty cents!" An enterprising Pvt. George W. Jones of the 24th Virginia Cavalry wrote, "My strong forte was molasses taffy and corn mush with blackstrap syrup . . . I could fry flapjacks so thin you could read through them and dilute the molasses so that it would run on a board. My price for a palatable dish was five hardtacks and a chew of tobacco."[38]

Fortunately for Jones, business ventures like his profited from a steady customer base created by the continual arrival of prisoners. He later reported that while on a detail assigned to paint the newly constructed prison hospital buildings, he made a fortunate discovery. Near one building, he noticed a pile of discarded coffee grounds. Gathering them, Jones put his find to use. "With my stock of coffee grounds, I would have a kettle full [of coffee] every morning. I would stand on the street in front of my tent and cry: 'here's your coffee! Cupful for a cracker!' . . . [Y]ou could see the boys coming from every direction with a cup in one hand and a cracker in the other."[39]

38 Keiley, *In Vinculis,* 75; Jones, *In Prison at Point Lookout,* 2–3.

39 Ibid. 6-7.

Prisoners operating a prison restaurant. *Point Lookout State Park Collection*

Another prisoner claimed that his primary commodities consisted of apples, tobacco, and a "concoction of burnt bread and water which was used as a substitute for coffee." His warehouse and place of business was a cracker box, which he set up next to his tent to display his goods. "I would call in a loud voice, 'Here's your apples, hot coffee, and tobacco' . . . I would sell a few of these little cuts or chews [of tobacco] for five cents." One prisoner even assumed the occupation of barber and walked through the camp announcing, "Here goes your good old Tar Heel barber, will shave you for a chew of tobacco. If anyone will shave you cheaper, I'll give you a chew to let me shave you."[40]

Prisoners constructed traps, nets, and snares to harvest crabs, fish, and ducks, which they sold either cooked or raw. Oysters were plentiful on both sides of the peninsula, and prisoners sold dredged oysters from their shanties, also offering them cooked or raw. Although illegal and considered contraband, prisoners managed to build stills to produce moonshine, though "only in small quantities." The liquor was distilled from corn and potato peels smuggled out of the prison slop barrels in the cookhouses. Crude forms of beer were also available.[41]

40 Beitzell, *Point Lookout Prison Camp for Confederates*, 97; John B. Ernul, *Life of a Confederate Soldier in a Federal Prison* (Vanceboro, NC, 1909), 13.

41 Letters by Wells, "James T. Wells."

Gambling was a daily activity that flourished both inside and outside the prison. Nearly all prisoner accounts of this pastime reference the gamblers and the gambling houses in operation. The gamblers "constructed booths . . . every morning and slept on every night . . . Here the dice rattled, and the cards were shuffled from morning till night; everything represented value, from a 'hardtack' up," with goods and rations freely offered and accepted as legitimate currency. Games of chance included keno, poker, seven-up, cut throat monte, faro, and chuck-a-luck, the most popular at the time. Gamblers accepted both hardtack and hard cash for the games they ran in camp. The booths were generally located on the beach along the Chesapeake Bay and were "always crowded." They were "decorated by a small fancy-colored streamer flying from the top. . . . The gambling went on seven days a week regardless of the Sabbath, which disturbed many of the more pious prisoners."[42]

In November 1863, Edward Spencer, a news correspondent for the *Overland Monthly and Out West Magazine,* was permitted to visit his brother, a prisoner at Point Lookout living in Company K of the Seventh Division. His brother gave him a tour of the principal areas of the prison. Spencer was escorted to the central market area, which the prisoners referred to as "Market Street." His brother explained that "this is the Wall Street—the grand centre of trade and barter; the mart and emporium of traffic." The wide, hard-packed road was also called "Pennsylvania Avenue" and was bordered on either side by prisoner shelters facing each other.[43]

The entire street served as the general marketplace for goods and services produced and sold by prisoners. Market Street was located in the open area between the last divisional street and the prison hospital at the southern end of the camp. This space was initially used for overflow purposes but was eventually converted into additional divisional streets after the prison hospital complex was relocated in June 1864.

In his article "Point Lookout," Spencer reported that one of the several steam engines, which "yielded its builder quite a handsome revenue, by grinding hard-bread, and turning bones and gutta-percha for the ring-makers," was situated next to vendors offering homemade coffee, lemonade, molasses taffy, crabs, fish, watermelons, and various other goods and services.

One prisoner displayed "a splendid pair of gloves,"

42 Keiley, *In Vinculis,* 78; Letters by Wells, "James T. Wells."

43 Edward Spencer to Gilman Marston, Jan. 10, 1864, accessed April 28, 2023, https://findingaids.lib.umich.edu/catalog/umich-wcl-M-1688poi; Spencer, "Point Lookout," 419.

> holding up a shrunken pair of black, worsted mittens, with mouse-nibbled fingers. Another announcing, "who wants to buy a boot?" a sole less, moldy, old calfskin was held up for admiration. "Cakes! Cakes!" cried another, with half a dozen stale ginger-cakes in a wooden tray hanging before him. "A ring for four bits! A ring for four bits!" "How many crackers for my trowsers?" yelled another, elevating the cast-off article.[44]

A *New York Times* reporter wrote that gambling "keeps the mind engaged and operates more effectually to prevent conspiracies and improper combinations among the men than discipline and guards." He observed prisoner industry firsthand:

> Passing down Pennsylvania Avenue . . . a small wooden house, built evidently of cracker boxes, with a sign over the door, "Chains, rings, &c., manufactured here at shortest notice." Within were seated two rebs at a work bench, making up these articles, with tools gotten up by themselves.[45]

## Brick Making

Another item manufactured within the prison was sun-dried bricks. These crude bricks were used to construct chimneys for prisoner shelters as well as for the guard force. They became a commodity that could be traded, sold, or used as credit with the sutler from the guards. Brick making grew into an industry worked by enterprising prisoners willing to dig the clay-like soil of Point Lookout. Prisoners reported that several clay pits were located inside the prison enclosure, allowing brick makers to produce piles of bricks.[46]

Spencer's article describes the enormity of the prison brickyard and part of the process of manufacture:

> Near the sutler's booth a brick-yard was located, where thousands of bricks . . . made of the stiff, white oak-clay [of] Point Lookout, were laid out in symmetrical

44 Spencer, "Point Lookout," 421.

45 "Prison-Camp at Point Lookout," *The Alexandria* [VA] *Gazette*, July 27, 1864, evening edition, accessed March 27, 2025, https://chroniclingamerica.loc.gov/lccn/sn85025007/1864-07-27/ed-1/seq-2/.

46 Franklin, Diary of James Franklin, 26.

> rows, to dry in the sun. These adobes were fabricated . . . for the hearths and chimneys of their shebangs.[47]

The bricks were also used by the Union garrison for their shelters in the camps. Private Martin Haynes of the 2nd New Hampshire stated that

> scores of the [prisoners] might be seen kneading the clay and sand, filling little square boxes with the mixture, and dumping it on the ground to dry in the sun. Some . . . made enough of these bricks to build themselves little adobe houses [it was reported that at least two or three "adobe houses" were made entirely of handmade bricks in the prison] and sold many to our men at fifty cents a hundred to build chimneys in our own camp.[48]

At its height, the Point Lookout brick-making industry came to an abrupt halt for security reasons. Officials discovered that one of the brick pits concealed an escape tunnel. The tunnel was closed, the culprits punished, and the clay pits were covered with lime and repurposed as camp latrines.

## Lice

Body lice are insects that thrive on individuals who enjoy little opportunity for clean clothing, bedding changes, or daily bathing. Infestations can spread rapidly in unhygienic, crowded living conditions. Lice bites can in turn facilitate the spread of typhus among a closely packed population like that at Point Lookout.

There was no escaping lice (also referred to by soldiers as cooties, crums, gray backs, pants rabbits, seam squirrels, blue bellies, and other names). Body lice were the ever-present companions to soldiers in the field, infesting every space they occupied. Whether a soldier arrived with the pests onboard or not, he soon became a host and joined the ranks of garment pickers. Soldiers described their daily combat with the pests as being under the "black flag," meaning they gave no quarter to their "enemy." The daily chore of picking lice off garments was an unwelcome part of the routine, but to make life tolerable, it had to be done.

Drowning this scourge in the bay or river was a common practice, as was boiling clothes. However, most soldiers resorted to picking lice off in a perpetual struggle to rid themselves of the pests. This task could be lengthy, depending on

47 Spencer, "Point Lookout," 418.

48 Haynes, *A History of the Second Regiment New Hampshire Volunteer Infantry*, 159.

the tenacity of the garment's owner, the size of the garment, and the number of inhabitants wearing it.

Prisoners wrote that waging war on gray backs was a daily chore, with the lice multiplying by the hundreds overnight. One prisoner stated that, "although he could change his underclothes weekly, lice still bothered him and 'make you feel mean all the time.'" Lice infested not only clothing but also blankets, as well as the boards and canvas of shelters. Spencer noted that he was directed by a prisoner who "pointed across to the sunny side of the inclosure [sic], where, seated under the lee of the fence, were some fifty or sixty men very busy indeed—some with their shirts off; some with their trousers in their hands [picking lice]."[49]

Washing clothes was another profitable business venture for those who had the vessels and soap to provide this service for a few pieces of hardtack. Those without the means to wash their clothes hired those capable of the chore. They were aptly dubbed "washer women" by the inmates. Private Keiley wrote that,

> another source of extensive profits in prison was . . . washerwomen . . . The labors of these . . . *ouvriers* were conducted on the beach at low tide . . . A bluff of two to three feet was created by the tides . . . A small hole of about eight inches was dug on top of the bluff and as many from the edge. A cavity was dug into the bluff beneath this hole creating a cavity making the stove. A fire was built within this cavity where the boiler would be placed on top of the hole. Wash water was then retrieved from the bay and boiled.[50]

One of the few Black prisoners held at Point Lookout, Dick Poplar, a company cook with the 13th Virginia Cavalry captured at Gettysburg, took advantage of his vocation by operating a small eatery in the prison. He was also known to double his income as a washer woman. Nevertheless, despite the most tenacious efforts to stem the scourge, lice remained a constant companion for both prisoners and guards. Unfortunately, there was no permanent remedy for eliminating this pest, and it continued to be a nuisance to all who occupied Point Lookout.[51]

## The Camp Bulletin Board

Prison authorities provided a bulletin board near the camp post office for posting war news, general prison announcements, and other advertisements.

49 Peyton, *A Civil War Record for 1864–1865*, 99–101; Spencer, "Point Lookout," 417.

50 Keiley, *In Vinculis*, 77.

51 Ibid., 82.

More importantly, this bulletin board displayed notices for prisoners who received letters and packages. Prisoners' names were posted to notify them to claim their mail at the assistant provost marshal's office. With permission, prisoners could post announcements or notices seeking family or friends who may also have been held at Point Lookout.[52]

Prisoners checked the bulletin board often, not only for mail but also for the list of prisoners to be exchanged or transferred, hoping to see their names posted. Instructions for exchanges or transfers included the specific assembly time for prisoners with their belongings by the main gate. Some wary prisoners hesitated to believe news about possible exchanges, as reports often proved false.

Point Lookout authorities posted war news on the bulletin board, specifically noting items such as northern victories, the fall of strategic coastal ports, and the sinking of the CSS *Alabama* by a "U.S. gunboat off the coast of France." The arrival of hundreds of recently captured Confederates in April 1865 confirmed that their cause was in a downward spiral and was communicated to inmates via the camp bulletin board.

## Prisoner Mail

Prisoner mail, even if weeks old, was the next best source of information. Prisoners longed for news from loved ones and friends, and next to being exchanged, nothing uplifted morale more than a letter or package from home. Newspapers, letters, photographs, clothing, and homemade food items provided vital connections, giving the despondent prisoner something to anticipate and raising spirits in confinement. Hoffman's 1862 circular stated that prisoners were "permitted to write and receive letters, not to exceed one page of common letter paper each and had to be of a private nature." Letters from home were to be "examined by a reliable non-commissioned officer, appointed for that purpose by the commanding officer before the letters were forwarded or delivered to the prisoners."[53]

Civil War soldiers on both sides were among the most literate in U.S. history up to that time. Factors such as social class or educational attainment meant literacy skills varied from soldier to soldier, but in general the armies were comprised of literate men. Approximately eight out of ten Confederate soldiers and nine out of ten Union soldiers could read and write to some degree. The abundance of letters and diaries preserved in museums and archives attests that

52 Lanier, *Tiger Lilies*, 204–206.

53 *OR* 7/2:7, 75.

Prisoners gather at the prison letter drop box and bulletin board. *Point Lookout State Park Collection*

writing was not only necessary for soldiers to communicate with loved ones, but a favored pastime as well.[54]

As early as 1860, a post office operated at Point Lookout, prior to the arrival of the U.S. Army. It was served by a mail steamer that traveled the Potomac River, running downstream one day and returning upstream the next. In December 1863, Butler requested that Postmaster General Montgomery Blair establish a more efficient mail and transport service by having the mail boat stop at Point Lookout more than once daily. Butler noted that steamships owned by the Bay Line Company passed Point Lookout while transporting mail between Fortress Monroe, Virginia, and Baltimore. He further requested that the mail run twice a day: once from Washington, D.C., and once on the regular run from Baltimore.[55]

54 Ian Delahanty, "Soldiers' Diaries and Letters," Essential Civil War Curriculum, Virginia Center for Civil War Studies at Virginia Tech, accessed March 27, 2025, https://www.essentialcivilwarcurriculum.com/soldiers-diaries-and-letters.html.

55 Regina Combs Hammett, *History of St. Mary's County, Maryland 1634–1990* (Self-published, 1991), 186; Benjamin F. Butler, *Private and Official Correspondence of General Benjamin F. Butler: During the Period of the Civil Way* (Norwood, MA, 1917), 4:256.

Administrative ledgers were kept by the provost marshal's office in each prison to record incoming packages, letters, and money sent to and received by prisoners. "Several rooms in the Provost Marshal's building were constantly occupied by clerks, some of whom were prisoners of war, detailed for the purpose of distributing the mail." Federal clerks were assigned to censor the hundreds of incoming and outgoing letters and packages. Items were logged as received before being inspected by the censors, and any money enclosed in letters was entered under the prisoner's name with the date and amount, then credited to the prisoner's sutler account. To control correspondence, prison authorities established a post office and letter box within the prison, next to the bulletin board.[56]

The mandatory censorship of all mail was ordered by Hoffman and reinforced by army regulations. The process was tedious but necessary for the security of Point Lookout, to prevent information deemed injurious to Federal policy from reaching the enemy. Lieutenant Everson stated that the volume of mail received at Point Lookout "was one of the largest in the country" and that the thousands of pieces of prisoner mail had to be inspected for content, money, and contraband. Letters containing information valuable to the enemy or anything objectionable were marked for the provost marshal's attention. In the course of his many duties, such letters were sometimes given "the go by" and consigned to the flames without further examination.[57]

The consigning of mail to the nearest fire likely occurred frequently, as it would have been impossible for the provost marshal or his assistants to attend to the hundreds, if not thousands, of letters moving in and out of the prison while also managing the daily functions of prison operations. The destruction of so many letters is troubling when one considers not only the deprivation suffered by prisoners and their families but also the loss of valuable material for future research.

Censored letters that reached their intended recipients were usually "distinguished by the imprimatur of a certain official outside the 'pen,' who stamps our correspondence 'Prisoner's Letter, Examined.'" Restricted to a single page, prisoners acquired a "telegraphic habit" of writing, forcing them to become adept at using the fewest number of words possible to convey messages to family and friends on the required single sheet of paper. Compliance made inspections brief and enabled letters to pass quickly from inspectors to their intended recipients.[58]

56 Everson, Papers No. 28/710/22, 25; Sutton, *Civil War Stories*, 69.

57 *OR* 4/3:153; Everson Papers No. 28/710/22, 25.

58 Keiley, *In Vinculis*, 90.

Prisoners wrote of their loneliness and longing for home. Requests often included clothing, stamps, food, and especially money, in the hope that families could spare something. They could not request more stamps, since prison regulations prohibited prisoners from receiving more than eight postage stamps from outside sources. On rare occasions, some prisoners sent photographs of themselves taken at one of the studios operating at Point Lookout. Other common topics included the conditions of the prison, food, and water, though opinions about these matters varied depending on the outlook of the prisoner. Prisoners also mentioned fellow inmates familiar to those at home, reassuring families and friends that, at least for the time being, they knew where their loved ones were or where to send mail. Unfortunately, this news was only as current as the moment the letter was written and received.

Prisoners informed family members where letters and packages could be sent, hoping that they would not be transferred elsewhere in the meantime. All mail had to be addressed specifically with the prisoner's name, division, company, and in care of the provost marshal. Prisoner Barnard Baker wrote to his mother on September 5, 1864, instructing her to "Write me but one page, like this, and strictly upon family affairs. Write my name in full."[59]

Prisoners displayed frugality when restricted to a small sheet of paper. Their handwriting was often reduced to the smallest possible size while still remaining legible. They also wrote along the margins of the page after filling the main body of the letter. Some clever prisoners attempted to evade the censors through ingenious methods of concealing text. They discovered that by "using condensed milk, mixed with a little water" they could write between the lines. "It did not show enough, after it was dry, to attract attention; but, when the paper was held to the fire, the writing between the lines became quite legible."[60]

Once Stanton rescinded his moratorium on prisoner packages, parcels began to arrive again but were required to conform to the established guidelines set forth by Hoffman and the prison's provost marshal. Packages that did not meet the prescribed criteria upon inspection were declared contraband and withheld from the prisoner.

Prisoners were permitted to receive items such as food, note paper, envelopes, and other articles not considered contraband by the authorities. Receiving

59 Letter by Barnard E. Baker, "Baker Family Correspondence, 1800–1907," n.d., Brief Container 1138.01 and Series 11/537/29-45, Baker Family Papers, South Carolina Historical Society, Charleston, SC.

60 Royall W. Figg, *"Where Men Only Dare to Go!" or the Story of a Boy Company* (Richmond, VA, 1885), 234.

clothing, however, usually came with a caveat. A prisoner could not obtain any article of clothing unless he could prove that he needed the requested items. It was to a prisoner's advantage to appear before the provost marshal and staff in ragged clothing and worn shoes, in order to persuade the examiners that he was deserving of replacement garments.

In one account, a prisoner satisfied the requirements of the provost marshal for much-needed clothing and food. After some time, to his immense joy, he saw on the camp bulletin board that his package had arrived and was waiting at the Adams Express Office, located by the south wall of the prison next to the sutler. After convincing the clerk of his identity and proving that the requested items were his, the prisoner, filled with anticipation, returned to his quarters with his inspected package. He soon discovered that it contained nothing more than "a beef tongue and can of solidified cream." Much to his chagrin, the package had been officially "inspected."[61]

## The Prison School and Mess Hall No. 9

Prison authorities permitted the use of Mess Hall No. 9 for various activities, including church services, debating societies, and plays. Mess Hall No. 9 was the northernmost building in the row of mess halls within the prison. The building was seldom used for ration issues and generally came into use only when the prison population exceeded the capacity of the other mess halls. It later served as a schoolhouse, providing prisoners with the opportunity to further their education.

With the arrival of Pvt. Alonzo Morgan of Lee's Signal Corps came the creation of the prison school and its library. With permission from the provost marshal, Morgan established a curriculum after acquiring materials donated from the Baltimore Ladies Society. He enlisted the services of at least eight other prisoners who were as educated as he was. The men volunteered to teach mathematics, grammar, geography, U.S. history, and "phonography" (shorthand). Morgan's instruction was available to all prisoners free of charge, and he received a small extra ration from prison authorities as a reward.

Despite Morgan's efforts, prisoner accounts state that only a little more than 100 men took advantage of the prison school. Several prisoners explained that they did not accept the offer of free education because they were "too hungry to study about anything except something to eat." Private Malachi Bowden of the 2nd Georgia recorded in his diary that he attended "the most advance class" but noted that "there were but few in attendance."

61 Keiley, *In Vinculis*, 93.

Morgan himself was more sanguine about his school. He wrote in one letter that the school conducted regular classes every day except for two snow days and one day of heavy rain. At that time, the school had 150 men "learning to read and nearly as many more in the writing classes." English grammar, algebra, Latin, and dictionary were so well attended that some classes were divided into three sections, each containing 50 or 60 pupils. Arithmetic was so popular that it was divided into seven sections. At the time of his letter, Morgan reported that he employed seventeen instructors, including himself.[62]

Considering the thousands of prisoners incarcerated at Point Lookout, the number of students may seem small. Morgan regarded daily attendance of 150 students per day as a measure of success, since participation was voluntary. As some prisoners left the classes, newly arrived prisoners took their places.

Morgan arranged with the provost marshal a series of bugle calls that announced the opening of exercises and classes as part of the daily routine. Prisoner E. H. Sutton of the 24th Georgia remembered "school hours were from 9 a.m. to 12 [p.m.] and from 1 [p.m.] to 3 p.m." and that "the opening of the exercises [was] one long [bugle] blast . . . the first lesson, one long blast and one short one . . . the second . . . one long and two short blasts, etc. These blasts could be heard all over the camp." Sutton stated that he attended classes for twelve months at Point Lookout, missing only one month after contracting smallpox. The school flourished and continued throughout the prison's existence, gradually dissolving as the population was released in May and June 1865. Morgan later played a key role as one of several prison commissioners appointed to distribute clothing to prisoners supplied by the Confederacy.[63]

## Religion

In September 1863, representatives of the United States Christian Commission requested that a "minister of the Gospel" be sent to work among the prisoners at Point Lookout. The commission assured the War Department that if their request were granted, their representative "would in no way embarrass the Government." Clergymen were permitted to deliver not only sermons but also supplies and letters from families, once the items passed the usual inspection. Services and religious instruction, as well as the distribution of religious materials, tracts, and Bibles, were carried out by the clergy and volunteers. Commission member Reverend Andrew B. Cross wrote to Hoffman on December 16, 1863,

62 Beitzell, *Point Lookout Prison Camp for Confederates*, 106.

63 Sutton, *Civil War Stories*, 52–54.

requesting permission to preach at Point Lookout. Anyone wishing to visit Hammond Hospital or the prison was required to obtain a pass either in advance or upon arrival.[64]

As a courtesy to the commission, Hoffman granted Cross's request, since orders had already been issued permitting clergymen to address the prisoners if the prisoners did not object to their visit. Hoffman insisted that there should "be no doubt about the unqualified loyalty of the clergymen admitted and their visits must be for religious purpose only and not to engage in political discussions." Cross arrived on January 22, 1864.[65]

He was troubled by what he witnessed in some areas of the prison camp, but he reported nothing that the authorities did not already know or had not been made aware of through earlier inspections. Cross's evaluation noted that many improvements had been made regarding prisoner welfare since the previous inspections. He completed his assessment and departed Point Lookout on March 17, 1864.[66]

When permitted, local Catholic priest Father Basil Pacciarini from the nearby town of St. Inigoes visited regularly on Sundays and, at times, during the week. From December 1862 until July 1865, Father Pacciarini, Reverend J. B. Meurer, Reverend Dr. J. A. Spooner, and the Sisters of Charity assigned to Hammond Hospital baptized numerous prisoners of war, Union soldiers, and government civilians. The Sisters of Charity conducted a recorded 17 baptisms, while Father Pacciarini and Reverend J. B. Meurer performed many more.[67]

Several prisoners from St. Mary's County were familiar with Father Pacciarini and welcomed his visits to the camp. Prisoner Sgt. James Thomas of the 2nd Maryland, whose family hailed from the St. Mary's County town of Chaptico, stated that he received money from home through Pacciarini. On his way to Point Lookout, Pacciarini would stop by to visit Thomas's mother, who lived at the nearby plantation De La Brooke Manor. On occasion, Father Pacciarini shared meals with Thomas as well as Sgt. Maj. William Laird of the 2nd Maryland, the

64 *OR* 6/2:363; Andrew B. Cross, "Military Prison at Point Lookout," in *The War and the Christian Commission*, Baltimore, Maryland, (1865), 19.

65 *OR* 6/2:363.

66 Cross, "Military Prison at Point Lookout," 25.

67 Edwin W. Beitzell, *The Jesuit Missions of St. Mary's County, Maryland* (n.p., 1959), 147; Edwin W. Beitzell, "Baptisms at Point Lookout," *St. Mary's Monthly Bulletin of the St. Mary's County Historical Society*, Feb. 1980, 7–9.

sergeant major of the prison camp. This connection permitted Pacciarini easy entry and access to the prison and its occupants.[68]

Prison authorities also permitted Alonzo Morgan to use Mess Hall No. 9 for conducting Sunday religious services. One eyewitness observed the makeshift sanctuary: "At one end is a little raised dais-like pulpit, which constitutes all the furnishing; there are no seats in it, and we have to take in the heavenly food just as we do our bean soup—take it standing." On July 10, 1864, the prisoners received permission to organize the "Christian Association of the Prisoners of War." The association conducted religious services at least twice each day in every divisional street of the prison and at least once each day in Mess Hall No. 9. The association flourished until the prison closed.[69]

References to Christmas celebrations are often found in the letters and diaries that emanated from Point Lookout. Soldiers on both sides longed for loved ones and home, but Christmas seemed to emphasize this yearning more than any other time. On the Federal side, sporting activities, banquets, and music filled the diary pages of the three New Hampshire regiments.[70]

On the evening of Christmas Eve, within the prison stockade, prisoners found little to be thankful for and little solace in the day's observance. Private James E. Hall of the 31st Virginia wrote, "Christmas eve! Damn such a place for Christmas to come." Another prisoner recorded that he read books for entertainment while cold and hungry, surviving on "a peace of Bread and a cup of coffee for Breakfast and a small slice of Meat and a cup of Soop and five Crackers for Dinner and supper I had non."[71]

A soldier of the 20th Veteran Reserve Corps wrote, "we had a baked goose and whiskey plenty. We all got to feeling pretty good . . . We kept 12 days of Christmas." On the other side of the prison fence, however, few were "feeling pretty good." These men were prisoners of war and were not expected to have a jolly time regardless of the season. Nevertheless, a few isolated accounts from more fortunate prisoners recorded that they enjoyed eating apples, biscuits, tea,

68 Thomas, "Third Book of Diary," 77, 103.

69 Neese, *Three Years in the Confederate Horse Artillery*, 341.

70 Haynes, *History of the Second Regiment New Hampshire Volunteer Infantry*, 155. Risdon, "Letters of Charles," 4–5; Charles Warren Hutt, "The Diary of Charles Warren Hutt," *St. Mary's Monthly Bulletin of the St. Mary's County Historical Society*, May 1970, 87.

71 James E. Hall, *The Diary of a Confederate Soldier*, ed. Ruth Woods Dayton, Lynchburg, OH, (1961), 93; Bartlett Yancey Malone, *Whipt 'em Everytime*, ed. William Whatley Pierson Jr. and Bell Irvin Wiley (Wilmington, NC, 1987), 94.

mince pies, fried chicken, fried meat, "corn" coffee, and hardtack, among other prison "delicacies."[72]

Interestingly, the religious side of Christmas was seldom, if ever, mentioned in the correspondence of soldiers on either side. Nevertheless, it is likely that Christmas services were conducted by the local priests, pastors, and regimental chaplains who were present during this most sacred commemoration. Point Lookout was a place where words of faith, solace, encouragement, and hope were greatly needed, regardless of uniform.[73]

## Tent Cutters

There were notorious groups of prisoners referred to as "tent cutters." Spencer reported that "there were . . . many desperadoes, who would not hesitate to cut through a man's tent and rob, or even murder him." The deprivations of prison life gave rise to these gangs, who indiscriminately preyed upon fellow inmates—particularly the sick and helpless—taking the easiest route to survive.[74]

These bands of thieves conducted reconnaissance of the divisional streets, noting the vigilance of the inhabitants—or lack thereof—as well as the contents in and around their shelters. The attacker would then swoop down on an unsuspecting target, either by assaulting him directly or slitting a tent open from whichever direction was most convenient. They would then reach in or enter the tent to rob the occupants of anything they could seize, before making a quick escape. Tent cutters often operated individually during the day to avoid the scrutiny of guards, regrouping later. Resistance to these assaults usually resulted in life-threatening injuries or, in some cases, murder at the hands of these unscrupulous marauders.

Night raids after taps posed greater challenges to tent cutters as they attempted to evade the vigilance of guard patrols. Prisoner Finley P. Curtis of the 2nd North Carolina wrote in February 1865 that while lying in his cot one evening, he "was aroused by . . . the noise of cloth being stealthily severed . . . A hand was slowly entering the cut tent cloth, groping blindly for my haversack, intending to rob . . . Warned by something . . . the hand was withdrawn . . . and well for its owner, for I should have surely ended its unlawful career."[75]

72 Hall, *The Diary of a Confederate Soldier*, 124.

73 Malone, *Whipt 'em Everytime*, 115–116.

74 Spencer, "Point Lookout," 422–423.

75 Finley P. Curtis Jr, "The Black Shadow of the Sixties," in *Confederate Veteran*, ed. S. A. Cunningham, 9th ed. (Nashville, TN, 1920), 24:404.

The success of these shameless forays soon transformed the perpetrators into brazen gangs of muggers and thieves. As tent cutting escalated, prisoners began lodging complaints with the provost marshal. After receiving numerous reports of theft, injury, and murder, prison authorities acted to suppress the brigandage.

The guard became increasingly vigilant and soon began arresting the raiders. Eventually, a substantial group of them was tracked down and captured. Prisoner Sgt. Bartlett Malone of the 6th North Carolina noted in April 1864 that some of the U.S.C.T. guards patrolling the prison at night caught a group of tent cutters. Their punishment was "to wear a barrel shirt and march up and down the streets with large letters on them; the letter was this, Tent Cutters." Private Charles Warren Hutt of the 40th Virginia recorded that "most of the gang are Virginians," with a mixture of men from other Southern states.[76]

It was fortunate for the bandits that the guards apprehended them before the prisoners did. As reprehensible as their actions were, many of the guilty claimed they acted out of a need for survival. Desperation often compels men to act at the expense of others. Capture by prison authorities usually resulted in corporal punishment, whereas being caught by fellow prisoners subjected them to prisoner justice.

## Punishment

The *Lieber Code* did not specify or define what modes of punishment could be used to deter recalcitrant prisoners from violating prison regulations. While prisoners who violated the rules were to pay a penalty for their contraventions, they were not to suffer undue or unreasonable punishment.

The methods of punishment for infractions were generally left to the discretion of prison authorities. This included the interpretation of standing rules and regulations as well as the means of enforcing discipline. Modes of punishment were generally common and considered within the boundaries of army standards. Captured escapees were usually shackled with a ball and chain fastened to the ankle. Prisoners guilty of other infractions were typically confined to the guardhouse. Penalties could include being sentenced to bread and water, forced to wear "barrel jackets," being made to stand on the edge of barrels, being bucked and gagged, or subjected to the most dreaded penalty—being hung by the thumbs.[77]

Private John Ernul of the 67th North Carolina was arrested by a guard who claimed he had violated an area restriction within the prison. The guard declared to

76 Malone, *Whipt 'em Everytime*, 100; Beitzell, *Point Lookout Prison Camp for Confederates*, 71.

77 *OR* 3/3:156.

Two prisoners wearing a ball and chain as punishment for an escape attempt.

*Point Lookout State Park Collection*

Ernul, "You need some jewelry, something like a twelve-pound ball and chain," which was promptly attached to his ankle. Ernul soon encountered a fellow prisoner who told him that he knew of another inmate "who had a file and would file a ball and chain off for a chew of tobacco." Ernul located the enterprising prisoner, completed the exchange, and made his way through the gates to the beach with a haversack full of the former ball and chain. Ernul later wrote, "That ball and chain is now resting on the bottom of the Chesapeake Bay."[78]

Two Confederate officers attempted to escape while being treated at the army hospital on Point Lookout. They were unsuccessful and were soon apprehended by the guard. Their punishment was the wearing of a one-piece overgarment made of brown blanket material, adorned with a row of buttons down the back and black stripes around the arms. This uniform was complemented by a stocking cap of the same material with a tassel fastened to the crown. To complete the ensemble, the prisoners were also fitted with a ball and chain.[79]

Punishment was swift for those arrested after a raid on a cookhouse. "The next day ten of the sergeants who had been conspicuous in the riot were tied by their hands to the posts of the [stockade] fence and given several hours in which to meditate on their sins." Both prisoners and guards wrote of punishments such as carrying knapsacks filled with stones, hauling a log, and riding the wooden horse.[80]

Next to the wearing of a ball and chain, the suspension of a prisoner by his thumbs was considered the most painful and cruel punishment. It was often employed as a deterrent to prison offenses. Many prisoners later recalled both the method and its effects:

> [A] small cord of sufficient strength was looped over each thumb and made fast to the beam overhead, which was then wound up like a windlass until the victim was compelled to rest the weight of his body either on his toes or on his thumbs; when . . . toes fail, the strain is all on the thumbs, when the pain often became unbearable and victim loses consciousness, the Sergeant . . . would order him lowered, and when consciousness returned the prisoner was either sent to the pen, or to the guard house, to nurse as best he could his lacerated thumbs . . . This punishment was considered the most severe.[81]

78 J. B. Ernul, *Life of a Confederate Soldier in a Federal Prison* (Vanceboro, NC, 1908), 10–12.

79 Robert E. Park, "Diary of Captain Robert E. Park, of Twelfth Alabama Regiment," in *Southern Historical Society Papers*, comp. Southern Historical Society and Rev. J William Jones (Richmond, VA, 1876), 2:236.

80 Haynes, *A Soldier Boy's Letter*, 154; Livermore, *Dates and Events*, 324.

81 Blue, *Hanging Rock Rebel*, 269.

The refusal to obey the orders of prison guards often proved to be a painful mistake. Haynes noted that a few prisoners, when ordered to perform work for the prison, swore "they would not do any work for the United States. They changed their mind when they were strung up [by their thumbs] without any parley, and the joke of the thing was that a good many of the prisoners were tickled to death to see them disciplined."[82]

The flogging of prisoners at Point Lookout was not among the methods of prison punishment, as neither diaries nor letters of prisoners or guards contain any mention of inmates being flogged or whipped there. The U.S. Army had abolished this cruelest of punishments by August 1861. Even though flogging was illegal according to army regulations, there were recorded incidents of it being used at other prisons.[83]

According to the *Lieber Code*, prisoners of war were not considered criminals. When it came to punishment, prison authorities exercised measures they deemed necessary to maintain discipline and security within the prison.

## Prisoner Justice

Prisoners were likewise resourceful when it came to enforcing indemnification for offenses committed by fellow inmates. The punishment of prisoners by other prisoners constituted a distinct form of policing apart from that imposed by the prison authorities. For the most part, the provost marshal and the prison police force discouraged inmates from administering punishment to one another. Nevertheless, as prisoners are wont to do, they often relied on their own devices and wits to maintain a semblance of law and order. Still, some became part of factions that embraced the unwritten prison rule that all was fair in the struggle for survival, regardless of the victim.

Prison justice was a common occurrence. Prison authorities offered little resistance to such activity. Eyewitness accounts report that guards sometimes chose not to interfere so long as offending prisoners were not physically harmed.[84]

When justice was slow in coming from the prison authorities, prisoners resorted to their own means of retribution. When an offender or group of offenders was apprehended, mock court-martials were convened to hear the

82 Haynes, *A Soldier Boy's Letter*, 133.

83 John M. Copley, *A Sketch of the Battle of Franklin, Tennessee; With Reminiscences of Camp Douglas* (Austin, TX, 1893; Widener, AR: Southern Heritage Press, 2012), 82.

84 *OR* 3/3:156, Article 75.

complaint of the aggrieved. Punishment pronounced at the end of the "trial" was carried out immediately.

Cases such as the theft of another prisoner's possessions were considered serious offenses, but not of the same magnitude as taking another man's food or his life. Food was the primary target of most thieves. "Flanking" during the ration issue was regarded as equal to stealing a man's rations. This practice involved someone illegally taking another's place in line, which resulted in one or more prisoners losing their share or being cut short of a ration.

Judgments meted out to prisoners by prisoners could be severe. One chosen instrument of punishment for a convicted prisoner was the use of the loathsome garbage barrels located behind the prison cookhouses. During the summer months, these barrels could sit for hours, festering and becoming fetid. They were havens for rats, flies, maggots, and gnats, and their stench was offensive even to the strongest stomachs. After a prisoner was found guilty, he was "dipped head and shoulders in one of these garbage barrels—a terrible punishment." To their credit, the Federal guards tried to prevent this practice, though they did not always succeed.[85]

Worse still was the use of the uncleaned "night boxes" or barrels, which had been used for prisoner offal during the overnight hours. "The other fellow stole a man's rations . . . and was taken by the crowd and dipped head foremost into one of the barrels of filth sitting in the street—a very severe and loathsome punishment . . . [H]e deserved it for stealing rations from a fellow prisoner."[86]

Malicious crimes such as tent cutting continued despite the severity of punishment. The struggle for survival meant that some prisoners would persist in testing the prison justice system. Capital crimes such as murder were eventually addressed by prison authorities, often resulting in the transfer of offenders to other prisons. Men continued to steal from one another and risk arrest for "flanking," fearing death by starvation more than a dunk in a waste barrel or a filth-filled night box. One prisoner lamented in his diary, "Existing here is worse than not existing at all. It is hell and damnation mingled."[87]

The daily routine was basic and varied little throughout the life of the prison. Those responsible for the welfare of the prisoners were officers accustomed to maintaining soldiers in the field, not thousands of prisoners of war. They were

85 Inmate, "Point Lookout," 2.

86 Figg, *"Where Men Only Dare to Go,"* 235; Hubbs, *Voices from Company D*, 384–385.

87 Hall, *The Diary of a Confederate Soldier*, 118.

generally inexperienced in the administration of a prison, and the inmates suffered from their lack of training and experience.

## Suffering from Boredom and Uncertainty

Several factors contributed to the poor living conditions at Point Lookout. Policies of the War Department, the Commissary General of Prisoners, and prison administrators were revised several times during the two years that Point Lookout operated as a prison. These changes, combined with insufficient rations, poor sanitation, and a contaminated water supply, had a profound effect on conditions over which the prisoners had no control. The lack of ventilation and circulation of air within the stockade, as well as inadequate shelter, must also be considered. Prison officials were forced to alter the layout of the prison at least three times due to overcrowding. Divisional streets were added, eliminated, and at times reestablished in response to the constantly fluctuating population.

Prison life was both monotonous and harsh. Many soldiers attempted to make use of the long, empty hours of confinement by creating a meager livelihood out of what little Point Lookout had to offer. Boredom and desperation often led to escape attempts, while others turned to theft, gambling, or even murder in order to survive. The result was an environment of extreme deprivation and suffering. Unsure of whom they could trust, prisoners joined with fellow inmates from their home, company, or regiment to find a shared camaraderie. Yet even within familiar bonds, inmates remained cautious about whom to befriend or admit into their inner circles. It was known that prison authorities planted Union guards disguised in captured Confederate clothing to gain the confidence of prisoners and uncover tunnels, weapons, and plans for mass escape.

Prisoners relied on their wits and natural skills for survival, hoping to avoid sickness, stabbing, robbery, or starvation. The threat of being shot by a guard was a constant fear. Navigating these ever-present dangers required effort that did not always prove successful. Some prisoners went so far as to isolate themselves from the larger population, focusing solely on their own survival. These men answered roll calls, collected rations, and performed work details while deliberately avoiding association with others, regardless of the shared circumstances that had brought them to Point Lookout.

Unfortunately, some prisoners gave in to their plight and sat idly for hours, doing nothing to improve their existence. In contrast, others made the best of their time by keeping both body and mind active by volunteering for work details, attending classes at the prison school, or reading the books and periodicals available to them. Since hunger was a constant condition, many inmates spent their days seeking ways to supplement their meager rations by gambling, working with their hands, or selling food items they had managed to concoct.

Prison restrictions and regulations could be both debilitating and challenging to the inmates. Physically, prison life could either strengthen men in mind and body or break them down entirely. Adaptation came more easily to those already conditioned by the deprivations of wartime campaigns. As a result, men who resolved to endure the hardships of prison life often excelled under the hope of eventual release or exchange, and they were known to encourage and strengthen those weaker in body and spirit not to abandon the fight.

Some prisoners became lethargic and despondent, falling into despair and resigning themselves to the possibility that they would never leave Point Lookout alive. At least one case of suicide was recorded at Point Lookout in mid-1864. It is nearly certain that this most tragic and desperate of acts occurred more than once. Recent studies by contemporary historians suggest that mental illness and related disorders proliferated during the war. Suffering was not confined to the post-war years, when soldiers were diagnosed with a somatic condition labeled "soldier's heart," but was also present during wartime, especially among those who endured both the horrors of combat and the debilitating existence of imprisonment.[88]

A search of medical records in national collections, along with surviving diaries and letters, would most likely reveal additional cases of suicide at Point Lookout or other prison camps. Prisoner George Neese wrote that during his imprisonment at Point Lookout, when about 10,000 men were confined there, "in that vast crowd I have not seen one smile or heard a hearty laugh since I have been here. Everyone moves around in almost sullen silence, with a sad countenance, and the whole crew looks as if they had just returned from a big funeral."[89]

The highlight of each day, if it could be called that, occurred only twice: the ration issue. Once roll call was completed, the hungry inmates marched in columns to the mess halls in the hope of receiving a bounty from their captors. More often than not, however, they were disappointed by what prison authorities and the Federal government deemed an adequate meal.

88 Holland Thompson, "Life in the Prisons," in *The Photographic History of The Civil War*, ed. Holland Thompson, Francis Trevelyan Miller, and Robert S. Lanier (Springfield, MA, 1911), 7:124; Everson, Papers No. 28/710/22, 26; Dillon J. Carroll, *Invisible Wounds: Mental Illness and Civil War Soldiers* (Baton Rouge, LA, 2021), 63, 176.

89 Neese, *Three Years in the Confederate Horse Artillery*, 345–346.

# Chapter 6

# Rations and General Supply

Battlefield captures and the cessation of exchanges created problems for both governments. The constant fluctuation of the population at Point Lookout led to inconsistencies in the quality and quantity of rations issued to prisoners. Commissary records indicate that the prescribed ration was distributed to prison cookhouses based on roll calls submitted before each issue. Prisoners "flanking" from company to company to receive extra rations were a constant problem for those expecting their full allowance. The term "flanking" referred to outmaneuvering an opponent—or in this case, fellow prisoners or guards—to gain an advantage. Prisoners employed this tactic to obtain additional food, often at the expense of others.

Eyewitness accounts describe the items issued, as well as the quantity and quality received. Variations in these accounts are attributable to the different periods during which individuals were confined at Point Lookout. Nevertheless, prisoner accounts consistently dispute the accuracy of official ration reports.[1]

## Prison Rations

There were two categories of rations described in the U.S. Army regulations of 1861. Soldiers received either a "marching issue" or a "camp" (garrison) ration. The marching issue consisted of a reduced quantity for the convenience of soldiers on active campaign. The camp or garrison ration was issued in greater quantity and was prepared by cooks in established camps or garrisons. Congress ordered that prisoners of war be provided the more generous camp (garrison) ration. The

1 *OR* 6/2:645–646; Thompson, "Life in the Prisons," in *The Photographic*, 7:72–74.

schedule of rations was based on specifications issued by the War Department, prescribing the items to be served and their amounts.[2]

Prisoner rations were issued twice daily at Point Lookout, once in the morning and once in the early afternoon, with a soft bread portion distributed between the two periods. Prisoner accounts seldom mention a third ration. When a third ration was issued, it usually consisted of bulk items such as hardtack and coffee. Prisoners noted a third ration during the final weeks of the camp in June 1865, but only when the population had been greatly reduced.

During August 1863, prisoners received the prescribed soldier's garrison ration. This would not remain the case after the first few months of Point Lookout's operation. A careful comparison of the basic ration issued at Point Lookout indicates that prisoners were more likely to receive a ration resembling the marching issue rather than the intended garrison ration. Private Simon Seward of the 13th Virginia Cavalry stated, "We received the rations of a regular soldier . . . Just imagine a Confederate soldier eating fresh loaf bread, good coffee with sugar . . . and beef and pork in abundance." By the following September, prisoners at Point Lookout noticed that the quantity of their rations began to decrease.[3]

A Federal commissary sergeant at Point Lookout recorded that in August 1863 the prisoners received a "soldier's ration" which caused some prisoners to be "picky" as to its contents. It is certain, however, that being picky was not the norm in most cases. One Federal officer noted that the commissary warehouses at Point Lookout were fully stocked and further stated that the guards ate the same as the prisoners. "When rations of fresh beef could not be had in full supply, our guards received it but once a week; the prisoners of war twice a week."[4]

The condition and quantity of rations also appear in many accounts written by the guards. Reports indicate that the garrison ration was, on occasion, reduced for short periods. One Union soldier claimed that by mid-1864 the bread ration had been cut for reasons unknown, forcing soldiers to conserve what they received. As a result, they purchased a third ration with their own money or supplemented it with funds from their company. The same soldier questioned the army's rationale

2 U.S. Department of the Army, *Revised United States Army Regulations of 1861*, Art. 746, 107, Sec. 13, 526; J. Britt McCarley, "Feeding Billy Yank: Union Rations Between 1861 and 1865," U.S. Army Quartermaster Museum, Quartermaster Museum, accessed March 29, 2025, https://qmmuseum.army.mil/research/history-heritage/subsistence/Feeding-Billy-Yank-Union-Rations-Between-1861-and-1865.html.

3 Simon Seward, "An Escape from Point Lookout," in *War Talks of Confederate Veterans*, ed. George S. Bernard (Petersburg, VA, 1892), 77.

4 Gerald J. Sword, "Sword House/Cove," *Chronicles of St. Mary's*, March 1954, 1; Everson, Narrative and Personal Notes, 38.

for the cutback and stated in exasperation, "If the rations had to be cut down, why did they not take it off the salt beef or pork? Then we would not have missed it."[5]

Private Haynes of the 2nd New Hampshire testified in September 1863 that "good rations, of the same quality as were dealt out to us, were given to the prisoners." Another guard stated in May 1864 that, "Their [prisoners] rations, in quantity and quality, were about the same as ours." John W. Adams, chaplain of the 2nd New Hampshire, remarked that, "nothing was more common than to hear our soldiers grumble that the rebels fared better than they."[6]

The fluctuating prison population created constant difficulties for cooks, servers, and commissary staff. At times the ration was so meager that prisoners often tried to save one portion long enough to combine it with the next to form a larger meal. This practice depended on the severity of their hunger and their need to replenish nutrients.

Prison rations eventually reached what Hoffman considered adequate levels of sustenance for a largely inactive prisoner population. On November 9, 1863, Hoffman informed Marston that prisoners were being supplied with provisions by the commissary department and therefore prohibited the delivery of boxes and packages of food from outside sources. To worsen the situation, Secretary of War Stanton ordered all prison camp commanders to discontinue trade and purchases between prisoners and prison sutlers. This directive was issued in retaliation for similar restrictions imposed by Confederate authorities on Union prisoners.[7]

By February 1864 authorities determined that this restriction did not exist in Southern prisons, and General Butler rescinded Hoffman's order. Southern prisoners were once again permitted to receive packages from home. Butler also revoked the sutler order and allowed purchases and trade to continue. What gave him the authority to override Stanton's directive is uncertain, but it was carried out nonetheless.[8]

Prisoners were expected to survive on the rations issued to them, and items sold by sutlers were not intended to supplement those rations. However, the Federal government recognized that encouraging prisoners to purchase food from sutlers could reduce both the quantity of food required for rations and the

5 Clifford B. Davids, "The Assassination of Abraham Lincoln and the Search for John Wilkes Booth as Written by Provost Guard John H. Matthews from Inside Point Lookout Prison, Maryland," Confessions of an Oral Historian (blog), Nov. 5, 2012, accessed March 29, 2025, https://ashevilleoralhistoryproject.com/2012/11/05/lincoln/.

6 Haynes, *A History of the Second Regiment New Hampshire Volunteer Infantry*, 157; Allen, *Forty-Six Months with the Fourth Rhode Island Volunteers*, 261; Adams, *My Experiences as Army Chaplain*, 6.

7 *OR* 6/2:489, 625.

8 Ibid., 973–975.

associated cost. Hoffman was ordered to authorize a modified list of items for sale through prison sutlers. Authorities, however, seemed to overlook the fact that most prisoners lacked the means to purchase such items in the first place.

By the end of November 1863, the prison population had risen to over 9,000 men. The supply system strained to keep pace with the rapid increase. Rations allotted for 10,000 prisoners would be nearly spartan if numbers suddenly rose to 12,000 within a week. Nevertheless, the cost-saving effects of Hoffman's prison fund system became apparent. In December, Butler notified the secretary of war that "I find that there has been the sum of $65,000 in cash saved from feeding the prisoners [at Point Lookout], over and above the allowance." Butler found it convenient to use the prison fund surplus to cover transportation costs for transferring prisoners rather than to provide them with adequate rations.[9]

Dr. William F. Swalm's lengthy report on Point Lookout stated that "I do think they [prisoners] received half the amount of meat they are entitled to, but with the crackers, &c, given they cannot suffer at all from hunger." Marston, in his rebuttal to Swalm's report, maintained that the provisions issued were adequate for the prisoners in his charge and had been furnished in the prescribed quantities according to his orders from Hoffman and to army regulations.[10]

To support his position, Marston ordered a report from Sgt. John H. Wilkinson, the commissary sergeant responsible for issuing rations to each cookhouse in the prison. In his report dated December 1, 1863, Wilkinson stated that the prescribed quantities of meat, beans, soup, soft and hard bread, as well as vegetables and molasses, had been issued in accordance with regulations during October and November 1863. However, when comparing Wilkinson's figures to the ration issue mandated by army regulations, it becomes clear that the rations provided did not equal the prescribed amounts. No explanation was given for the discrepancy other than the possibility of a sudden increase in the prison population. This detail is not mentioned in Swalm's report.[11]

In December 1863, Stanton ordered Butler to conduct a personal investigation into allegations of prisoner mistreatment at Point Lookout. Later that month, Butler replied to Stanton reporting that he found the prisoners "as well fed as the soldiers in our army." He further stated, "I do not mean to say that their ration is as large as our regularly issued ration, because of their state of entire inactivity." During his investigation, Butler interviewed six Confederate mess sergeants who

9 Ibid., 763.

10 Ibid., 578.

11 Ibid., 644.

worked in the various cookhouses of the prison camp. They generally agreed that Wilkinson performed his duties faithfully, remained fair in his dealings, and fulfilled their requests for rations. Nevertheless, there were several inconsistencies in the ration issue, which at times resulted in substitutions of items.[12]

Despite Butler's investigation, further reductions in rations followed. On May 19, 1864, Hoffman requested that the secretary of war consider his latest cost-saving proposal to reduce prisoner rations. His rationale was based on the supposed inactivity of prisoners. He stated that the reduction would still provide enough food "without depriving them [prisoners] of the food necessary to keep them in health . . . " Hoffman further ordered that if any food item was substituted for something on the ration list, the item replaced must be eliminated or reduced so that the substitution could be purchased with the savings generated from the elimination.

No extra funding was permitted for the substitution of rations that might not be available to the commissary department. Any savings realized from reduced ration items or substitutions made at a lower cost were to be returned to the Subsistence Department. Hoffman ensured that a prison fund surplus was maintained. His proposed ration reduction plan was approved by his chain of superiors (excluding the president) and made effective on June 1, 1864.[13]

An additional recommendation was made by Gen. Joseph K. Barnes, acting surgeon general, who was included in the approval of the reduction. In his endorsement, Barnes stated that the reduction "could be carried out except for the ration for the sick and wounded, who would require that as proposed by Col. Hoffman or more than its equivalent in medicine and hospital items," and he emphasized that rations for the sick should not be reduced. The ration reduction ordered by the Office of the Commissary General of Prisoners applied both to Confederate prisoners and to Union soldiers confined in northern parole camps.[14]

Dr. James H. Thompson, the Federal surgeon in charge of the prison hospital, was permitted some latitude in determining which vegetables were needed to combat the diseases ravaging the prison population. Items issued to the sick often included additional vegetables, vegetable-based soups, and beef broth. In August, General Barnes included in his monthly report to Hoffman a recommendation

12 Ibid., 754–755, 763–768.

13 *OR* 7/2:183–184.

14 Ibid., 151.

that he review Thompson's request to further modify the ration. Barnes noted that Thompson's suggestions "deserve careful consideration."[15]

Prisoner accounts depict inconsistencies in the items issued within the prison and its hospital. The only apparent explanation is that Hoffman believed the cost of feeding inactive prisoners was excessive. Some Federal authorities argued that Confederate prisoners were being "coddled" and even preferred captivity because they were receiving better care than they would receive in the field. Meigs accused prison authorities of treating the inmates "as southern gentlemen" rather than as prisoners of war.[16]

Several ration items appeared more frequently than others. Pork, beef, coffee (coffee was temporarily eliminated by Federal authorities in retaliation for the alleged elimination of coffee to Union prisoners), hardtack, soft bread, and bean soup seem to have been the constants in many ration issues. Other foods were substituted for prescribed rations depending on shortages and availability. Prisoners reported that mule and horse meat, white sugar, cornmeal, flour, mackerel, salted codfish, molasses, and mutton were served only sporadically. In early 1865, prisoner George Neese of Chew's Battery wrote that he had once been issued the "upper part of a sheep's head," which included both the eyes and wool. He recorded, "I shaved the wool and ate the eyes, lids and all; the eyes were certainly delicious."[17]

Prisoners suffered from scurvy from the time the prison opened until its closing. Fresh vegetables were necessary supplements to prevent the outbreak of this dreaded illness. A variety of vegetables, including vinegar, were issued whenever they could be acquired or made available, but the supply was never sufficient to curb the disease. Often, vegetables were provided in soups consisting of, as one prisoner wrote, "a combination of mixed vegetables such as turnips, cabbage, [and] carrots."[18]

A type of soup concocted by the army, considered at times appealing to some but repulsive in taste and odor to others, was served to the prisoners. The cooks prepared a pot of hot water containing the meat ration to which they added

> other green garden vegetables, cooked and pressed into large squares [commonly known as desiccated vegetables] . . . [T]he soup was made of potatoes, beans

15 Beitzell, *Point Lookout Prison Camp for Confederates*, 60; *OR* 7/2:184–185.

16 James I. Robertson, *Tenting Tonight: The Soldier's Life* (Alexandria, VA, 1984), 114–115.

17 Neese, *Three Years in the Confederate Horse Artillery*, 349.

18 *OR* 6/2:473–489.

> and onions, the potatoes were not peeled, and the onions were not sorted and frequently they were spoiled, when the blocks of pressed vegetables were thrown in after the meat being cooked it was good.[19]

The boiling broth caused the squares of compressed vegetables to break apart and mix into the liquid, creating a variation of soup.

The increased issue of vegetables was an obvious attempt by prison authorities to stem scurvy. As late as March 25, 1865, Hoffman encouraged Barnes to dedicate eight acres of open ground for prisoners to plant and cultivate vegetables to counter the disease. There is no record of whether this was implemented, but as the war was winding down, it most likely was not. Despite these efforts by prison authorities, scurvy continued to bedevil prison operations.[20]

Prisoner accounts mention that fish, such as mackerel and codfish, were usually issued either raw or salted. The Quartermaster Department purchased fish and vegetables from local watermen and farmers, which were incorporated into the ration issue. Soldiers of the guard force were also permitted to purchase these items to supplement their rations. In most cases, prisoners lacked the means to cook the raw fish. Even if they had wood to spare, open fires were prohibited within the prison by mid-1864 (though this order was later rescinded that year), forcing prisoners to consume the fish raw or to trade or sell other raw rations to fellow prisoners.[21]

Starving prisoners consumed anything they could find, regardless of its source or how it was acquired. Eye-witness accounts describe prisoners eating potato peelings from slop barrels kept by the cookhouses. One prisoner attempted to boil grass growing between the mess halls, mistakenly thinking it was rye or oats, only to find that "the longer it boiled the tougher it became and the less fit it was to eat." Another prisoner wrote that he "received permission to go to a large [syrup] kettle near the road." Finding it "filled with odds and ends of rusty bacon boiled to a jelly . . . I fished out and filled my haversack with the best of this putrid mess and carried it into the prison." Men scavenged ditches for refuse from any source to satisfy their hunger. Private John Stevens of the 5th Texas recalled "cases

19 John R. King, *My Experience in the Confederate Army and in Northern Prisons* (Clarksburg, WV, 1917), 29.

20 Hunter, "Warden for the Union," 161.

21 John W. Stevens, *Reminiscences of the Civil War: A Soldier in Hood's Texas Brigade, Army of Northern Virginia* (1902; repr. Middletown, DE, 2017), 144.

of dog eating . . . I can't tell you anything about it except that I am satisfied that it was done."[22]

In July 1864, prisoner rations were reduced for a third time when Gen. Henry W. Wessels temporarily replaced Hoffman (Hoffman was transferred in November 1864; it was rumored that he was suffering from health problems). Wessels issued General Order No. 1, dated January 13, 1865, which stated that rations issued to prisoners who were sick and in prison hospitals were to be increased for certain items. Regardless, rations for the general prison population were to be reduced, effective February 13, 1865. This general order also modified what was issued to prisoners as compensation for employment in the construction of fortifications and government structures. This inclusion created an incentive for prisoners to vie for the details required for fortification construction. Hoffman returned east to replace Wessels in February 1865.[23]

Despite the overwhelming number of prisoner statements testifying to hunger and insufficient rations, some accounts present a different perspective, which can be confusing. Certain prisoners stated that they ate as well at Point Lookout as they did in their armies. This suggests that their rations might have been equally spartan in the field. Some claimed that at Point Lookout they occasionally received double rations and at other times refused one ration item to accept another. One prisoner stated that he never knew of anyone starving to death, though this statement likely reflects the particular period and circumstances of his confinement. Nevertheless, evidence indicates that many prisoners suffered from the effects of malnutrition, leaving them vulnerable to nutritional diseases that ran rampant throughout the prison.[24]

## Issuing Rations

During the first three months of prison operations, rations were issued after the ritual of roll call. Once roll was verified, the men were permitted to draw their rations from the issuing facilities within the camp. Because the stockade and mess halls were still under construction, the men cooked at their shelters with the necessary vessels and utensils provided to them. Prisoners who cooked for themselves wasted valuable firewood, and the practice was soon curtailed.

22 Holliday, "Vain Efforts," in *Confederate Veteran*, 28:383; Ernul, *Life of a Confederate*, 9; A. J. Cone, "Prison Commander at Point Lookout, M.D.," in *Confederate Veteran*, ed. S. A. Cunningham, 11th ed. (Nashville, TN, 1912), 20:525; Stevens, *Reminiscences of the Civil*, 146.

23 *OR* 7/2:1117; *OR* 8/2:62–63.

24 Inmate, "Point Lookout," 2; Sutton, *Civil War Stories*, 54.

Cooking was transferred to the cookhouses as they became available. As each cookhouse opened, every company within the divisions sent "details of 10 or 12 men under a sergeant . . . [that were] assigned to each house whose duty it was to cook the rations and issue them." Rations were then distributed to their respective companies.[25]

The duties of the mess hall sergeants were to ensure that rations were received as ordered from the commissary and to oversee that they were cooked and served as directed. Variations could occur because the cooks and their practices were not standardized. Army regulations required Federal authorities to be present when rations were weighed and measured before being issued. A few surviving prisoner eyewitness accounts state that the officer of the day at the prison inspected the rations prior to issue.

By late 1863, the procedure for preparing and issuing rations had been modified from earlier months because of the increasing numbers of prisoners arriving weekly. As more cookhouses and mess halls prepared food for more prisoners, greater distribution organization became necessary. Prisoners were formed into lines alphabetically within their divisions before receiving their rations by company. Men whose last names began with the letter "A" often received a pint of watery broth, while those at the end of the line obtained a cup of soup richer with beans or vegetables from the bottom of the pot.

The men were formed into ranks in their streets and marched four abreast by division to their assigned mess halls, escorted by their first sergeant and his Federal counterpart. Each mess hall could receive approximately 500 men, accommodating three to four shifts and thus serving 1,500 to 2,000 men per ration. Each company sergeant and Federal NCO stood at the mess hall door to prevent "flankers" from slipping in, counting each man as he entered. Prisoners then lined the tables, standing over a tin plate and cup that had been preset with a ration.

The serving tables were approximately "fifteen inches wide, in the shape of a long hollow rectangle with a few cooks scattered in the hollow" to distribute food and to ensure no one touched a ration until instructed. On signal, each prisoner took his ration and marched out of the building, led by his company sergeant. As they exited, "lines were broken, and everyone went out and did as he pleased." The second and final ration was generally issued at 2:00 or 3:00 p.m., when the same routine was repeated after the last roll call of the day.

After breakfast, bread wagons arrived at the front gate of the stockade filled with fresh bread baked in the massive bakery near the army hospital. Prisoner

25 Letter by Wells, 11.

Prison artist depiction of prisoners at a Mess Hall. *Point Lookout State Park Collection*

Neese remembered that at "[a]bout nine o'clock in the forenoon a detail from each company goes to the cook house and draws the bread for the company . . . after the bread arrives at the company every two men draw one loaf and the man that divides the loaf always gives his comrade first choice of pieces." The bread ration was baked in sheets or layers using large molds that produced multiple loaves for expediency. After cooling, the sheets of bread were stacked in the wagons and delivered. The bread was subdivided into loaves upon issue. Although part of the ration, baker's bread was never a constant daily issue, its availability sporadic at best.[26]

## "It was root, pig, or die": Flanking to Survive

Reduced rations often forced prisoners to do whatever was necessary to survive. Private George W. Jones of the 24th Virginia Cavalry wrote that, "Every

26 Neese, *Three Years in the Confederate Horse Artillery*, 337–338.

conceivable trick was resorted to in order to make buckle and tongue meet." Jones observed that the "various occupations, the scheming, the tricking, the hustling for grub, the flanking . . . and trading for rations, were the issues, which required no oratory, no preaching, but chicanery and trickery." Prisoners referred to this as having "a possum eyed time," and many were deprived of their rations by such tactics.[27]

Individual survival was paramount and "selfishness rules the hour and sways the whole camp." Prison officials intervened when flanking became common and disruptive to other prisoners. In December 1863, all prisoners were moved by division to the open area between the two stockade fences. They passed through the gate into the prison as roll calls were taken and verified. Rations were then issued to those who answered by company, while flankers were removed and dealt with.[28]

Private George Peyton of the 13th Virginia recorded, "I reckon they found out that the sergeants were drawing more rations than they had men . . . If a man goes to the hospital, he [his company sergeant] leaves his name on the roll book for several days after he leaves." One prisoner apprehended by the guard stated, "all is fair in love and war!" but punishments were still administered. If prisoners were caught stealing a fellow prisoner's ration, the penalty could be nearly fatal. Few offenses committed against a fellow prisoner were considered worse than stealing another man's ration.[29]

## Prison Cooks and Food Preparation

Select prisoners cooked and served rations at Camp Hoffman. Many vied for these coveted positions, sought by thousands who wished to perform such services. Fellow prisoners dubbed those fortunate enough to be chosen "cookhouse rats." Prison cooks were generally untrained and inexperienced in meal preparation. It is unlikely that they possessed the skills necessary to prepare the vast quantities of food required to feed thousands. They were supervised by the Federal officer of the day as well as members of the guard force who most likely lacked the same experience.[30]

Preparing and serving rations for thousands must have been a daunting task for inexperienced prison cooks. This is not to suggest that some were not conscientious

27 Jones, *In Prison at Point Lookout*, 2.

28 Sutton, *Civil War Stories*, 57.

29 Peyton, *A Civil Record for 1864–1865*, 101; Sutton, *Civil War Stories*, 57.

30 Clay W. Holmes, *The Elmira Prison Camp: A History of the Military Prison at Elmira, N.Y., July 6, 1864, to July 10, 1865* (1889–1890; repr., Wilmington, NC, 1993), 6:360.

and dedicated to their duties, but they were likely overwhelmed by the vast numbers to be served and restricted by limited cooking facilities and equipment.

Food preparation was similar to the basic procedures used by the army in the field. The meat ration was first boiled in large forty-gallon cauldrons. After the meat was removed from the pots, beans and vegetables were dumped into the broth to produce soup. At the very least, the water that was normally unsafe to drink was boiled during the cooking process, eliminating some bacteria before the prisoners consumed the final product.[31]

With few exceptions, prisoners described the issued bean soup as so thin that they could see the shiny bottom of their cup through it. Because the pots were seldom stirred during distribution, the heavier contents sank to the bottom, producing what many prisoners called "slop water." Sergeant William Izlar of the Edisto Rifles, South Carolina, claimed that he secured a friend a position as a cook in one of the cookhouses, and "he kept me well supplied with the thick part of the bean soup" that had settled at the bottom of the large kettles.[32]

Providing thousands of rations in large quantities expeditiously restricted the time available to properly clean the equipment used to handle and serve food for each shift. This also meant that the mess halls were left unclean after thousands of hungry men passed through them. The lack of sanitation undoubtedly contributed to the illnesses experienced by prisoners. The facilities were also havens for countless disease-carrying rats.

Being a prison cook carried clear advantages. Prisoners recognized that "a cook has good warm quarters to sleep and stay in and they take good care of number one and help themselves to all the rations that they can devour." Sergeant Joseph H. Wilkinson, commissary sergeant in the prison, observed that those who complained about the cooks were usually seeking to become cooks themselves. He stated, "The cold weather coming on renders this position desirable." During the colder months, cooks were permitted to sleep in the rafters of the cookhouses to stay warm. The fires required for the cauldrons substantially heated the buildings, making them far more comfortable in winter than the much colder prison shelters. Summer months, however, posed a different challenge, but even then, being assigned to a cookhouse offered advantages over residing in a leaky tent.[33]

31 Stevens, *Reminiscences of the Civil War*, 144.

32 Curtis, "The Black," in *Confederate Veteran*, 24:404; William Valmore Izlar, *A Sketch of the War Record of the Edisto Rifles, 1861–1985* (Columbia, SC, 1914), 124.

33 Neese, *Three Years in the Confederate Horse Artillery*, 339–340; *OR* 6/2:645.

## Rats

Medical inspectors were thorough in their reporting of discrepancies at Point Lookout. Reports frequently noted the lack of sanitation, limited water supply, and the presence of lice. However, none mentioned the hordes of rats that infested the prison or expressed concern about their possible effect on the population. The presence of thousands of free-ranging rats became more than a nuisance, as described by the soldiers. According to testimonies by both guards and prisoners, rats existed in enormous numbers throughout Point Lookout, thriving from the opening to the closing of the prison camp.

How the rats arrived is speculative. They likely came on the ships that transported visitors or in the cargo holds of vessels delivering supplies. Regardless of their origin, rats were an affliction that became an extreme problem for the occupants of Point Lookout.

Driven by hunger, prisoners took advantage of the vast population of rats. Many, desperate to stave off hunger, resorted to eating the rodents, a practice neither common nor desirable among the inmates. Nevertheless, it occurred often enough that Pvt. John Ernul of the 67th North Carolina State Troops recalled he had been in prison only a few days when he began to suffer from hunger: "I saw some of the boys eating broiled rats, they smelled very appetizing, but I could not get any to eat. I decided that I must either find something to eat or starve."[34]

The overlooked consequence of the rat infestation—and the consumption of flea-infested rats—was the spread of disease. Rats transmit a variety of illnesses that endangered the population of Point Lookout. Contamination of food supplies and water by rat feces, urine, or saliva, as well as scratches or bites, could spread diseases such as salmonella (food poisoning), fevers, and typhus, while also transmitting other ailments that could be misdiagnosed. Diseases carried by rats often produced symptoms resembling those of illnesses already familiar to physicians at Point Lookout. Leptospirosis, for example, can exhibit symptoms similar to malaria and other conditions. Infected individuals suffered headaches, meningitis, muscle pain, fevers, and severe pulmonary bleeding. The disease also causes rash, jaundice, and ultimately kidney failure.[35]

The mobility of rats produced widespread infestation throughout Point Lookout. Locations where rations were stored—barrels, cloth or burlap sacks, or wooden crates—provided sustenance for rats. Prisoner John W. Stevens of the 5th

34 Ernul, *Life of a Confederate*, 8.

35 Alan J. A. McBride, et al., "Leptospirosis," *Current Opinion in Infectious Diseases* 18, no. 5 (2005): accessed March 31, 2025, https://doi.org/10.1097/01.qco.0000178824.05715.2c.

Prisoner selling rats to fellow inmates. *Point Lookout State Park Collection*

Texas observed that the cookhouses within the prison were "hot beds for rats." He saw that "all along at the side of these houses the earth was perforated with rat holes where they burrowed under the [mess] house."[36]

Rat hunting among the prisoners became a kind of sport that provided not only entertainment and occupation but also an additional source of food:

36 Stevens, *Reminiscences of the Civil War,* 145.

Private John W. Stevens, 5th Texas,
Hood's Texas Brigade
*Texas Heritage Museum, Hill College*

> The rats would come out by the hundreds . . . and the boys would get sticks and take their stand at these rat holes . . . then one man would walk down among them, and they would "rats" to their holes then the killing act would be played—a dozen, twenty, maybe fifty would be killed. The men then gathered and stored their quarry in a barrel. Not long after this initial killing spree . . . [the rats] would be . . . as thick as ever again . . . The killing and gathering process would continue until the hunters filled their barrel. They would let the barrel remain until morning and then the skinning and frying act would begin. The next day, the men would manage to secret some grease from one of the cookhouses. Using a canteen half [a canteen split in half at its outer seams] as a frying pan, when . . . five to eight men . . . are skinning some are frying, some are eating . . . this "Ratting" act is played until the whole "catch" is consumed . . . I have seen it often at Point Lookout . . . there were not many who would eat rats, but there were enough of them to make it very unhealthy for the rodents.[37]

Rats were sold along Market Street by prisoner entrepreneurs. Sergeant James Wells of the 2nd South Carolina claimed, "We also had eating houses with very little to eat in there; but you could get a good cup of coffee and a piece of fried rat for 25 cents . . . rats were eaten with much gusto."[38]

The Union garrison was not exempt from the swarms of rats. Private Haynes of the 2nd New Hampshire exclaimed, "Rats! Rats! Rats! We are overrun with them. They swarm everywhere and are big enough to waylay a cat. They run over us as we lie in our bunks, and the other night one dropped plum in my face from

37 Ibid., 145–146.

38 Letter by Wells, 32.

the upper bunk." The following January, Haynes recorded that after the former slaves were relocated to government farms in the county, their camp was ordered demolished. He noted that thousands of rats scattered as his work party carried out the demolition:

> The ground where the [contraband] camp stood is a labyrinth of rat holes. Rat hunts are a standard amusement and bushels of them have been unearthed and killed. . . . In the regimental camps, they are thicker than flies in summer time, and an awful pest, running over everything and everybody at night. And stealing everything eatable they can get their teeth onto.[39]

Lieutenant Everson wrote that "it has been charged that in their [prisoners] hunger they ate rats of which by the way there were about enough at Point Lookout to ration the entire Chinese Army." He recorded that the commissary building of his regiment was so infested with rats that they undermined the floor. In a desperate attempt to curb the problem, Lieutenant Stewart, who oversaw the commissary of the 20th V.R.C., gathered all the dogs in camp he could find for "a great rat hunt." Stewart had the floor of the shed suddenly raised, scattering swarms of rats that immediately fled toward the waters of the bay. "Seeing the rats take to the water [his dog] lay down on the beach, waited till they came ashore . . . then dispatched them instanter. In this manner, he killed the hundred and forty-two that were counted."[40]

Confederate prisoner Pvt. Barry Benson of the 2nd Battalion, South Carolina Sharpshooters, recorded that a fellow prisoner named Williams and his pet terrier "made unceasing war upon rats . . . [T]he rats were fed to the dog, the skins sold to make gloves." Given the thousands of rats that populated the prison environs, Benson later wrote that during his imprisonment at Elmira, New York, "our drinking water came from wells, into which the rats used to fall and drown. The water becoming so unbearable that somebody would have to go down and clean them out; it seemed to me that we were always cleaning out the wells." With the overwhelming rat population at Point Lookout, it is almost certain that the same situation occurred there as well.[41]

Prisoner George Neese of Chew's Battery wrote about a seller of rats who promoted his trade throughout the prison: "There is a rat vendor going along the

39 Haynes, *A Soldier Boy's Letters*, 151, 157.

40 Everson, Narrative and Personal Notes, 38, 52.

41 Barry Benson, *Berry Benson's Civil War Book: Memoirs of a Confederate Scout and Sharpshooter*, ed. Susan Williams Benson (Athens, GA, 1992), 91.

street carrying three large rats by the tail . . . I hear him cry: 'here are your rats, fresh and fat! I just caught them at the commissary department, and I warrant them to be in fine order.'" Private Malachi Bowden of the 2nd Georgia recalled that the Black guards were heard to shout at lights out, "Rats to your holes, or I will shoot you," comparing the prisoners to the thousands of rats within the stockade.[42]

## Firewood

By September 1863, firewood sources at Point Lookout rapidly neared depletion. The sudden influx of prisoners challenged what resources were available from the barren peninsula. Tons of seasoned firewood were required to cook food and provide warmth for the growing population during the cooler months. As supplies diminished, the commanding officer at Point Lookout authorized expeditions to retrieve firewood from neighboring Virginia.[43]

A consistent supply of firewood became a problem. Private Robert Craddock of the 1st Virginia described the details of five prisoners from each company assigned to retrieve firewood from designated areas miles beyond the garrison. Post orders prohibited prisoner work details from entering new ground for wood, forcing them instead to collect stumps and roots from areas already worked by earlier details.[44]

The permitted boundaries inside which to secure firewood were soon extended beyond Point Lookout Creek. Marston ordered that no work details were permitted to advance beyond the picket line, seven miles from the northern border of Point Lookout's fortifications, for any reason. Timber was not to be cut or removed from local civilian farms without the permission of the commanding officer. This order restricted accessible areas. Eventually, a contract was negotiated for the woodlot of local farmer James Richardson of nearby Ridge, authorizing the cutting of trees for firewood. Because no conveyances were used to haul it back, prisoners assigned to this detail carried the gathered wood themselves, often losing along the way much of what they had managed to bring.[45]

During the colder months, prisoners often suffered without wood to burn for warmth. To help alleviate the firewood shortage, they were permitted to bring in sticks and chips of coal collected while on work details. These were either used

42 Neese, *Three Years in the Confederate Horse Artillery*, 145; Beitzell, *Point Lookout Prison Camp for Confederates*, 98.

43 "Reunited at Gettysburg," in *Confederate Veteran*, 30:445–446; Haynes, *A Soldier Boy's Letters*, 168.

44 "Prison Life," 1–2.

45 *Book No. 251*, General and Specials Orders Aug. 1863–Aug. 1865.

for themselves or sold to other prisoners. Though meager, many prisoners relied on this source when firewood details yielded little. With the onset of winter in 1863, assistant quartermaster Capt. Nelson Plato solicited bids for "8,000 cords of Wood . . . four feet long and split to the usual sizes . . . to be delivered on the wharf at Point Lookout." The wood was to be delivered within a specified period.[46]

As the winter of 1863–1864 gave way to spring and summer, the use of firewood shifted from heating to primarily cooking. Eventually, prison authorities permitted firewood details to venture further north into St. Mary's County. Under heavy guard, they advanced beyond the picket line to secure additional supplies. This meant an arduous trek of eight miles or more back to the prison, with prisoners carrying only armloads of wood. To encourage participation, authorities offered extra rations as an incentive for this detail.[47]

By June 1864, camp orders prohibited open fires in the prison streets. One prisoner speculated that this was to prevent befouling the prison or keep the vision of guards on the catwalks free of veiling smoke. More likely, the order represented an attempt by authorities to conserve firewood. Regardless of the reason, it was short-lived, as wood was sparingly issued during the winter months and fires were again permitted for prisoner use.[48]

Prisoner accounts state that on a few occasions a cord of wood was issued to each division by the quartermaster's department. This was most likely the result of Captain Plato's firewood contracts. During the final months of prison operations, firewood was delivered to Point Lookout from locations further north. Prisoners assigned to the unloading details were permitted to carry armloads of wood from the wharf back to the prison.

In November 1864, Private Peyton of the 13th Virginia declared, "They now give us a cord of wood a day for each division, but as we have not a stove, we cannot have a fire," which reflected the situation of many prisoners throughout the camp. Although a cord of wood represented a substantial amount of firewood, a division of 1,000 to 2,000 men could consume it within only a few days, particularly during the winter months. A short time later, Peyton noted, "Our division has

46 Nelson Plato, "Proposals for Wood," *Daily National Republican* [Washington D.C.], Sept. 4, 1863, evening edition, Proposals, 1, accessed March 31, 2025, https://www.loc.gov/resource/sn86053570/1863-09-04/ed-1/?sp=1&r=0.106,0.865,0.343,0.209,0.

47 William B. Styple, ed., *Writing and Fighting from the Army of Northern Virginia* (Kearny, NJ, 2003), 273.

48 Keiley, *In Vinculis*, 96.

only five companies [500 men] so we get twice as much per company as the others which have ten companies."[49]

The distribution of firewood revealed the clear pecking order in the camp. Peyton recorded that by December 1864, "the Yankees did not give us any wood today. The supply is small, and the Yankees have the first grab at it." Given the circumstances, this outcome was hardly surprising.[50]

## Water

The availability of firewood may have been sporadic, but the water situation remained abysmal throughout the prison's existence. No matter what measures prisoners, guards, or authorities attempted to remedy the problem, water remained scarce, barely tolerable, and at times fatal. Only in the final months of the prison did Federal authorities establish a supply of fresh water for the relief of those residing at Point Lookout—or so they believed.

From the beginning, officials considered the water at Point Lookout safe to drink, since resort residents had consumed it prior to the war. As early as July 1862, attendants at the hospital reported that wells were going dry, months before the facility reached capacity. It should have been evident to authorities a year later that if the wells were failing in 1862, they would face the same problem once thousands of prisoners and guards arrived.[51]

The problem was not the scarcity of water, since it could be obtained by digging almost anywhere at Point Lookout. As soon as the first prisoner tents were erected in August 1863, wells were dug for both the prison and guard camp areas. As the complex expanded, Capt. Nelson Plato directed prisoner details to dig as many as 16 wells throughout the Point. All were hand-dug, with depths ranging between 11 and 15 feet. These shallow wells left the supply close to the surface, causing the water to become brackish and unfit for human consumption.

Prisoners described the water as "deleterious, rendered so by percolating through drifts of impure vegetable matter in the alluvial sand." It was a mixture of groundwater tainted by seepage from the bay and river. Because the drinking water was unfiltered, sand and bits of shell often passed directly to the users. In contrast, according to Point Lookout State Park authorities, the present-day

49 Peyton, *A Civil War Record for 1864–1865*, 103.

50 Ibid., 108.

51 Gibbons, *Life of Abby Hopper Gibbons*, 1:355–356.

wells that provide filtered, potable water to park visitors extend more than 700 feet in depth.[52]

Prisoners stated that they suffered more from the lack of good drinking water than from the want of food. Each day long lines of thirsty men stood at the pumps with cups, pans, and bowls in hand for a drink of unfiltered groundwater. This often led to fights when others tried to reach the wells before they were exhausted. Private Luther Hopkins of the 6th Virginia Cavalry described the scrums around the wells. "During the four months that I was there," he remembered, "the [water] pumps were always surrounded by a thirsty crowd of from 40 to 50 prisoners, each with his tin cup, trying to wedge his way in, that he might quench his thirst." Prisoners sometimes satisfied their thirst by attempting "to catch the drip of rain water from tents or sit out with cups, pans, cans, buckets and any vessel that could hold water" during storms.[53]

Water pumps were placed near each cookhouse as well as along the main thoroughfare at the heads of the divisional streets. Another stood just inside the officers' stockade. The varying qualities of water from pump to pump tasted of sulfur, isinglass, and copperas, "all a mixture and all bad." Contaminated water became a major contributor to the ailments of thousands of Point Lookout's occupants. Widespread dysentery and diarrhea resulted from the bacteria that thrived in the drinking supply.[54]

Clothes washed in this water turned black and yellow and it was also blamed for discoloring teeth. Prisoners described it as having a "sweet" taste, a reference to its impregnation with "copperas," a mineral with a metallic flavor. The contaminated water emitted a foul odor and displayed a range of colors, from a copper tint to darker shades, often leaving a thin surface film on which "someone could almost write their name." It was also known to leave a coating on tinware, staining it unless boiled or thoroughly cleaned, and when left overnight, a green scum formed on the surface.[55]

52 Neese, *Three Years in the Confederate Horse Artillery*, 340; Eric Barnes, interview by the author, Point Lookout, MD, June 16, 2019.

53 Freeman W. Jones, "Addendum to an Escape from Point Lookout," in *War Talks of Confederate Veterans*, comp. George S. Bernard (Petersburg, VA, 1892), 85; Luther Hopkins, *From Bull Run to Appomattox*, Florence, MA. (2012), 95; Flinn, "A Southern Soldier's Experience in a Northern Prison," 16.

54 Thomas, "Third Book," 73.

55 Letter by Wells, 13; Jones, "Addendum to an Escape," 85; King, *My Experience in the Confederate Army and in Northern Prisons*, 13; N. F. Harman, "Forbes Lost His Rations," 1907, in *Confederate Veteran*, ed. S. A. Cunningham, 9th ed. (Nashville, TN, 1907), 15:400.

Consuming contaminated water caused widespread and uncontrollable digestive disease throughout the prison population. One prisoner noted that the water gave him consistent "digestive discomforts." Another prisoner recalled that "the second day after I arrived here the water made me sick with a violent diarrhea." Without exception, the population of Point Lookout suffered.[56]

Despite the efforts of prison authorities, wells remained the most convenient solution to the problem. In December 1864, Barnes informed Hoffman that three additional wells had been dug, followed by another 12, which were expected to provide a projected 500 gallons of water per day. Even with these additions, production was still insufficient to supply the facility's needs.

Hoffman did take additional measures, for example ordering the quartermaster's department to arrange for and provide 20,000 gallons of fresh water from springs in the Washington, D.C., and Baltimore areas. As a result, Barnes reported that a water supply began arriving regularly by boat and barge. The casks and barrels were shipped by vessel and then conveyed to the camps, prison, and hospitals. Barnes was informed that "the steamer Ide will bring this week . . . 20,000 gallons. [The] Commodore Foote is expected daily, and . . . will bring as much more."[57]

By April 1865, as the war was nearing its end, one prisoner noted, "the crowding, quarreling, squirming and fighting around the pumps is now broken up and each company is furnished a barrel which is filled up early in the morning and set out for the use of the company." By this time, Federal authorities had requisitioned water-producing condensers. Their arrival, however, came too late to offer an effective solution.[58]

## Prisoner Clothing

Most prisoners arrived in badly worn uniforms, usually either barefoot or wearing worn-out shoes. This did not deter the guards from confiscating extra blankets and clothing from the new arrivals, despite its prohibition by army regulations. According to Article 72 of the *Lieber Code* (General Order No. 100), "[prisoners'] extra clothing, are regarded by the American Army as the private property of the prisoner . . . and the appropriation of such . . . is considered

56 Keiley, *In Vinculis*, 113; Neese, *Three Years in the Confederate Horse Artillery*, 40.

57 *OR* 7/2:985.

58 Hubbs, *Voices from Company D*, 373.

dishonorable and is prohibited." Regardless of the code, such seizures by the guards continued without fear of repercussion from their authorities.[59]

The condition of enemy uniforms, regardless of how badly worn, cannot be attributed to neglect within the Federal prison system. In his November 1863 report, Swalm stated that the appearance of the prisoners

> was ragged and dirty[, most] very thinly clad . . . one the fortunate possessor of an overcoat, either a citizen's or the light blue ones used by our infantry . . . Others . . . are well supplied as regards underclothing, especially those are from Baltimore . . . Some are without shirts, or what were once shirts hanging in shreds . . . the entire back or front will be gone . . . Their clothing is of all kinds and hues . . . the light and dark blue of our infantry all in a dilapidated condition.[60]

Dr. Augustus Clark reported in his December inspection that prisoners were wearing condemned U.S. Army clothing, adding that their clothing was "sufficient except [for] overcoats and underclothing." The two reports clearly reflect the differences of opinion between civilian and military inspectors regarding the condition of prisoner clothing.[61]

Correspondent Edward Spencer described the prisoners as including both "men well-clad, and men in rags," noting that the men from Maryland (as did Swalm) "were as scrupulously neat, sweet, and clean in their persons . . . as if they had just emerged from a bandbox." At the same time, he depicted many prisoners as dirty, ragged, and worn. He detailed the condition of one Tarheel, writing "war has not used him kindly . . . shoes are soleless; his carroty hair steals out through the broken places in his straw hat . . . clothes are worn through, stained, draggled, besmeared, and his grimy person is the very incarnation of dirt."[62]

Hoffman instructed the prison commander at Camp Morton, in Indianapolis, that "so long as a prisoner has clothing upon him, however much torn, you must issue nothing to him." According to the *Lieber Code*, the government was obligated under Articles 76 and 79 to both feed and care for the medical needs of sick or wounded prisoners of war. Nowhere, however, was there any specification requiring the government to provide clothing. By adhering to this general order,

59 *OR* 3/3:156.

60 *OR* 6/2:577.

61 Ibid., 742.

62 Spencer, "Point Lookout," 417.

Hoffman ensured that the Federal government did not fund clothing for a prisoner without his explicit approval.[63]

On April 20, 1864, in a reversal of policy, Hoffman issued an updated version of the July 1862 circular. Article XII directed that the commanding officer order his quartermaster to make clothing requisitions to the nearest depot for "such clothing as may be absolutely necessary for the prisoners and approved by the commanding officer." The circular clearly established how to requisition clothing for prisoners; however, it did not require camp commanders to distribute it. Although customary by international standards, the provision of clothing to prisoners of war was not mandatory. According to Hoffman, items were to be issued only at the discretion of the camp commander, and then only when deemed "absolutely necessary." The circular, however, gave no definition of what constituted "necessary."[64]

Clothing available in bulk quantities for issue consisted of uniforms rejected by the quartermaster's department. The issuing of new Federal uniform parts was forbidden unless the articles were first modified, as prescribed in Hoffman's circular. The cost and time required to refashion Federal clothing would have been exorbitant. Moreover, authorization for the destruction of such clothing could only be granted with Hoffman's approval.

The quartermaster's department at Point Lookout lacked the resources to supply thousands of enemy soldiers, and the government was not in the business of replacing the worn-out uniforms of its foes. Nevertheless, Hoffman recognized that most prisoners were in dire need of clothing and began permitting requisitions for garments from familial sources, provided the requests were submitted by the prisoners themselves. Hoffman specified that "The material for outer clothing should be gray or some dark mixed color and inferior quality."

Hoffman further stipulated that "any excess of clothing over what is required for immediate use is contraband" and would be confiscated. Donations proved cost-effective for Hoffman's budget and that of his prison quartermasters. Simple, generic, and clearly non-military items such as hats, shirts, drawers, socks, and shoes were supplied by the government, though they were issued infrequently. Ample documentation exists describing which items were distributed and when they were replaced.[65]

63 *OR* 3/3:156–157.

64 *OR* 7/2:74.

65 Ibid., 74–75.

Private Keiley complained, "You could receive nothing in the way of clothing without giving up the corresponding article which you might chance to possess." Barefooted men begged for or purchased shoes—regardless of condition—from other prisoners so that they would have a pair to exchange. The same requirement applied to any article of clothing. Regulations, however, did not apply to those items supplied directly by the quartermaster's department, which did not require an exchange.[66]

Prisoners recorded sporadic issues of items such as shoes and shirts during November 1864, with many others also receiving shoes and trousers. Prisoner Sgt. John Locke of the 14th Tennessee wrote multiple entries noting that clothing was issued to him and thousands of others during his confinement. On January 14, 1864, he wrote, "some divisions are drawing clothes." He did not specify which items, but the reference to "divisions" suggests that several thousand men were supplied. Two days later, Locke noted, "We march to the gate [main gate] and draw clothes," and again, two days after that, he recorded, "Our division drew clothes today. I got a pair of pants."[67]

Hoffman had previously received direction from Meigs as early as August 1862, that "it would be almost a direct issue to the Southern Army, as the prisoners will take their places in the ranks immediately on their arrival south in new clothing." As a result, it was decided not to release prisoners who had been issued new clothing while in confinement. To enforce this mandate, on August 1, 1864, Butler ordered the provost marshal at Point Lookout to confiscate "all surplus clothing from prisoners when [they are] exchanged," thereby denying the former prisoners any additional garments. This practice not only saved the expense of surplus clothing but also reserved supplies for future distribution to other prisoners.[68]

By November 1864, a negotiated program between the Union and Confederate governments went into effect to address the lack of clothing and blankets for prisoners on both sides. Under the agreement, a Southern representative was to act as a purchasing agent, authorized to sell 1,000 bales of cotton released by the Confederate government at auction in New York. The proceeds from this sale were to be used by an appointed agent to purchase and distribute blankets

66 Keiley, *In Vinculis*, 69.

67 Thomas Griffin Read to Martha White Read [wife], "Point Lookout, MD," Oct. 19, 1864, Box 1, Folder 19 MSN/CW 5015-19, Read Family Correspondence, Hesburgh Libraries University of Notre Dame, Notre Dame, IN; John Franklin Locke, John Locke Diary (unpublished typescript, 1861), 51–52.

68 *OR* 4/2:406; Peyton, *A Civil War Record for 1864–1865*, 101.

and clothing for Confederate prisoners of war. In return, General Grant selected two imprisoned Union officers to serve in the same capacity, supplying Union prisoners held in the South.

This arrangement became known as the "Beall Commission," named for Confederate Gen. William N. R. Beall, who had been selected as the Confederate representative. Beall performed in this capacity until his release in August 1865, after taking the Oath of Allegiance and Amnesty. Although short-lived, the Beall Commission achieved modest success, providing thousands of items to prisoners held in Northern prisons.[69]

## "For my part, I never saw any one get enough of anything"[70]

Point Lookout differed little from other prisons. The resources needed to sustain a population that fluctuated monthly created persistent deficiencies in the quartermaster's supply system. Rations were inadequate in both quantity and nutritional value. The hunger produced by insufficient rations forced men to do whatever was necessary to survive. Supplementing their meager fare by consuming cookhouse refuse, hunting rats, or stealing from one another became common practices. Malnutrition caused thousands to suffer from scurvy and other diseases.

Prisoners suffered crippling effects from consuming the contaminated water drawn from shallow, hand-dug wells. The lack of a reliable source of fresh water persisted until late 1864, when a flotilla of boats and barges began delivering sufficient supplies. The Beall Commission—though it came almost too late—also provided critically needed clothing and blankets during one of the harshest winters on record in southern Maryland.

Point Lookout did provide prisoners with an opportunity to bathe and wash their clothes by granting access to the Chesapeake Bay. Some took advantage of the bay's bounty, supplementing their rations or selling what they caught to others. The bay also offered relief from the stagnant air of the stockade, while occasionally presenting a means of escape for the brave or foolhardy.

Prisoners often vied with one another for transfer, hoping for better conditions at another prison, only to discover that circumstances were frequently no better elsewhere. Exchange was another possibility, though it came with a caveat. Before an exchange could take effect, a prisoner was required to accept parole, which meant first taking the Parole of Honor oath, which was a promise a captured

69 *OR* 7/2:1117, 1199–1200; *OR* 8/2:13–14, 21–22, 241, 748–749.

70 Keiley, *In Vinculis*, 66.

soldier made to not fight again until officially exchanged. The Federal government also offered another alternative: enlistment into the U.S. Army or Navy.[71]

An exchange of prisoners offered a means of leaving captivity, but it usually meant an eventual return to the battlefield. The exchange process had evolved into a convoluted and inequitable system, rarely satisfying either side. Accusations of fraud and disputes over the physical condition of exchanged men were among the factors leading to the breakdown of the system. By mid-1863, the Confederate government's refusal to recognize captured Black soldiers prompted retaliation by the Federal government and resulted in a suspension of exchanges.

The debilitating effects of languishing in prison caused needless misery, undermining both the mental and physical well-being of prisoners. Hardships persisted because of the inability—and, at times, the unwillingness—of both governments to negotiate an equitable system of exchange. As each side waited for the other to yield, prisoners on both sides suffered and died in what became a deadly contest of wills.

71 *OR* 5/2:306–307.

## Chapter 7

# Exchange, Parole, and "Swallowing the Bitter Pill"

An exchange cartel was an agreement mutually established by opposing belligerents. It was both economical and practical to exchange paroled prisoners promptly, returning them to their respective armies. Cartel agreements, however, were only as binding as the commitment of each side to honor them. According to international law, if one side ceased to recognize or uphold the agreement, the cartel was considered non-binding by the opposition. Prisoner exchanges occurred at the discretion of the captors, with no obligation for either party to participate. According to *International law*, it is illegal to coerce the enemy into such an agreement through the suffering of prisoners held by either side.[1]

From the outset of the 1861 crisis, the Lincoln administration refused to recognize the seceded states as a newly organized and sovereign Confederate nation. Lincoln labeled the opposition as rebels and, in some cases, pirates. Only after the Confederate government began holding captives from both the Union army and navy did the administration acknowledge them as prisoners of war, doing so as a concession rather than as a matter of legal right. As the war escalated, the unexpected accumulation of prisoners forced both belligerents into establishing an exchange cartel.[2]

It was not until the issuance of General Orders 49 (February 1863) and 100 (the *Lieber Code*, April 1863) that the administration formally outlined

1 Thompson, "Life in the Prisons," in *The Photographic*, 7:98; George B. Davis, *Outlines of International Law with an Account of Its Origin and Sources and of Its Historical Development* (New York, 1898), 1.

2 Anna Price, "Pirates, Privateers, and Civil War Maritime Laws," In Custodia Legis Law Librarians of Congress (blog), May 20, 2020, accessed April 3, 2025, https://blogs.loc.gov/law/2020/05/pirates-privateers-and-civil-war-maritime-laws/; Guelzo interview.

conditions of parole, including specifications for prisoner parole and exchange. General Order 100 also detailed the circumstances under which parole could be granted and identified who bore responsibility for the release and care of captives. It further declared that a belligerent was not obliged to parole prisoners of war. In the early phases of the conflict, exchanges of soldiers and sailors between the two governments were conducted rank for rank, and at times one body for another.[3]

Incarcerating prisoners for extended periods could weaken the host government's available manpower and strain resources by requiring a large guard force. The growing number of Confederate prisoners initially deprived the Northern armies of combat-experienced men, who were reassigned as prison guards.

Due to prolonged imprisonment, prisoners suffered from declining health, poor living conditions, and disease. Homesickness and separation from loved ones further weakened their resolve and often proved unbearable. An overwhelming sense of abandonment by their government, combined with the debilitating conditions of prison life, sometimes worsened their physical and mental decline. No longer willing to live under such circumstances, some Southern prisoners reluctantly accepted the oath of allegiance, often referred to as "swallowing the bitter pill" or "swallowing the eagle."[4]

Prisoners were encouraged to desert their respective armies and take the oath of allegiance, which offered either amnesty or the possibility of recruitment into their captor's army. Taking the oath was the first step required of a Confederate prisoner to obtain his parole. If he violated his oath and parole by returning to his army and was recaptured under arms, he was subject to execution.[5]

In response to the Confederate proclamation (General Orders No. 111 issued by Confederate President Jefferson Davis December 23, 1862), President Lincoln issued General Order No. 252 on July 30, 1863. Known as the "Retaliation Order," Lincoln's directive denounced the Confederate proclamation and suspended participation in the mutually agreed Dix-Hill prisoner exchange cartel until the Confederate government recognized captured Black U.S. soldiers as legitimate prisoners of war. The termination of the exchange cartel led to the cessation of prisoner exchanges on a substantial scale, prolonging the suffering of all prisoners.

3 *OR* 3/3: Sections VI and VII.

4 Gary Emerson, "Swallowing the Eagle: The Question of Loyalty at the Elmire Prison Camp," *The Chemung Historical Journal* 2, no. 2 (2016): 6962.

5 *OR* 8/2:239-240; *OR* 3/3:160, Article 124; *Deserters, Prisoners Exchanged, Received and Released, Refugees, 1863–1865* (Point Lookout, MD, n.d.), NARA Microfilm rolls, 369–370, 369–373, 598.

The absence of an exchange program also increased the prison populations in both the North and the South.[6]

If it was discovered that a prisoner or group of prisoners applied to "swallow the eagle," they often faced severe retribution from more steadfast inmates. This knowledge made the decision to take the oath difficult. Committees of prisoners sought potential oath takers, issuing sanctions from verbal threats to bodily harm. Sergeant James Wells of the 2nd South Carolina stated that,

> fear of death either by disease or . . . of the negro guards forced . . . soldiers to think of taking the oath . . . [it] had to be done with great secrecy as the participators in it, if known, would have been severely punished. Meetings were held in . . . camp and various schemes devised to prevent the depletion of our ranks in this manner.

Wells further described instances where some of these measures had little effect on an oath taker and "more vigorous measures had to be adopted." As soon as word of an oath taker spread through the prison grapevine, or "the grape,"

> a party would proceed to his tent the night previous, call him out, and administer a severe flogging. They even went as far as to clip the ears of one fellow prison mate . . . the parties who did this work were completely disguised.

Such measures influenced the number of prisoners considering whether to "swallow the bitter pill," as they feared severe punishment from their fellow inmates.[7]

To be sure, not all inmates felt the same way. Many well understood the hard choices involved. Private E. H. Sutton of the 24th Georgia stated, "I have nothing to say against those who went out [to take the oath] to keep from starving . . . [M]en esteem life more then all things besides and that death is so dreaded we will do almost anything honorable or not to avoid death." At Point Lookout, taking the oath increased one's chances of survival, freedom, and an eventual return to home and family.[8]

For their protection, oath takers were promptly removed from the prison by authorities after the completion of the ceremony. However, in some cases authorities sent the newly minted U.S. citizen back into the population to gather

6 Doris Kearns Goodwin, *Team of Rivals: The Political Genius of Abraham Lincoln* (New York, 2005), 550–552.

7 Letter by Wells, 25–27.

8 Sutton, *Civil War Stories*, 62.

his belongings, demonstrating that the reward for taking the oath was a new set of clothes and a good meal before release. This return to the prison population could prove hazardous, however.

## The Second Wave of Prisons

As the war continued into 1863, the influx of Confederate prisoners overtaxed Northern prisons. The elimination of the exchange cartel forced Hoffman to reopen prison camps he had previously closed. While these prisons resumed operation, additional depots were established to alleviate the sudden overcrowding. Point Lookout was opened for use for less than four months before the establishment of the prison at Rock Island, Illinois, in December 1863. A year later, in July 1864, another prison opened at Elmira, New York. Despite this second wave of new prisons, the overwhelming numbers continued to strain the Federal prison system to its limit.

At the conclusion of the meeting on the *River Queen* between Confederate Vice President Alexander Stephens and President Lincoln in February 1865, Stephens appealed to the president that if they could not agree on anything else, at least something be done to relieve the suffering of prisoners. Lincoln agreed to Stephens' request and ordered Grant to reopen a general prisoner exchange. Although Grant understood that curtailing the exchange cartel had denied the Southern forces the battle-experienced men they needed, he nevertheless complied by continuing a limited exchange. As the renewed exchange progressed, Hoffman observed that by April 1865 thousands of prisoners arriving at Point Lookout for exchange far outnumbered those whom Grant had ordered released, thereby preventing an equitable exchange between the governments.[9]

Until this time, Hoffman transferred prisoners to other sites to alleviate overcrowding. Prisoner Louis Leon of the 1st North Carolina stated that 400 prisoners left Point Lookout for "some other prison as there were too many here." While Point Lookout transferred prisoners elsewhere, new arrivals destined for other camps reached the prison and often remained for weeks before proceeding. This created additional mouths to feed, along with the needs of boat crews who stayed while their transport ships were refueled. At times, transport ships were diverted elsewhere, leaving their prisoners at Point Lookout until further orders.

Additional shelters were also required. Barnes brought this situation to the attention of his superiors, Generals Augur and Hoffman, informing them that he preferred prisoners to continue directly to Aiken's Landing or other points of

9 Walter Stahr, *Seward: Lincoln's Indispensable Man* (New York, 2012), 426.

exchange and, if necessary, to other prisons, provided their layover lasted a day or less. Barnes's concerns were acknowledged but disregarded, as the reply was simply to send more prisoners.[10]

By this time, Point Lookout was in a constant state of transit. Thousands of prisoners arrived from the front destined for other prisons, while hundreds—even thousands—more were transferred to or from different sites. In early March 1865, over 4,500 paroled Confederate prisoners destined for exchange arrived at Point Lookout, eventually departing later in the month for their original destination to City Point, Virginia. In the meantime, these additional men increased the prison population of Point Lookout to more than 11,000.[11]

On April 8, 1865, General Barnes reported to Hoffman that Point Lookout held 13,500 prisoners, further claiming, "We can take care of three or four thousand more." This statement indicates either poor record keeping or a deliberate attempt by Barnes to inflate numbers to secure a surplus of supplies and tentage. The returns for the end of the month of March reported 11,332 prisoners present. Regardless, Hoffman complied by sending several thousand additional prisoners to the camp. By April 15, Barnes reported that the prison was holding more than 22,000 men. He immediately requested more tents to house the newly arrived. If additional shelter was required, it was certain that rations were once again being spread thin among the population.[12]

## Lieutenant General Grant and Prisoner Exchange

In the spring of 1864, Grant instructed General Butler, special agent of exchange, that if the Confederate government did not comply with the terms of parole after the capitulations of Port Hudson and Vicksburg, "not another prisoner of war will be paroled or exchanged." In response, Southern exchange agent Judge Ould warned Grant of possible Southern retaliation for such an action. Grant nevertheless remained steadfast in his conviction against further exchanges. He stated to Secretary Seward, "We ought not to make a single exchange nor release a prisoner on any pretext whatever until the war closes. We have got to fight until the military power of the South is exhausted, and if we release or exchange prisoners captured it simply becomes a war of extermination." Prisoners became convinced

10 Leon, *Diary of a Tar Heel*, 66; *Book No. 257*, vol. 4, *District of St. Mary's, Press Copies of Letter and Telegrams Sent* (Washington DC, n.d.), 180–182.

11 Ronald S. Coddington, *Faces of the Confederacy: An Album of Southern Soldiers and Their Stories* (Baltimore, 2008), 53, 87; *OR* 8/2:991.

12 *Book No. 257*, 276. *O.R.* 8/2: 991.

that Federal authorities preferred to imprison them instead of fight them. General Halleck agreed, noting that it was cheaper to feed them than to fight them.[13]

Colonel William E. Doster, provost marshal of Washington, D.C., stated that the prison system suffered from one major drawback regarding the status of civilian prisoners: "It [the system] operated like a rat trap . . . in other words, plenty of provision for arresting people, but none for trying them or disposing of their cases . . . Just about anyone and everyone had the power to arrest, but no one could release a prisoner without stepping on someone's toes." (Secretary Seward created the "Treason Bureau," manned by a team of detectives under the State Department. From its inception until February 1862, the bureau ordered 864 arrests. After February 1862, responsibility for internal security transferred from Seward to Stanton and the War Department.)[14]

Authorities in St. Mary's County arrested civilians and held them at Point Lookout for various offenses, including blockade running and speaking out against the Federal government. Many locals were captured by Federal patrols or the U.S. Navy for suspicious activities such as transporting intelligence, recruits, mail, supplies, and weapons, or for running blockades to and from neighboring Virginia.[15]

The status of arrested civilians eventually became a conundrum for Point Lookout commanding officer Col. Alonzo Draper. On July 5, 1864, Draper requested instructions from the secretary of war regarding how to treat civilians who refused to take the oath of allegiance. He reported that many civilians, despite imprisonment, refused the oath and, being civilians, were less likely to be exchanged. Draper requested permission to expel them from his district to other locations. Although some were released after taking the oath, others who demurred were transferred from Point Lookout to the Federal penitentiary in Washington, D.C., and the Old Capitol Prison until their fates could be decided. As explained by Col. William E. Doster, they were caught in the proverbial "rat trap."[16]

13 James McPherson, *Ordeal by Fire: The Civil War and Reconstruction* (New York, 1982), 455; *OR* 6/2:709, 711–712, 768; *OR* 7/2: 62–63, 606–607; *OR 7/2*: 614-615, 606–607; Peyton, *A Civil War Record for 1864–1865*, 100; *OR* 8/2:239–240; Richard E. Beringer, et al., *Why the South Lost the Civil War* (Athens, GA, 1986), 369.

14 Neff, *Justice in Blue*, 156–157;*OR* 3/3:150; Neff, *Justice in Blue*, 160–161; Tobin T. Buhk, *True Crime in the Civil War: Cases of Murder, Treason, Counterfeiting, Massacre, Plunder, and Abuse* (Mechanicsburg, PA, 2012), 5. Secretary Seward created the "Treason Bureau" manned by a team of detectives under the state department. From its start until Feb. 1862, 864 arrests were ordered by the State Department. After Feb. 1862, the responsibility of internal security was transferred from Seward to Stanton and the War Department.

15 Thompson, "Life in the Prisons," 7:345.

16 *Book No. 253*, 422.

Confederate sailors and marines imprisoned at Point Lookout faced a similar ordeal. Lincoln's secretary of the navy, Gideon Welles, stated that Secretary of War Stanton "assumed that the Navy was secondary and subject to the control and direction of the military branch of the government" (in other words, under the control of the War Department), despite the fact that their respective departments were considered equal. Although Welles was always ready to cooperate with the armies, Stanton believed that the War Department had overall control of all military aspects of the war, including prisoner exchanges. Stanton and Welles often disagreed about which branch of the service should have priority.[17]

Correspondence between Welles and his Confederate counterpart, Stephen Mallory, failed to produce immediate results regarding the exchange of imprisoned naval personnel. To complicate matters further, Stanton consistently maintained that the army should manage all prisoner exchanges, leaving the status of captured naval personnel to be addressed later.

Acting upon presidential inquiry on October 4, 1864, Secretary Welles informed Lincoln that there had been no exchange of naval personnel for 14 to 15 months between navies and that while exchanges between the armies had sporadically continued throughout this time, "no naval prisoners had been embraced." An exchange finally occurred in early October by an arrangement between Butler and Ould for all Confederate naval officers and sailors presently held at Point Lookout, Elmira, and Fort Delaware. All were transferred to Point Lookout before sending them to Savannah, Georgia (Venus Point), to affect the exchange.[18]

That same month, Butler was transferred to a field command and replaced by his assistant, Maj. John E. Mulford, as the primary agent for prisoner exchanges. Mulford immediately arranged the exchange of 90 Confederate naval officers and enlisted men, receiving 323 officers and men of the U.S. Navy in return. This exchange demonstrated that prisoner transfers continued to occur as needed under the Lincoln administration.[19]

On at least two occasions, Secretary Stanton diverted prisoner transfers originally destined for Point Lookout, citing security concerns related to the prison's precarious location. Colonel Hoffman shared these concerns, noting that the inadequate guard force was vastly outnumbered by the massive prisoner population held there.[20]

17 Gideon Welles, *The Civil War Diary of Gideon Welles: Lincoln's Secretary of the* Navy, ed. William E. Gienapp and Erica L. Gienapp (Urbana, IL, 2014), 683.

18 Butler, *Private and Official Correspondence of General Benjamin F. Butler*, 4:266–267.

19 *Book No. 257*, 36, 38–39.

20 *OR* 6/2:1015–1016.

As early as May 1864, Hoffman notified then-post commandant Colonel Draper that Point Lookout would soon receive upwards of 10,000 additional prisoners. Draper responded by proposing to the secretary of war that "it might be prudent to add one or two militia regiments to our present force" to guard the thousands of new prisoners. At that time, Point Lookout had barely 1,500 men, most being members of the Veteran Reserve Corps, to guard upwards of 12,000 prisoners—a ratio of roughly eight prisoners for every guard. Draper received little additional support from Washington.[21]

By October 1864, Southern armies were forced to fight on multiple fronts, resulting in thousands of captured soldiers being sent to northern prisons. The prison at Point Lookout expanded its footprint to accommodate this influx of prisoners. In response, the Lincoln administration devised a plan intended to reduce prison populations while simultaneously adding more men to the Union army.

## The United States Volunteers or "Galvanized Yankees"

Pennsylvania Republican Congressman Thaddeus Stevens stated, "When a country is at open war, with an enemy . . . you have a right to use every means which will weaken him." The cessation of prisoner exchanges was one clear method to accomplish that goal. Captured Confederate soldiers who were not exchanged were prevented from rejoining their armies and continuing the fight. This strategic calculation was fully understood by the Lincoln administration.[22]

In December 1863, General Butler reported to Secretary of War Stanton that he had recently sent 500 prisoners from Point Lookout to City Point for exchange, but the request was refused by his Confederate counterpart. As an alternative, Butler informed Stanton that he believed a substantial number of prisoners at Point Lookout would enlist in the U.S. Army once discharged. He inquired whether there were any objections to enlisting "as many prisoners as may desire to do so . . . either in the regular or volunteer force of the United States or that of any State."[23]

Lincoln believed that some prisoners had been coerced into Confederate service and deserved the opportunity to enlist and serve the United States. He therefore issued Proclamation No. 108 (December 1863), which stated that once a prisoner was pardoned, it furnished the Federal government the legal means to recruit the former prisoners into United States service. As had been practiced in

21 *Book No. 253*, 40.

22 Louis P. Masur, *Lincoln's Hundred Days: The Emancipation Proclamation and the War for the Union* (Cambridge, MA, 2012), 22–23.

23 *OR* 6/2:768.

European wars for decades, recruiting soldiers from one's enemy was not a new tactic and had already been attempted by both armies earlier in the Civil War.

This proclamation created an additional source of manpower previously inaccessible to the Union by further providing rules for releasing and recruiting prisoners. It listed two categories: those willing to take the oath of allegiance, and those who would take the oath, be discharged, and reside within Union lines. John Hay, the president's secretary, delivered the necessary instructions and documents to Generals Butler and Marston.

On December 27, 1864, both Lincoln and Secretary Stanton visited Point Lookout to personally inspect the camp and determine if any prisoners were willing to take advantage of the president's proclamation. The *New York Tribune* reported that both men had satisfied themselves that not less than a thousand prisoners were prepared to enter Federal service.[24]

The new recruits were transferred westward to secure and protect supply and communication lines frequently disrupted by Native American tribes. These newly enlisted soldiers were not to be used against their former government out of concern for potential retribution if captured. Butler's plan received endorsement from Lincoln, who viewed it as a means to reduce prison populations, add soldiers to the Union army, and begin the process of national healing.[25]

Butler had already received permission the previous year from Stanton to begin recruiting prisoners from Point Lookout. Before proceeding, Butler was required to obtain authorization from the provost marshal general in Washington, D.C., to assure prison commandants that his recruitment efforts were officially sanctioned. Otherwise, commandants could be held liable for the escape of recruits who had formerly been confined under their watch.[26]

On January 8, 1864, Butler informed Marston that he was directed to "enlist from the rebel prisoners under your command all those who may desire to enlist in the service of the United States either in the Army or Navy . . . upon taking the oath of allegiance and the parole as prescribed in General Orders, No. 49." The following day, Butler instructed Marston to require each prisoner at Point Lookout to answer one of four specified questions after hearing them all. Marston was further directed to use designated forms from the accompanying book, ensure

24 Abraham Lincoln, *Nov. 5, 1863–Sept. 12, 1864*, Vol. 7, *Collected Works of Abraham Lincoln* (New Brunswick, NJ, 1953).

25 The American Presidency Project, "Abraham Lincoln Event Timeline," The American Presidency Project, UC Santa Barbara, accessed April 3, 2025, https://www.presidency.ucsb.edu/documents/abraham-lincoln-event-timeline.

26 *OR* 6/2:802, 1090; Guelzo interview.

each prisoner's signature was witnessed, read the oath and parole to them, and pose the questions to each individual separately from other prisoners. Every prisoner in the stockade was to be interviewed, with their answers recorded according to instructions and their names attached to the responses.[27]

By March 11, 1864, Butler notified Hoffman that Point Lookout could accommodate up to 20,000 prisoners and requested the transfer of additional prisoners from Fort Delaware. Butler based his assessment on the expectation that more prisoners would participate in the enlistment program at Point Lookout. He reported that every prisoner had responded to one of four specified questions and that he had nearly recruited a regiment, anticipating further additions with incoming prisoners. Secretary Stanton denied Butler's request for the large-scale transfer, reportedly due to concerns about concentrating several thousand enemy soldiers near the nation's capital.[28]

Approximately 1,100 inmates of the 8,500 incarcerated at Point Lookout applied for enlistment under the president's proclamation. The group, officially designated as the "First Regiment of United States Volunteers" (U.S.V.), was recruited and enlisted at Point Lookout between January and April 1864. Recruitment for the 4th Regiment U.S.V. commenced in October of that year, resulting in the enlistment of only six companies. Of the 1,100 former prisoners initially recruited for the 1st Regiment, 700 were deemed fit for service and subsequently mustered into the new regiment.[29]

After the ranks of the newly established 1st United States Volunteers—also known as Galvanized or Whitewashed Yankees—were filled, approximately 200 additional eligible recruits were permitted to join three New Hampshire regiments. Individuals deemed unfit for Federal service were sent to a "reject camp," from which they were subsequently dispatched north to assist with government fortification projects. Additionally, the remainder of the original 1,100 recruits were offered the opportunity to enlist in the navy, with several accepting the offer.[30]

Marston appointed Capt. Thomas Livermore of the 5th New Hampshire as the inaugural commanding officer of the 1st U.S.V. Livermore accepted this

27 *OR* 4/3:15.

28 *OR* 6/2:823, 1033–1034, 1079.

29 Abraham Lincoln, "Proclamation 108—Amnesty and Reconstruction," The American Presidency Project, University of California Santa Barbara, accessed April 4, 2025, https://www.presidency.ucsb.edu/documents/proclamation-108-amnesty-and-reconstruction. President Johnson would follow by issuing General Order No. 85 (May 8, 1865) for those captured prior to the fall of Richmond below the rank of Colonel; Dee Alexander Brown, *The Galvanized Yankees* (Lincoln, NE, 1985), 112–117; Haynes, *A Soldier Boy's Letters*, 160.

30 Bartlett, *History of the Twelfth Regiment New Hampshire Volunteers*, 148.

responsibility and commenced the process of transforming his recruits into U.S. soldiers. Upon his arrival, he encountered nearly 1,000 newly released prisoners assembled outside the prison gate.

Livermore promptly relocated his new recruits to an appropriate encampment site on the Chesapeake Bay side of Point Lookout, adjacent to his former regiment. Upon arrival, he issued orders for the men to change out of their gray clothing, bathe in the bay, receive haircuts, and don new Federal uniforms. He subsequently implemented regular drills and enforced military discipline. According to his account, there was never a need for serious disciplinary measures, nor did any soldier desert; all remained in camp as instructed. The newly established 1st U.S. Volunteers soon experienced improved living conditions and began receiving rations equivalent to those provided to the guard force.[31]

Notably, as the president anticipated, many new recruits did not identify the South as their home before the outbreak of war. Among the several hundred who joined the 1st U.S.V., 57 came from ten Union states, 31 from three border states, and 52 from ten foreign nations. Many reported being in the South when hostilities began, at which point they were conscripted, drafted, or otherwise compelled into Confederate service. Some volunteered independently but later changed allegiance after receiving an offer of repatriation.

Unfortunately for Livermore, after his arduous work in forming these men into soldiers for the Union, he was denied promotion to colonel and command of the 1st U.S.V., and he was soon replaced by Col. Charles Dimon (formerly of the 30th Massachusetts and 2nd Louisiana), a personal selection of General Butler. The provost marshal of Point Lookout, Maj. Harrison G. O. Weymouth (18th Massachusetts), was relieved of his duties and placed second in command of the 1st U.S.V. under Dimon. It was army politics as usual, with both men from the same state as Congressman Butler.[32]

General Butler initially anticipated that these men would not serve as guards at Point Lookout. However, General Edward Hinks (who had succeeded Marston), organized a new Police Guard of the provost marshal, and directed Dimon to detail two second lieutenants, two sergeants, six corporals, and fifty privates from the 1st U.S.V. to this guard. The next day, Capt. H. Sargent, the ordnance officer, received instructions from Hinks to supply "100 stand of arms" (rifles, cartridge boxes, and bayonets) to the men assigned to this duty. These personnel served as guards until their transfer. On April 23, 1864, approximately 619 officers and

31 Livermore, *Dates and Events*, 325–326.

32 *Book No. 251*, General Order Aug. 1863–Aug. 1865.

men of the 1st U.S.V. departed Point Lookout for Norfolk, Virginia, where they relieved the 4th Rhode Island. The 4th Rhode Island, in turn, moved to Point Lookout to reinforce the guard force.[33]

As many as 6,000 former prisoners of war were recruited into the United States Volunteers. The initiative to enlist former adversaries into Federal service represented a notable and unconventional experiment. However, the program did not produce the results anticipated by the president and Secretary Stanton, nor did it resolve the problem of overcrowding in the prisons as intended. After the 1st U.S.V. left Point Lookout, several recruits deserted at the first opportunity. Despite these challenges, many remained in service for the duration of the war, with some reenlisting and later retiring after full army careers.

### "Turning our backs on this miserable place."[34]

No standardized procedure for selecting prisoners for exchange existed at Point Lookout. According to prisoner accounts, authorities sometimes notified individuals of upcoming exchanges through postings on the prison bulletin board. Those eligible were instructed to prepare their belongings and report to the prison gate the following morning for parole and exchange.

Once prisoners completed the parole process, they were escorted to the wharf near Hammond Hospital. There, another roll call was conducted to verify each man's identity against the official roster and to ensure that no "flankers"—those attempting to assume another's identity or hide among the departing—were present. To support the reintegration of prisoners of war into the Union, the Federal government established several avenues for parole. Prisoners could request inclusion on a list to take the oath of allegiance and be paroled under various presidential proclamations and general orders.[35]

Prisoners from Point Lookout were transferred by a flag-of-truce ship, often the side-wheeler *New York*, to designated exchange sites between the lines of the opposing armies. On the East Coast, these sites included City Point, Aiken's Landing, Cox's Wharf, and Boulware's Wharf on the James River. Fortress Monroe initially served as an exchange point, but its use ended when General Butler returned to field command in May 1864. After exchange, Confederate prisoners were sent to Richmond for care and possible reassignment. On one

33 *Book No. 255*, 50, 52; Michèle Tucker Butts, *Galvanized Yankees on the Upper Missouri: The Face of Loyalty* (Boulder, CO, 2003), 52.

34 Hubbs, *Voices from Company D*, 386.

35 Lincoln, "Proclamation 108—Amnesty," The American Presidency Project.

Flag of Truce boat, *S.S. New York*. *Library of Congress*

occasion, sick prisoners from Point Lookout were exchanged at Venus Point near Savannah, Georgia. Over time, Venus Point and Aiken's Landing became major exchange locations.

On February 8, 1865, Sgt. James Wells of the 2nd South Carolina saw a notice on the prison bulletin board stating that "those captured at Gettysburg should hold themselves in readiness" for exchange. After the provost marshal determined eligibility, the selected men were moved to a pen next to the one they had occupied for eighteen months, where they were informed they would be paroled. Selection for exchange was not always random; Sgt. James Thomas of the 2nd Maryland noted that by paying $50 to a clerk, he and four others secured places on the exchange list, which led to their parole. Thomas was among those who, after leaving Point Lookout through exchange, were recaptured and returned 16 days later. He remarked that Union soldiers recognized him and commented on his quick return.[36]

36 Letter by Wells, 42–43; Thomas, "Third Book," 82.

The parole and exchange process began with prisoners lining up outside the main prison gate, where the provost marshal counted them and recorded their personal and capture details. This information was entered in the prison roll for those being exchanged or released. Prisoners leaving Point Lookout could also convert any remaining sutler check balances into greenbacks, which signaled their imminent departure.[37]

Another stockade had been built as a holding area for exchanged and released prisoners a short distance from the main stockade and the new prison hospital. After receiving their parole, these men were transferred to the newly established parole camp, which required guards only at its entrance. One exchanged prisoner described the pen as having "mud ankle deep" and noted the difficulty of finding solid ground on which to rest. Because the men were on parole status, no shelter was provided. With the addition of the officers' stockade and the construction of the parole pen, the overall size of the Point Lookout prison expanded to 45 acres.[38]

Before departure, prisoners underwent a final roll call to confirm their identities before boarding the exchange ship. Each man was ordered to squat, respond to his name, stand, and proceed to the ship; this prevented impersonation or illegal additions to the ranks. If more than one prisoner answered to the same name, the impostors were sent back and punished. Prisoners received two or three days of rations for the journey to the exchange point.[39]

Men who chose to take the oath of allegiance left Point Lookout as soldiers, sailors, or citizens of the United States. Those who remained endured the harsh conditions at Point Lookout as best they could. Some attempted escape by tunneling, joining work details, or adopting false identities; however, these efforts often led to recapture, punishment, or death at the hands of Federal guards. Despite the risks and uncertain outcomes, many considered the pursuit of freedom preferable to remaining in captivity under conditions of illness, malnutrition, or other severe hardships.

37 Keiley, *In Vinculis*, 115.

38 Charles T. Loehr, "The Treatment of Prisoners," in *Southern Historical Society Papers*, ed. R. A. Brock (Richmond, VA, 1890), 18:119; Thomas, "Third Book," 77.

39 H. W. Graber, *A Terry Texas Ranger: The Life Record of H. W. Graber* (Austin, TX, 1987), 120–121; Jones, *In Prison at Point Lookout*.

## Chapter 8

# Breakouts and Escapes

Prisoners of war were expected to escape by any means in order to return to their armies. According to the *Lieber Code*, escape attempts were not considered crimes. Nevertheless, failed escape attempts often resulted in corporal punishment. Methods of escape at Point Lookout ranged from simple to ingenious. Some prisoners attempted tunneling, bribing guards, walking away while on work details, or assuming the identity of a former or deceased prisoner. Others feigned fatal diseases, concealed themselves aboard boats and barges moored at the wharf, or hid among the dead.[1]

Some bold prisoners attempted to bribe members of the guard force with currency or jewelry they had smuggled upon arrival or acquired later. They hoped that bribing the guards would ensure the sentinels looked the other way if tunneling operations or other escape attempts were discovered. It was a gamble, but many believed it was worth the risk.[2]

Even though Article 77 of the *Lieber Code* defined a difference between an "attempt" and an "escape," the guards at Point Lookout rarely differentiated between the two. If escaped prisoners were recaptured alive, their punishments varied and could be excruciatingly painful. At times, prison authorities employed creative methods of punishment to discourage future attempts. The *Lieber Code* did not forbid punishment and did not describe its limitations or methods.[3]

1 Bartlett, *History of the Twelfth Regiment New Hampshire Volunteers*, 149. The *Laws of Nations* were more guidelines than laws and were difficult to enforce. However, they were cited when it was necessary and convenient to warring governments. This included the *Lieber Code* which was not enforceable.

2 Leon, *Diary of a Tar Heel*, 66.

3 Letter by Wells, 15–17.

## Schemes and Spies

As the prisoners soon learned, the provost marshal had informants embedded within the prison, disguised as fellow inmates. Federal soldiers wearing captured Confederate uniforms alerted authorities to escape plans, tunnel digging, and other breakout schemes. These operatives sometimes baited prisoners into attempting escape by suggesting the best means and routes, only for a prearranged party of guards to be waiting for those they had deceived. Although there were several successful escapes, most attempts were thwarted.

Lieutenant John Blue of the 11th Virginia Cavalry discovered firsthand the existence of informants when he and others devised a plan to escape. Blue described a fellow prisoner, "a wolf in sheep's clothing," who advised them on the supposed best time, place, and method for their attempt. Trusting their "friend," Blue and his party put the plan into action, only to realize their mistake. Once clear of the prison stockade, they were quickly captured by a squad of Union guards waiting for them.[4]

Visiting correspondent Edward Spencer wrote that loose talk about escape plans was discouraged, as no one truly knew who their friends were. "There was little or no kindliness or fellow feeling among prisoners," he reported. "A sauzve-qui-peut, rule prevailed . . . there was but little open talk, or free confidence . . . There are so many spies in camp." Many men listened for such schemes to secure the payoff of an extra ration or two in exchange for information. In prison survival was paramount, and brotherhood extended only so far. A breach of trust was a serious matter.[5]

There was always the risk that informants would uncover escape plans, but prisoners also dreaded the possibility of tunnels collapsing or flooding during excavation. Solid ground had to be located, as tunnels could easily collapse at any stage of construction. Escape-minded prisoners were forced to dig through sand and clay, hoping their burrows would not fill with water from the high-water table, which caused further soil instability and flooding. To detect tunneling operations, guards routinely sounded the ground around the camps with a heavy maul, like those used for paving streets, to determine whether hollow areas lay beneath the surface.[6]

4 Blue, *Hanging Rock Rebel*, 266–267.

5 Spencer, "Point Lookout," 418.

6 Everson, Narrative and Personal Notes, 14.

Guards and roving patrols remained constantly alert for suspicious piles of surplus dirt appearing in or around the prison and its shelters, as these could indicate tunneling activity. Prisoners devised ways of disposing of the soil without drawing attention. Private Albert G. Warfield of the 1st Maryland Cavalry managed to carve out a tunnel using nothing more than his pocketknife. He discovered that he could fill his pockets with the excavated dirt and broadcast it throughout the prison grounds, rather than leaving conspicuous piles exposed to scrutiny. Warfield then constructed a crude boat to cross the Potomac River once he cleared the stockade. However, as he emerged from his tunnel with the boat, he found he had been betrayed, for elements of the Federal cavalry were waiting. Ignoring warnings to halt, he continued his escape toward the river. A musket ball fired after he refused to stop ended the escapade, though not his life, when it glanced across the top of his head and exited near his ear.

Undeterred by the this failure, Warfield devised another scheme that took advantage of the smallpox quarantine. Feigning smallpox was another ruse sometimes used by prisoners hoping to escape captivity. The contagion appeared soon after the prison was established in 1863. Smallpox could be deadly, and those afflicted were quarantined outside the stockade at the "pest house," away from the main prison population and camps.

While recovering from his head wound, Warfield observed that each day at three o'clock the smallpox hospital wagon passed through the prison to collect prisoners designated by surgeons for removal to the hospital. He procured a piece of baling wire and discovered that, by heating it until red hot, he could burn and blister his skin to resemble the pustules of smallpox. His ruse deceived the prison surgeons into believing he was in the early stages of the contagion, and he was soon placed on the ambulance bound for the smallpox hospital.

As soon as Warfield was out of sight of the camp and guards, he fled the ambulance and took refuge in some bushes until dark, after which he made his way south. Warfield managed to put eight miles between himself and the prison before he was again apprehended by Federal soldiers searching for him after discovering his absence. This time, Warfield was punished for his escape attempt by being suspended by his thumbs. The authorities sought to force him to reveal the names of any accomplices who might have aided in the scheme, but he refused to betray a friend.[7]

Once a tunnel was discovered, the guards usually forced the guilty prisoners to fill it in and destroy their work. They then demolished the shelter from which

7 Geo. W. Booth, comp., *Illustrated Souvenir Maryland Line Confederate Soldiers' Home* (Pikesville, MD, 1894), 37–38.

the tunnel originated, after which the prisoners served a penalty appropriate for the act. One such escape attempt ended with more than the destruction of a tunnel. Several prisoners who lived together collected wood for the construction of boats capable of carrying two to three men each, disguising the effort as an attempt to enlarge their shelter. Concealing the boat parts within their shebang, they even bribed guards in advance to ensure access out of the stockade when the time came. Prison authorities, having been informed of the plot, prepared an armed reception for the escapees.

As the party waited for nightfall to begin their exit, the provost marshal dispatched a guard to the shelter. The guard uncovered the boats, set the crafts and the shebang ablaze, and left the occupants to depend on the charity of their fellow prisoners for lodging. The tunnel was then filled in by the miners.[8]

Tunneling was one method of escaping beneath the stockade fence, but those inclined to leave Point Lookout more quickly attempted to scale the 12-foot wooden plank wall. Several enlisted men sought to use two long tent poles to construct a ladder. Over time, they secreted lengths of rope to fashion the rungs. They soon discovered, however, that despite their craftsmanship, the rungs were too weak to support even their meager weight.

The prisoner recalled that they waited until the guards were at their furthest distance apart on the catwalk. He was the first to scale the ladder, and he quickly went up and over the stockade fence to freedom. His comrade who followed was not as fortunate. Halfway up the ladder, a rung broke, cracking one of the tent poles with a sound like a rifle report within the stockade. The sound quickly drew the attention of the two guards, and the man was soon captured. The rest of the party seized the remains of the ladder and escaped back into the vast sea of tents, later burning the remaining rungs to eliminate the evidence. The ringleader was eventually recaptured and further "ironed and chained to a wall" of the prison for his efforts.[9]

Humor was seldom found in the life of a prisoner, yet one bid for freedom ended in the amusement of the guards. Lieutenant Everson recalled that one evening an unlucky squad of prisoners, after digging several hundred feet underground, emerged in the middle of a tent where a Union officer was entertaining his friends. They were immediately apprehended and returned to the prison.[10]

8 Keiley, *In Vinculis*, 73.

9 G. N. Saussy, "In Memory of Lee," *Savannah Morning News*, Jan. 20, 1901, 4, accessed April 4, 2025, https://chroniclingamerica.loc.gov/lccn/sn89053684/1901-01-20/ed-1/seq-4/.

10 Everson, Narrative and Personal Notes, 14.

Some members of the Union guard force displayed the same disloyalty as the prisoners they guarded. Many of these unscrupulous men, recruited as substitutes and draftees during the Federal draft of 1863, longed to desert as badly as the prisoners wished to escape. After these substitutes arrived to fill the ranks of the New Hampshire regiments, desertion attempts increased, with many taking the opportunity to flee during their transport to Point Lookout. Once at the prison, their frequent desertion attempts became a persistent problem for their commanding officers. On occasion, guards and prisoners even coordinated efforts to escape together. Some of these joint efforts, however, ended in failure. Sergeant James Wells of the 2nd South Carolina recorded in late 1863 that he heard firing on the bay side of the prison one night, "and next morning the bodies of several Confederates and Yankees were seen lying upon the beach and near them a boat."[11]

During the early months of the prison, waste from both the prisoner and guard camps was disposed of in the Potomac River or Chesapeake Bay. This included not only raw refuse but also the many empty wooden crates and barrels used for food packaging and shipping. Each morning, a prison cleaning detail deposited collected waste in the enclosed area of the deadline that extended into the bay from the beaches. Prisoner Luther Hopkins of the 6th Virginia Cavalry remembered that when men were swimming in the bay, they would take advantage of "any empty barrel or box that happened to be floating by." A prisoner would wait for his chance to slip beneath one, hoping not to be noticed by a guard. He would then float out "with the tide as the container drifted up the bay . . . The prisoner would then keep near the shoreline until he got beyond the line of guards and pickets and then make his escape."[12]

According to prisoner accounts, alarm bells were located in the guards' quarters north of the 5th New Hampshire camp on the Chesapeake Bay side of the point. Rumor held that these noisemakers were attached to a series of wires, spaced apart and extending from the beach into the water, anchored by stakes driven into the seabed. Their reported purpose was to alert the guards to the presence of prisoners attempting escape along the beach. Prisoner Barry Benson claimed that during his escape he passed the guards' quarters when he saw a stake in the water. "Curiosity prompted me to find out whether there were really any wires as [a prison acquaintance] had said. I waded up to it, felt all around and found there were no wires." Simon Seward of the 13th Virginia Cavalry stated that during his escape he passed outside the blockhouse, where the guards had

11 Letter by Wells, 31.

12 Hopkins, *From Bull Run to Appomattox*, 95.

allegedly strung wires connected to bells in the guardhouse on shore. Neither Seward nor any other escapee reported encountering such an obstacle during their escape along the Chesapeake Bay side of the point.[13]

Prison authorities placed a "calcium light" on the bay shoreline to detect activity after dark. This spotlight allowed the guards to illuminate the beach at night whenever prisoner movement was suspected outside the stockade. To further aid visibility, lamps or lanterns were positioned on both the external and internal sides of the stockade fence at intervals of about 50 yards. These lights provided the illumination necessary for the guards to monitor the prison interior, highlight suspected nighttime activity, and watch the deadline areas.[14]

Prisoners devised a clever, though elaborate, means of escape by assuming the identity of another inmate or even a deceased prisoner. If successful, they could literally walk out of Point Lookout undetected by the provost marshal. The ruse generally involved adopting the name of a deceased prisoner, often someone who had lived in a company several streets away. A prisoner would take note of the man's name, regiment, and company in the Confederate army, then patiently wait for that name to be called for an exchange. At that point, he would step forward and take the man's place.

The practice of assuming another's identity was common, though if discovered, the impersonator was returned to confinement. This stratagem required considerable cunning, patience, and planning; yet the risk of detection and punishment was considerably less than that faced by tunneling. One prisoner observed, "There were some . . . who had rather stay [in prison]; they dreaded the fighting that might come again." When such a man was called out for exchange, another would assume his identity. The "substitute" would answer all pertinent questions of identification in the hope that the deception would succeed. "When the man's name was called," one escapee reported, "[I] replied and quickly answered the necessary questions. The officer in charge said, 'pass out.' The scheme had worked."[15]

Methods of soldier identification during the Civil War were virtually non-existent, which made verification difficult. A prisoner's own word, and perhaps the testimony of acquaintances who knew him, formed the primary basis of identification in prison. When a prisoner presented himself to a clerk, it was generally assumed that the information he provided was correct and accurate. If the

13 Benson, *Berry Benson's Civil War Book*, 93–95; Seward, "Perilous Escape," in *Confederate Veteran*, 19:42.

14 Everson, Papers No. 28/710/22, 35.

15 Beitzell, *Point Lookout Prison Camp for Confederates*, 98.

number of men matched the number ordered to be transferred or exchanged, the requirement was considered fulfilled. The information offered by the prisoner—name, rank, and regiment—whether true or false, was typically accepted. In this way, a man could walk out of prison without lifting a shovel or risking a guard's bullet. If the attempt failed the first time, it was not unusual for prisoners to try the ploy several times until they achieved release or transfer.

Prisoners competed for assignment to the work details that took them outside the prison stockade. Such duties not only provided opportunities to gather items that might make life inside more tolerable but also offered potential avenues of escape. Prisoner George Tanner of the Richmond Hussars, Cobb's Legion recalled being on a detail outside the stockade when he "saw a very good chance to escape by going out on this [firewood] detail . . . dressed myself in a Yankee uniform, threw a blanket around me to hide it." Once beyond the Federal picket line, "I handed a friend my blanket and turned right round and made out like I was a Yankee going back to camp. The guard did not halt me; they were marching one way and I the other . . . I soon found friends to put me across the Potomac."[16]

Using the crowded beach as a diversion, prisoners sometimes distracted the guards while others buried themselves in the sand. Each evening a bugle signaled prisoners to return from the beach to the stockade, closing it for the day. A squad of guards, bayonets fixed, then advanced in a skirmish line along the shore, stabbing the sand in search of anyone who might have concealed himself in the soft layers to attempt escape. One prisoner recalled being hidden in this way with the help of fellow inmates who "diverted the attention of the guard," while they concealed the fact that "one of them dug a hole in the soft sand and buried himself, being carefully covered by the rest, and leaving only an aperture to breathe through." After he was buried, the others dispersed, leaving him to "work out his plan as best he could."[17]

## Overcrowding and a Breakout

As the number of prisoners increased, the possibility of a mass breakout became a major concern for the authorities. As early as October 1863, Marston discovered that the prisoners were planning just such an attempt. The chronic shortage of guards was, and would remain, a constant problem throughout the life of the prison. His existing force was not large enough to prevent a mass escape. As a precaution, Marston ordered that prisoners were no longer permitted to

16 Ibid., 149; Styple, *Writing and Fighting from the Army of Northern Virginia*, 273.

17 Seward, "An Escape," 42; Allen, *Forty-Six Months with the Fourth Rhode Island Volunteers*, 269.

gather in groups of three or more, hoping thereby to reduce the chance of guards being overpowered.[18]

Following this directive, Hoffman soon ordered that prisons implement a nighttime roving guard to patrol the prison streets, ensuring security and compliance with regulations—particularly the rule requiring all prisoners to remain quiet after taps and inside their shelters until reveille. Corporal Allen of the 4th Rhode Island recalled that their orders were to maintain security and keep the camp quiet throughout the night. The patrols were authorized to fire at "the least sign of insubordination" by the prisoners. Typically, the guards entered the pen quietly "about 9 o'clock at night and came out at daybreak the next morning."[19]

The guards considered these nighttime patrols the most dangerous assignment. Outnumbered, they could easily be overwhelmed by the massive prison population should the inmates attempt a breakout. This knowledge was disconcerting to the roving guards, especially since their only means of defense were single-shot rifles and bayonets. Such limited weapons left them vulnerable to attack by overwhelming numbers of desperate men. The placement of nighttime roving guards within the prison only temporarily addressed the problem.[20]

Concerned with the vulnerability of the guards, Hoffman sent a communication in November 1863 to the secretary of war recommending that the nighttime prison patrols be armed with revolvers instead of single-shot rifles. The increased firepower, he argued, would allow a guard to better defend himself if several prisoners attempted to overpower him. Hoffman noted that a guard armed with a revolver "gives him the strength of two or three men without such arms." He further recommended that "400 revolvers, with accoutrements complete, and 25,000 rounds of ammunition be sent" to the prisons. Point Lookout was designated to receive 200 revolvers and 10,000 rounds of ammunition, with all accoutrements. Soon thereafter, the night guards at all prisons—including those at Point Lookout, who were also issued cutlasses—were armed with revolvers for their defense.[21]

When news of a suspected breakout attempt in December reached Hoffman, he recommended to Stanton that a battery of artillery be added to the guard force at Point Lookout. Accordingly, Battery F, 1st Rhode Island Artillery, was detached on December 23, 1863, sailing from Yorktown, Virginia, and landing

18 Haynes, *A Soldier Boy's Letters*, 143.

19 Allen, *Forty-Six Months with the Fourth Rhode Island Volunteers*, 263.

20 Ibid., 263–264.

21 *OR* 6/2:584.

the next day at Point Lookout. A few weeks later, the 2nd Battery, Wisconsin Independent Light Artillery, arrived to relieve Battery F. Authorities expected that the addition of artillery would compensate for the Federal guard force's lack of small arms. Prison officials strategically positioned artillery to provide crossfire on the prison as well as coverage of all land approaches to the peninsula. Although the Federal government operated only the approximate 400 acres containing the prison and hospital, they were effectively defending the entire peninsula and its approaches, measuring five miles wide by six miles long, to the lighthouse.

When rumors of another possible breakout surfaced, Captain Bartlett recorded that patrols, mounted and on foot, "patrolled at night and the gunboat squadron has been reinforced until we now have ten vessels here ready for any emergency." Bartlett further worried that, "though armed, [if the guards were] taken by surprise [prisoners] would have had more than even chances of exchanging the fortunes of war and making prisoner of those who were guarding them."[22]

At no time during the operation of Point Lookout was the guard force adequate to control thousands of prisoners or to prevent the possibility of a mass breakout. For extended periods, the prisoner-to-guard ratio stood at no less than eight to ten prisoners for every guard. Escaped prisoners could also count on assistance from citizens of southern Maryland, as Point Lookout was bordered to the north by three counties—Charles, Calvert, and Prince George's—where pro-secessionist sentiment was strong. For this reason, on several occasions Stanton deferred the transfer of additional Confederate prisoners to Point Lookout. In his view, it was neither safe nor prudent to confine so many thousands of enemy soldiers in an area so close to Southern-leaning counties, neighboring slave states, and the nation's capital. His one assurance, though questionable, was that Point Lookout lay firmly behind Union lines. Even so, a mass breakout nearly came to fruition in early February 1864.

By the opening months of 1864, conditions at Point Lookout had deteriorated to such an extent that the prisoners resolved they would no longer endure them. Foul water, reduced rations, disease, lack of firewood, and inadequate shelter were more than they could bear, and men continued to die under these conditions. To prison authorities, this prospect was more alarming than any escape attempt by tunnel or by assumed identity. The camp stood on the verge of a forced breakout—a collective, organized assault by desperate men against a minimal guard force.

Confederate officers were confined within the Hammond Hospital complex, including one of the two boarding houses or the general hospital itself. They

22 Chase, *Battery F, First Regiment Rhode Island Light Artillery*, 114; Bartlett, *History of the Twelfth Regiment New Hampshire Volunteers*, 148, 153.

were sequestered from the Confederate enlisted men to prevent communication between the two groups, in accordance with regulations. In February 1864, the officers were relocated to the newly constructed pen assigned to them, with the transfer completed by March 21. Because of the proximity of the two prisons and their inmates, officials remained on constant alert for schemes to organize a mass breakout. The problems of overcrowding and the threat of escape were resolved sooner than anticipated, and largely by chance.[23]

Confederate officers quickly took advantage of the proximity of both the enlisted and officer prison pens. They devised a system of communication by tying messages to rocks and tossing them over the stockade walls from one pen to the other. In February 1864, despite the apparent success of this method, one evening a message thrown from the officers' pen fell short of its intended target and landed on the open wagon road that separated the two stockades.

The errant message was recovered by a vigilant guard and immediately delivered to the commanding officer of Point Lookout. This discovery confirmed what prison officials had long suspected and feared: Confederate officers were organizing a breakout of all prisoners. Informants further verified rumors of an all-out attempt by approximately 9,000 prisoners to overpower the garrison. Federal authorities recognized the severity of such a plot and its potential consequences.[24]

Eyewitness accounts from the guard force testified that prison authorities reacted swiftly to the threat. The post command could take some assurance from the fact that the force on hand included a substantial number of combat veterans and was led by a corps of experienced officers. The artillery pieces protecting the garrison were capable of inflicting heavy casualties with each discharge should a breakout occur. A successful escape would have required great determination and heavy losses on the part of the prisoners. The guard force soon gave the prisoners the appearance of being aware that something was developing. Before the plan could be realized, prison officials acted immediately by conducting a surprise inspection of the camp to thwart the plot at its outset. The men of the 2nd and 12th New Hampshire were ordered to the prison with loaded muskets to oversee operations while all prisoners were marched out of their quarters. A thorough inspection of shelters then followed. Federal accounts state that two pieces of artillery, double-shotted with canister, were placed outside the prison gate "so as

23 Evans Atwood, Evans Atwood Diary, 1861, SMC-004-005, Evans Atwood Diary, Arkansas State Archives, Little Rock, AR.

24 Everson, Papers No. 28/710/22, 6.

to sweep the gateway while the prisoners were all marched out of their quarters a company at a time."[25]

The inspection revealed that a tunnel had been dug "nearly to the outside of the stockade," disguised as one of the clay pits excavated in camp for brick making. After the discovery, brick making, which had been flourishing, was prohibited by prison authorities and all brick pits were converted into prisoner latrines.[26]

As a result of the inspection, prison authorities reported that they had recovered several muskets. (One Federal statement estimated that 75 muskets were recovered. It remained a mystery to the authorities how the prisoners had acquired them. However, no mention was made of any required accoutrements being recovered with the muskets.) Several bunks were discovered to be boats whose "sides and cracks [were] filled with grease and soap to render them watertight." Searchers also found parts of Federal uniforms hidden in prisoner shelters. With the exception of the muskets, all items were destroyed, including the tunnel. Some regimental officers believed that less scrupulous substitutes from the New Hampshire regiments may have supplied the weapons and uniforms to the conspirators.[27]

Officials sought a solution to prevent further breakout attempts on such a scale. At the conclusion of this incident, procedures were modified to increase the vigilance of the guards. Prison authorities maintained a heightened state of alert due to the ever-growing prison population. Efforts to secure Point Lookout, despite the reduced guard force, were intensified to protect against a repeat attempt. Many of the incoming prisoners were recent captures from the battlefields and remained physically capable of resisting prison authority. The persistent problem for the garrison force was that it was seldom sufficient in number to resist thousands of prisoners should an attack or breakout occur.

General James Barnes, soon issued a standing order that if at least one rifle shot was fired between sundown and sunrise, the "long roll" was to be beaten for all troops to assemble on the "color line" with rifles and equipment, "without regard to appearances." As the population grew, this order was later modified to apply at all hours, day and night. By this time, a minimum of 160 men stood guard at the prison, including its catwalks, main gate, and auxiliary areas. Under this order, guards were permitted to fire into the prison if prisoners attempted to escape.[28]

25 Bartlett, *History of the Twelfth Regiment New Hampshire Volunteers*, 149.

26 Ibid., 149.

27 Haynes, *A History of the Second Regiment New Hampshire Volunteer Infantry*, 204.

28 Everson, Papers No. 28/710/22, 8; Bowditch, Family Papers, Aug. 7, 1864.

Federal authorities recognized the severity of escape threats and their potential consequences. This reality was also understood by the government in Richmond. In the months following the breakout attempt, Secretary of War Stanton ordered Hoffman to conduct a personal inspection of conditions at Point Lookout. In his report, Hoffman particularly emphasized the overcrowded state of the prison. By May 1864, the prison population was approaching 13,000 prisoners, far exceeding the planned 10,000-man capacity established in the construction of the enlisted stockade.

Hoffman reported that, in accordance with regulations, Confederate officers were kept in a separate stockade from the enlisted men, but in his opinion, too much space had been allotted to the few officers held there. He therefore recommended that the officers be transferred elsewhere. Such a transfer would allow at least one of the two stockade walls dividing the pens to be removed, thereby incorporating the two prisons into one. Including the space of the separating wagon road would further enlarge the enlisted pen, potentially easing the overcrowding problem.[29]

Stanton ordered the move, with Hoffman expeditiously sending instructions to Colonel Draper that all Confederate officers fit for the voyage be immediately transferred. On June 24, 1864, approximately 656 Confederate officers were sent from Point Lookout to Fort Delaware. This transfer not only frustrated further plots by the officers to plan escapes but, more importantly, added eight much-needed acres in which to relocate the prison hospital. The move created additional space in the enlisted prison for new divisional streets. The consolidation of the two stockades alleviated overcrowding in the enlisted prison, at least temporarily.[30]

## The Attack on Point Lookout

In June 1864, Point Lookout underwent another administrative change. It was removed from the Department of Virginia and North Carolina under Butler's command and placed under the command of Maj. Gen. Christopher C. Augur, commanding the XXII Corps, responsible for the defenses of Washington. Augur considered Point Lookout part of those defenses following the transfer of authority. By July 1864, a higher level of vigilance was ordered at Point Lookout than had been in effect earlier in the year. Federal authorities were receiving intelligence regarding a possible Rebel attack on Point Lookout to release the prisoners held there. A prominent Richmond newspaper, *The Richmond Times-*

29 *OR* 7/2:154.

30 Ibid., 389; Keiley, *In Vinculis*, 96.

*Dispatch,* had somehow obtained information about the raid and published it before the opening movements of the campaign.[31]

It was further reported that the attack would be conducted in conjunction with Confederate Gen. Jubal Early's raid into Maryland. By July 2, 1864, Brig. Gen. James Barnes arrived to assume command of Point Lookout, relieving Colonel Draper, who immediately returned to command the 36th U.S.C.T. On July 8, Augur began taking precautions, sending a telegram to Barnes stating that Butler had reported the possibility of an attack and further adding, "that a rebel deserter reports that Early intends, among other things, to attack Point Lookout and release the prisoners there."[32]

As a precautionary measure, Augur ordered cavalry patrols on July 5, 1864, to range into southern Maryland in search of "anything like small bodies of cavalry (rebels) going down that way [towards Point Lookout] and to see that the telegraph line is not disturbed." Augur also instructed Barnes to be "on his guard" and to "notify the gun-boats and keep some of your cavalry well out." At the same time, Secretary of the Navy Gideon Welles ordered Cdr. Foxhall A. Parker, commander of the Potomac River Flotilla patrolling that region, to "take additional precautions relative to covering the camp of prisoners at Point Lookout and its approaches by your gunboats."[33]

On July 12, Hoffman arrived at Point Lookout to inspect Barnes's defensive preparations and to assure the War Department that the "command of Point Lookout is in safe hands, and that all proper measures will be taken for the safety of the post and the security of the prisoners." Hoffman reviewed the defenses established by Barnes and recorded his recommendations. To deprive the attacking force of potential reinforcements should the assault achieve any measure of success, Hoffman ordered Barnes to begin reducing the prison population, which at that time held just under 15,000 prisoners, by transferring inmates to the newly opened prison at Elmira, New York.[34]

It did not take an experienced officer such as Barnes long to begin strengthening his vigilance and defenses. He reported to Augur that he was working in conjunction with naval forces from the Potomac River Flotilla, noting that two additional gunboats had been on patrol around the point the previous

31 James H. Bruns, *Crosshairs on the Capital. Jubal Early's Raid on Washington, D.C., July 1864—Reasons, Reactions, and Results* (Havertown, PA, 2021), 175.

32 *OR* 40/1:3:90.

33 *OR* 37/1:2:62; *OR* 40/1:3:90; United States, Naval War Records Office, comp., *War of the Rebellion: Official Records of the Union and Confederate Navies* (Washington, D.C., 1894), 10:458.

34 *OR* 7/1:462; *Book No. 254,* 93.

night and that he had extended the defenses of Point Lookout to all possible approaches. He also readjusted the positions of his guard forces, and his fieldworks were significantly expanded by adding an outer picket force and digging a chain of rifle pits. Regardless of these efforts, as late as July 15, 1864, Barnes remained concerned about his lack of defenders. Approximately 1,000 men of the 36th U.S.C.T., who had formed a major part of his guard force, had been transferred to Yorktown the previous June. They were soon replaced by the arrival of the 5th Massachusetts (Colored) Cavalry, now dismounted and serving as infantry. Barnes also reported that he had lost an additional "[t]hree hundred and thirty men with eleven officers" who had been detailed as guards for the prisoners he was transferring to Elmira. He concluded by stating, "It leaves me rather short."[35]

Apparently, General Lee was relying on outdated intelligence regarding the defensive works and the troops stationed at Point Lookout. He presumed that "most of the garrison at Point Lookout was composed of negroes. I should suppose that the commander of such troops would be poor and feeble. A stubborn resistance, therefore, may not reasonably be expected." By this time, however, the 1,000 men of the 5th Massachusetts (Colored) Cavalry and their officers had already experienced combat around Petersburg, Virginia.[36]

Neither Lee nor Early knew that elements of the VI and XIX Corps had recently sailed past Point Lookout on their way to defend Washington against Early's attack. These same elements, or portions of them, could readily backtrack either to defend Point Lookout or to cut off the two main routes leading into Point Lookout, thereby blocking Johnson on his return march north should he reach southern Maryland.

Recently promoted to brigadier general, Bradley Johnson was assigned by his commanding officer, Maj. Gen. Jubal Early, to command the raid into Maryland. Lee believed that Bradley, a native of Maryland, could rally the various pro-secessionist factions of southern Maryland to aid him in his rescue attempt on Point Lookout. Nevertheless, he informed Early that he regarded his assigned task as "utterly impossible for man or horse to accomplish," since he had been given only four days to disrupt communications, railroads, and to free the prisoners at Point Lookout. The plan envisioned that once Brig. Gen. Bradley Johnson freed the prisoners, they would march north, where he expected his new force to be "armed and equipped from the arsenals and magazines of Washington."

35 *OR* 40/1:3:275.

36 *OR* 37/1:1:767.

They were then to reinforce Early on campaign. Despite the long odds, Johnson resolved that he "would do what was possible for men to do" in the time allowed. Before attempting to move into southern Maryland, he deployed scouts to St. Mary's County to observe the roads and potential enemy forces there. He likely recognized that riding deep into southern Maryland and returning by the same roads would present serious risks for his command.[37]

The timetable Early had given to Johnson, along with the timing of his attack and return, would be crucial factors in the success of the venture, and a considerable amount of coordination was required for such an undertaking. There was no way

37 Bradley Johnson, "My Ride around Baltimore in 1864," in *Southern Historical Society Papers*, ed. R. A. Brock (Richmond, VA, 1902), 30:218.

for Johnson to know that Point Lookout was already on alert. The approach of such a force would be detected well before he reached striking distance.

Even if he succeeded in liberating the prison, additional time would be required to organize the return march of thousands of men whose physical condition, whether on foot or horseback, was unknown to him. Certainly, the sick and wounded would have to remain behind, and provisions to care for the mass of starving prisoners on the move would also have to be considered.

It may also be assumed that Federal forces would have moved to cut off his retreat, since no bridges existed to allow his command to cross the Potomac into Virginia from Point Lookout. These factors, among others, contributed to Johnson's reluctance to undertake this part of his mission.[38]

Additionally, other troops assigned to the defense of Point Lookout included the men of the 5th Massachusetts (Colored) Cavalry, the 11th and 20th Veteran Reserve Corps, the 4th Rhode Island, and the 139th Ohio Volunteer Militia, which had arrived in May 1864. Companies A and C of the 10th V.R.C. were also present, along with the men of the 2nd Wisconsin Independent Battery. These additions brought the number of available effectives to approximately 2,100. Barnes's defenses also included eight pieces of artillery, positioned not only to defend Point Lookout from attack but also trained upon the prison as a deterrent against escape attempts. In addition, companies of both the 2nd and 5th U.S. Cavalry were posted about 20 miles north, in Leonardtown, as a provost force. Barnes increased the assigned cavalry detachment from 20 mounted men to 80, extending their range further into St. Mary's County under Hoffman's orders.

Lee could not have known that the Potomac River Flotilla (Potomac Squadron), along with elements of the U.S. Navy's North Atlantic Blockading Squadron, had also been placed on alert. On the evening of July 14, Barnes reported to Stanton that there were "Five gun-boats on duty last night" at Point Lookout. These included the USS *R.R. Cuyler* (10 guns), USS *Massasoit* (10 guns), the newly commissioned USS *Saco* (11 guns), USS *Mackinaw* (10 guns), and the USS *Minnesota* (41–44 guns). In total, more than 80 naval cannon of various calibers were available and on station for the defense of Point Lookout. As the *Minnesota* drew too much water, she soon returned to her regular station in the Chesapeake Bay and the Atlantic Ocean, once the USS *Roanoke*, a six-gun triple-turret ironclad, arrived on July 25, 1864, to take her place off Point Lookout.[39]

38 Ibid., 225.

39 *OR* 40/1:3:222, 251.

To further reduce the area requiring defense, Barnes consolidated his forces. He ordered the only unit remaining outside the fortified areas of Point Lookout, the 5th Massachusetts Cavalry, to relocate its camp within the protection of the two stockade walls guarding the approaches to Point Lookout, south of Point Lookout Creek.

In preparation, the naval gunboats began training their heavy guns on the approaches to Point Lookout, firing from both the bay and the river. Captain Charles Bowditch of the 5th Massachusetts Cavalry recorded on July 15, 1864, that he had been told they would have to move their camp closer to the prison, as a sizable force of Rebels was rumored to be approaching Point Lookout down the peninsula, "and, as the gunboats wanted to shell across the place where our camp was, the only thing to do was move our camp." The massive steam frigate, USS *Minnesota*, "has steamed up abreast the fortification [prison] and is prepared to throw broadsides into any rebs that may appear."[40]

The Johnson-Gilmor raid, as it later came to be known, never reached as far south as Point Lookout. Both Johnson and Major Harry Gilmor were ordered to return to Early's army by July 12, aborting the rescue attempt. Approximately two weeks later, Barnes once again ordered the 5th Massachusetts (Colored) Cavalry to move farther down the Point. On August 6, Bowditch recorded "that they are building defenses around here, and are going to rout us out of this camp to build a fort."[41]

## How Many Escapes?

Final statistics, as recorded in the *War of the Rebellion: Official Records of the Union and Confederate Armies,* show that, according to monthly returns, Point Lookout reported 50 prisoner escapes between July 1863 and June 1865. The highest number of escapes in a single month was 12, recorded in December 1863. No escapes were reported from January through April 1864, likely due to the heightened state of alert imposed by prison authorities following the attempted mass breakout in February of that year. Two escapes were reported in March 1865, with no further escapes after that month. Overall, the trend shows an increase in escapes between May and October 1864, followed by a decline from November

40 Bowditch, Family Papers, July 15, 1864.

41 Ibid., Aug. 6, 1864.

1864 through February 1865. No records were kept of the many failed attempts, so it is impossible to contextualize the data we do have.[42]

There are two likely explanations for the absence of reported escapes between November 1864 and February 1865. The first was the seasonal conditions, notably, the winter of 1864, one of the harshest in years. The shoreline of the Chesapeake Bay was often covered with ice extending several yards into the water, and the bay's temperature by then would have been near freezing. The Potomac River was generally frozen during the winter, and keeping the shipping channels open was a continual challenge for vessels and their crews traveling to and from Point Lookout.

The second explanation may lie in the prison administration's lack of proper record keeping. Prisoners often employed ingenious methods to manipulate the system in their favor. False identities and the substitution of one man for another would undoubtedly have affected the numbers submitted in the monthly returns. Of the approximate 52,000 prisoners who passed through the prison gate at Point Lookout, it is doubtful that such a small number of reported escapes represents an accurate accounting. Regardless of the security measures imposed by the prison or the heightened vigilance of the guard force, the figure appears unusually low for a facility that at one point held more than 22,000 prisoners guarded by a reduced force of no more than 2,000 men.

Despite these considerations, thousands of prisoners came within a hair's breadth of escaping from Point Lookout on two separate occasions. Had either breakout succeeded, the consequences for Northern morale could have been devastating. The release of thousands of prisoners in secessionist southern Maryland, behind Union lines, would have created chaos for the Lincoln administration and undermined the morale of Federal forces. Moreover, such an event might have triggered a ripple effect, inspiring prisoners in other camps to attempt similar breakouts once the news spread.

The motivations behind the February breakout attempt remained unchanged even after the revolt was thwarted. The fortunate interception of the communication by a lone Union guard demonstrated that prison authorities had come close to catastrophic disaster. Those with the power to implement reforms at Point Lookout did little to improve conditions despite having narrowly survived the crisis. Few improvements to prison life were made, and conditions in fact worsened following an ordered reduction in prisoner rations. To the already deplorable environment was added the constant fear of being shot by a guard

42 *OR* 8/2:991.

with little provocation. With the arrival of additional Black infantry units, life for prisoners of war at Point Lookout descended into a continual nightmare.

Throughout the existence of the prison at Point Lookout, inmates endured the debilitating conditions of confinement through various means of their own. Ill treatment by the guard force was no exception to the challenges they faced in their struggle for survival. It must be remembered that this was war, and they were prisoners of that war. Such treatment, therefore, was not unexpected.

However, limits were set by the regulating *Lieber Code* regarding the penalties permitted and measures allowed. Even so, infractions by prisoners at Point Lookout were swiftly punished, as in any other prison. It would have been unrealistic for prisoners to expect kind or humane treatment from the guards, particularly given the constant animosity fueled by racial tensions and the political divisions between the two warring factions. Although some accounts describe occasional acts of kindness by the guards, more often prisoners faced punishments: the "ball and chain," suspension by the thumbs, even death from a jumpy guard's bullet.

## Chapter 9

# Prisoner Treatment and Shootings

---

Prisoners could be the target of guards enforcing prison regulations beyond their intent and official duty. Frequent acts of retribution prompted commanding officers of Point Lookout to revise standing general orders and regulations to curb violations committed by the guard force. Despite varied testimonies, most prisoners generally agreed that treatment by the guards, both Black and White, particularly by Black soldiers, could at times be brutal, and harsh. This is unsurprising, given that a substantial number of the guards had formerly been enslaved.

However, what has often been forgotten by those who recorded guard abuse is that this was war, and they were prisoners of that war, subject to the treatment of their captors. Nevertheless, guards often demonstrated what any fair observer would identify as excessive measures.

Section III of the *Lieber Code* contains approximately 33 articles directed toward the treatment of prisoners of war. Incidents of abusive treatment by the Federal guard force at Point Lookout clearly violated Articles 28, 56, and 75. Specific articles stated that no revenge was to be taken against prisoners with the intent of causing bodily harm, disgrace, cruelty, or any other barbarity. A prisoner could be confined or imprisoned to assure him of his safety but was subject to no further misery or indignity. Retaliation was to be undertaken only if an act was proven to warrant and justify such a response.[1]

Some prisoners recalled occasional acts of kindness, but such incidents were rare. It was often assumed that soldiers, even on opposing sides, might feel a sense of camaraderie from the shared experience of battle, but many prisoners

1 *OR* 3/3: General Order No. 100, Articles 28, 56, and 75.

at Point Lookout discovered this was not the case. Prisoner William Flinn of the 17th Mississippi wrote that "The guard generally treated the prisoners badly—especially if the guards themselves had been soldiers on the battlefield." Private George C. Tanner of Cobb's Legion wrote that the treatment he received from the guards was generally as he expected. Even so, he dreaded the soldiers of the 12th New Hampshire in particular, as "They never let the prisoners know their orders . . . They would soon let you know, however, by sending a ball after you." Some shootings by White guards were committed by substitutes or draftees rather than veterans. Some seemed intent on shooting a Confederate, reasoning that it was safer to do so from the prison wall than on the battlefield.[2]

Sergeant James Wells of the 2nd South Carolina attributed his mistreatment to the Federal government. "As a general rule, the treatment by the White soldiers was not so bad and it would have been much better had it not been for the cruelty of the Gov[ernment] and the stringent orders to have that policy carried out." Wells did not specify what policy he referred to. His assertion appears speculative, as he did not explain how he became aware of such a policy, if it indeed existed. By contrast, many prisoners attributed a greater share of mistreatment to retribution carried out by the formerly enslaved now serving in the U.S. Army. Some believed that the former slaves were deliberately using their new authority over Southern prisoners as a means of retaliation for their prior condition.[3]

The arrival of the first U.S.C.T. units was met with intense resentment by the thousands of Confederate prisoners held at Point Lookout. Many prisoners regarded this as a deliberate insult by the Lincoln administration, intended as retaliation for the mistreatment of Union prisoners in the South. Prisoners wrote of their resentment at the arrival of Black infantry soldiers, stating that it "caused a good deal of indignation." One astonished prisoner wrote, "They were the first black soldiers I had seen," and as they replaced the White guards, he added, "It was a bitter pill for Southern men to swallow, and we felt the insult very keenly. They were impudent and tyrannical, and the prisoners had to submit [to] many indignities."[4]

Luther Hopkins of the 6th Virginia Cavalry described the shared animosities of his fellow prisoners, stating, "I think that there were about 15,000 prisoners at this camp guarded by Black troops which made our Southern blood boil . . .

2 Flinn, "A Southern Soldier's Experience in a Northern Prison," 29–30; Styple, *Writing and Fighting from the Army of Northern Virginia*, 273.

3 Letter by Wells, 27; Bryant, *The 36th Infantry United States Colored Troops in the Civil War*, 80–81.

4 Drake, *The Annals of the Army of Tennessee and Early Western History*, 1:271; Holliday, "Vain Efforts for Avoid Prison," in *Confederate Veteran*, 28:383.

The bottom rail had got on top." The guards often warned the Southerners not to cross the deadline or approach the stockade wall, "or they would shoot." This was commonly followed by the taunt, "the bottom rail be on top now," referring to the fact that the former slave was now in authority over the Southern soldier. Prisoners dreaded the third day of the guard rotation, knowing that on this day Black guards would be assigned to duty.[5]

It angered the prisoners to look up at the former slaves who now paced the stockade catwalk above them. This not only incensed many of them but also deepened their animosity toward the Federal government. Private Jarrett Morgan of the 4th U.S.C.T. recalled, "I had to walk back and forth on a high scaffolding from which I could look down upon them. They did look terrible. Filthy, dirty, ragged, starved, miserable." By the time of their transfer—less than a month in April 1864—the regimental historian claimed that they had not shot a prisoner for any offense while stationed at Point Lookout. This was, indeed, a rare occurrence.[6]

As time passed, animosity between the Black guards and White prisoners intensified. Wells recalled a pitiful scene when "[a] negro sentry . . . one hot afternoon fell off the parapet and broke his neck. He was immediately surrounded by a parcel of the bathers [prisoners] who danced around his corpse." The crowd was soon dispersed by a squad from the guard. One prisoner, Anthony Keiley of the 12th Virginia, ran afoul of the guard while attempting to cook his meager meat ration. Keiley claimed that while small fires were permitted along the beach on the bay side to heat water for washing clothes, he had built a fire to "cook the raw meat we were furnished with at the mess room." A guard soon warned him to put out the fire "or I'll put you out dam quick" and "convinced me of the propriety of obedience by certain manipulations of his musket."[7]

The issue of revolvers to the guards who patrolled the prison during the evening hours caused further anxiety among the prisoners. Lieutenant Everson complained to Barnes of the "carelessness of the patrol and other armed parties" that entered the prison pen at night. For a time, standing orders required the entire garrison to turn out if any weapons were discharged between sunset and sunrise. According to Everson, "the guard of the 20th V.R.C. has been turned out

5 Hopkins, *From Bull Run to Appomattox*, 94; Kimmel and Musick, *I Am Busy Drawing Pictures*, 92; Letter by Wells, 19.

6 Longacre, *A Regiment of Slaves*, 65.

7 Letter by Wells, 41–42; Keiley, *In Vinculis*, 97.

The bottom rail on top. *Point Lookout State Park Collection*

Present-day view from stockade catwalk. *Author*

and the regiment aroused nearly every night through the carelessness of the patrol in their discharging of their revolvers."[8]

Many prisoner accounts report that the Black guard units patrolling the camp at night were more than diligent, often carrying out their duties beyond the scope of their instructions. Acts of harassment by the Black guards against the prisoners became commonplace and were carried out at nearly every opportunity. Freeman Jones of the 56th Virginia stated with perhaps a bit more innocence than the case warranted, "We did not object [to] having colored soldiers guard over us on the regular posts, but when they were sent to patrol the camp at night . . . [n]o man was allowed to show his head out at night no matter how urgent his business." George Peyton of the 13th Virginia, wrote, "the negro patrol made several men pray for old Abe last night. At 9 o'clock all lights must be out . . . the negroes come in and march up one street and go down the other . . . if they catch a

8 *Book No. 258*, Endorsements Sent, Mar. 1864–July 1865, Register of Letters Received, Jan. 1864–July 1865, General Orders and Special Orders Received, 1864, Register of Orders Received, Registers of Applications for Furloughs and Discharges, Oct. 1863–Apr. 1864, 38.

prisoner on the street, they make him double quick up and down the street or do something else."[9]

Private John J. Omenhausser of the 46th Virginia, known for his watercolor portrayals of prison life, recorded many scenes of alleged mistreatment in the portfolios he produced during his confinement. Abuses committed by the Black guards were the subject of several renderings, which depicted prisoners carrying Black guards on their backs, prisoners double-timing in place at gunpoint, and prisoners forced to kneel and pray for the president of the United States. By contrast, no surviving Omenhausser picture contains renderings of physical abuse or harassment by the White guards, even though such incidents certainly occurred.[10]

Lieutenant Everson could not ignore the abuses he witnessed by the Black soldiers against their charges. He recorded in his diary,

> another outrage had been practiced sometime before being discovered[,] was to force prisoners in their night garments to climb the rickety chimneys built of mud and sticks, of their huts and tents and to kneel upon them . . . and pray for the President of the United States and the welfare of the Union.[11]

Eventually, the Black guards were removed from after-hours patrol duty. In an order dated December 2, 1864, Barnes directed Colonel Henry S. Russell, commanding officer of the 5th Massachusetts (Colored) Cavalry, to discontinue his regiment's participation in the night patrols. From that point forward, the night patrols were conducted by the newly organized guard of the provost marshal.[12]

Not long after the removal of the 5th Massachusetts (Colored) Cavalry from the night patrol, Colonel Russell received another order from General Barnes, informing him that the complement of troops he was to provide for the grand guard each day would be reduced. This was followed by another order directing that the 50 men of the 5th Massachusetts Cavalry detailed to the mounted patrol stationed at nearby Leonardtown were to be relieved of this duty as well. Barnes had apparently grown weary of the complaints registered against the men of the 5th Massachusetts.[13]

9 Jones, "Addendum to an Escape from Point Lookout," 85; Peyton, *A Civil Record for 1864–1865*, 106.

10 Kimmel and Musick, *I Am Busy Drawing Pictures*, 93–95, 98.

11 Everson, Narrative and Personal Notes, 8.

12 *Book No. 255*, 289.

13 *Book No. 255*. 323, 325.

By the end of the war, all White guard units had been transferred from Point Lookout, either back to their home states for discharge or to Louisiana and Texas in response to the possible invasion of the United States from Mexico under Emperor Maximilian, the Austrian archduke. Companies from several other U.S.C.T. units were detached and sent to Point Lookout, where prison authorities deemed their presence necessary for the safety and security of both the garrison and the prison.

Despite frequent prisoner complaints of abusive treatment by the U.S.C.T., their use as guards continued until the official closing of Point Lookout. The inclusion of Black guards at Point Lookout from the beginning proved to be a challenge for successive commanders.[14]

## Prisoner Shootings

In a communication to Hoffman on June 10, 1864, Colonel Draper, commandant of Point Lookout and commanding officer of the 36th U.S.C.T., remarked, "I think the colored troops are the only guards from whom no prisoners have escaped, and they, as you are aware, are very prompt to use their pieces [rifles], perhaps too prompt."[15]

Prisoners were again prohibited from gathering in groups of more than three during the daytime. Further, in General Order No. 25, issued May 24, 1864, Draper directed that prisoners were strictly forbidden to gather outside their shelters after dark, nor were they permitted to pass "from tent to tent or to any other place than the night sinks [latrines]." If any prisoners violated this order and were seen outside their shelters after taps, sentinels were instructed to take into custody "any individuals violating this rule; and when the violation is by several persons, if persisted in after being distinctly warned, the sentinels will fire upon them, at the same time calling for the guard."[16]

Draper's directive was certainly an extension of basic guard procedure, but it apparently became necessary for him to elaborate the orders in such detail that little room was left for discretion by the guards. A review of prison records, diaries, and eyewitness accounts reveals that more shootings occurred than were officially reported during the war. Sergeant Bartlett Y. Malone of the 6th North Carolina alleged that there were several shootings by both Black and White guards

14 Everson, Narrative and Personal Notes, 7.

15 *Book No. 253*, 254.

16 *OR* 7/2:165–166.

Soldier of the United States Colored Infantry. *Library of Congress*

while he was at Point Lookout. Between November 1863 and August 1864, 19 prisoners were either killed or wounded by gunshots inflicted by the guards.[17]

There were instances in which guards fired at prisoners without inflicting casualties. It is certain that these incidents were investigated each time a guard discharged a firearm, as the sound of a weapon being fired immediately raised the alarm. However, such events were not recorded in the official reports of the prison when no casualties resulted. Private John W. Stevens of the 5th Texas recalled, "They shot frequently but missed more often than they hit." Regardless of the guards' accuracy, such incidents left prisoners wary and in continual fear of being shot, day and night.[18]

John King of the 25th Virginia stated,

> negroes who guarded us were not accustomed to having authority over the white people and the defenceless prisoners suffered at their hands. Numbers of scars were left on the frame work of the closets made by negroes firing at the prisoners. Often their threats became true . . . during the night, when they quarreled with some poor fellow who had displeased them, we in our tent hugged the ground very closely expecting to hear a bullet sing at any moment.[19]

17 Beitzell, *Point Lookout Prison Camp for Confederates*, 56–58.

18 Stevens, *Reminiscences of the Civil War*, 153.

19 King, *My Experience in the Confederate Army and in Northern Prisons*. Clarksburg, WV. 28.

Prisoner James Huffman of the 10th Virginia insisted that in one occurrence, a prisoner made the mistake of "getting to the edge of this Negro's beat, [and] the latter fired into the crowd, killing one man and wounding four or five others. 'I'll show you, I'll let you know,' were his exclamations. This happened right by my side." Firing into a crowd of prisoners as a means of control without any immediate threat is difficult to justify, yet such actions appear to have occurred. This act clearly violated the mandates of the *Lieber Code*.[20]

During his short tenure as prisoner at Point Lookout, Lt. Col. Edwin Drake, 4th Tennessee, recorded an incident that involved the guards from the 36th U.S.C.T.:

> One of the greatest horrors of our life here was the daily dread of being shot by the negro guards. I remember one day starting toward a group collecting around the detail then coming in, but before I reached the place a negro guard raised his musket and fired into the crowd; two of the party fell dead, and another was wounded . . . These guards were from North Carolina [36th U.S.C.T.] and claimed that their conduct was in retaliation for bad treatment from their former masters. Fifteen or twenty prisoners were killed or wounded by them during our stay . . . the slightest noise after tattoo . . . was sufficient to provoke a shot from the walls.[21]

Drake was imprisoned at Point Lookout for approximately two and a half months, from May 17, 1864, before being transferred to Elmira, New York, on July 30, 1864. This timeline suggests he may have embellished his claim of the shooting of "fifteen to twenty prisoners . . . during our stay." It appears that Drake may have concealed his rank and avoided reporting as an officer, as he was placed in the enlisted men's stockade. Since all officers at Point Lookout were housed in the adjacent prison, Drake could not have witnessed so many shootings if he had not been within the enlisted camp. Moreover, all officers were transferred to Fort Delaware by June 25, 1864, about a month before Drake claims to have been transferred to Elmira—a transfer that surely would have included him had he been residing in the officers' prison. Although his claim regarding the number of prisoners shot is disputable, his presence at Point Lookout cannot be denied.

20 Huffman, *Ups and Downs of a Confederate Soldier*, 91.

21 Drake, *The Annals of the Army of Tennessee and Early Western History*, 1:272–273. The "tattoo" that Drake mentions was the evening bugle call given by the army to signal all prisoners to be in their shelters, extinguish lights, and maintain silence in the camp until the hour of reveille the next morning. This call was a standard military procedure used at Point Lookout and elsewhere to enforce curfew, promote discipline, and ensure security during the night hours in the prison camp.

Nevertheless, his assertion of witnessing so many shootings in such a short period is highly improbable.

Prisoners were often blamed for incidents perpetrated by White guards and would "pay the penalty by being fired into on more than one occasion." Even though both Black and White guards wore the same uniform, it did not erase more than a century of racial animosity between the races. This racial bias and the resulting antagonism between Black and White Union soldiers was an inescapable part of the experience of a Confederate prisoner of war.[22]

Reports of numerous shooting incidents prompted the authorities in Washington to investigate, initiating letters of inquiry from the commissary general of prisoners and from civilian organizations. Although shootings by members of the Black guard force received considerable notoriety, records show that several shootings by White guards were also investigated. Martin Haynes, a guard in the 2nd New Hampshire, evocatively described one incident in a letter home:

> Two prisoners were shot yesterday. The Fifth's [New Hampshire] drum corps was playing "Dixie" . . . the Rebs crowded up to the fence and gave "three cheers for Dixie!" The demonstration soon became riotous and threatening . . . passing beyond all control when the Twelfth [New Hampshire] man on guard at that point fired into the crowd.[23]

Lieutenant Everson also witnessed a shooting by a White guard from the 139th Ohio Volunteers, a short-term unit temporarily assigned guard duty at Point Lookout:

> In the autumn of 1864 one prisoner was shot at Point Lookout for passing beyond the "dead line." The guard who did the shooting was a member of an Ohio "100 days regiment." The soldier had been placed in arrest and an investigation followed and closed all further inquiry into the affair. None were ever shot by the Veteran [Veteran Reserve Corps] guards.[24]

Regardless of Draper's efforts to regulate the prison and its guards, shootings by guards continued. Private William Flinn of the 17th Mississippi testified that "a negro guard shot into a crowd of men at the door of the mess barracks because those behind in mere sport were pushing those in front out of the line too near

22 Letter by Wells, 29.

23 Haynes, *A Soldier Boy's Letters*, 148–149.

24 Everson, Papers No. 28/710/22, 28.

the guard." The recurrent shooting of prisoners prompted Draper's successor, James Barnes, to issue General Order No. 46 on August 29, 1864, with further instructions for the guard force. This order reiterated the necessity of compliance with orders by the guards, as outlined by his predecessors.[25]

Regardless of these additional regulations, prisoner shootings continued. Private Samuel Pickens of the 5th Alabama recorded in his diary an incident on May 26, 1865, more than a month after the war ended:

> Negro police came in last night carrying pistols about, halted everyone on the street—cursed and ordered them back to their tents. I hear the report of one of which was fired at a man in the street by the guard missed him and passed thro' the thigh of a poor fellow who was lying asleep in his tent and caused the amputation of his leg.[26]

By the time Pickens wrote this, many White guard detachments were being transferred elsewhere, returning U.S.C.T. men to prison guard duty.

Prisoners reported witnessing shootings at all times of the day, at varying distances, and in different locations within the prison, including divisions other than their own. In some cases, prisoner accounts of harassment and shootings should be taken with caution. Phrases such as "I was told" and "it's been said" offer little credibility to many accounts. If an incident did not happen to the person telling the story, if he was not a witness, or if he cannot identify the exact circumstances, readers may properly suspect both the source and the account. This is not to say that shootings and abuses by the guards did not occur.

As in the case of the shooting of Private Mark Lisk, the attending physician, Dr. James Thompson, Federal surgeon in charge of the prison hospital, stated in his testimony regarding the shooting that "he was told" how the incident supposedly occurred by another prisoner who had not witnessed it. This illustrates why prisoner accounts should be subjected to scrutiny and not always trusted. Nevertheless, in many cases, testimony by the offending guard was believed over that of prisoners. What cannot be denied is that many shootings took place, and the resulting horrors were real.

25 Flinn, "A Southern Soldier's Experience in a Northern Prison," 30; *Book No. 251*, 46.

26 Hubbs, *Voices from Company D*, 383.

## Chapter 10

# The Prison Camp Hospitals and Death

Soon after the battle of Gettysburg, Federal authorities planned to transfer captured and wounded prisoners to Hammond Hospital at Point Lookout. Officials considered relocating Union soldiers already at Hammond to hospitals in Baltimore, Philadelphia, and New York, thereby making room for new prisoners. Confederate wounded were to be placed at Hammond only where space could be found, since the care of wounded and sick Union soldiers clearly took precedence over that of prisoners of war. A few weeks later, Federal authorities reconsidered their plan to incarcerate prisoners at Point Lookout, leading to the creation of the prison camp and its hospital.

The *Lieber Code* guaranteed that wounded prisoners were entitled to receive medical attention "according to the ability of the medical staff." This was reinforced by Hoffman's circular of July 1862, Article 3, which placed the prison hospital under the authority of the senior surgeon, who was responsible for the care of the prisoners and the facility itself. He was also aided by two assistant surgeons. The medical staff at Hammond Hospital, as well as at the prison hospitals, met the requirements prescribed both by Lieber and Hoffman by treating all prisoners in need of medical attention.[1]

To care for the sudden influx of prisoners suffering from diseases such as pneumonia, dysentery, and smallpox, hospitals were established in the prison camp as soon as the first tents were erected. With little time to prepare for the unexpected arrival of large numbers of sick prisoners, the medical staff worked to limit the spread of disease and endeavored to ease their patients' suffering.

1 *OR* 3/3: Article 79, 156; *OR* 7/2:73.

Over the next two years, the prison hospital expanded steadily in response to the increasing number of sick and injured prisoners at Point Lookout.[2]

## The Prison Hospital

Treatment was provided to all prisoners to the extent possible. As beds at Hammond became available, the most serious cases were sent there to free space in the prison hospital. Before anyone could anticipate, the number of sick and wounded from both armies filled to capacity the 1,400-bed Hammond Hospital and its satellite facilities. This forced prisoners, regardless of the severity of their illness, to remain in the crowded prison hospital or, when no space was available, to convalesce in their tents and makeshift shelters.[3]

By November 1863, with the completion of the new prison stockade, 10 divisional streets were established within the prison, running north to south. The remaining open area in the southeastern portion of the compound was designated for the prison hospital, as this section had not yet been used for any other purpose. The hospital was organized in the manner of a field hospital and was initially administered by Surgeon Sylvanus Bunton of the 2nd New Hampshire. The facility soon expanded with the arrival of more prisoners. In this early phase, regular army hospital tents were erected and fitted with wooden floors and pallets arranged as beds for the sick. A makeshift pharmacy, cooking facilities, a laundry, and a well for water were also established for the use of staff and patients.

In his comprehensive inspection report, Sanitary Commission Inspector Dr. William Swalm described the prison hospital as consisting of nine wards, each made up of 18 hospital tents arranged in pairs, end to end, and placed in two rows. This layout created a broad street between the rows, with a cook and dining tent at the eastern end facing the street. The arrangement was short-lived and soon expanded due to the increasing number of sick prisoners. Swalm noted that, apart from five or six prisoners, all 100 patients in the prison hospital at that time were on mattresses in raised bunks, each with a single blanket.

He further remarked that "no attention was given to the separating of different diseases. Wounded and erysipelas, fever, and diarrhea, were lying side by side," with chronic diarrhea being the most prevalent illness. Other diseases being treated included consumption (tuberculosis), typhoid fever, peritonitis, pneumonia, apoplexy, rheumatism, and measles, among others. Prisoners were detailed to serve as stewards, nurses, cooks, and in other necessary roles within

2 Barnes, et al., *The Medical and Surgical History of the War of the Rebellion*, 1.3:64–65.

3 *OR* 6/2:740.

the prison hospital. According to Swalm, "the stewards comprised of prisoners, were found to be generally uncompassionate and incapable of taking care of the needs of their fellow prisoners." He also noted that the army hospital [Hammond] received an average of twenty to thirty prisoners per day from the camp hospital and that post-mortem examinations showed nearly all who died had succumbed to diarrhea, often complicated by pneumonia.[4]

Cooking for the sick was carried out by fellow prisoners, as was the case for the general population. There were no stoves in the hospital tents, and the sick endured the cold of the winter months while limited to a single blanket. The dispensary existed in name only, consisting of poor, insufficient, and dirty equipment with little, if any, medicine. The grounds around the hospital had apparently not been policed for some time, as filth was accumulating in many areas and sinks (latrines) were not provided. The "great amount of the misery experienced in the hospital and throughout the camp might be obviated if a little more energy was displayed by the surgeon in charge," Swalm noted caustically.[5]

Shortly after the arrival of the 5th New Hampshire on November 14, 1863, the administration of the prison hospital and its facilities was temporarily placed under the charge of surgeon Maj. William Child, MD, of the 5th New Hampshire. Child described the hospital as consisting of 14 wards, each formed by three hospital tents placed end to end with their curtains rolled back and including board floors. His account illustrates how rapidly the prison hospital had expanded following Swalm's recent report. Child was assisted by eight Confederate army surgeons, as well as civilian surgeons among the prisoners, who served in the same capacity. He routinely inspected each patient twice daily, in the morning and evening, and made a full inspection of the entire hospital and camp once a week. Hospital rations, according to some prisoner patients, varied based on condition and prescribed diet.[6]

During his follow-up inspection on December 17, 1863, Dr. Augustus M. Clark, acting medical inspector of prisoners of war, confirmed Child's description of the prison hospital and noted the improvements made since Swalm's inspection the previous month. Clark reported that as many as 217 prisoners occupied the hospital, which had been designed to care for 225 patients, with an additional 380 prisoners sick in quarters, bringing the total to 597. At the same time, 1,196 sick prisoners were housed in Hammond Hospital at Point Lookout.[7]

4 Ibid., 575.

5 Ibid., 576.

6 Child, *Letters from a Civil War Surgeon*, 246–247; Stevens, *Reminiscences of the Civil War*, 156.

7 *OR 6/2*:742.

Clark further reported that Surgeon James H. Thompson arrived on November 13, 1863, and relieved Child as head of the prison hospital. Thompson was later assigned the position of surgeon-in-chief of the District of St. Mary's, a post he held until July 1865. He stated that upon his arrival, the camp held "nearly 10,000" prisoners. Clark confirmed that Thompson quickly brought the prison hospital into excellent condition, providing sufficient proof of the efficiency of the surgeon in charge. Thompson was assisted by "at least twelve doctors who were prisoners of war that were deemed competent by the ranking medical authority at Point Lookout."[8]

Dr. James Thompson was a young but knowledgeable physician, formerly an assistant surgeon of the 12th Maine. He arrived at Point Lookout on November 13, 1863. The following day, he was appointed head surgeon of the prison hospital, responsible for the care and welfare of the prisoners.[9]

Thompson faced the enormous task of improving the substandard conditions of the prison camp hospital during his time on post. Although an ample staff of surgeons and physicians assisted him, he was also permitted to employ Confederate prisoners who had served as surgeons before and during the war. Even with this additional help, efforts were insufficient to care for the overwhelming number of patients, which filled the prison hospital beyond capacity.

Thompson achieved mixed results during his tenure at Point Lookout in improving prison conditions. Despite his efforts, he never brought the hospital to the standard for which he labored. He repeatedly petitioned authorities for better rations, clothing, water, and additional hospital facilities to meet the staggering number of sick and wounded sent daily to him. Ironically, conditions began to improve as the war ended. Though suffering from bouts of dysentery himself, Thompson remained in this position while the last of his charges were released or transferred to other hospitals, both up to and after the end of the war. Until then, Surgeon Thompson was fully occupied with the care of thousands of prisoners of war as well as the patients of Hammond Hospital.

The Confederate doctors mentioned by Clark and Thompson were held at Point Lookout in accordance with Article 56 of General Order No. 100 (*Lieber Code*), which granted commanding officers the authority to retain Confederate medical staff, apothecaries, hospital nurses, and servants who had been captured or surrendered, even though they were not considered prisoners of war. At the time of Clark's inspection, Thompson assigned nine of the 12 physicians to various

8 *Book No. 258*, Thompson Letter, July 17, 1865; *OR* 6/2:743.

9 *Book No. 258*, Thompson letter.

Dr. James H. Thompson
*Maine State Archives*

divisions in the prison camp, with two more employed in the prison hospital. As additional physicians arrived, they were assigned to the smallpox hospital. Another served as a dentist for the prison. Private John Stevens of the 5th Texas confirmed this arrangement, stating, "there were two physicians there from my regiment—Dr. W. P. Powell and Dr. Roberts. They were both on hospital detail."[10]

Regardless of the number of inspections, overcrowding in the prison hospital and its inadequate facilities remained a constant problem from the time it opened. Luther Hopkins of the 6th Virginia Cavalry recorded in mid-1864 that, due to overcrowding, he had to wait a week to 10 days for a vacancy in the prison hospital before being admitted. By that time, he was so weakened by illness that he had to be carried in on a stretcher. He stated that the hospital then consisted of "long tents that each held about thirty cots and as soon as a patient died, he was taken to the dead house, the sheets changed, and another [patient] brought in . . . the nurses were all men, chosen from among the prisoners."[11]

## Expansion and Improvement

The footprint of the prison hospital changed at least three times before the end of the war due to the overwhelming increase in patients. In May 1864, Hoffman recommended to the War Department that permission be granted to construct permanent hospital wards (or sheds) to replace the inadequate temporary facilities.

10 Stevens, *Reminiscences of the Civil War*, 156.

11 Hopkins, *From Bull Run to Appomattox*, 98–99.

The existing hospital tents were described as so worn that they could not be repaired, and no replacements were available. Hoffman proposed dimensions of 125 feet by 25 feet for each ward, which would accommodate up to 75 patients.[12]

Hoffman stated that additional auxiliary buildings were necessary to accommodate attendants, a dispensary and storeroom, as well as an eating room and kitchen to replace the tents then in use. These structures were to be constructed by prisoners, with funding drawn from the prison fund. After receiving authorization, Hoffman instructed the commanding officer of Point Lookout on June 6, 1864, to begin immediately the construction of at least one ward, with the other buildings, apart from the cookhouse, to follow, replacing the deteriorating tents. He stated that one building would be sufficient for the time being, with the others to be constructed "from time to time as they become necessary."[13]

Hoffman did not appear to appreciate Thompson's situation. While one ward was under construction, Thompson wrote to the acting assistant adjutant general of the District of St. Mary's on June 23, 1864, formally complaining of the continual overcrowding of the prison hospital. He exceeded Hoffman's initial request by further requesting that the hospital be expanded with a barracks capable of accommodating at least 200 men. At that time, Thompson had 200 sick men convalescing in their tents due to the lack of space in the hospital.[14]

Fortunately for Thompson and his overcrowded hospital, on June 24 plans were set in motion to transfer several hundred Confederate officers from Point Lookout to Fort Delaware, making their former stockade available for the long-needed expansion of the prison hospital. Officials immediately enlarged the enlisted stockade, allowing Thompson to relocate the hospital into the former officers' prison and make use of its eight acres. The tents previously occupied by the Confederate officers temporarily housed the sick while the new hospital sheds were under construction.

By early July 1864, Thompson's expansion of the prison hospital ward and associated buildings was underway as ordered. In his weekly report for September 4, 1864, Provost Marshal Brady informed Barnes that "the [prison] hospital is now being removed to a locality separated from the prison camp by a high fence." In December 1864, drawings by prison artist Pvt. John J. Omenhausser depicted at least three completed hospital sheds. These sheds were raised several feet off the ground, included windows on both sides, and had doors at both ends. Like all

12 Quartermaster, "Drawings and Inventory," map.

13 *OR* 7/2:182–183, 200–201.

14 Ibid., 399–400.

Water color depiction of the prison hospital. *Point Lookout State Park Collection*

other structures, they were whitewashed, with felt paper-covered roofs, air vents, and chimneys along the peaks, indicating the presence of stoves for heating.[15]

As overcrowding of the prison hospital continued, additional wards were needed and requested—this time by the Point's commanding officer, General Barnes. On January 26, 1865, orders were issued to Barnes to begin construction of three additional hospital wards. Lieutenant Everson reported that by the time he transferred from Point Lookout in May 1865, seven large frame buildings had been erected for sick prisoners within the prison. By war's end, the hospital comprised 10 wards (25' x 140'), each containing 60 beds, along with a cookhouse (25' x 140') and an additional 120 hospital tents, all equipped with wooden floors and cots.[16]

15 Letters, Lists of People, Prisoner Financial Records, Prisoner Lists, Vessels Boarded, 1864–1865, M598 Roll 126 (Washington, D.C., n.d.), microfilm, 376–378:100–110; James Barnes, *Rebel Prison Scenes Point Lookout, MD, 1864*, Color portfolio of Point Lookout Scenes by J. J. Omenhausser. The Historical Archive.

16 Everson, Narrative and Personal Notes, 23; Barnes, et al., *The Medical and Surgical History of the War of the Rebellion*, 1.3:60.

## The Smallpox Hospital

It was the overcrowding at Fort Delaware, Fort McHenry, and the Old Capitol Prison in Washington that led to the conversion of the acreage at Point Lookout into a new prison. Prisoners were quickly transferred there, but with their arrival came contagious diseases that spread rapidly through the population. As early as October 1863, Marston complained to Hoffman that he had received 26 cases of smallpox in a shipment of prisoners from Fort Delaware. Soon after, the prison population began to experience outbreaks of various diseases, with smallpox spreading quickly. Measles, typhoid fever, and other communicable diseases followed, appearing in camps throughout the prison. The list of illnesses also included scurvy, typhus, and chronic diarrhea.[17]

Smallpox was one of the leading causes of death at Point Lookout for both prisoners and guards. Its transmission, described at the time as "crowd poisoning," was highly contagious, particularly in closely confined populations. The disease spread rapidly and seemed almost unstoppable. Out of necessity, a "pest house" was established within the prison pen to quarantine those afflicted. Even so, the pest house was soon filled to overflowing.[18]

As a result of overcrowding, it became necessary to quarantine smallpox cases immediately to prevent further spread of the disease. Medical authorities selected a larger site that would consolidate both Union and Confederate cases thereby containing the contagion. This smallpox hospital was established outside the main prison and away from the guard camps. The new facility replaced the smaller pest house and made use of an abandoned brick house along the northern shoreline of Point Lookout Creek (north of today's Lake Conoy). Dr. Sylvanus Bunton of the 2nd New Hampshire, already the lead physician at the prison hospital, administered the smallpox hospital as well. Bunton was assisted by assistant U.S. Army surgeons Broadbent, Russel, and Walton and, eventually, by seven acting Confederate medical assistants serving in both hospitals. The new smallpox hospital area was heavily guarded and separated from the more populated portion of Point Lookout by Point Lookout Creek, accessible only by bridge.

In his report, Swalm noted that within the first two weeks of operating the separate smallpox hospital, "133 cases were sent there, at which time 33 deaths had occurred." The abandoned brick house was soon overwhelmed, forcing prison

17 *OR* 6/2:435; Franklin, Diary of James Franklin, 26; Clay W. Holmes, *The Elmira Prison Camp: Read by Clay W. Holmes of Elmira, Companion by Inheritance, February 7, 1912. Personal Recollections of the War of the Rebellion,* 4th ed., ed. A. Noel Blakeman (Wilmington, NC, 1992), 368.

18 Barnes et al., *The Medical and Surgical History of the War of the Rebellion*, 1.3:46, 65.

authorities to expand the hospital with wedge tents, placing three patients to a tent, each lying on straw on the ground with only a blanket and a half per man. While improvements were underway at the main prison hospital, conditions at the relocated smallpox hospital continued to worsen.[19]

Surgeon Maj. William Child, MD, who replaced Bunton as head surgeon of both the prison hospital and the smallpox hospital, reported in mid-November 1863, that "There are now about five hundred cases of smallpox in hospital . . . As many as fifteen a day have died. Five or six is the usual number." He further stated, "An epidemic of smallpox continued for many weeks in the prisoners' camp. For these cases, a special and isolated hospital was arranged beyond the stockade in an old house." This facility was in operation less than three months after the opening of the prison.[20]

Crowded prison confinement soon brought the disease to epidemic proportions. As late as June 1864, smallpox continued to plague the camp. Sergeant James Wells of the 2nd South Carolina stated, "Fever in every shape abounded and smallpox was epidemic . . . almost every tent had one or two cases of small pox. The hospital could not accommodate all the sick and they were left in their tents."[21]

## Disease and Other Maladies

Along with smallpox, outbreaks of scurvy appeared as early as the latter months of 1863. Scurvy is a slow, debilitating disease caused by insufficient intake of vitamin C, or ascorbic acid, compounded by a poor and restrictive diet lacking essential nutrients. "Diarrhea and scurvy in a chronic form were doing fearful work among the men," one prisoner noted in October 1863, "30, 40 and probably more were dying daily." This figure was an approximation, but there is no doubt that scurvy ran rampant at Point Lookout.

If left untreated, scurvy is both painful and fatal. The same prisoner described scurvy as the formation of "great scabby sores on the outside of the thighs and on the shoulders and arms; it became almost as loathsome as leprosy. Finally, it reaches the bowels . . . Death then ensures in a very short time." Another prisoner stated that scurvy had taken his appetite and caused pain in his joints, forcing him to go to the hospital: "[M]y gums sloughed away from my teeth. With my fingers

19 *OR* 6/2:581.

20 Child, *Letters from a Civil War Surgeon*, 183, 247.

21 Letter by Wells, 23.

I could remove any tooth from my mouth without pain." Outbreaks of diarrhea, caused mainly by the consumption of contaminated water drawn from the wells, often accompanied these diseases.[22]

To stem the outbreak of scurvy, the post commander, General Edward Hinks, issued Special Order No. 108 in mid-April 1864. The order increased the distribution of potatoes, or an equivalent of fresh vegetables, to every 100 rations daily. It also included cornmeal when flour was unavailable and increased the allotment of hominy or beans, "not to exceed 10 quarts per 100 rations." This increase, as ordered by Hinks, was a significant addition to the prisoners' vegetable ration, but it was short-lived. On June 1, 1864, Hoffman recommended a newly reduced ration which lowered Hinks's allocation of 40 pounds of potatoes to only 15 pounds per 100 rations. This drastic reduction in the prisoners' ration further promoted scurvy in the camp. Cases continued to rise through 1864 and persisted into 1865, afflicting the population until the end of the war.[23]

Yet another ailment endured by prisoners came from a surprising source. The condition, referred to as "moon blindness," was more of an inconvenience and nuisance than an actual disease. Temporary blindness resulted from the combination of the sun's reflection on the sand and the tentage that blanketed the cramped prison during the daytime hours. Some men were unable to endure the glare. Those suffering the temporary blinding effects required their comrades to lead them around camp from dusk until dawn, until their eyesight readjusted and was naturally restored. "Nothing was done by the authorities . . . excepting the issuing of green shades for the eyes and planting some small spots with oates [sic], rye, etc. so that the eye might have something green to look upon." One notable request made by a prisoner in correspondence with a friend was "a pare of green spectacles if you will be so kind . . . please let me here from you soon. I am Sun Blind (Blind at knight.)"[24]

## Diarrhea and Dysentery (The "Bloody Flux")

The drinking water available to the prisoners and guard force came from hand-dug wells. This unfiltered and contaminated water produced violent cases

22 Stevens, *Reminiscences of the Civil War*, 146; Holliday, "Vain Efforts for Avoid Prison," in *Confederate Veteran*, 28:383.

23 *Book No. 251*, General Order Aug. 1863–Aug. 1865, Special Orders Aug. 1863–Aug.1865, Special Order No. 108 issued April 18, 1864.

24 Hopkins, *From Bull Run to Appomattox*, 96; Letter from Wells, 27–28; J. B. Nelson to W. P. Johnston, July 17, 1864, Letter Collection of Eleanor Ford, Point Lookout State Park, Point Lookout, MD.

of diarrhea and, in extreme instances, death among both prisoners and guards. Contaminated water remained a persistent problem throughout the existence of Point Lookout, affecting the military post as well as the prison depot. Nevertheless, water was not the only cause of chronic diarrhea.

Modern research on starvation offers alternative explanations for the causes of prisoner deaths, which prison physicians could have misdiagnosed. In his report, Inspector Swalm described the "poor emaciated creatures suffering from diarrhea [which] is the most prevalent disease." By this time, rations were being reduced for the prison population. Swalm perceived the general filthiness and lack of personal hygiene as laziness, but in some cases, these conditions could have been symptoms of severe starvation.[25]

Medical studies conducted before and after the Civil War distinguished "famine dysentery" from ordinary dysentery. Famine dysentery resulted from prolonged starvation and indicated that the sufferer was near death. It could kill quickly and proved fatal to undernourished patients recovering from smallpox who were suffering from what became known as "putrid dysentery," often accompanied by fever. Doctors discovered as early as the American Revolution that those seemingly recovering from smallpox sometimes died from this form of dysentery due to neglect and undernourishment.[26]

Famine diarrhea could be confused with dysentery in the final stages of starvation. In this last and fatal stage, diarrhea could become relentless, killing a sufferer within weeks or even days. Weight loss intensified with diarrhea, and this interplay created a debilitating cycle, with the afflicted dying in "extreme cachexia" (unintentional weight loss). Prisoners at Point Lookout were undernourished and consumed fewer calories than necessary to maintain their health. This persistent nutrient deficiency consistently starved them of the essential nutrients required for survival.

Private John Stevens of the 5th Texas, for instance, reported that he weighed approximately 222 pounds upon entering Confederate service. After his capture at Gettysburg, he was sent to Fort Delaware and soon transferred to Point Lookout. Stevens claimed that due to "short rations . . . [d]iarrhea is a prevailing disease." He also stated that he suffered from rheumatism and scurvy while a prisoner. In October 1864, Stevens was paroled and transferred from Point Lookout as part of an exchange of sick prisoners. Upon completion of his journey to Fort

25 *OR* 6/2:576.

26 Brian Patrick O'Malley, "What Killed Prisoners of War? A Medical Investigation," *Journal of the American Revolution*, last modified Sept. 21, 2020, accessed April 8, 2025, https://allthingsliberty.com/2020/09/what-killed-prisoners-of-war-a-medical-investigation/.

Monroe, Stevens claimed his weight had been reduced to 141 pounds, reflecting a significant loss during his imprisonment.[27]

A list of diseases suffered by both prisoners and guards would included erysipelas, pneumonia, typhoid fever, consumption (tuberculosis), cholera, and several illnesses contracted from disease-laden rats. Thompson and his staff faced the enormous task of saving as many sick men as possible while attempting to improve conditions within the prison. Unfortunately, he fought an uphill battle against the overwhelming number of prisoners arriving daily, the lack of supplies and proper facilities, and the effects of contaminated drinking water.

Deaths occurred faster than accommodations could be constructed to manage all the sick and dying prisoners at Point Lookout. As the number of dead increased, available space for cemeteries grew scant, and recording the dead became part of the routine for both the hospital and prison staffs.

## The Dead House and Burials

The procedure for collecting and burying the deceased varied over time, influenced by the increasing numbers of dead. Prisoners such as George Peyton of the 13th Virginia recalled the dread regularity of the interments: "The burial hour here is daily at four o'clock in the afternoon." This timing is corroborated by other prisoner accounts. In some cases, autopsies were performed, but as the number of deceased grew, this procedure became rare. Burials were generally conducted by prisoners or by former slaves who had taken refuge at Point Lookout.[28]

Federal authorities established at least two graveyards for deceased prisoners. Other cemeteries were designated for smallpox victims, Black refugees and their families, and Federal soldiers. These areas eventually suffered from erosion, fire, and the passage of time. Until recently, most remained unidentified.

A detail of prisoners gathered the dead from the prison and conveyed them by wagon to the dead house. The "dead house" was sometimes a Sibley tent and at other times a wooden building. According to prisoner accounts, one was located adjacent to the wharf on the Hammond Hospital end of Point Lookout. However, both prisoner and eyewitness accounts state that to facilitate the burial of deceased prisoners, stacks of coffins were kept by the gate of the prison near the

27 Stevens, *Reminiscences of the Civil War*, 155–158.

28 Peyton, *A Civil War Record for 1864–1865*, 347.

assistant provost marshal's office. Another tent used as a dead house existed in the parole stockade.[29]

As the number of deceased prisoners began to overwhelm the prison dead house, bodies were taken directly from the prison to one of the designated graveyards for burial. Private Luther Hopkins of the 6th Virginia Cavalry recorded this somber memory in his diary: "Once a day a two-horse wagon came in, and their bodies were laid in it like so much cord wood, uncoffined, taken out and buried in long trenches. The trenches were seven feet wide and three feet deep, and the bodies were laid across the trench side by side and covered with earth."[30]

As expected, this was not the case for deceased Union soldiers at Point Lookout. In May 1863, Surgeon-General William Hammond wrote a letter of complaint to General Meigs, stating that, "the [Union] graveyard [at Point Lookout] is without fence or protection, the graves only marked through the kindness of friends or wardmasters; not a single properly marked headboard has been put up by the Quartermaster." Hammond's complaint prompted action. During his inspection of Point Lookout on July 9, 1863, Surgeon Charles T. Alexander reported that Union soldier interments were being conducted properly, with each grave marked by a headboard bearing the name, rank, company, and regiment. A year later, on June 26, 1864, Colonel Draper, commanding officer of Point Lookout, ordered provost marshal Maj. W. G. O. Weymouth to locate another burial ground higher up the peninsula. Specifications required graves to be "dug 6 ft. deep and every grave to be applied with a headboard marked with the name, rank and regiment of the deceased." However, the post-war National Reburial Program discovered that at some point, this procedure was discontinued, and, in many cases, graves were found to be disgracefully maintained.[31]

## The Death Toll of Point Lookout Prison

According to Hoffman's army circular of July 7, 1862, all prison commanding officers were responsible for the daily recording of various prisoner activities and changes, including deaths, transfers, sickness, arrivals and exchanges, oaths and paroles, and prisoner correspondence. These daily reports were consolidated monthly and submitted to the office of the commissary general of prisoners. The

29 Letter by Wells, 25; Adams, *A Cycle of Adams Letters 1861–1865*, 2:214; Jones, *In Prison at Point Lookout*, 9.

30 Hopkins, *From Bull Run to Appomattox*, 99.

31 Hunter, "Warden for the Union," 155; Sword, "Where the Union," 237; *Book No. 255*, vol. 3, 141.

same information was entered into the various ledgers required by that office at each prison depot. In the post-war years, the government published Hoffman's monthly reports as a public record.

The prison hospital information compiled by Thompson and the medical staff included prisoner deaths, patient vital statistics, cause of death, and place of interment, which was to include a grave number if known. The names of the deceased were recorded by rank, company, regiment, and state, if this information was known. Given incomplete record keeping at the time, many deaths at Point Lookout were recorded without this information. The personal effects of deceased prisoners were recorded and turned over to the commanding officer. Valuables, money, credit balances remaining in the deceased prisoners' sutler accounts, and monies received from the sale of the deceased prisoners' effects were placed in the prison fund according to regulations. Serviceable prisoner clothing was to be turned into the quartermaster for reissue.

The accuracy of record-keeping by prison authorities has been a point of dispute since the prison closed in July 1865. Contentious topics include the number of deceased (both known and unknown), cemetery locations, and unmarked graves. Unfortunately, the sources—both official and later investigations—have disagreed on the death count since the end of the war. This disagreement includes prison authorities and the prison hospital. Estimates of death rates at Point Lookout appeared periodically in memoirs, diaries, and letters from former prisoners. Some estimates varied significantly from the numbers recorded in the official records. Attempts to ascertain an accurate count have repeatedly fallen short, as new data continues to be uncovered. A definitive figure is likely to remain elusive despite the best efforts of historians.

The prison camp at Point Lookout operated from July 1863 to June 1865, during which time more than 50,000 prisoners, both military and civilian, were held. The *Official Records of the War of the Rebellion* report a death toll of 2,950 from September 1863 to June 1865, while the *Medical and Surgical History* records, covering the same period, report 3,704 deaths. Additionally, the *Official Ledger of the Dead* from the prison lists 3,431 deceased prisoners, though no timeframe is provided. Estimates vary widely in memoirs, letters, and other sources, with some contemporary accounts suggesting even higher mortality numbers, possibly exceeding 4,000. The discrepancies between these sources have led to ongoing disputes among historians, and despite extensive research, no consensus on the death count has been reached.[32]

32 *OR* 8/2:992–1002; Barnes et al., *The Medical and Surgical History of the War of the Rebellion*, 1.3:46; *Register of Confederate Soldiers, Sailors and Civilians Who Died in Federal Prisons and Military*

Prisoners at Point Lookout were held in multiple locations, including the stockade, the prison hospital, and Hammond Hospital. Federal authorities were aware that prisoners living and dying in multiple locations complicated the accurate keeping of records. Hoffman's circular of July 7, 1862, accounts for this by noting that reports from such institutions presented only a partial picture of the prisoner population and deaths.

Consequently, the figures in both the *Official Records of the War of the Rebellion* and *The Medical and Surgical History of the War of the Rebellion* reflect incomplete data. These publications explicitly state that their statistics represent prisoners held in separate facilities and did not fully capture the total number of prisoners under U.S. custody. This disclaimer preempted accusations regarding discrepancies in reporting and record-keeping. The demand for these records from Washington, combined with the immense workload required to maintain multiple ledgers tracking thousands of prisoners coming and going, placed a heavy burden on the inexperienced soldiers drawn from the guard force and prison population to serve as clerks.[33]

Prisoner accounts claimed that between 19 and 30 deaths occurred per day at Point Lookout. These estimates were likely based on hearsay and the limited time the writers were present, as they were probably neither privy to nor witnesses of the actual daily figures. In a post-war address in 1890, former prisoner Charles T. Loehr of the 1st Virginia recalled, "It was not unusual to hear it stated that sixty or sixty-five deaths had occurred in a single day; and it is said that eight thousand six hundred dead Confederates were buried near that prison." Clearly, Loehr's statement was founded largely on rumors, hearsay, and speculation rather than verified data. Unfortunately, figures such as Loehr's have often been accepted as truth, fueling controversy throughout the post-war years over the actual death rate at Point Lookout. Usually made at second-hand, such statements add little to the historical record.[34]

In June 1864, prisoner Private James E. Hall of the 31st Virginia was appointed clerk to the surgeon assigned to his division in the prison. Hall was thus in a favorable position to witness prisoner mortality. "The sickness appears to be increasing and the deaths average eight every day," Hall later reported. "I've quit clerking for a division in camp and have a clerkship now in the [prison] hospital."[35]

---

*Hospitals in the North. 1861-1865*, 530-612. Washington D.C.: National Archives Microfilm Publications, 1972. Microcopy Roll# 918 Roll-1.

33 Barnes et al., *The Medical and Surgical History of the War of the Rebellion*, 1.3:46.

34 Loehr, "The Treatment," 18:2.

35 Hall, *The Diary of a Confederate Soldier*, 118, 122.

Other eyewitness accounts were even more harrowing. Prisoner movements between prisons were primarily facilitated by transport boats to ensure security and expediency. Private John Stevens of the 5th Texas witnessed a disturbing incident during his transfer by boat to another prison. Stevens wrote that approximately 150 men out of the 500 transported with him died at sea. According to Stevens, these men were disposed of over the side of the ship while in transit. This account raises questions about whether these deceased prisoners were properly identified, accounted for, and recorded by the responsible officials during transit or upon arrival at their destination.[36]

The reporting of information was a necessary but massive task for the clerks of a prison camp the size of Point Lookout. To alleviate some of the statistical backlog, prisoners were detailed to assist Federal clerks with these duties. Relying on prisoners to accurately record vital statistics was a risk taken by prison authorities. One Federal eyewitness account stated that a prisoner working for the provost marshal took advantage of his temporary position by holding some of the logbooks hostage, concealing them in exchange for extra privileges. This same clerk soon regretted his transgression with a prolonged stay in the guardhouse, living on bread and water until the ledgers were surrendered. The accuracy and reliability of such prisoner clerks should therefore also be taken with a grain of salt.[37]

Nevertheless, according to the accumulated monthly statistics reported by the medical officer at Point Lookout, the principal causes of death among prisoners were dysentery and diarrhea, which accounted for over 2,000 deaths. Pneumonia and pleurisy were the second leading causes, with 425 deaths reported, followed by eruptive fevers (smallpox) at 333 deaths. The total number of deaths reported at Point Lookout was 3,704, out of 44,934 combined reported cases of all illnesses and injuries suffered by prisoners. However, this figure is contradicted by the voluminous *Official Records* covering the 23 months of operation. Notably, the statistics for the entire month of August 1863 were omitted from both the *Medical and Surgical History* and the *Official Records*.[38]

## Death's Numbers

One early account, published in 1912, figured a 9 percent death rate at Point Lookout based on a reported figure of 3,446 deceased prisoners. This figure was

36 Stevens, *Reminiscences of the Civil War*, 121–122.

37 *OR* 8/2:991-1002; Everson, Papers No. 28/710/22, 14.

38 Barnes et al., *The Medical and Surgical History of the War of the Rebellion*, 1.3:46.

based on total prison population of 38,053. However, we know that the recorded total population for that period was actually 44,600 prisoners. This account illustrates some of the difficulties in reaching firm numbers. Prison populations were never static. Prisoners were constantly transferred between prisons, paroled, or exchanged. Some were incarcerated for a month or two, and some were imprisoned longer than a year, maybe even two years. Hence determining a death *rate*, let alone total number of deaths, is nearly impossible.[39]

Another post-war publication, the *Confederate Handbook* published in 1900 by Colonel Robert C. Wood, C.S.A., of New Orleans, Louisiana, reported on "Confederate Prisoners in Federal Prisons and Number of Deaths in Each." Wood compared the lists of dead from northern prisons and claimed 38,073 deaths across the system. He repeated the figure of 3,446 deaths at Point Lookout as referenced in the 1912 publication, with no specific period stated.[40]

The *Official Register of the Dead,* maintained by prison authorities at Point Lookout during the war, has listed names of deceased prisoners that are absent from the names displayed on the present federal monument at Point Lookout. To date, over 600 deceased prisoners whose names should appear on these tablets have not been accounted for. Recent studies of private collections and publications have added more names to this tally.[41]

None of these figures account for individuals who died after their release, but from causes attributable to their period of incarceration. One such case is that of Pvt. James W. Kidwell, Company G, 8th Virginia, who died on April 6, 1865, while returning home after serving three months at Point Lookout. Private Kidwell represents the hundreds, or more, who likely succumbed to the effects of prison life after their release.

In his monthly April 1865 report to Barnes, provost marshal Maj. Allan Brady stated that "the average rate of mortality for the week was 4½ prisoners per day." Brady's report reflected the return for March 1865, which listed approximately 7,595 prisoners at the beginning of the month. An additional 3,373 prisoners arrived before the month's end, raising the total to 11,332. The returns for March recorded a total of 175 prisoner deaths, which suggests that an average of five to six

39 Holmes, *The Elmira Prison Camp*, 6:255.

40 Robert C. Wood, comp., *Confederate Handbook: A Compilation of Important Data and Other Interesting and Valuable Matter Relating to the War between the States, 1861–1865* (New Orleans, LA, 1900), 38.

41 *Register of Confederate Soldiers, Sailors, and Citizens Who Died in Federal Prisons and Military Hospitals in the North.* Microfilm Roll M-918. NARA, Washington D.C.

Major Allen Brady, Provost Marshal, Point Lookout Prison. *Library of Congress*

deaths per day for that month would have been a more accurate figure.[42]

Just as the living prisoners required maintenance, so did the deceased. Camps, wells, hospitals, and prison stockades demanded extensive space on the limited peninsula of Point Lookout. Additional acreage was also necessary for the interment of the deceased—Union, Confederate, and civilian prisoners alike—posing further challenges for depot authorities. Several relatively small cemeteries were established, stretching from the lighthouse area northwards to beyond the protective palisade walls of the prison. An act of Congress later established a national program to identify the deceased and consolidate numerous military graveyards into Federally protected national cemeteries for servicemen from both the North and South. Those assigned to this unenviable task soon arrived at Point Lookout to recover and properly inter those who perished there during the war.

Unfortunately, the total number of prisoners who died at Point Lookout will never be known. Efforts to establish an accurate count have consistently fallen short, thanks to the inadequacy of record keeping by prison authorities. No official source has ever agreed with another on these numbers, whether recorded by prison authorities or the prison hospital. Estimates of death rates at Point Lookout have appeared over the postwar years in memoirs, diaries, and letters from former prisoners, all differing from the official figures submitted from Point Lookout. Compared to the overall Civil War death toll, a definitive accounting remains elusive, especially as new names of the deceased continue to emerge from newly discovered sources.

42 *OR* 8/2:463. 991–1002.

Chapter 11

# The Cemeteries and the National Reburial Program

General Order No. 33, issued on April 3, 1862, required all commanding officers to ensure the burial of those who died under their command. They were directed to designate burial grounds so that remains would be interred with headboards bearing numbers and, when practicable, the names of the deceased. The directive applied not only to battlefield burials but also to those near hospitals and prison camps, such as Point Lookout. The order sought to secure proper and recorded interments, with registers corresponding to the marked graves, thereby preserving the identity and dignity of the deceased.[1]

As a result of the Quartermaster Department's success in locating the dead and buried, Congress created the National Reburial Program in early 1866 to finance the relocation process. The program served the dual purpose of identifying and reinterring Union and Confederate dead. To support the quartermaster department's efforts, the War Department ordered that the bodies of deceased Confederates not be removed from any cemetery without a permit. This order ensured the maintenance of records for all Confederate bodies that were removed from cemeteries.[2]

## The Cemeteries of Point Lookout

In April 1866 government officials learned that the bodies of deceased Confederates were being removed from Point Lookout without permits, or with

1 Appendix I, Section VI, National Cemeteries," in Proclamations and Orders (National Park Service, n.d.), 2:504, accessed April 10, 2025, https://www.nps.gov/subjects/legal/proclamations-and-orders-volume-2.htm.

2 *Death and the Civil War*, directed by Ric Burns (American Experience, 2018), DVD.

permits issued by departments other than the War Department, in violation of its mandate. In July 1866, E. Edward Gilbert, a civilian agent for the Quartermaster Department, and his staff were ordered to Point Lookout as part of the Reburial Program. Reports of the unlawful removal of Confederate dead from the site likely prompted the government to direct Gilbert to secure and survey the cemeteries located there and to end the unauthorized removal of remains. The principal cemetery containing many of the Confederate dead was situated on land owned by W. P. Smith in the Tanner's Creek area. Those removing bodies trespassed on Smith's property without his consent, often leaving graves open and the surrounding ground disturbed.

During this period the government discovered that a group of entrepreneurs, who claimed exclusive rights to remove Confederate dead at Point Lookout, had been exhuming bodies without permits or proof of identification. For a fee of 30 dollars, they provided a body and coffin to anyone willing to purchase their services. The government soon forced this group to end its unlawful operations. The number of bodies removed while the business operated was never recorded. This omission significantly affected Gilbert's reported count of recovered bodies, which differed from the higher numbers recorded by other government sources and from the figure displayed on the present monument.[3]

Gilbert's initial report to his immediate superior, acting assistant quartermaster Bvt. Lt. Col. Elisha E. Camp, stated that he found deceased prisoners of war interred in several cemeteries at Point Lookout, all in varying states of disrepair, storm damage, flooding, and overgrowth. On July 12, 1866, Gilbert reported that the first Confederates reinterred at Point Lookout were removed from a plot north of the prison pen, which he designated on his map of the site as Rebel Graveyard No. 1. This graveyard contained 63 known burials and no unknowns and was likely the first used as a prisoner cemetery because of its close proximity to the prison. Those interred there were later reburied at one of the other two Confederate cemetery locations. Today much of the area designated as "the Peach Orchard" (the name referencing the well-known Peach Orchard at the battle of Gettysburg) is either densely wooded or submerged. The site covered approximately 90 feet by 89 feet.

Gilbert then moved his operations north to the area of the smallpox hospital and cemetery. While exhuming bodies from that site, he discovered an additional 70 unknown burials of White and Black Union soldiers and Confederates near

3 M. Ludington to Montgomery Meigs, "Cemeteries for Union and Confederate Soldiers," June 12, 1866, Record Group 92, Entry 576, Box 57, Records of the Office of the Quartermaster General, National Archives and Records Administration, Washington D.C.

the cemetery grounds. He proposed enclosing them by taking "down some of the fencing around the old pens." This remark indicates that remnants of the prison stockade were still standing during Gilbert's visit. He declared his intention to consolidate all recovered bodies from four burial sites—the Peach Orchard, the smallpox cemetery, and two others—into two designated locations. The Tanner's Creek site, the first of these, encompassed just over an acre. The smallpox hospital cemetery covered approximately two and one-quarter acres.[4]

There is no evidence regarding the disposition or final location of these unknown bodies after Gilbert's report, nor any explanation for why they had been placed outside the cemetery boundaries. Gilbert stated only that he had discovered them and included their number in his final report. His account suggests that the unknown bodies were removed by his workers and reinterred at either the Tanner's Creek cemetery or the adjacent smallpox hospital cemetery.

The 70 unknown soldiers may or may not be represented among the names inscribed on the present-day monument or in the Register of the Dead maintained by Federal clerks at Point Lookout. The smallpox hospital cemetery contained 60 graves of Union, U.S.C.T., and Confederate soldiers, which, unlike the others, were not enclosed. Gilbert's recoveries in this area reflected inadequate record keeping and careless work by the original grave-digging details.

Gilbert further reported that the smallpox hospital cemetery and the area he designated Rebel Graveyard No. 1, located approximately 200 yards north of the prison, contained 1,190 known burials and 10 unknowns. A third Confederate graveyard on Tanner's Creek, situated on the eastern side of the smallpox hospital grounds, allegedly contained 1,444 known and 60 unknown soldiers. Gilbert stated that the total number of Confederate bodies recovered was 2,697 known and 70 unknowns, for a combined total of 2,767, when he completed his survey and reinterments in these areas.[5]

Gilbert further reported that the Union graveyard along the Potomac River contained 457 known and 175 unknown remains, all enclosed by fencing. Outside the fence lay an additional 33 known and 17 unknown burials. His report described a neglected burial ground in disrepair and damaged by storms, while also noting his receipt of the requested "25 blankets, 400 headboards, 2 dozen lettering pencils and 25 coffins" to assist in the repair and recovery effort. He reinterred the recovered Union dead within the cemetery boundaries, thereby avoiding the expense of constructing additional fencing. Despite

4 Beitzell, *Point Lookout Prison Camp for Confederates*, 115, 117.

5 Gerald J. Sword, "Confederate Cemetery: Point Lookout," *St. Mary's Chronicles*, Dec. 1979, 2.

these efforts, Gilbert soon discovered that natural forces would continue to hinder his work.[6]

He reported,

> [t]he U.S. yard is situated close to the beach on the river side and the fence being open the sand that drifts upon the shore during a blow, will settle on this place and undoubtedly covered up a good many of the head boards or they may have been carried away. A good many of the coffins are within a foot of the top of the ground.[7]

Gilbert's count of bodies recovered as of this date was as follows:

| | |
|---|---|
| Union Graveyard No. 1 | 457 known—175 unknowns (632) |
| Outside of the Union Graveyard | 17 known—33 unknowns (50) |
| Colored burying ground | 17 known—27 unknowns (44) |
| Rebel ground No. 1 | 63 known (63) |
| No. 2 | 1190 known—10 unknowns (1200) |
| No. 3 | 1444 known—60 unknowns (1504) |

Gilbert's report shows a final recovery count of 2,767 (2,697 known, 70 unknown) Confederate deceased. If he discovered or moved more, he does not say.

Total deceased Confederate prisoners recovered: 2,767
Total all others: 726
Total figure of bodies recovered by Gilbert: 3,493

Gilbert reported that he had provided the best information available to him, stating that "the grass and weeds together with the marshy ground prevents me from being more positive." His total count of recoveries cannot be regarded as the full number of deceased prisoners, since his figures conflict with the final totals reported by prison authorities in the *Official Records of the Rebellion,* which listed 2,950. According to Gilbert, he and his workforce reinterred the Confederate dead in the two cemeteries designated on his map. He may have recovered more remains, but he did not record them. In a follow-up report dated July 14, 1866, Gilbert stated that his men had begun moving the bodies of Union soldiers buried outside Union Graveyard No. 1. He also intended to transfer the smallpox dead to

6 Beitzell, *Point Lookout Prison Camp for Confederates,* 116.

7 Sword, "Where the Union Slept," 2.

the other burial grounds. Work was continuing on the consolidation of remains into the two designated cemeteries.[8]

Internal Quartermaster Department communication in November 1867 revealed that there were over 3,000 bodies interred in the two final Confederate cemeteries, of which one-third were unknown as a result of headboards being effaced by weather and by the manner in which they had been marked. Officials determined that the Union cemetery at Point Lookout not be considered for National Cemetery status under the criteria established in the National Cemeteries Act, approved by President Johnson on February 22, 1867.[9]

"The location . . . is not desirable for a National Cemetery being liable to be washed in seasons of high tide. I would therefore respectfully recommend the removal of the bodies to the Arlington Cemetery," according to one memorandum. Reinterring the bodies of the Federal soldiers in Arlington Cemetery would cost the government less than paying for a ward master, new headboards, and the continued maintenance of a remote cemetery subject to severe weather conditions.[10]

None of this was surprising, as the Union cemetery had already begun to suffer from the severe weather conditions for which Point Lookout was known. Reports also noted that "one of the two cemeteries [Tanner's Creek] was unfit for use as it was subject to the overflow of the tides." Gilbert suggested that additional space remained available in the other cemeteries.[11]

The Quartermaster Department eventually granted approval for the relocation of Union soldiers to Arlington Cemetery. The removal and reinterment of the Union dead took place between December 30, 1867, and January 3, 1868. Of the 678 recorded Union burials, 212 were unidentified. Gilbert reported that some of these 212 graves contained the remains of more than one soldier. This indicated that, as with the Confederate dead, not all Union burials had been properly conducted or recorded. These circumstances reflected inadequate record keeping and negligent burial practices for both Confederate and Union soldiers.

The remains of U.S.C.T. soldiers were also relocated to Arlington Cemetery. Confusion surrounds the exact number of deceased among both U.S.C.T. soldiers and Black civilians. Arlington's interment records indicate that 30 soldiers and 18 "contrabands" were buried there. However, the quartermaster's final list recorded 22 U.S.C.T. soldiers. Gilbert's 1866 report stated that he had identified

8 Beitzell, *Point Lookout Prison Camp for Confederates*, 115, 117.

9 Asa P. Blunt to John C. McFerren, "Point Lookout, MD," Nov. 11, 1867, RG 92, Stack Area 8002, Box 829, Quartermaster Files, National Archives and Records Administration, Washington, D.C.

10 Blunt to McFerren. "Point Lookout, MD."

11 Sword, "Confederate Cemetery, Point Lookout." 2–3.

seven known and 27 unknown U.S.C.T. burials at Point Lookout, a total of 34, not including Black civilians. The three sets of interment records for the deceased Black population at Point Lookout conflict with one another, clearly demonstrating that little attention was given to the burial and documentation of U.S.C.T. soldiers and Black civilians. The remains of all Union soldiers from Point Lookout are now interred in Sections 13 and 27 of Arlington National Cemetery in Arlington, Virginia.[12]

On February 21, 1868, assistant quartermaster and inspector of national cemeteries Bvt. Col. Charles W. Folsom reported to his superiors that one Confederate cemetery at Point Lookout was enclosed by a fence and another only partially enclosed. Folsom recommended that both be fully enclosed. It is unknown whether this was ever completed. The federal government acquired the two parcels of land containing the cemeteries in June 1868. Even if the fences had been completed, they likely would not have survived the marsh fire that swept through the cemetery in 1868 or 1869. John T. Calleghen, president of the Confederate Veterans Association of the District of Columbia, visited the site during the summer of 1870 and reported that the marsh fire "destroyed, to our regret, all vestige of the identification of the little pine-plank headboards [of the prisoners cemetery]."

On March 4, 1871, William L. Thomas, a member of the board of Trustees appointed by the Maryland Assembly by law in 1870, for the creation of a cemetery for the Confederate deceased, requested permission from Secretary of War William W. Belknap to relocate the remains of Confederate soldiers and sailors at Point Lookout once again. Belknap granted permission on the condition that the move incur no cost to the government. The trustees—Thomas, Joseph Forrest, J. Parran Crane, James Langley, Thomas Martin, Dr. John Brome, George Thomas, and George Garner—requested the necessary funding from the Maryland General Assembly. The Assembly responded that such funding had already been provided in the Act of 1870 for the exhumation and reinterment of the 3,444 bodies of Confederate prisoners of war buried at Point Lookout. The cost of placing an iron fence around the cemetery was also expended.[13]

12 Sword, "Where the Union Slept," 3.

13 Sword, "Confederate Cemetery, Point Lookout." 3. This number clearly inflates Gilbert's final count of recovered Confederate bodies (2,767) by at least 600 or more, and their reply does not explain why the higher count. Regardless, their number could be based upon the final accounting as found in the official document entitled, *List of Confederate Soldiers and Sailors Who, While Prisoners of War, Died at Point Lookout,* which number is stated as 3,431 deceased. List of Confederate Soldiers, Sailors and Civilians Who Died While Prisoners of War, Died at Point Lookout, Maryland," in *Register of Confederate Soldiers, Sailors and Civilians Who Died in Federal Prisons and Military Hospitals in the North, 1861–1865* (Washington, D.C., 1972), 530–612, 918.

The cemetery consisted of a common grave measuring 24 square feet with a three-foot-high mound. The monument was erected with funds raised by the citizens of St. Mary's, Calvert, and Charles Counties through a series of tournaments, fairs, balls, and other entertainments. Commonly known as the Tanner's Creek Cemetery, the monument—constructed of granite quarried in Baltimore—was dedicated in 1876 and stood at the center of the cemetery. The dates 1910–1911 displayed on the monument reflect its relocation to its present site, adjacent to the Federal monument outside the present-day state park. This monument records 3,004 prisoner deaths and bears the dates March 1, 1864–June 30, 1865. No explanation has been found for why these particular dates were chosen, as the brief period inscribed does not represent the full span of the prison's operation at Point Lookout.[14]

Although the recovery and reinterment of deceased Confederate soldiers fell under the provisions of the National Cemetery Act, the marking of Confederate cemeteries and their graves was treated separately. In 1906, Congress passed Public Act No. 38, which authorized the marking of the graves of Confederate army and navy soldiers and sailors buried in Northern cemeteries. The act also established the Commission for Marking Graves of Confederate Dead. The Commission operated from 1906 to 1912 and again from 1914 to 1916, under the leadership of four former Confederate officers.[15]

Because of its proximity to the Chesapeake Bay, Tanner's Creek Cemetery was subject to severe tidal erosion. It soon became evident that the cemetery, and the Confederate remains it contained, would again need to be relocated. In 1909, four of the original trustees prepared legislation for presentation to the Maryland legislature in January, requesting that the Confederate cemetery at Point Lookout be transferred to the care of the U.S. government. The reinterment occurred just in time, as the original Tanner's Creek cemetery site is now underwater.

Although Federal law authorized the marking of Confederate graves with individual markers at government expense, the authorization carried a caveat. On May 12, 1910, Congress passed another bill stipulating that the Maryland Assembly must relinquish and convey its rights to the U.S. government before federal markers could be provided. Maryland officials refused to permit individual markers as outlined in the Public Act of 1906. They eventually consented to a single monument

14 Sword, "Confederate Cemetery," 3; Beitzell, *Point Lookout Prison Camp for Confederates*, 117–118.

15 National Cemetery Administration, comp., Federal Stewardship of Confederate Dead (Washington D.C., 2016), 5, accessed April 12, 2025, https://www.cem.va.gov/docs/wcag/history/Federal-Stewardship-Confederate-Dead.pdf.

bearing tablets inscribed with the names of deceased Confederates. The law was amended to authorize one monument placed over a mass grave.

A joint Resolution passed by Congress on December 23, 1910, proclaimed:

> That where it has been, or shall hereafter be, found impossible to identify the individual burial place of Confederate prisoners of war, the Secretary of War is hereby authorized to cause to be erected central masonry construction, or monument, upon which bronze tablets shall be placed containing the names of the deceased prisoners of war who are buried in its immediate vicinity.[16]

The 85-foot monument erected in 1910 by the Federal government marks the final resting place of the Confederate dead at Point Lookout. The contract for its construction was awarded to the Van Amringe Granite Company of Boston, which built the structure. The monument is composed of reinforced concrete faced with North Carolina granite. It displays, in alphabetical order, the names of 3,384 deceased prisoners—including soldiers, sailors, and civilians—together with the company and regiment of each, inscribed on eight bronze plaques.[17]

In 1910, while the monument was under construction, the Maryland state monument was relocated once again. Under the terms of the monument contract, the Van Amringe Granite Company was required to move the Maryland monument and its surrounding wrought-iron fence from its Tanner's Creek site back to the cemetery north of the former prison (Gilbert's Rebel Graveyard No. 1). Shortly after this move, the board of trustees of the Point Lookout Confederate Monument found the monument and surrounding grounds again in neglect, as no caretakers had been assigned.

In 1932, the Federal government declared the two vacant burial plots surplus property and sold them at auction. In 1938, after standing in its previous location for more than 20 years, the Maryland monument was moved once again to its final site, where it now stands beside the federal monument within the present-day boundaries of the wrought-iron fence.

The total cost of construction, the relocation of the Maryland state monument to its original location, fencing, and related expenses was $22,104.06.

16 Sword, "Confederate Cemetery, Point Lookout." 4.

17 "Shaft to Confederates: War Department to Erect Monument at Point Lookout, MD," *Evening Star* [Washington, D.C.], Sept. 19, 1910, 3, accessed April 14, 2025, https://www.loc.gov/resource/sn83045462/1910-09-19/ed-1/?sp=3&q=point+lookout%2C+md&r=0.08,0.88,0.575,0.347,0; M. C. Meigs, "Proposals for Iron Head Blocks," *The National Republican* [Washington, D.C.], Nov. 13, 1866, 3, accessed April 12, 2025, https://www.loc.gov/resource/sn86053571/1866-11-13/ed-1/?sp=3&st=image&r=0.288,0.502,0.344,0.207,0.

Monuments marking the final resting place of the remains of Confederate prisoners of war.

*Author*

Although the earlier cemetery of 1876 had been dedicated during the National Centennial Celebration on July 4, 1876, no evidence exists that the final cemetery and its new monument were ever officially dedicated after construction was completed in May 1911.[18]

18 National Cemetery Administration, Federal Stewardship, 186.

All the Confederate remains that could be recovered from the Tanner's Creek site were relocated to their final resting place beneath the present-day Federal monument. It is incorrect to rely on that monument for an accurate final number of deceased prisoners of war. The remains buried beneath the obelisk had been moved at least twice, if not more, before being placed there. The likelihood of losing remains, as well as the difficulty of determining identities, was compounded by the multiple reinterments. An eyewitness account by local citizen Albert Greenwell Jr. stated that his father told him the prisoners' remains from Tanner's Creek were moved to the present site in 1910 by two local workers, William Shorter and Yaret Hewlett, who had been hired to carry out the task. According to this account, the skulls, arms, and legs of the deceased were separated and placed in three boxes, which were then buried beneath the front and back of the monument.[19]

It was rare for a prisoner—or any soldier, for that matter—to possess formal identification. When a man's name was unknown, fellow prisoners often referred to him simply by his home state. The identity of a deceased prisoner could sometimes be provided by another inmate who had known him in life. With luck, that identification was entered into the proper register by a diligent clerk or nurse when the prisoner was admitted to Point Lookout or one of its hospitals.

The discrepancies in the recorded numbers of deceased prisoners can be attributed to faulty record keeping and the constant fluctuation of prisoner totals due to exchanges, releases, and transfers. Prison clerks often depended on the accuracy of reports made by prison and hospital staff, as well as the honesty of prisoners themselves. It is also likely that the figures varied with the condition and status of the sick and wounded across the three hospitals. This raises the question of how much cooperation or coordination existed between prison officials and hospital authorities in reporting statistics to the office of the commissary general of prisoners and the medical department.

Clerks often relied on incoming or outgoing prisoners to verify their identities. Examination of the handwriting in the surviving ledgers reveals that multiple clerks recorded entries on the same days. Evidence also shows that names were frequently entered phonetically—provided the prisoner gave his correct name in the first place. Such practices ensured that inaccuracies in both numbers and prisoner information were inevitable. In many cases, if a clerk had a name and a man claiming it, his task was considered complete, with no further follow-up by the provost staff. As a result, the prisoner lists and numerical records, along with their accuracy, must be regarded as highly suspect.

19 Sword, "Confederate Cemetery, Point Lookout." 5; Beitzell, *Point Lookout Prison Cap for Confederates*, 198.

The exact number of deceased at Point Lookout will most likely never be known. The identification discrepancies produced by the Civil War system gradually diminished as procedures improved with the introduction of dog tags, identification cards, and fingerprinting. These methods lay in the not-too-distant future, but not soon enough for the prisoners at Point Lookout.

As research continues and additional deceased prisoners are identified, the recorded number of deaths at Point Lookout will likely rise. Undoubtedly, names still await discovery in diaries, letters, attics, or family Bibles. Present-day visitors to the cemetery have occasionally reported that an ancestor died there, though the name does not appear on the extensive lists displayed on the national monument. There are also claims that some names inscribed on the monument as deceased are incorrect, and that those individuals in fact survived both the prison and the war.

The deceased prisoners at Point Lookout were treated in the same manner as other enemy prisoners of war. Mass graves were not uncommon, as trenches became necessary in some areas because of the sandy soil that composed the peninsula. Unfortunately, these mass graves were seldom marked individually, unlike other cemeteries where individual graves were provided. Burial efforts were likely further hindered by the high-water table at Point Lookout, which caused graves and trenches to flood as they were being dug.

As demonstrated, the records produced by the Reburial Program did not correspond to the official records of the government or prison authorities. This discrepancy extends speculation regarding the true number of those who died while imprisoned at Point Lookout. The death of any prisoner or soldier is a tragedy, but to be forgotten is worse. Many left their homes for war, confident they would return as heroes—or at the very least be remembered by their families as having fallen on the field of honor. For many at Point Lookout, however, remembrance came only in the form of a stark prison roll marked simply, "Died."

Before thousands of prisoners of war were released from Point Lookout to begin their journey home, many were first required to swear an Oath of Allegiance and Amnesty to secure their release papers. Those who accepted government-provided transportation to the South were assembled at the wharf for the journey home. The former prisoners departed joyfully, relieved to leave behind a place of death, deprivation, and misery. Many speculated during their return about what awaited them in the future. Yet thousands never left Point Lookout, their remains permanently confined there.

## Chapter 12

# The Fortifications of Point Lookout

The near success of the February 1864 breakout attempt inspired Confederate plans to liberate the prisoners at Point Lookout. The incident also served as a wake-up call for Federal authorities in Washington, demonstrating the urgent need to strengthen the post's security and defenses. A successful attack and mass escape would be devastating to the Northern war effort, precisely what the Rebels were hoping. In response to the threat, Federal authorities stepped up their readiness and fortified the defenses at Point Lookout.

Though the February breakout failed, prison authorities undertook new measures to prevent further attempts. Beginning in late July 1864, additional artillery was emplaced, followed by the construction of three earthen redoubts with supporting works. These fortifications served as a visible deterrent, signaling to the prisoners that security had been reinforced. Prisoners were warned that any renewed effort to overpower the guard force would be answered with gunfire at the slightest provocation. Coupled with the firepower of patrolling naval gunships, these new defenses made clear that any future uprising would be met with devastation.

Externally, and from the outset, the defense of Point Lookout constituted a major concern for Federal authorities. After the breakout attempt, the possibility of a Confederate attack to liberate the prisoners became an urgent priority. Defensive planning took advantage of the natural geographic restrictions created by the site's position on Maryland's southernmost peninsula. The relatively small guard force assigned to protect Point Lookout and its surrounding areas could defend it effectively once strategically deployed with the support of the U.S. Navy.

The two main roads leading onto the peninsula eventually converged and passed through the center of Point Lookout, terminating at the lighthouse.

From there, these same roads extended north, connecting with a central route that continued on to several larger towns before reaching the major cities of Washington and Baltimore.

There was no bridge across the lower Potomac River connecting southern Maryland to the distant Virginia shoreline, while the Eastern Shore of the Chesapeake Bay lay more than 20 miles away. Point Lookout, situated on a narrow peninsula, could be defended effectively by a determined force against attack from either land or water. This reality was not lost on the succession of officers who commanded the post or on the Army Corps of Engineers. Both recognized that the successful defense of Point Lookout depended on fully exploiting its geography, the type of fortifications constructed, and the proper deployment of troops and artillery.

A coordinated defensive position would be paramount in the event of either an enemy attack or a prisoner breakout. Equally critical were secure lines of communication between defending units. As early as September 1863, General Marston, assisted by Captain Francis U. Farquhar of the U.S. Army Corps of Engineers, began constructing rudimentary defensive works across the northern portion of the peninsula to fortify these strategic approaches.[1]

During the early phase of construction, soldiers of the 2nd and 12th New Hampshire regiments were assigned to build the first defensive works. In September 1863, Private Haynes of the 2nd New Hampshire recorded in his diary: "We are building a stockade across 'the neck' [Potomac River side], a narrow strip of sand connecting the Point with the mainland." The Potomac River approach was secured by a log palisade wall—referred to by the guards as a "stockade"—pierced for small-arms fire. This palisade stood approximately 12 feet high. About 100 yards to the north, soldiers constructed a lunette to mount an artillery battery.[2]

The bay-side approach was secured by an earthen berm, a log blockhouse, and a ditch 15 feet wide and equally deep, spanned by a bridge. Corporal George Allen of the 4th Rhode Island observed that an earthwork was built "capable of accommodating a battery of field artillery [six cannons]." By early 1864, this position was further fortified with an additional 10 artillery pieces covering the stockades across the causeway. The blockhouse and palisade were flanked on both sides by rows of closely set posts extending into the bay on one side and into Point Lookout Creek on the other. For added strength and stability, the

1 *OR* 33/1:667.

2 Haynes, *A Soldier Boy's Letters*, 142.

bases of the palisade walls at both land approaches were entrenched 3 to 4 feet into the ground.[3]

At the same time, work began on a blockhouse located just outside the prison gate, intended both as a deterrent to prisoner escape and as protection for the guard force. Private Haynes noted that a blockhouse was already under construction that "would have a howitzer mounted in it to command the main entrance to the prisoner's camp and double as a guard house." In time, two 12-pound howitzers were mounted to reinforce the log blockhouse.[4]

Confederate prisoner accounts attest to these improved defensive measures. Prisoners confirmed the presence of a heavily guarded palisade fence, reinforced with two cannons positioned to face the prison pen as a deterrent against mass escape. They also noted that one or two naval gunboats were regularly anchored on the river with their guns trained on the prison as an additional precaution. Point Lookout was also defended by multiple strategically positioned artillery pieces, supported by fortified earthen works.[5]

Still, as late as April 1864, commanding officer General Hinks complained to Butler that the existing works were inadequate, adding that they would not fully protect the Point from attacks by enemy forces or from "revolts" by the prisoners. Any such action would devastate the hospital and much public property. The threat extended to the contraband camp, as well as to civilians and patients in the hospital.[6]

Hinks's concerns were well founded. At the time of his communication to Butler, more than 6,000 prisoners were confined at Point Lookout, a number that would rise to over 15,000 within the next two months. Hinks proposed placing a small work on the peninsula along the Chesapeake Bay side near the palisade and blockhouse, to be manned by a regiment of infantry, and a "redoubt constructed on the Potomac River side near the Murphy Farm to be strongly armed and fully manned." He further recommended that the peninsula between the Potomac and Point Lookout Creek (present-day Lake Conoy) be "strongly stockaded." He concluded by recommending that the "rest of the garrison remain in the camp upon the ground now occupied by the 2nd N[ew] H[ampshire] Vols. [Potomac River side] and the 5th N[ew] H[ampshire] [Chesapeake Bay side] regiments."

3 Allen, *Forty-Six Months with the Fourth Rhode Island Volunteers*, 267; *Book No. 253*, Vol.1, 261; Letter by Everson, "Letters," 33.

4 Haynes, *A Soldier Boy's Letters*, 145.

5 Holliday, "Vain Efforts," in *Confederate Veteran*, 28:383.

6 *Book No. 253*, Vol.1, 2–5.

These camps protected not only the approaches to the Point but also the flanks and approaches to the prison.[7]

The defense of the point was strengthened by the additional support of gunboats from the Potomac Flotilla and elements of the North Atlantic Blockading Squadron. Vessels normally employed in deep-water navigation, along with craft more suited to shallow waters, were rotated in and out of Point Lookout. They either lay at anchor or patrolled just off the point in the bay, the Potomac River, and surrounding rivers and creeks.

The defenses of Point Lookout extended beyond the point itself, as far north as the town of Leonardtown. Located approximately 20 miles north of the point, Leonardtown was then, as now, the county seat of St. Mary's County. An office for the provost marshal was established in the courthouse, and his force encamped nearby in an area known as Sheep Pen Woods. In January 1863, companies A, B, and M (totaling 150 men) of "Scott's 900," later officially designated the 11th New York Cavalry, arrived in Leonardtown under the command of Maj. Seth P. Remington. Later that year, companies of the 2nd and 5th U.S. Cavalry were assigned to replace this force. Both units shared the duties of provost marshal and patrol.[8]

The 20-man mounted force from Point Lookout augmented the cavalry detachments assigned to patrol St. Mary's County. In addition to the camp at Leonardtown, several mobile camps were established at strategic locations throughout the county, including Piney Point, Colton Point, the town of Hollywood, and as far north as the town of Benedict. Although the primary focus of the mounted patrols was St. Mary's County, they were also known to operate as far east as Calvert County and west into Charles County, searching for contraband, protecting the telegraph line, and monitoring for signs of enemy activity.

The advanced guard force north of Point Lookout consisted of several vidette and picket post locations. This perimeter extended as far north as the village of Ridge, approximately seven miles from Point Lookout, and guarded the major roads leading northeast (Route 235, or "Three Notch Road") and north (present-day Route 5, also known as "St. Inigoes Road") toward Washington and Baltimore through Ridge.

As the threat of an attack on Point Lookout grew more imminent, Hinks's warning to Butler in early April 1864 served as a wake-up call that could no longer be ignored. When the danger lessened by mid-July 1864, the War Department

7 *OR* 8/2:991; *Book No. 253*, Vol.1, 2–5.

8 Thomas West Smith, *The Story of a Cavalry Regiment "Scott's 900" Eleventh New York Cavalry, from the St. Lawrence River to the Gulf of Mexico, 1861–1865* (Chicago, IL, 1897), 66.

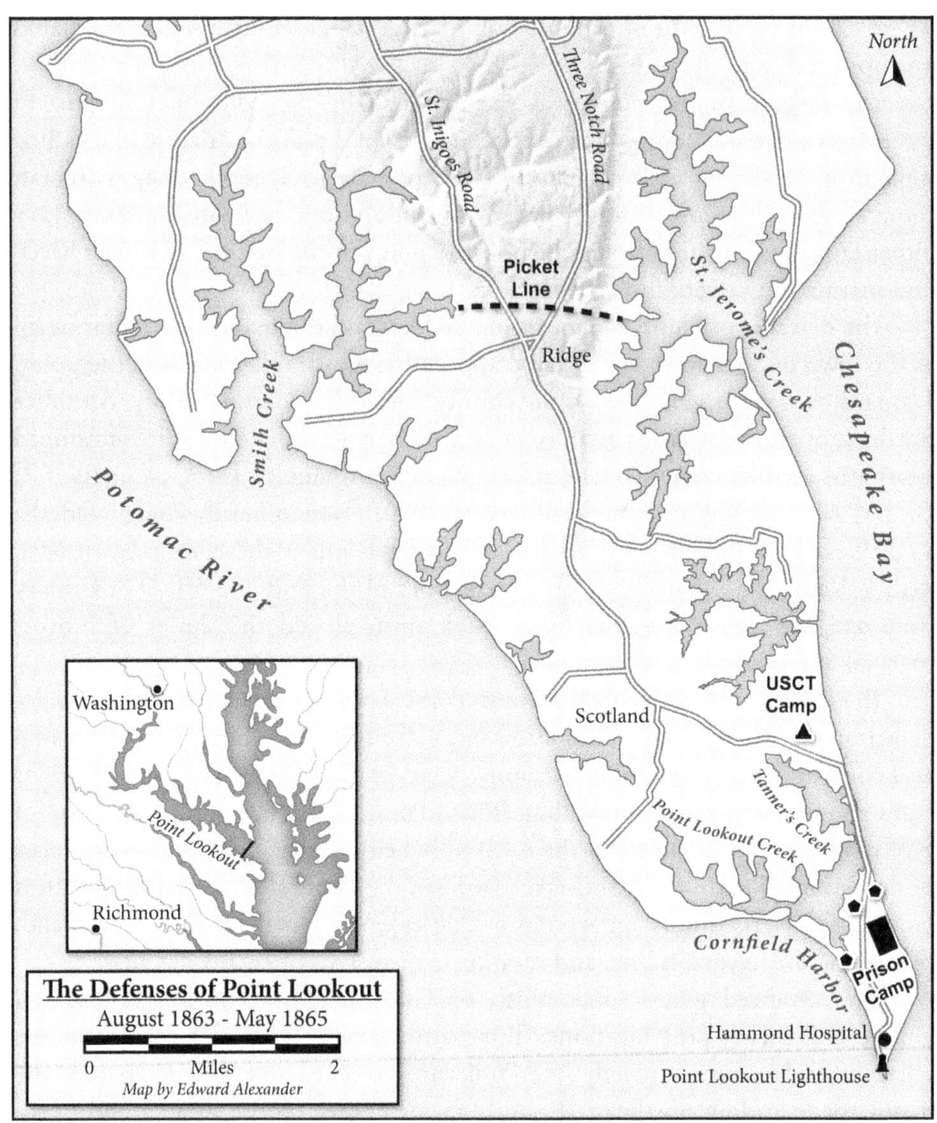


recognized that it had narrowly avoided an enormous catastrophe. An aggressive program to strengthen the defenses of Point Lookout was immediately begun.

In July 1864, General Barnes ordered entrenchments constructed along the shoreline south of Point Lookout Creek. The creek and adjoining swamp covered the central approach between the two connecting necks of land, making an assault through this point nearly impossible. Additional rifle pits defended the gap between the palisade wall on the Potomac River, and the palisade wall and blockhouse on the Chesapeake Bay. These defenses could be quickly manned from the northern guard camps in the event of an attack. Barnes reported to the War Department in his daily telegram of July 11 that the defensive works he had initiated were nearly completed.[9]

Nevertheless, these measures did not satisfy officials in Washington. The War Department ordered him to strengthen his defenses, as his current fortifications were judged inadequate to protect against either a prisoner breakout or an external attack. Soon after, Point Lookout was incorporated into Washington's overall defenses by the new department commander, Major General Augur. If Point Lookout were captured by enemy forces, it would place a formidable hostile presence not only behind Union lines but also along an open avenue to the nation's capital. Despite Barnes' objections, Secretary of War Stanton ordered the construction of more substantial fortifications to prevent any attempt to liberate the prisoners of Point Lookout by force.

## The Fortifications of Point Lookout

Major Charles S. Stewart of the U.S. Army Corps of Engineers arrived at Point Lookout on July 16, 1864, under orders from Brig. Gen. Richard Delafield, chief engineer of the U.S. Army, to evaluate the defensive works at Point Lookout and to select sites for earthen redoubts. On July 20 Stewart was further directed to "make Point Lookout perfectly secure from within and without by defensive works." The fortifications Stewart proposed considered both the existing defenses and their weaknesses. His plan emphasized expediency and simplicity of construction, using materials that could be readily obtained on site by the available workforce.[10]

On July 22, Stewart submitted his report and recommendations to Delafield, including a hand-drawn map of Point Lookout's existing defenses. The map depicted three recommended redoubts, numbered 1, 2, and 3, with a fourth fort proposed near the main entrance of the prisoners' camp. Although recommended, the fourth redoubt was never constructed. Instead, a massive two-story log guardhouse erected at the main gate of the prison served the same purpose and was accepted in its place. Stewart's evaluation and proposed plans were approved and acted upon immediately. Officials determined that three redoubts would be the most expedient to construct for the defense of Point Lookout.[11]

9 *Book No. 253*, Vol.1, 482.

10 "Point Lookout State Park" March 30, 1994; Charles S. Stewart to Richard Delafield, telegram, July 20, 1864. DeGrange Index, Library of Congress, Washington, D.C., S-9228, RG 77.

11 Charles S. Stewart to Richard Delafield, "Point Lookout, MD," DeGrange Index, Library of Congress, Washington, D.C. RG 77, S-9233, July 22, 1864.

Stewart was concerned that recruiting a workforce from the standing guard for the construction of the redoubts would prove insufficient. At least half of the guard force was drawn from two units of the Veteran Reserve Corps, composed of men unable to endure the rigors of active campaigning. The guard force was already strained to near exhaustion by rotations, patrols, and other fatigue duties necessary for prison operations and security. Stewart noted this in his report to Delafield, stating that he could obtain few soldiers from the guard since they were not physically capable of performing heavy labor in soil composed largely of clay and sand. The project, he judged, would proceed slowly and at great cost.

Barnes, Stewart, and the engineer officers under his command decided that, in the interim, a small detachment of the guard force would be spared as laborers until a more suitable solution could be found. This arrangement was short-lived, as the number of prisoners rose to 15,000 by the end of July. Because of this sudden increase, Union guards were exempted from working on the fortifications. Although a token guard force was required for security during construction, it was far fewer in number than those needed to perform the actual labor.

Stewart stated in his report that it would be costly for the army to hire outside laborers, noting "it will not be possible to procure them at less than, if at all, $1.25 a day & a ration in addition, & we will have to encamp them." As construction plans advanced, there remained uncertainty regarding who would perform the physical labor on the fortifications. Regardless of who undertook the work, a substantial labor force was required to construct the three redoubts within the time demanded by Stanton and Delafield. Ultimately, however, a labor force was already present at Point Lookout—fed, housed, and encamped—and could provide the necessary work at little cost without the need for additional compensation.[12]

However, permission to employ the Confederate prisoners was required and Stewart soon requested it. In late July, Stewart inquired

> whether there is any objection to the employment of rebel prisoners, who are willing in throwing up the defensive works here. The prisoners are allowed a small sum for each day's work, the amount being placed to their credit, or made up to them in some article needed by them. It is believed that quite a number would willingly work for us for the sake of the small allowance made them as well as from a desire to be occupied.[13]

12 Stewart to Delafield, "Point Lookout." DeGrange Index, Library of Congress, Washington, D.C. RG 77, S-9234. July 23, 1864.

13 "Point Lookout State Park," March 30, 1994.

Many prisoners readily volunteered for this detail, tempted by the various forms of compensation offered by the provost marshal. The cost of paying the sutler for the items used as prisoner compensation amounted to approximately $1,000.[14]

Hundreds of prisoners vied for selection in the three construction projects. For the prisoners, the primary appeal was that the work offered relief from the tedium of confinement inside the stockade, in addition to the compensation being provided. Stewart's proposed earthen works, as originally designed, would take months to complete, requiring thousands of man-hours and considerable funding to realize his plan. Private James Elliott of the 56th North Carolina wrote in March 1865 that "the largest detail was known as the fort detail, building, and sodding a fort on the Potomac side [Redoubt No. 3]. About three hundred men were worked on it."[15]

From the outset, Stewart directed the construction operations, assisted by engineer officers Capt. Samuel M. Mansfield and Lieutenants John T. Cantwell and William A. Jones. Assistant civil engineer John Bogart served as overseer, supported by several hired civilian carpenters. Despite Barnes's objections to the additional fortifications, work on the three proposed earthen redoubts began with preliminary preparations on July 24, 1864, followed by actual construction commencing on July 27 with a token detachment of Union soldiers. On July 30, authorization was received to employ prisoner labor, relieving the small force of soldiers, who were eager to return to their guard duties.[16]

## Construction of Redoubts 1, 2, and 3

The redoubts were constructed diagonally on a northeast-by-southwest axis. In this arrangement, artillery from all three positions could cover the approaches to Point Lookout by land and sea, including any attack on an individual redoubt, without interfering with one another's fire. The northernmost position, Redoubt No. 2, was located on the Chesapeake Bay side. Redoubt No. 3, the most southerly fort, stood on the shore of the Potomac River, while Redoubt No. 1—also known as the "Central Fort"—was situated between the two. Redoubts No. 1 and No. 2 were placed on either side of the main entrance road into Point Lookout.

14 Henry Brewerton to Richard Delafield, Nov. 16, 1864, RG 77, File Number 857, DeGrange Index 1864–1865, National Archives and Records Administration, Washington, D.C.

15 James Carson Elliott, *The Southern Soldier Boy: A Thousand Shots for the Confederacy* (Raleigh, NC, 1907), 30.

16 *OR* 3/3:156. According to Article 76 of the Lieber Code, prisoners could be required to work on any details found necessary by prison authorities that "may be required for the benefit of the captor's government, according to their rank and condition."

Construction of Redoubts No. 1 and No. 2 began first. The garrison christened these two positions as Fort Stanton and Fort Lincoln, respectively. They were soon followed by work on the remaining earthwork, Redoubt No. 3, which retained only its numerical designation, as it was never completed to the same stage as Forts Stanton and Lincoln. All three redoubts were designed with barbette, or cannon, platforms that allowed unrestricted, multi-directional fire for light field artillery.

Engineers' calculations for the three proposed redoubts had to be precise when constructing the moats, their surrounding walls, and the internal formations. The removal of the correct amount of earth from the moat was necessary to construct the redoubt walls, platforms, traverses and powder magazines to their proper heights and thickness. The moats of each redoubt measured approximately 20 feet wide by 15 feet deep providing enough earth to construct what was required including the walls of the redoubts that measured 8 feet in height by 22 feet at their base.

An additional measure was necessary in building the works: several areas of the redoubts were sodded to stabilize the earthen walls and prevent erosion caused by heavy summer rains. Sod cut from the local marsh grass proved effective. Because of the engineered slope of the walls, the sod covering would, by its weight, naturally settle back and reinforce the structure.[17]

On November 8, Col. Henry Brewerton of the U.S. Army Corps of Engineers relieved Stewart and took command of construction operations at Point Lookout. In one of his final reports, dated November 3, 1864, Stewart noted that Redoubt No. 1 would be completed first, as it did not include the additional two-gun barbette platforms with which Redoubts No. 2 and No. 3 were designed. This modification made the Central Fort a four-gun position, in contrast to the other two, which could each mount six guns. Shortly thereafter, a company of the 20th V.R.C. garrisoned Redoubt No. 1.[18]

Brewerton reported on January 5, 1865, that the Point Lookout quartermaster had placed a temporary one-story wooden barracks, accommodating about 90 men, on one of the faces of the parade ground in Redoubt No. 1. Barnes requested that similar structures be erected in Redoubts No. 2 and No. 3 for the same purpose. It was Barnes's intention that, in the event of a mass prisoner breakout, all three forts could house as much of the garrison as possible in order to defend Point Lookout.[19]

17 Beitzell, *Point Lookout Prison Camp for Confederates*, 54; Charles M. Stotz, "Defense in the Wilderness," in *Drums in the Forest*, 2nd ed., by James Alfred Proctor, Historical Society of Western Pennsylvania, and Charles Morse Stotz (Pittsburgh, 2005), 162.

18 Eicher, Eicher, and Simon, *Civil War High*, 144; Henry Brewerton to Richard Delafield, Nov. 9, 1864, RG 77, File Number 837, DeGrange Index 1864–1865, National Archives and Records Administration, Washington, D.C.

19 Colonel Henry Brewerton to Brig. Gen. Richard Delafield, January 5, 1865.

Present-day view of the interior of Fort #3. *Author*

A guardhouse was constructed adjacent to the main gate, which opened to the sally port and gorge (the principal entrance) of the redoubts. Each redoubt could accommodate at least two barracks for enlisted men, along with two officers' quarters located on the northern face of the inner works. Positioned in the northernmost corners, these buildings completed the complement of structures required for each redoubt.

The buildings were simple in nature and basic in design. They were easy to construct and equally easy to dismantle once their purpose had passed. Built in the balloon-frame method of the period, they followed the same construction style used for all structures within the complex. Roll-felt roofing was commonly applied; however, evidence suggests that tar pitch, along with pea gravel and sand from the nearby beaches, was also used to seal the roofs of some buildings. The walls of each structure were coated in whitewash. Each redoubt was designed to contain a powder magazine. Because neither brick nor stone was readily available to meet immediate construction needs, each magazine was built with an internal wooden framework and covered with local materials such as earth and clay. Marsh grass from the nearby swamp was used as sod to render the structures bombproof. The magazine entry doors were wooden and painted with whitewash.[20]

20 Charles S. Stewart to Richard Delafield, "Point Lookout, MD," Nov. 2, 1864, RG77, S9351, DeGrange Index, Library of Congress, Washington, D.C.

Each wall of the redoubts featured a palisade revetment, which Brewerton reported as being constructed of "breast-height planking"—horizontal wooden boards lining the inner walls. This design, however, presented problems due to the unstable composition of the earthen walls. Torrential rainstorms compounded these difficulties, causing the support planking to warp and wash out sections of the palisade, which required additional time to repair.[21]

By May 1, 1865, Brewerton concluded that hostilities had effectively ceased, based on the steady reduction of his labor force as men were released by federal order. He transmitted inquiries to Delafield regarding the continuation of the fortification project, noting that he had received no instructions from his superiors in Washington on how to proceed now that the war was ending. While awaiting an official reply, Brewerton began shutting down his operations, relying on reports in the *New York Herald*—"which I had presumed to be true"—concerning the cessation of hostilities.[22]

Brewerton reported to Delafield that he was completing several projects and paying off the hired workers. He further stated, "I have telegraphed to my assistant Mr. Bogart, at Point Lookout, Md. to suspend all work on the field defenses . . . and collect tools and materials preparatory to sending them to [Fort Monroe]." By this time, the three forts were operational but remained incomplete as originally planned. The internal support buildings had been constructed, as requested by General Barnes. Brewerton received Delafield's reply two days later, on May 3, 1865, officially concluding the fortification project and leaving the forts in their unfinished state. On June 12, 1865, Brewerton notified Delafield from Fortress Monroe that his responsibility at Point Lookout "was brought to a close on the 4th of May 1865."[23]

In Brewerton's final report for the year ending June 30, 1865, he included his final dispositions for the three earthen redoubts at Point Lookout:

> During the past year three redoubts have been constructed at Point Lookout, Md. commanding the approaches to the prisoner's camp and the camp itself. These earthen redoubts are square, and of the same size: having sides of sixty yards in length. Two of these redoubts, No. 1 and 3 are provided with platforms for four field guns [It was intended that Redoubt No. 3 was to have a double barbette as drawn but was not completed]. In all fourteen guns can be placed in position.

21 U.S. War Department, U.S. Army Corps of Engineers, Annual Report, B1692.

22 Colonel Henry Brewerton to Brig. Gen. Richard Delafield, May 5, 1865.

23 Henry Brewerton to Richard Delafield, May 3, 1865, RG 77, File Number B1318, DeGrange Index 1864–1865, National Archives and Records Administration, Washington, D.C.

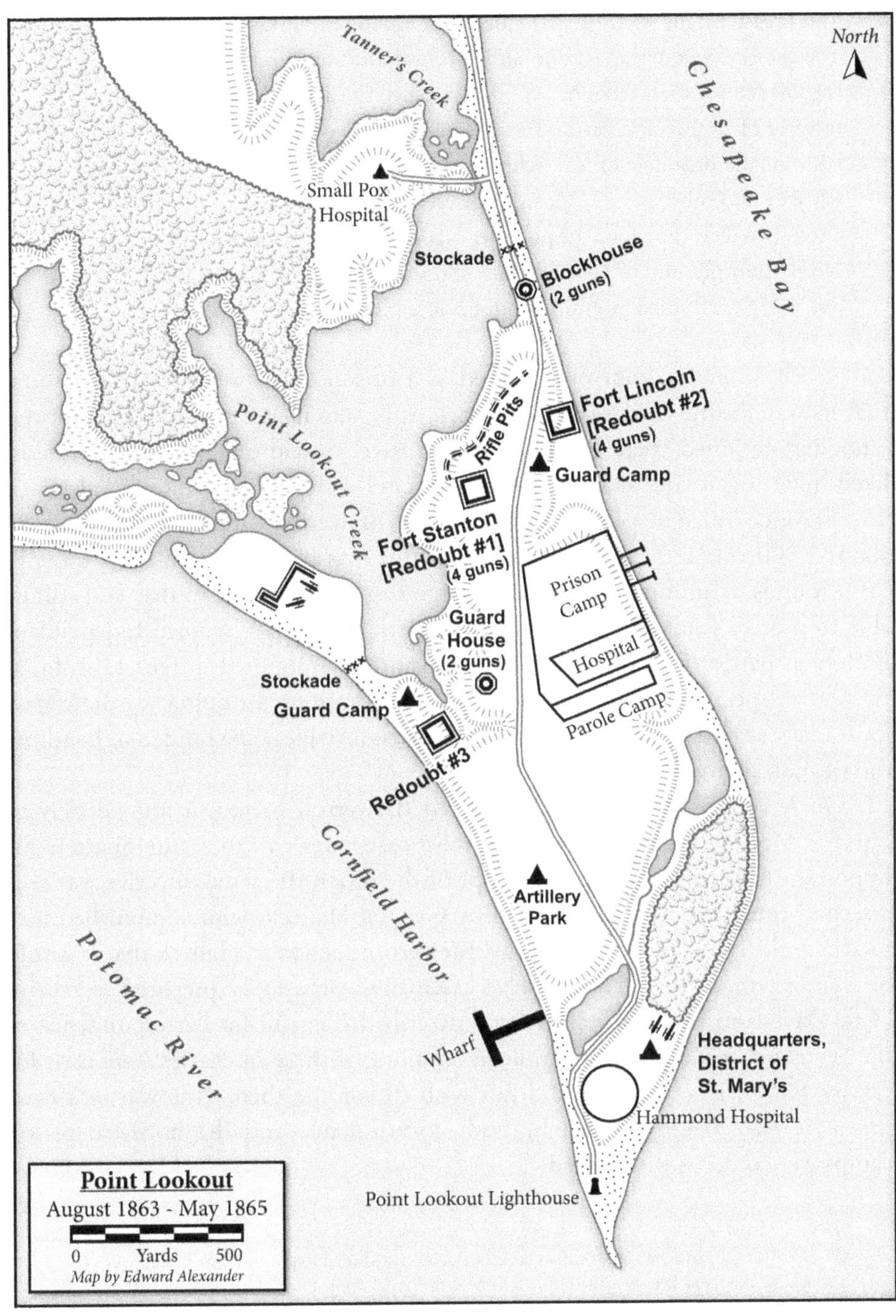
North
Tanner's Creek
Chesapeake Bay
Small Pox Hospital
Stockade
Blockhouse (2 guns)
Point Lookout Creek
Rifle Pits
Fort Lincoln [Redoubt #2] (4 guns)
Guard Camp
Fort Stanton [Redoubt #1] (4 guns)
Prison Camp
Guard House (2 guns)
Hospital
Stockade
Guard Camp
Parole Camp
Redoubt #3
Cornfield Harbor
Artillery Park
Potomac River
Wharf
Headquarters, District of St. Mary's
Hammond Hospital
Point Lookout Lighthouse
Point Lookout
August 1863 - May 1865
0 Yards 500
Map by Edward Alexander

> The breast height of these redoubts is of wood, the other slopes being earth. The exterior wooden magazine underground and made bomb-proof with earth is provided for each redoubt . . . The entrance to each redoubt is defended by a traverse of timber and earth. These redoubts were constructed by the volunteer labor of the prisoners of war, which labor was paid for by a small allowance of whiskey and tobacco . . . Operations were brought to a close on the 3rd of May 1865, at which time four, 12 pounder Napoleon guns were mounted in Redoubt No. 1 [Fort Stanton or Central Fort] and three 12 pounder brass howitzers, and one 4-1/2-inch rifled gun in Redoubt No. 2 [Fort Lincoln].[24]

When Point Lookout first opened as a prison, Marston reported to Butler that its waterborne defense against attack or breakout was provided by a mortar schooner stationed there by the Potomac River Squadron. Marston was most likely referring to the USS *Sophronia*, a vessel classified as a mortar schooner. The 4.5-inch rifled siege gun mentioned in Brewerton's report had a range of about 1,900 yards. Butler specifically sent this massive weapon to Marston with "100 rounds of ammunition . . . on a large siege carriage . . . so that you will be able to protect yourself." The gun arrived with the 2nd Wisconsin Independent Battery as part of its armament and was eventually mounted in Fort Lincoln, as Brewerton specified in his closing report of operations. In doing so, Brewerton most likely spared the men of the 2nd Wisconsin Artillery the burden of handling the weapon themselves.[25]

On May 15, 1865, Delafield ordered Brewerton to return immediately to Fortress Monroe to "prepare ten or twelve casemates . . . to secure quarters for important prisoners." To ensure receipt of the order, the same directive was sent a second time directly to Brewerton by General Halleck, who admonished him to accomplish the task without delay. Brewerton replied to Halleck that it would be done at once. The "ten or twelve casemates" were to be prepared to receive "Jeff. Davis and his crew," as Halleck described them in his correspondence to the Secretary of War. Ultimately, however, none of these casemates were used for Davis's family, since Halleck did not wish to confine them. The war was over, prisoners were being released by both governments, and the northern prison camps were ordered dismantled.[26]

24 U.S. War Department, U.S. Army Corps of Engineers, Annual Report for Year Ending 30th June 1865, by Col. Henry Brewerton, RG 77, Fort Monroe, Fort Wool, and Field Works at Point Lookout b1692 (New York City, NY, 1865).

25 *OR* 33/1:667; *Book No. 255*, Vol.3, 112.

26 *OR* 49/1:2:773.

# Chapter 13

# The Final Days of Point Lookout

By April 1865, Union victory was in sight with the announcement of the surrenders of Robert E. Lee and Joseph Johnston. This was followed by news of the flight of Confederate President Jefferson Davis and his cabinet, and the dissolution of the Confederate government. Point Lookout averaged fewer than 100 prisoner releases from January to April 1865. Exchanges, however, continued, removing almost 8,000 prisoners between January and March. Despite this activity, no significant release of prisoners occurred until April.

Despite this long-awaited outcome, Federal authorities were reluctant to implement a wholesale parole of prisoners of war. This decision reflected uncertainty about the possible repercussions of thousands of paroled soldiers roaming freely in the North. As a result of the retention order, the population of Camp Hoffman rose to more than 22,000. Another factor driving Federal reluctance was the devastating news that reached Point Lookout by telegram on the morning of April 15, 1865.[1]

## Assassination

Flush with the news of Lee's surrender and the capitulation of the Army of Northern Virginia, most Americans were thrown into shock upon learning that the president and commander in chief had been assassinated. Reports also stated that simultaneous attempts on the lives of Secretary of State Seward and Vice President Johnson had been made, but both failed. These heinous acts enraged the surviving administration members and military leadership. Many immediately assumed

1 *OR* 8/2:1000–1002.

that the former leaders of the dissolved and fleeing Confederate government were complicit in the plot; they were urgently pursued for their possible involvement.

Many awaited the reaction of the United States military, which had only recently witnessed Lincoln's second inauguration. News of the assassination ignited a slow-burning fuse in an army awaiting orders from its leaders on what action to take. As Stanton dispatched contingents of Federal cavalry and detectives in search of the conspirators, he also ordered military commanders to maintain control of their armies, fearing the possibility of wholesale retaliation and the destruction of their former enemies.

There was a real possibility of reprisal by the Federal guard as news of the assassination reached Point Lookout. In the early morning hours of April 15, Halleck sent a series of telegrams to Barnes relaying the devastating news and issuing instructions. Reports suggested that conspirators might cross the Potomac into Virginia, perhaps seeking sanctuary in friendly southern Maryland territory. Barnes was ordered to immediately increase mounted patrols throughout St. Mary's County and to coordinate with the ships of the Potomac Flotilla in monitoring the many possible crossing points of the Potomac River, the Chesapeake Bay, and adjacent creeks and tributaries into Virginia. He further ordered his personal guard boat to detain the mail boat, which normally carried dispatches to Leonardtown, Maryland, and Washington in the event of a telegraph failure.[2]

The fear of retaliation by the prison guard force was evident in accounts recorded by many prisoners. Several, including Pvt. David Johnston of the 7th Virginia, had the misfortune of arriving at Point Lookout that same day. Johnston and his fellow captives were informed by the guard what would happen to them should there be any signs of celebration:

> Saturday the 15th, found our vessel anchored off Point Lookout . . . [We] were soon convinced that some fearful catastrophe had taken place, as the flags on the shipping were at half-mast . . . [W]e became satisfied that the report of Mr. Lincoln's death was true, the federal soldiers informing us that any signs of exultation would result in the opening of the batteries on us. We saw that the guns were pointed at the prison.[3]

2 *OR* 46/1:3:802–803.

3 David Emmons Johnston, *The Story of a Confederate Boy in the Civil War* (Portland, OR, 1914), 339.

Prisoner George Neese of Chew's Battery described the sudden change in demeanor among the guards at morning roll call. By then, it was clear that the guards knew of the death of their president and commander in chief. Prisoners soon recognized the possibility of reprisal as they observed the guards' angry reactions during the morning evolutions. Neese noted that the flags were at half-staff and recorded, "the Yankee sergeant came in to superintend the roll call he tried to look sad, but from his snappish demeanor I at once saw that the biggest bunch of his grief was entirely composed of anger."

After the roll was called, a prisoner asked the sergeant, "why are the flags floating at half-mast this morning?" The sergeant, visibly angry, replied, "Some of you Rebels killed President Lincoln last night." His agitation was clear in the quick repartee of a prisoner who replied, "We did not do it, for we were here in this pen all night." Private Samuel Pickens of the 5th Alabama wrote, "The flags have been at half-mast all day . . . we first heard it was for the death of Abe Lincoln who was assassinated in a theatre last night in Washington City. We were all right uneasy too, lest the Yankees might retaliate on us."[4]

The news spread throughout the point despite Barnes's request to his officers to suppress the information for at least 24 hours. Lieutenant Everson of the 20th V.R.C. understood what reaction could be expected from the guards should they perceive even the slightest sign of a celebration given by the Confederate prisoners in their charge. "It was the endeavor of Gen. James Barnes . . . to keep the news of the assassination from the prisoners for a day or two," Despite Barnes' efforts to delay the announcement, Everson observed. "The guards and the guarded were in possession of the details the morning after it occurred."[5]

By the next morning, what Barnes and his staff feared most was evident in the faces of the Union soldiers. The guard force had already heard the news. Everson wrote that the Union soldiers were out of their tents, walking about their camps, "their hands in their pockets . . . there is no doubt that the minds of all were engaged with the same thought. The pulling of a few lanyards would have sent from those two earthworks [Redoubts 1 and 2] death and destruction beyond estimate."[6]

The trappings of a nation in mourning were already appearing at Point Lookout. In to a letter written by Pvt. John H. Matthews of the 11th V.R.C. to his brother, Matthews reported that "all the officers of both the Army and Navy . . . were

4 Neese, *Three Years in the Confederate Horse Artillery*, 353; Hubbs, *Voices from Company D*, 372.

5 Everson, Papers No. 28/710/22, 31–32.

6 Ibid., 31–32.

wearing black crepe on their left arms and on their swords. The Post Quarter Master has furnished black crepe to hang in front of all the offices and Public Headquarters on the Point. And as to the door fronts on the side of the Wharf."[7]

He later wrote that while the funeral for the slain president was taking place in Washington, "it was the stillest day that I have witnessed on Point Lookout. All business was stopped, and scarcely a man was to be seen anywhere from his private abode . . . [A]ll boats [were] searched before they can pass this Point, all try to detect and arrest the murderer John Wilkes Booth or any of the conspirators concerned in the assassination." Anyone who did not have a proper pass to travel, or who could not positively identify himself, was arrested by order of Halleck and Stanton.[8]

## Prisoner Release

Prior to his death, President Lincoln had issued a series of proclamations outlining the legal avenues by which former Confederates could return to the Union and regain citizenship without penalty. General Grant continued the slain president's work by issuing General Order No. 85 on May 8, 1865. This order directed that all who had asked to take the Oath of Allegiance prior to the fall of Richmond on April 2, 1865, were to be allowed to do so and then released, with transportation provided to their homes. It further stated that, "In respect to all other prisoners of war further orders will be issued." Grant desired a peaceful and steady transition toward reunion, but the war was still not officially concluded. To flood the Union with its former enemy all at once could have proved a serious mistake.[9]

President Johnson soon followed these actions by issuing Proclamation No. 134 on May 29, entitled, "Granting Amnesty to Participants in the Rebellion, with Certain Exceptions." Proclamation No. 134 was consistent with the Oath of Allegiance proclamations that President Lincoln had issued, namely Proclamation No. 108 of December 8, 1863, and Proclamation No. 111 of March 26, 1864.

7 John H. Matthews, "The Assassination of Abraham Lincoln and the Search for John Wilkes Booth," Confessions of an Oral Historian, Clifford B. Davids, accessed April 16, 2025, https://ashevilleoralhistoryproject.com/2012/11/05/lincoln/.

8 Ibid.

9 *OR* 8/2:538, General Order No. 85.

Proclamation No. 134 provided a final opportunity for individuals to accept the amnesty terms being offered without retribution.[10]

Between May and June, more than 20,000 prisoners were released from Point Lookout through a simple yet time-consuming procedure. The requisite paperwork slowed the process to an agonizing crawl for the prisoners, who were anxious to board the boats waiting at the wharf to transport them home. The delay was caused by the wait for two important documents issued by the provost marshal's office: the Oath of Allegiance and Amnesty, and the release forms signifying that they were officially freed from prison.

It was essential that a released former Confederate prisoner possess proof that he had taken the Oath of Allegiance and Amnesty and received his release forms. Without them, a soldier had no evidence that he was legally released and officially paroled by the Federal government. This paperwork permitted travel across Union lines to return home without interference. It was also required to gain access to government railroads for transportation and to receive rations or clothing at U.S. Army provost marshal's offices or quartermaster depots. It further proved that they were protected by Grant's General Order No. 85 and his Special Order No. 215. Former prisoners arrested without proof of release and parole risked being returned to Federal prison in close confinement.

It was apparent that the days of Point Lookout as a prison, like those of all other prisons, were ending. The remaining prisoners knew with certainty that the war was over, having witnessed the release of thousands of their fellow captives. By the end of May 1865, nearly 1,600 men were released from Point Lookout under General Order No. 85. This was soon followed by General Order No. 98, issued on May 27, which specified that civilian and Confederate military prisoners tried and sentenced by military tribunals during the war were to be released upon taking the Oath of Allegiance. As rapidly as the prison at Point Lookout had been organized in August 1863, it was closing just as swiftly almost two years to the day.

The general release was not restricted to those in the prison stockade alone but extended to the prison hospitals as well. At Hoffman's request, Barnes provided an accounting of the prisoners remaining in the hospitals. Barnes reported that as of May 16, 1865, approximately 1,859 men were in the prison hospitals. He noted that at least "1,600 of them were disabled by a loss of limb or by wounds and the

10 The American Presidency Project, "Proclamation 134—Granting Amnesty to Participants in the Rebellion, with Certain Exceptions," The American Presidency Project, UC Santa Barbara, accessed April 3, 2025, https://www.presidency.ucsb.edu/documents/proclamation-134-granting-amnesty-participants-the-rebellion-with-certain-exceptions.

expense of any further care for them at Point Lookout would be considerable." He further stated that "200 to 300 were not in condition to be furloughed at that time, but the others were able to take the Oath of Allegiance." On May 30, Stanton granted permission for their release and authorized the transfer of the sick and wounded to exchange and release points located in Mobile, Alabama, Wilmington, North Carolina, and Savannah, Georgia. Point Lookout was beginning to shut down.[11]

These decisions were immediately followed by General Order No. 104, issued on June 2, 1865, by the adjutant general, which directed the quartermaster department to "furnish all prisoners of war, and citizen prisoners who have been or may be released from confinement . . . with transportation to their homes, or to the nearest points thereto which it may be practicable to reach by the usual routes of water and railroad transportation." As a provision of this order, a list of destination ports was announced, similar to those previously designated by Stanton. This list included Alexandria and Richmond, Virginia; Wilmington, North Carolina; Charleston, South Carolina; and Savannah, Georgia, by steamship. Prisoners could also choose to travel by various railroad systems to their home states, provided the rail lines had been repaired and were in operation.[12]

As a further measure to expedite the release process, President Johnson issued Presidential General Order No. 109 on June 6, 1865, entitled "Order for the Discharge of Certain Prisoners of War." Of particular importance to prison camp commanders, Article IV of this order directed that prison commanders release daily "as many of the prisoners hereby authorized to be discharged as proper rolls can be prepared for, beginning with those who have been longest in prison and from the most remote points of the country."[13]

This order effectively opened the floodgates for the former Confederate prisoners still held at Point Lookout. As a result of this directive, the largest release of prisoners from the prison occurred during June 1865, when approximately 18,836 men were discharged. While thousands of prisoners left the camp, several hundred sick men who were unable to walk out on their own were transferred to Hammond Hospital, to be released later during June and July.[14]

11 *OR 8/2:*557–558, 582.

12 R. Hugh Simmons, "Discharges from Fort Delaware April 1865 through January 1866," Fort Delaware Society Going Home, Fort Delaware Society, accessed April 16, 2025, https://www.fortdelaware.org/Going%20Home%20-%20The%20War%20is%20Over.htm; *Book No. 257*, 461.

13 Johnson, "Executive Orders," The American Presidency Project.

14 *OR* 8/2: Serial No. 121, 1002.

## The Prison Guards

On April 26, 1865, Headquarters, Department of Washington, XXII Corps issued General Order No. 56. Title I, Article 3, specified that a newly created

> District of the Patuxent [was] to embrace the country between the Potomac and the Patuxent Rivers and south of the Piscataway, and all troops serving therein, except Point Lookout and immediate vicinity, with headquarters at or near Port Tobacco. Col. H. H. Wells, Twenty-Sixth Michigan Volunteers, temporarily in charge.

Article IV, Section II further affected the status of Point Lookout, stating, "The District of St. Mary's is hereby discontinued. The commander of Point Lookout will report direct to these headquarters." After receiving these instructions, Barnes issued orders for his detachment commanders stationed in Leonardtown, Piney Point, and Blackistone Island to return to Point Lookout for reassignment as soon as the commanding officer of the new District of the Patuxent relieved them.[15]

The reduction of the guard force continued. The various companies of the 10th, 20th, and 28th United States Colored Troops, along with the 29th Connecticut Colored Infantry, were transferred from Point Lookout in May, followed by the 2nd Wisconsin Independent Light Artillery in July. The 11th and 20th Veteran Reserve Corps Regiments were discharged from Point Lookout and Washington by companies between August and November 1865. One company of the 24th U.S.C.T. arrived at Point Lookout on July 1 with orders to guard the station and assist in closing the post. They were transferred back to their regiment on July 17.[16]

Other companies of the U.S.C.T. that had been stationed at Point Lookout were transferred to Texas or Louisiana to protect the southwestern border between Mexico and the United States. These transfers were carried out in response to concerns raised by Secretary of State William H. Seward regarding a possible invasion of the southwestern United States by Emperor Maximilian of Mexico, who sought to exploit America's internal divisions.

The Mexican question may also have influenced the disposition of some reserve forces. Private George F. Risdon of the 20th V.R.C., a member of the mounted patrol encamped at Piney Point, Maryland, wrote to his sister that he hoped to be discharged and return home now that the war was over. He also

15 *OR* 46/1:3:962.

16 *Book No. 255*, Vol. 3, 498–500.

feared that this would not happen as soon as he wished. "It looks as though we would soon have peace once more, but I think it will not be of long duration, for we have got another little job to do down in Mexico with the French which will take six months or a year."[17]

According to several prisoners, many of the transferred U.S.C.T. soldiers were not pleased with the sudden change of theater. On May 28, 1865, Samuel Pickens of the 5th Alabama wrote, "The negro soldiers were sent off from here today . . . to be sent to Texas. Their place was taken by other Black troops who came from Washington." They resented the idea of being sent west instead of being discharged, as many White soldiers were, while Grant began demobilizing the army. In contrast, Black units were not considered volunteer organizations like many of the other guards, but instead were enlisted in the regular service, the same as the U.S. Regulars, bound by formal terms of enlistment.[18]

Regardless of which troops were arriving or departing, there were still prisoners to guard. By this point, guard duty had become more of a formality than a necessity. While many prisoners enjoyed release and began the journey home, others waited to be called out. Samuel Pickens, one of the last prisoners to be released, wrote on May 30, 1865: "The negro guards have been taken out and Rebels substituted. A company of forty or fifty prisoners of war have been formed with [prisoner Alonzo Morgan] as captain and Glover as one of the corporals. They are unarmed, but I suppose the men will willingly obey them." By then, prisoners were more concerned with release and transportation home than with planning an escape.[19]

## Oath of Allegiance, Parole, and Release

To expedite the release process, prison authorities began using Mess Hall No. 9, located at the northwest end of the prison and the last in the row of mess halls. Prisoners often described this building as devoid of furnishings, with no seating other than the bare floor. A stage was constructed to assist schoolteachers during classes and to serve visiting priests or ministers during religious services. The large mess hall provided the provost marshal and his clerks with the necessary space to administer the oath to large numbers at once.

17 Risdon, "Letters of Charles," 58–59.

18 Hubbs, *Voices from Company D*, 384–385.

19 Ibid.

The building soon became crowded with anxious prisoners hoping for release. The procedure began by calling squads of prisoners across the now-neutral deadline, allowing them to enter the building two at a time. They were ordered to stand at tables where clerks recorded their personal information, including name, rank, company, regiment, place and date of capture, date of arrival at Point Lookout, and a physical description such as height, weight, complexion, and the color of their hair and eyes.

They were then formed into a crescent-shaped line to accommodate as many men as possible at one time and to ensure that all prisoners properly performed the ceremony of parole. They stood with their hats removed and placed their right hand on a Bible, one for every four men, as the oath was administered. Overhead, a large United States flag, measuring 20 by 30 feet, formed a canopy under which the oath takers stood. After swearing the oath, each man received his completed oath and parole form, which he was required to sign or mark. The forms were then signed and witnessed by one of the clerks.

The release process slowed agonizingly for the thousands of prisoners now ordered to be freed. B. T. Holliday of Chew's Battery recorded that he was taken to an extension of the prison enclosure where "we remained for several days while our names were being enrolled on the books, and we signed our parole not to take up arms until exchanged . . . [T]he work of paroling was slow." Once this part of the process was completed, prisoners were moved into the stockade to take the Oath of Allegiance. Holliday noted in mid-June that they were placed in groups of 16 men. By the time Private George Neese of Chew's Battery went through as one of the last by the end of June, he remarked that they had been placed in groups of 32 to expedite the procedure.[20]

To exacerbate the situation further, it was announced in early June that, to maintain an orderly release process for the thousands who remained, the procedure would be conducted alphabetically rather than by date of capture. Prisoners whose last names began with the letters A, B, or C were to report to the provost marshal as the first to be released. Private David Johnston of the 7th Virginia remembered that on June 15, "as soon as it was announced that men's names beginning with the letter 'A' would repair to headquarters then it seemed to all appearances that half the prisoners had names beginning with the letter 'A.'"

20 Holliday, "Vain Efforts," in *Confederate Veteran*, 28:383–384. They were then required to kiss the Bible. Holliday further stated, "how fortunate that he knew nothing concerning "germs" in those days for thousands of dirty men kissed the same Bible; Neese, *Three Years in the Confederate Horse Artillery*, 354–355.

The required release and parole forms included a personal description of the prisoner based on the observations of the clerk completing the paperwork. In addition to noting the height and color of a prisoner's hair and eyes, the forms also recorded weight. In practice, weight was to be measured on the quartermaster's scales used for ration weighing, providing the clerk with an approximate figure. Many prisoners observed, often with some humor, the inaccuracy of the information gathered by clerks in their haste to move the process forward. Johnston claimed that upon his oath and release forms, "the reader may be interested to know that I have grown a full inch in height and gained more than 80 pounds in weight."[21]

Each form was required to be signed by the provost marshal, Maj. Allen G. Brady, to ensure its validity. The requirement that Brady personally sign every form would have delayed the process considerably. To alleviate this potential bottleneck and expedite the procedure, clerks were provided with rubber stamps bearing Brady's signature. A clerk affixed Brady's name to the form in acknowledgment of the prisoner taking the oath. The stamp was the final step in the paperwork.

The names of the departing prisoners were registered in two books. Once this was completed, each man marched out the opposite end of the building until 50 or more men had been assembled into a squad, which was then marched to the adjacent parole pen located beside the prison stockade. There they received three days' rations and were loaded onto boats bound for a release point of their choosing in the South, provided such a boat was available. Prisoners who did not wish to travel by boat were released to find their own way to their destination.[22]

By June 28, prisoners serving as nurses and patients who were able to walk were processed and released from the prison hospital in the same manner as others. On that day, John J. P. Murphy of the 34th North Carolina stated that at "about 10 a.m. all the 'J's' in the hospital had taken the Oath of Allegiance of America." The following day, Murphy wrote, "They made a clean sweep. Taken every man out of the Bull Pen [prison stockade]. I have no doubt very pleasant to the prisoners that was last getting out of the prison." On June 30, 1865, Murphy recorded, "By 12 M. [noon] every Confederate prisoner of war was a citizen of the U.S.A."[23]

21 Johnston, *The Story of a Confederate Boy in the Civil War*, 341, 344.

22 Hubbs, *Voices from Company D*, 386.

23 John Joseph Pledger Murphy, "Diary of John Pledger Murphy While in a Union Prison," Georgia American Genealogy and History Project, GA AGHP, accessed April 16, 2025, https://ahgp.org/ga/Diary2.html.

### "As we left the prison incolsure for the boat, we remembered Lot's wife and never looked back"[24]

After the release process was completed for each group of prisoners, they were held in the adjacent parole stockade. This reduced the risk of missing those who refused to take the oath and attempted to conceal themselves among the others. As one group exited, the next entered. Once marched to the parole area, they waited for transportation home as provided by General Order No. 104. Private David Johnston of the 7th Virginia noted that, "steamers were at the wharf and as soon as it was known that a sufficient number of those whose destination was Richmond were discharged to load the vessel. We went aboard landing at Richmond the evening of June 29."[25]

Some prisoners questioned the legality of being required to take the oath before their release. Sergeant James Thomas of the 2nd Maryland, along with a committee of fellow prisoners, believed they were being unlawfully forced to swear to a vow they considered unconstitutional and could not be compelled to take. To address their grievance, Thomas and his committee requested a meeting with General Barnes, who consented to hear their objections. Barnes allowed them to present their protest, after which he explained his position and the instructions he had received from his superiors in Washington for such cases. He stated that "The oath taking was made a matter of necessity. Orders came from the war department at Washington that all who would take the oath should be sent home; that those who refused should be sent to Washington to be placed in solitary confinement, or close confinement."[26]

Barnes further explained to the committee that he would be required to arrest them and send them, along with any others, to the federal penitentiary in Washington where "we might lie there and rot while Congress decided what to do with us." Thomas stated, "believing the war over and nothing to be gained by refusing, few failed to go up as their time came." For Thomas and his comrades, discretion proved the better part of valor that day.[27]

Some prisoners of foreign birth believed they were exempt from taking the Oath of Allegiance, reasoning that they had never been citizens of the United States and were therefore not obligated to swear it. Washington officials, however, were

24 Holliday, "Vain Efforts," in *Confederate Veteran*, 28:384.

25 Johnston, *The Story of a Confederate Boy in the Civil War*, 344.

26 Thomas, "Third Book," 83.

27 Ibid.

unsympathetic, declaring that regardless of national origin or circumstance, such prisoners were placed in the same class as all other Confederate prisoners under the various presidential proclamations. Congress determined that those who claimed foreign birth but had served the Confederacy were equally bound, alongside native-born Americans, to take the oath. Those who refused were subjected to the same confinement as explained to Thomas and his comrades, as directed by Congress. To federal authorities, foreign birth or residence made little difference.

The publication *War of the Rebellion: Official Records of the Union and Confederate Armies* states that of the more than 52,264 prisoners of war who passed through the gates of the Point Lookout prison camp during its existence, 15,192 were exchanged and another 22,810 were classified as released. On June 30, 1865, Barnes notified Hoffman by telegram that 279 prisoners had been released that day, further stating, "This completes the discharge of all prisoners of war confined at this Post."[28]

Now a former prisoner, George Neese recalled the moment he and his comrades walked out of Mess Hall No. 9 at the Point Lookout prison camp for the last time. "After we were through with the oath-taking we were turned loose on a green grassy sward outside of the prison gate and the men went so wild with joy that old veterans playfully tumbled and rolled on the grass like young schoolboys."[29]

## Closing the Books

On July 5, 1865, newly promoted Maj. Gen. William Hoffman wrote to General Grant, informing him that all prisoners held at Point Lookout, both military and civilian, had been released except for the sick and wounded, who were transferred to Hammond Hospital. Barnes and his one remaining aide, Sgt. Charles Rambo of Company D, 20th V.R.C., were ordered to oversee the closing of the post and the submission of its records.

On July 14, 1865, Barnes wrote to Hoffman stating that, "his [Barnes] duties at Point Lookout are discontinued as well as his connection with your dept . . . it will be necessary for Maj[or] Brady Prov[ost] Marshal to remain for the purpose of winding up the records of his office . . . and will soon be completed . . . it will be necessary for Sgt. Rambo 20th V.R.C. to remain with him for a few days."[30]

28 *OR* 8/2:991; *Book No. 257*, Vol. 4, 134.

29 Neese, *Three Years in the Confederate Horse Artillery*, 354–355.

30 *OR* 8/2:700–701; *Book No. 257*, 178–179.

Before Barnes could relinquish his command and depart Point Lookout, he was required to complete the final accounting and submit the prison fund. On August 2, Barnes wrote to Hoffman that, "The prison fund property (except the buildings) has been sold at auction." General Barnes and Sergeant Rambo then closed the books on Point Lookout and forwarded all records to Washington. Barnes, Brady, and Rambo transferred elsewhere later that month.[31]

Before departing, Barnes amended his final return report of the Point Lookout prison fund on August 6, 1865. As of that date, he stated that the closing and final accounting of operations at Point Lookout and Hammond Hospital had been concluded. The prison fund had originally begun with a budget of $550,418.00. After all final expenses were paid, a deficit of $5,861.69 brought the remaining balance to $544,556.31.

In his final report, Barnes included the prison fund account with the sales of prison fund and public properties ($2,511.81), along with the remaining balance of Hammond Hospital $25,845.49 (equal to $513,690.78 in 2025). After all outstanding invoices were satisfied, the final amount returned to the office of commissary general of prisoners totaled $572,917.44. With this final tally submitted, Point Lookout officially closed as a prison.[32]

On October 19, 1865, Hoffman returned the final balance of the total prison fund (which included that of all prisons and hospitals) to the commissary general of subsistence amounting to $1,845,125.99 (equal to $36,673,407.22 in 2025). He reported to Congress later on November 24, that, "32 forts, as well as prisons barracks, camps and hospitals have been well subsisted having received a sufficient portion and variety of the ration to insure health, leaving in the hands of the several issuing commissaries as savings that portion of the ration not deemed necessary for persons living in entire idleness."[33]

Hoffman's apparent penchant for thrift and cost-cutting practices ultimately cost both the prison system and Confederate prisoners of war dearly. Although he encouraged prison camp commanders to make purchases at their discretion, many may have been reluctant to spend as freely as necessary under Hoffman's restrictions, regulations, and strict scrutiny of expenditures.[34]

31 *Book No. 257*, Vol. 4, 178–179, 184.

32 *Book No. 257*, Vol. 4, 184–186. Barnes's account was sent Aug. 2, 1865, and an amended report Aug. 6, 1865; *OR* 8/2:767–768.

33 *OR* 5/3:522.

34 Leslie Gene Hunter, "Warden for the Union: General William Hoffman (1807–1884)" (PhD diss., University of Arizona, 1971), 158. "His [Hoffman's] concern with economy became a virtual obsession when dealing with the prison fund. While the fund accumulated large sums at some

As a result of his administration of a department that had been dormant for nearly 50 years, Hoffman was awarded the brevet rank of major general, backdated to March 1865. After the Civil War ended, he went on to command a regiment in St. Louis, Missouri, and at Fort Leavenworth, Kansas, from 1865 to 1868. Before the end of his career, Hoffman became superintendent of the general recruiting service for the U.S. Army. The office of the commissary general of prisoners officially ceased to exist on November 3, 1865, after which its records were transferred from the Quartermaster Department to the Adjutant General's Office in Washington.

## The Disposal of Civil War Point Lookout

On August 2, 1865, Point Lookout was officially closed, nearly three years after it had first opened as a military hospital and prison camp. One year later, on August 20, 1866, President Johnson issued Proclamation No. 157, declaring the late rebellion officially over. At the close of the proclamation came the sentence that thousands had long awaited through four agonizing years of war: "And I do further proclaim that the said insurrection is at an end and that peace, order, tranquility and civil authority now exist in and throughout the whole of the United States of America." Many of those still on parole from Point Lookout were at last free of their obligation.[35]

On December 23, 1865, General Grant recommended to the secretary of war "that the government buildings at Point Lookout be sold at as early a day as practicable." Stanton approved the order six days later. Brevet Major General Marshall I. Ludington, chief quartermaster in the Quartermaster General's Office, was assigned responsibility for the disposal and sale of the government buildings at Point Lookout. The property was publicly advertised for auction and included the massive hospital complex and its outbuildings, each with a complete description of their construction and materials. The sale, however, was suspended for one week while Congress considered repurposing Hammond Hospital as an asylum for wounded and sick soldiers and sailors.[36]

After the estimated cost of damages incurred during the federal occupation of Point Lookout was deducted, the government owed $128,104.50 in back rent to

---

prisons, much of this money was not expended." He generally left the expenditure of this money to the discretion of the prison camp commanding officers.

35 Johnson, "Proclamation 157," The American Presidency Project.

36 Ulysses S. Grant to Edwin W. Stanton, Dec. 23, 1865, RG 92, Entry 576, Box 57 W.305, National Archives and Records Administration, Washington, D.C.

the property's most recent owner, Chicago philanthropist Dauphine P. Baker. On March 6, 1865, Baker received a charter to establish an asylum for the nation's veteran soldiers and sailors in the former Hammond Hospital and its complex. She purchased the property using a combination of private funds and a government grant, securing the grounds and its structures in the hope that the site would be selected by the newly created National Asylum for Disabled Volunteer Soldiers and Sailors Board. Her purchase included Hammond Hospital, its surrounding cottages, the hotel, the land on which they stood, and the massive wharf. This acquisition temporarily delayed the disposal of the property while the managers of the newly created board debated whether to use Point Lookout as the asylum site.[37]

On March 21, 1866, the government conveyed the property to the asylum managers, after which Baker transferred her rights to the trustees of the Asylum of Point Lookout. The managers ultimately decided, however, that despite the advantages the location offered, the property was not suitable for the asylum. They declared that the site of a former Confederate prisoner-of-war camp was unfitting to honor their disabled Union veterans. The auction of the hospital and its structures proceeded during the latter months of 1866 and continued into 1867.[38]

In accordance with Ludington's orders, the property was to be sold at public auction to the highest bidder. A contingent of the military guard was to remain on site and oversee the buildings for 15 days after the sale. Purchasers were granted 20 days to remove their purchases from the location. All structures included in the auction—such as buildings, the prison stockade walls, fortifications, and other government facilities—were considered surplus property and sold accordingly. The sale began on January 18, 1866, with several buildings sold within two days.

By the end of the year the remaining eight rebel cookhouses in the prison had been purchased by James H. Bell, while all other remaining buildings were bought by William Bayard of New York City. A few days later, on December 19, the paper reported that surplus items—including "30,000 bricks, shingles, stockading, slab fencing, timber, a log building, 1 lot of manure (about 50 cords), and the entire wharf"—were still to be auctioned by the Quartermaster Department.[39]

37 L. P. Brockett and Mary C. Vaughan, *Women's Work in the Civil War: A Record of Heroism, Patriotism and Patience* (Chicago, IL, 1867), 4; Sword, "Hammond General," 7–9.

38 Trevor K. Plante, "The National Home for Volunteer Veteran Soldiers," *Prologue Magazine*, Spring 2004, accessed April 16, 2025, https://www.archives.gov/publications/prologue/2004/spring/soldiers-home.html?_ga=2.59680484.856080889.1662406601-1899690746.1662406601.

39 Sword, "Hammond General," 8; "Announcement," *The National Republican* [Washington D.C.], December 28, 1866, 3, accessed April 16, 2025, https://www.loc.gov/resource/sn86053571/1866-12-28/ed-1/?sp=3&q=Point%2BLookout%2C%2BMd.&r=0.786,0,0,0,0.

Six months later, Ludington informed the authorities in Washington that the unsold structures were rapidly depreciating in value. On September 14, 1866, Maj. Gen. Edward R. S. Canby, then commanding officer of the District of Washington, D.C., recommended that the remaining buildings be sold outright, with the proceeds reserved for the asylum at Hammond Hospital. In October 1866, Stanton was informed that the civilian asylum managers no longer wished to purchase the land. As a result, he ordered Ludington to transfer all buildings that could not be sold on-site to Washington for government use or for public sale.

In a follow-up report dated January 17, 1867, Ludington stated that "several buildings have been sold and all the rest of them torn down and that the materials of which the latter were constructed have all been either brought to the city or sold at public sale at Point Lookout." However, one barge load of materials was diverted to Baltimore to be sold at public auction. It was estimated that the federal government had spent approximately $50,000.00 (equal to $990,944.79 in 2025) to construct the buildings at Point Lookout. War Department reports stated that Point Lookout was occupied by the Federal government from July 4, 1862, through January 4, 1867. By mid-1867, much of the military presence at Point Lookout had disappeared from the landscape.[40]

Former Confederate prisoner Simon Seward returned to Point Lookout in 1899 and described his journey. He wrote that during his visit to the former prison site, a wire fence now enclosed the field where the prison once stood. The lighthouse was still in operation, and the open white-sand beaches of both the Chesapeake Bay and the Potomac River remained a defining feature of the site.[41]

By the late 1800s, Point Lookout had returned to the barren peninsula it had been before the war. By then, only the lighthouse, two farms, and a few cottages remained. Over time, those last cottages, along with the hotel and boarding houses, disappeared through vandalism, arson, and neglect. What endured were reminders to the residents who had either lived there themselves or were the children and grandchildren of those who once occupied Point Lookout. It was not until the mid-20th century that the area experienced a resurgence as a place for recreation and leisure.[42]

40 Sword, "Hammond General," 8–9.

41 Beitzell, "Story of an Escaped Confederate," 170.

42 Sword, "Hammond General, Point Lookout, Maryland," 9.

# Conclusion

There were 150 prisons and holding areas designated for political and military prisoners during the Civil War. Historians have classified these facilities into seven categories, though many additional sites were used as expedients until prisoners could be transferred to more secure locations. At times, barns, covered bridges, and even captured enemy vessels served as temporary prisons. Point Lookout fell into the fifth category—an open enclosure with only temporary structures for shelter.[1]

The features that distinguished Point Lookout from most other Civil War–era prison camps were its construction, organization, acreage, and location. Most notable of all was its size: Point Lookout was the largest prison camp of the war, both North and South. Yet despite these distinguishing features, its purpose was the same as any other prison camp of the era. Built in an area where no substantial structures had previously existed, it became part of a prison system that utilized warehouses, forts, penitentiaries, and former training camps. According to the findings of the U.S. Medical Department in 1870, few prison camps were reported to be in better condition than the depot at Point Lookout.[2]

Because of its location in pro-secessionist southern Maryland and its proximity to Virginia, Point Lookout caused considerable concern for Secretary of War Edwin Stanton. The chronic shortage of guards remained a constant worry for Stanton, Hoffman, and the camp's commanders. Thousands of enemy prisoners were confined only miles from the nation's capital, in a camp that incarcerated and processed more captives than most other Union prisons.

1 Speer, *Portals to Hell*, 9–10; *OR* 3/3:292, 327–328.

2 Barnes, et al., *The Medical and Surgical History of the War of the Rebellion*, 1.3:59.

At the beginning of the war, neither side intended to mistreat prisoners. Prison camps, however, were never meant to provide comfort. The prison at Point Lookout reflected the reality of a conflict that pitted a nation against itself, fought under circumstances for which no clear rules had yet been established. Accusations of deliberate starvation and shootings were leveled against prison camps and their administrations on both sides, supported by numerous accounts. In truth, both the Union and the Confederacy bore equal guilt and responsibility for the thousands of prisoner deaths that occurred during the war and in its aftermath.

If there was any positive legacy from Point Lookout's two years as a prison, it was the influence it had on the future organization and administration of prison camps. The prisoner-of-war system in the United States saw little improvement from the mid-nineteenth century until the nation's entry into World War I. It was not until the Geneva Convention of 1929 that the Federal government formally adopted significant reforms in the treatment of prisoners. The later system of prison depots was shaped by both the successes and the failures of the hastily established Civil War camps, with Point Lookout serving as one of the most influential examples.

The experience gained from operating a camp as large as Point Lookout led to the development of a more effectively managed and organized prison system than the ad hoc arrangements of the Civil War. This improved system brought advances in prison security, logistical supply, and expanded use of prison labor. Greater oversight was established, resulting in more humane treatment, a reduction in prisoner abuse, and an enhanced system for prisoner identification and graves registration. These improvements were direct responses to the failures experienced by the United States government during the Civil War across many prison camps, including Point Lookout.

The conflict prolonged far beyond initial expectations, leaving neither government prepared for the extended incarceration of prisoners. It took at least a year to develop a system capable of supplying and administering the numerous camps necessary to secure the many thousands of captives. As the war dragged on and prisoner numbers surged, additional camps were established—facilities once thought unnecessary. Individual survival depended on a prisoner's ability to endure the harsh conditions of the camp, often while competing against fellow prisoners struggling for the same goal. Prison camps became places of misery, physical deterioration, and, for many, needless death.

Prison administrators at Point Lookout accused of acts of retribution against prisoners were, in most cases, diligently following orders and regulations prescribed by the government. Despite allegations from both sides, the reality is that neither government was blameless. Both bore responsibility for the failures of their prison systems. The lack of compromise between the governments resulted in unnecessary hardships and the deaths of thousands, promoted by retaliatory orders and acrimonious directives. It became clear that lessons regarding prisoner treatment from previous American wars were either forgotten, ignored, or both.

Blame for the poor conditions at Point Lookout has often been directed at Maj. Gen. William Hoffman, commissary general of prisoners. However, evidence suggests that much of the fault attributed to Hoffman—and to Point Lookout itself—was generated by the so-called "Lost Cause Myth." Generations after the Civil War, advocates of the Southern cause have attempted to load Northern officials with opprobrium and Point Lookout, like those officials generally, has been obliged to shoulder a blame it does not entirely deserve.

Historical records indicate that Hoffman acted in accordance with his military training from the U.S. Military Academy, government restrictions, and army regulations. This does not fully exonerate him, as some of his decisions remain questionable. To his credit, Hoffman was on record encouraging prison camp commanders to use the prison fund as intended, following directions from War Department officials. Yet his strict enforcement of regulations and insistence on accountability may have made camp commanders hesitant to spend funds, due to his close oversight and rigorous justification requirements for each expenditure.[3]

Hoffman, while a prisoner of war, was appointed commissary general of prisoners in October 1861, reviving an office that had been dormant since the War of 1812—even while his parole was still active, as he would not be exchanged until mid-August 1862. He reluctantly accepted the newly reactivated position, which had no precedent or established guidelines. Tasked with reviving and updating a department lacking regulations, Hoffman was charged with creating standards to reform a previously moribund prison system. Although Hoffman has often been blamed for prisoners' suffering, many post-war prisoner accounts clarify that few of these conditions were caused by him alone. His regulations and policies were implemented only with the consent, approval, or direct orders of Quartermaster General Montgomery Meigs and, especially, Secretary of War Edwin Stanton.

Multiple requests for barracks construction at Point Lookout were submitted on two separate occasions by the camp's commanding officers. Hoffman forwarded these requests to Washington with his endorsement and regulatory recommendation. However, Stanton held the authority to approve or deny such construction and expenditures, which Hoffman did not possess. Any disapproval from Stanton had to be communicated to the camp commanders through

3 Hunter, "Warden for the Union," 161.

Hoffman. Despite these protocols, many have mistakenly attributed the denial of the barracks construction requests solely to Hoffman, which is inaccurate.

Official records show that Hoffman was responsible for proposing and recommending multiple ration reductions for prisoners. However, these reductions were implemented only with approval from his superior officers, not solely at his discretion. Regardless, no prisoner would have known of Hoffman's involvement in these decisions or been privy to them. Many accusations against Hoffman were likely influenced by post-war revisionism and rumors. Hoffman dutifully managed his office as a professional U.S. Regular Army officer trained at the West Point Military Academy, adhering strictly to government regulations.

The newly established Point Lookout complex was placed under the command of a single commanding officer responsible for both the prison and the general hospital operations. This command was further divided into subcommands, with the vast Hammond Hospital administered by senior medical officers and the prison camp overseen by the provost marshal. It was assumed that successive commanding officers of Point Lookout were experienced administrators selected for their command expertise, with the expectation that their duties would closely resemble field operations. However, this assumption proved incorrect, as none of these officers had training in managing a prison camp or caring for thousands of prisoners.

Much like Hoffman's initial situation, the first commanding officer of Point Lookout, Gen. Gilman Marston, faced similar circumstances. Marston was ordered simply to "establish a camp," aligning with the guidelines set forth in Hoffman's circular issued on July 7, 1862. From Marston to Gen. James Barnes, the last in the line of commanding officers, all dutifully carried out their assignments as directed by the army, government officials, and federal regulations.

The basic responsibilities of the camp commanders at Point Lookout included not only the protection and welfare of thousands of prisoners of war but also the maintenance of a guard force composed of infantry, artillery, and cavalry troops. Their duties extended to administering a major army hospital, overseeing a camp of more than 2,000 civilian refugees, managing four government farms, and supervising a provost marshal's office located 20 miles away. Despite these extensive responsibilities, the camp commanders were often unfairly blamed for shortcomings in their performance.

Records show that the camp officials did their utmost to provide what they were permitted to, in accordance with army regulations. In this sense, it can be said that they fulfilled their duties as ordered, just as soldiers were expected to do; Point Lookout was no exception. If anyone should be held accountable for negligence, retaliation, and the overwhelming suffering endured by countless prisoners, it would be the officials of both governments.

Prisoner and guard eyewitness accounts reveal that Southern prisoners at Point Lookout sometimes suffered acts of vengeance by the very guards responsible for their safety and security, who occasionally abused their authority. Prisoners often described guards as spiteful, prejudiced, and at times overzealous in carrying out their orders. This assessment is undoubtedly accurate, as prisoners endured persecution and violence from guards enforcing prison regulations often beyond the intended scope of their duties. Records and investigations reveal clear racial bias and conflict within the guard force—both between White and Black soldiers and between Black guards and the Southern prisoners of war.

Despite these accounts, records also show that Point Lookout was guarded by a force that was chronically understrength, forcing authorities to combine regiments of infantry and cavalry troops. It is also documented that this same guard force endured extended tours of duty, along with the physical and mental strain of camp responsibilities. These conditions frequently exhausted the soldiers beyond their limits. Given that an army camp never sleeps, this constant demand applied clearly to the men tasked with maintaining round-the-clock security and protection for Point Lookout and its prison population.

Although accusations of mistreatment by the guards increased over the years, it is often overlooked or forgotten that these men were enemy prisoners of war, not long-lost friends, brothers, or comrades from the battlefield. Private Frank Wilkeson of Battery A, 11th New York Artillery, lamented, "A military prison, it matters not what people keep it, is not a place where life is enjoyed. The prisoners are enemies, and their keepers care little for their lives or comfort."[4]

Although there were numerous incidents of prisoners being shot by White guards at Point Lookout, records show that these were fewer than the acts committed by Black soldiers within the guard force. The frequent acts of retribution by certain elements of the guard prompted each commanding officer at Point Lookout, from the first to the last, to reissue and modify standing orders aimed at better regulating the guard force to ensure the protection and safety of the prisoners. Due to multiple reports of abusive treatment and harassment of local citizens, General Barnes, the last commanding officer, eventually removed the Black soldiers from the nighttime prison guard rotation and from the county-wide mounted patrols.

4 Frank Wilkeson, *Turned Inside Out: Recollections of a Private Soldier in the Army of the Potomac* (Lincoln, NE, 1997), 224.

The selection of Point Lookout, for both hospital and prison facilities, was dubious at best. In a post-war evaluation, the Medical Department described Point Lookout as an unfit site for habitation which should never have been chosen for either purpose. The site lacked shade during the oppressive summer heat and offered little warmth against the numbing cold of what became record-setting winters. Its water source was often contaminated, leading to unsanitary conditions and deadly, frequently fatal illnesses. Due to its low-lying, sea-level geography, Point Lookout suffered prolonged flooding from storms and high tides, combined with blinding, wind-blown sand. The marshy areas surrounding the prison bred clouds of disease-carrying mosquitoes, lice, fleas, and flies, along with colonies of thousands of rats that were a constant pestilence throughout the year.

To say that the government was negligent in its care of prisoners may be partially true. However, considering that authorities at Point Lookout were responsible for caring for prisoners at a newly established site, the care they provided was considerable compared to other prison facilities in both the North and South. In farm fields lacking any provisions for either sick or healthy prisoners, authorities hastily constructed a prison and hospital that continuously expanded to accommodate an ever-growing population exceeding 10,000 prisoners. Of the more than 52,000 prisoners of war who passed through Point Lookout during its two-year operation, records indicate that 11,872 were transferred to Hammond Hospital. This means approximately one in every five prisoners held at Point Lookout was sent to the massive Hammond Hospital, which was primarily designated for treating Union soldiers.[5]

Despite post-war accusations, ample evidence, including prisoner testimony, shows that the medical staff at Point Lookout made exceptional efforts to combat common maladies such as smallpox, pneumonia, and scurvy. The medical personnel also diligently cared for prisoners who arrived wounded, as well as those injured by the guard force. While medical science in the 1860s was advancing, it was not yet able to eradicate the many diseases experienced by prisoners at Point Lookout.

Article 79 of the *Lieber Code* stated that "Every captured wounded enemy shall be medically treated according to the ability of the medical staff." This article, and no other within the *Lieber Code*, specifically obligates prison authorities or medical staff to treat the sick and extends only to the wounded received. In this context, it is evident that the medical staff at Point Lookout, motivated by

5 Hammond General Hospital, park information sign, Point Lookout, MD.

compassion and their oath, treated all sick and wounded prisoners of war to the best of their ability.[6]

Despite its remote southern location, Point Lookout was not as isolated from the outside world as it might appear. The Point was connected by an active telegraph line that facilitated a constant flow of messages to nearby Leonardtown, the War Department in Washington, and even as far as Baltimore. While guerrilla activity rarely interrupted the line, any damage that did occur was quickly repaired by Federal forces.

Point Lookout reflected broader changes in national culture involving new and innovative ideas and programs. Despite its remoteness from Northern states and its location in a pro-secessionist border region, the camp was strongly influenced by Federal policies and legislation. One such pivotal order was the Emancipation Proclamation, which went into effect a few months before Point Lookout opened. This landmark proclamation paved the way for recruiting approximately 180,000 Black men, who would comprise nearly 10 percent of the Union Army and Navy during a critical phase of the war. Units such as the 36th U.S. Colored Troops (U.S.C.T.), the 5th Massachusetts (Colored) Cavalry, and various companies from other U.S.C.T. units were assigned to Point Lookout as part of the guard force. Additionally, several hundred former slaves were recruited locally from Point Lookout into these units, including the newly formed 38th U.S.C.T.

Whether willingly or not, Southern prisoners and Union guards at Point Lookout became participants in, and in some cases beneficiaries of, these new and innovative policies. Point Lookout was the first prison camp to recruit Confederate prisoners of war for service in the U.S. armed forces. This program alone provided nearly two infantry regiments—approximately 1,500 men for the 1st and 4th U.S. Volunteers—as well as numerous recruits for the U.S. Navy.

The government further utilized Union soldiers who were no longer considered fit for active field duty by creating a reserve force to support the regular troops in campaign. The 11th and 20th Regiments of the Veteran Reserve Corps (V.R.C.), along with various other V.R.C. companies, filled roles such as guards, artillerymen, escorts, mounted patrols, and hospital stewards at Point Lookout. Like the U.S.C.T. units, elements of the V.R.C. actively recruited at Point Lookout. These two innovative approaches provided additional manpower, supplementing not only the guard force at Point Lookout but also the broader U.S. armed forces in their path to final victory.

Finally, Point Lookout became part of the National Reburial Program for the reinternment of both Union and Confederate dead immediately after the war's

6 *OR* 3/3:157.

conclusion. Just outside the boundaries of Point Lookout State Park today, the remains of prisoners of war rest on approximately one acre of land managed by the Federal government. These former prisoners are memorialized by a monument provided and maintained by the U.S. Department of Veterans Affairs.

Prison camps did not exist to offer succor or sanctuary to the enemy. Their purpose was the detention and rehabilitation of captives, with treatment determined by the captor. Prisoners had no authority to dictate how they were to be treated. What occurred at Point Lookout was no different from conditions at other prisons during the Civil War, whether in the North or South.

The joy expressed by released Southern prisoners proved short-lived. Returning soldiers came back to a South devastated by war and a home changed from the one they had left behind. Men proud to be called "Rebels and Confederates" were found to be changed. Many former prisoners became profane, depressed, distrustful, and bitter, bearing the humiliation of imprisonment, the defeat of their cause, and the fear of the South's total destruction.

For former Southern soldiers, the transition from soldier back to private citizen proved to be a difficult process for many. One soldier remarked that the world he knew before the conflict was over. He felt no ambition and struggled to accept emancipation and the end of slavery. These former Confederate soldiers now lived under military governors and under the constant, resentful watch of their former enemies—often Black soldiers patrolling their towns, cities, and countryside. This stark reality drove home the point that the Confederacy was no more.[7]

The sudden transition from soldier and prisoner to civilian life proved difficult for most during the post-war years. Private E. P. Rucker of the 11th Virginia, who had been a prisoner at Point Lookout for nearly a year, expressed his feelings about prison life in a letter dated mid-May 1865. He summed up his experience by writing, "I do not think that you can possibly conceive the distress of a prison camp." Indeed, many could not then—and still cannot now—fully understand what these soldiers and prisoners endured during the war.[8]

This condition was known as "Soldier's Heart" and would later be referred to as "Shell Shock," "Combat Fatigue," and "Post-Traumatic Stress Disorder" (PTSD). Since medical professionals of the time were not as aware of this condition as

7 Kevin M. Levin, *Searching for Black Confederates: The Civil War's Most Persistent Myth* (Chapel Hill, NC, 2019), 71.

8 Frank Vetelanna, "Private E.P. Rucker," e-mail message to author, June 5, 2023.

they would eventually become, very little was recorded to allow for symptom comparison between then and now.[9]

However, it is safe to say that this condition certainly existed, though undiagnosed. A Union officer stationed at Point Lookout reported that a prisoner had committed suicide in the camp, while another prisoner wrote about contemplating the act. These were certainly not isolated cases. Further in-depth investigation of prisoner diaries and letters, conducted in preparation for this work, reveals that several prisoners alluded to such desperation within the camp's population—and incidents of self-annihilation have been undoubtedly overlooked or ignored in post-war accounts.

This work is not intended to be the final word on Point Lookout as a military prison. Rather, it is hoped that it will inspire further interest—not only in Point Lookout but also in the broader subject of Civil War prisons. As William Hesseltine succinctly stated in his book *Civil War Prisons*, "the student of the times must pick his way carefully among the passionate and partisan documents of the era in order to arrive at a true picture of the prisons north and south, how they were administered, [and] what life for the captured soldiers was like." This was the goal of this work, and hopefully, it has contributed to a clearer and more accurate understanding of the significant role Point Lookout's prison camp played during the American Civil War and its immediate aftermath.[10]

9 Dillon J. Carroll, *Invisible Wounds: Mental Illness and Civil War Soldiers* (Baton Rouge, LA, 2021), 63.

10 William B. Hesseltine, *Civil War Prisons* (Kent, OH, 1972), back of dust jacket.

# Epilogue

During the post-war years, there was an effort to restore Point Lookout to its former status as a recreational destination, but this attempt was short-lived. The old Fenwick Hotel, which had enjoyed brief success before the war, burned down in 1878. The resort area and several cottages used as hospital wards soon fell into disrepair. It appeared that Point Lookout was destined to remain a barren, swampy peninsula—primarily suited for farming and hosting the lighthouse service.[1]

After the war, all government-owned structures at Point Lookout—excluding the lighthouse—were either sold at public auction or dismantled, with materials returned to the quartermaster department. Former prisoners wrote of making the long journey back to Point Lookout, now of their own free will, to visit the site of the erstwhile prison camp. They described seeing the last remnants of the prison, now enclosed by a wire fence, including the remains of water pumps that once provided contaminated water, and the prisoner cemetery.

With no apparent value and little use to local farmers, the prison remained as it was when abandoned by the Federal government. Perhaps out of respect for the thousands of prisoners incarcerated there, or as a reminder of the suffering and death it witnessed, local inhabitants chose not to disturb the site. It would be halfway through the next century, and another generation or two later, before the land was returned to the open fields it had been prior to the war. In 1866, the quartermaster reburial detail had used portions of the stockade wall to fence in parts of the cemeteries during the reinterment and marking of various burial grounds. Ultimately, the fate of what remained of the prison camp—including its

1 Sword, "Hammond General, Point Lookout, Maryland," 17.

The Point Lookout Lighthouse. *Author*

stockade and the three earthen forts—would be determined by the occupants of the Point and by the forces of nature.

Over time, developers found other uses for Point Lookout. The Point Lookout Land Developers erected a wind-powered generator on part of the western walls of Redoubt No. 2 (Fort Lincoln). Eventually, the power plant failed, and the structure was converted into a cottage, which was later razed. The remaining walls of Fort Lincoln were also destroyed during the same hurricane that caused havoc along the bay shoreline in 1933. As late as 1976, the outlines of the fort's ditch, or moat, could still be seen on the bay floor; however, currently, there are no visible remains of the fort. Coastal storms and high tides would extensively erode the shoreline on the Chesapeake Bay side of the peninsula, further diminishing its landscape.[2]

In 1926, the Edgemoor Real Estate Company, owned by Walter Tuckerman, purchased several hundred acres of Point Lookout. Tuckerman undertook various development initiatives before his business venture at Point Lookout ultimately

2 Sword, "The Civil War Forts of Point Lookout Prison Camp for Confederates," 5.

dissolved. His proposed plans envisioned blocks of over 1,000 homes to be built from the lighthouse area extending north, spanning from the shores of the bay to the river. These homes were to be constructed on land that, just a few decades earlier, had housed thousands of soldiers in the army hospital and prison camp during the Civil War. In July 1955, Tuckerman sold 650 acres of Point Lookout for $150,000 to the newly formed six-member board registered as the Point Lookout Grand Hotel Company, which had established its offices in Washington, D.C.[3]

Fortunately, before completing the sale of his holdings to the Point Lookout Grand Hotel Company, Mr. Tuckerman recognized the historical significance of the surviving Redoubt No. 3 site and its need for protection from the impending development. Prior to the final sale, on July 8, 1955, Tuckerman deeded 4.5 acres of land to St. Mary's County, deliberately excluding it from the sale; this land included what is now Redoubt No. 3. He did so in memory of his wife, with the condition that St. Mary's County preserve the fort site as a public park within a specified time. Thanks to Tuckerman's foresight and generosity, Redoubt No. 3 was spared from the bulldozers. However, it remained hidden and overgrown by trees and brush for years.[4]

The earthen walls of Redoubt #1 or "Fort Stanton" was used in 1940 as part of a W.P.A. project to construct Route 5 after the Hurricane of 1933. The W.P.A. or "Work Projects Administration", was a government initiative that provided employment through public works during the Great Depression.

In 1965, the Point Lookout Grand Hotel Company sold much of its property to the state of Maryland, retaining 17 acres that included the Grand Hotel and its complex. The Point Lookout Grand Hotel and its cottages flourished until the hotel's closure in 1971. The state's primary reason for the purchase was to establish a new state park for recreational purposes. Following standard procedure, the Maryland Park Service commissioned a Master Plan in December 1966 for the newly established Point Lookout State Park. As the county failed to act within the allotted timeframe stipulated by Tuckerman, his heirs subsequently deeded additional land adjoining the original gift, including Fort #3, to the state of Maryland on September 29, 1967.

While offering recommendations for the development of the land for recreational use, the state's master plan's author stated that restoring the prison camp site "does not appear to be warranted," although an appropriate marker could

3 "D.C. Men Plan to Build Resort at Point Lookout," *Evening Star* [Washington D.C.], Sept. 5, 1955, 1, accessed April 16, 2025, https://chroniclingamerica.loc.gov/lccn/sn83045462/1955-09-15/ed-1/seq-42/.

4 Sword, "The Civil War Forts of Point Lookout Prison Camp for Confederates," 5-6.

be erected to identify the site. Strangely, there is no mention or acknowledgment of either the fort or hospital sites, even though the fort is depicted in the maps included.

As a result, there were no plans to restore or interpret any of the historic sites at Point Lookout. With the recent memory of the Civil War centennial celebration still fresh in the minds of many, the refusal of the park system to not consider the ground's historical significance cannot be an oversight. The plan specifically excluded the development or recognition of the historic areas, noting that a monument already existed outside the northern border of the park. Consequently, it was deemed unnecessary to mark the prison, and no budget was allocated for preserving or interpreting the historical aspects of Point Lookout.[5]

So, why preserve Point Lookout as a historic site? Statistics show that it was the largest prison camp during the Civil War. Its total prison population alone rivaled the size of a small city, virtually outnumbering that of the county in which it was located. Although often accused of being a place of misery and death, it is important to remember that one of the largest state-of-the-art hospitals—along with separate prison and smallpox hospitals—operated there, treating Confederate and Union soldiers as well as civilians. Point Lookout was also a place of sanctuary for thousands of refugees and formerly enslaved individuals seeking freedom in the North. These are just a few reasons why Point Lookout should be preserved and why it deserves to be remembered.

The revised master plan for the Point Lookout Park Land Unit, issued in 1996, finally recognized the significance of the Civil War sites. It acknowledged restoration efforts at what would later be identified as Redoubt No. 3, the prison, and the site of Hammond Hospital. The plan also highlighted the area's extensive history, noting occupation by Native Americans, colonial settlers, and British crown forces during both the American Revolution and the War of 1812. Further research revealed that the U.S. Army and Navy conducted invasion exercises there in the months preceding the D-Day invasion of Europe in 1944. Notably, President Abraham Lincoln and Gen. Ulysses S. Grant had also visited the site.[6]

Since its acquisition by the state of Maryland, various volunteer groups—including the Youth Conservation Corps, local Boy Scout troops, Frederick Community College Vocational School, the Friends of Point Lookout, and the

5 *Department of Natural Resources, Department of Public Improvements, Master Plan of Development Point Lookout State Park St. Mary's County, Maryland*, comp. Rummel, Klepper, & Kahl (Baltimore, MD: Consulting Engineers, 1966), 3.

6 *Maryland Department of Natural Resources, Point Lookout State Park Land Unit Plan* (Annapolis, MD, 1996), 11, 17.

Reconstructed enlisted men's barracks of the guard. *Author*

staff of Point Lookout State Park—have undertaken extensive preservation and reconstruction projects. Their efforts have successfully restored Redoubt No. 3 and its buildings to reflect the design created by the Army Corps of Engineers in 1864. Additionally, this work has involved interpreting the remains of the prison site, known as Camp Hoffman, as well as the site of Hammond Hospital.

Approximately two-thirds of the original area that once comprised the prison pen has suffered significant erosion due to a series of storms and the tidal forces of the Chesapeake Bay. The present-day fishing pier occupies approximately the back third of the pen. The front third, where the main gate and mess halls once stood, remains accessible. Maryland State Highway Route 5 traverses this tract, separating the cookhouse area from the section that once housed the prisoners' encampment and divisional streets. Park staff and the Friends of Point Lookout have constructed a faithful recreation of the prison's southwest corner with its gate, through which over 52,000 prisoners passed. The remains of the deep ditch and Main Thoroughfare, which ran directly in front of the mess halls, are still discernible. However, the remnants of the divisional streets are now permanently covered by forest, water grass, and pine needles.

View of reconstructed prison gate of Camp Hoffman (Point Lookout). *Author*

No remains of the massive Hammond General Hospital survive today. The many cottages that once dotted the area north of the lighthouse were abandoned and eventually fell victim to vandalism. Considered ahead of its time in both design and function, the army hospital provided medical care for sick and wounded patients from both the Union and Confederate sides. It also offered sanctuary and support to those escaping enslavement and seeking freedom in the Northern states. Today, only the lighthouse stands as a reference point to where the hospital once stood, commemorated by a flagpole, interpretive sign and a small monument honoring its existence.

Although the wooden piers have long since disappeared, the massive wharf area located just a few yards west of Hammond Hospital has lost little shoreline. Today, visitors can easily imagine the vast numbers of boats and ships that once tied up or anchored there. Ships, boats, and barges transported incoming and outgoing prisoners and Union troops, as well as the large quantities of supplies needed by both the hospital and garrison.

Remnants of the old country road, once traveled by thousands before, during, and after the war, weave through the heavily wooded areas of the park, now identifiable only by the park's trail signs. Interpretive markers designate sites where thousands lived during the war and, in some cases, even earlier. Markers also designate the smallpox hospital and cemetery areas.

Today, Point Lookout has grown to approximately three times its original war-time size of 400 acres. Over 1,100 acres encompass both historic and recreational areas, including Point Lookout Creek and Lake Conoy.

Most traces of where thousands suffered and died during that catastrophic time in our national history have been erased by time and progress. Point Lookout has survived years of economic hardship and the devastation of civil war. Fortunately for our country, Point Lookout and its history were saved from oblivion through the chance donation of a benevolent citizen from St. Mary's County, along with the dedication of many others committed to its preservation. With continued efforts, Point Lookout and its history will endure the forces of nature and progress for generations to come.

## Appendix A

# Additional Maps of Point Lookout

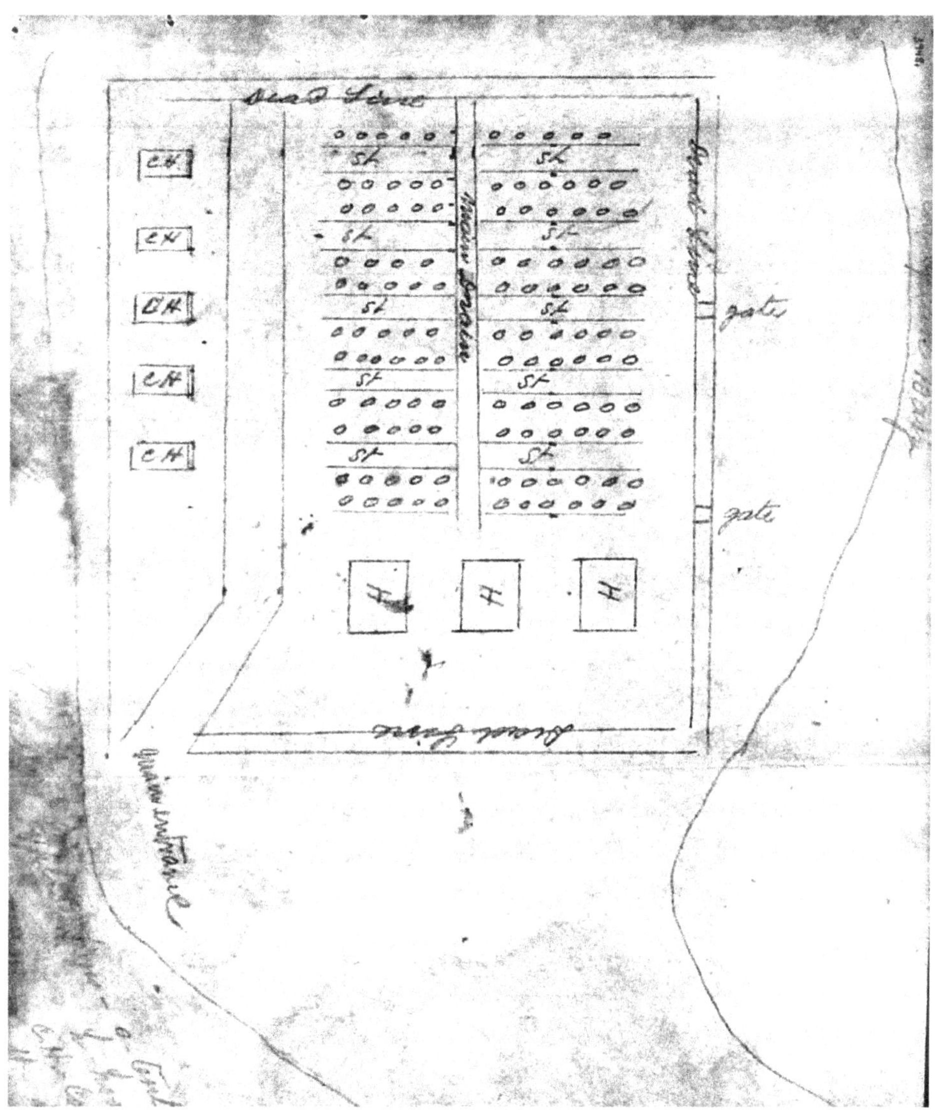


Depiction of Camp Hoffman drawn in late 1863 by prisoner Sgt. James T. Wells, 2nd South Carolina. Wells depicts five divisional streets (St). By March 1864, the prison would almost double in size to ten or more streets. (CH=Cookhouses H=Prison Hospital. Potomac River (east) left side/Chesapeake Bay (west) right side of map. *James T. Wells Papers, South Caroliniana Library*

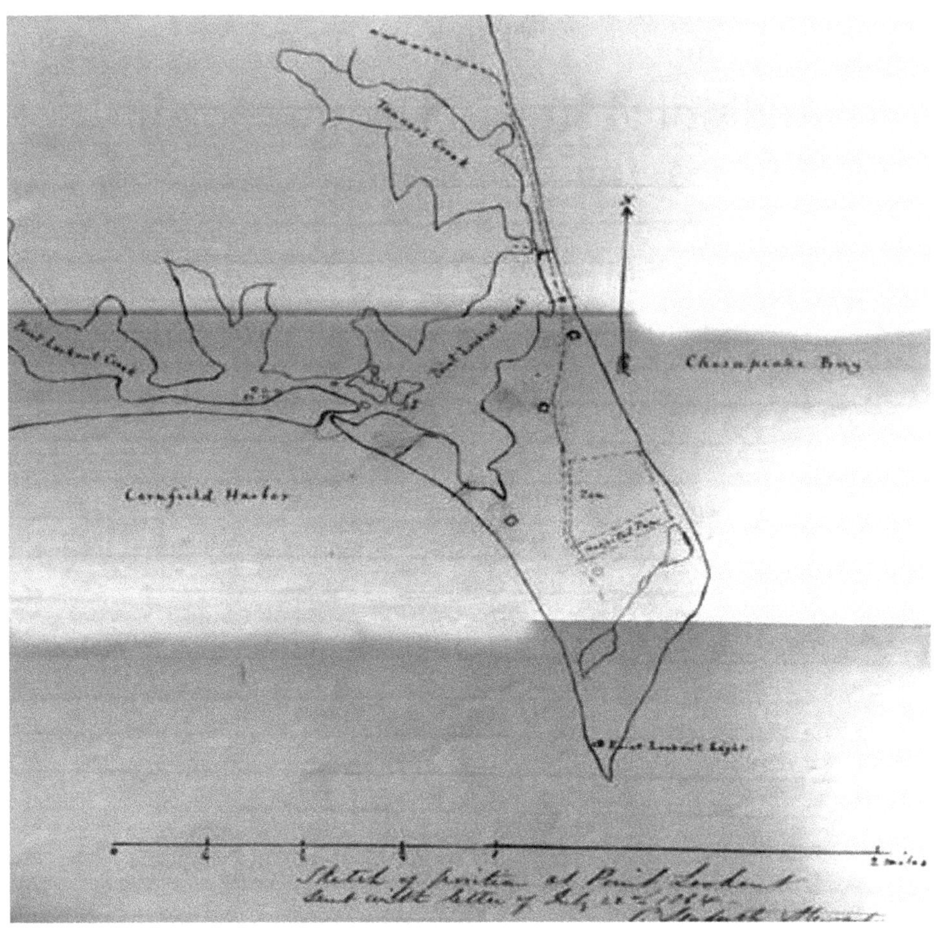

Map as drawn by Maj. Charles S. Stewart, Army Corps of Engineers, July 22, 1864, depicting the proposed earthen redoubts at Point Lookout. Stewart shows three squares representing the forts diagonally from northeast to southwest, including an additional fourth fort southwest of the prison gate. *Library of Congress*

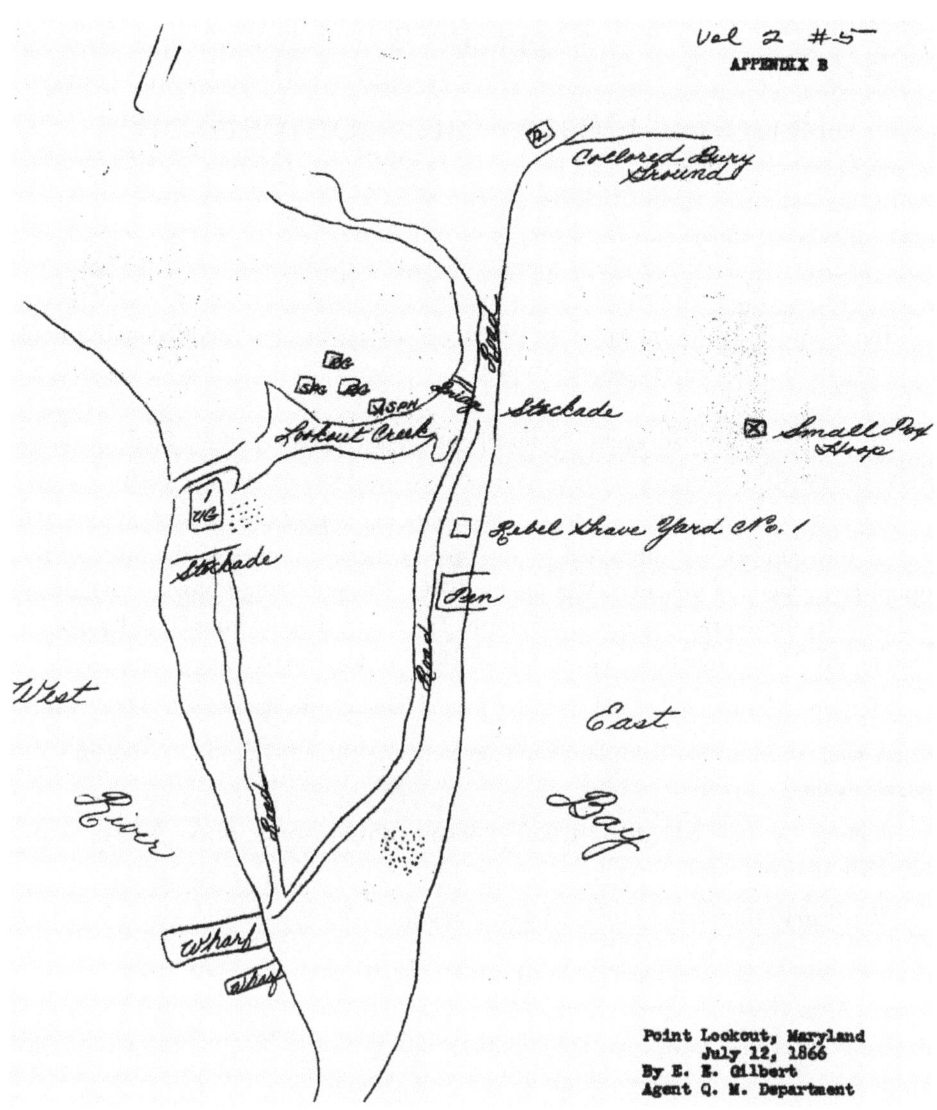


Map of cemeteries by contractor E. E. Gilbert, Quartermaster Department.

*National Archives and Records Administration*

# Appendix B

# Prisoner Death Rate Comparison

The following is a compilation of primary sources that have reported numbers of deceased prisoners at Point Lookout Prison:

E. E. Gilbert, civilian agent. National Reburial Program (1867): 2,767 prisoner bodies recovered.[1]

*War of the Rebellion. Official Records of the Union and Confederate Armies* (1899): 2,950 deaths. This number was submitted by the provost marshal's office to the office of the commissary general of prisoners, Washington, D.C. This publication provides the lists of final statistics for all prison camps in the north. The recorded figure from Point Lookout is based on the 23 monthly reports from August 1863 to July 1865.[2]

Maryland Monument located at present federal cemetery site dated 1876: 3,004 deaths.

Federal monument at Point Lookout Cemetery (1910): 3,389 deaths. (Listed on eight bronze plaques).

Register as maintained by Point Lookout Prison Authorities: 3,431 deaths (National Archives).

*The Elmira Prison Camp* (1912): 3,446 deaths.[3]

1 Gerald J. Sword, "Confederate Cemetery. Point Lookout," *St. Mary's Chronicles*, Dec. 1979, 2.

2 United States War Department, comp., *War of the Rebellion: Official Records of the Union and Confederate Armies, Prisoners of War* (Washington, D.C., 1880), 8:991–1002.

3 A. Noel Blakeman, ed., *Personal Recollections of the War of the Rebellion* (New York, 1912), 363.

The following three editions of *Confederate Veteran Magazine* all differ in death counts at Point Lookout:

*Confederate Veteran Magazine,* vol. 5, estimate 3,404 deaths.[4]

*Confederate Veteran Magazine*, vol. 12, estimate 3,446 deaths.[5]

*Confederate Veteran Magazine* vol. 19, estimate 3,384 deaths.[6]

*Medical and Surgical History of the War of the Rebellion (1861-1865).* (1880): 3,704 deaths (*Medical and Surgical History of the Rebellion* as published by the federal government in 1880 Volume I. Part 3. Section IV. This number was submitted by the prison hospital.)

| Death estimates as of 2024 | |
|---|---|
| Point Lookout Prison Camp and Hospital | 3,905[7] |
| Author's Collection (additional names) | 160 |
| Present estimated total from recent accounting | 4,065 |

At present there are only 3,389 names listed on the Federal monument, a difference of 676 names missing from the monument and a difference of 1,115 names of those deceased unaccounted for from the official Federal count. This calculates to a death rate of approximately 8 percent. As more names of deceased are found this percentage will undoubtedly increase.

4 Bradley T. Johnson, "Confederate Dead in Maryland," 1897, in *Confederate Veteran*, ed. S. A. Cunningham, 12th ed. (Nashville, TN, 1897), 5:622.

5 "Marking Graves of Confederate Prisoners," 1897, in *Confederate Veteran*, ed. S. A. Cunningham, 3rd ed. (Nashville, TN, 1897), 12:102.

6 "Monument at Point Lookout, MD," 1897, in *Confederate Veteran*, ed. S. A. Cunningham, 3rd ed. (Nashville, TN, 1911), 19:123.

7 Richard H. Triebe, *Point Lookout Prison Camp and Hospital: The North's Largest Civil War Prison* (Wilmington, NC, 2016), 91–92; includes 428 additional names.

# Appendix C
# Commanding Officers

The following were assigned Commanding Officers of Point Lookout and the District of St. Mary's in order of succession. There were instances where the commanding officer temporarily left the Point on business requiring a temporary commanding officer as a substitute. As a result of his absence, the senior regimental commanding officer present at Point Lookout, was ordered to take his place. They were to enforce orders and policy only, and not issue or supersede any orders in place. They are not considered assigned but appear in this list denoted as "temporary."[1]

**Captain G. W. P. Smith** (Smith's Independent Company, Cavalry (Maryland): May 1862–August 1863.

**Captain H. J. Van Kirk** (Company A, 85th Pennsylvania Infantry): Arrived September 1862–November 1862.

**Captain Nicholas Hager** (Company F, 85th Pennsylvania Infantry): November 1862. Relieved December 2, 1862.

**Captain Anthony S. Woods** (Commanding G, 8th New York Militia) (Engineers). July, 1862.

**Assistant Surgeon Clinton Wagner** (United States Army Chief Surgeon in charge of Hammond General Hospital) July 1862–February 1863.

**Major John Carter Brown** 3 companies of "Enfans Perous" ("Lost Children"), (Independent Battalion, New York Volunteer Infantry): December 4, 1862, until February 1863.

**Brigadier General Henry Hayes Lockwood** (1st Delaware Infantry): February to June 1863. In Late June, he was appointed and transferred to command of the 2nd Brigade, 1st Division, XII Corps, Army of the Potomac. Commanding Officer of the "First Separate Brigade" headquartered in Southern Maryland/Point Lookout.

**Brigadier General Gilman Marston** (2nd New Hampshire Infantry): Arrived July 31, 1863. First official commanding officer of Point Lookout with combined prison camp and

1 Further information regarding the listed commanding officers can be found in their respective regimental histories, General/Special Orders Volume I, District of St. Mary's National Archives, Washington D.C. or in *War of the Rebellion: Official Records of the Union and Confederate Armies.* 128 vols. Washington, D.C.: Government Printing Office 1899. Harrisburg, Pa: Historical Times, Inc.1985.

general hospital. Relieved April 1864 and transferred to Norfolk, Virginia, as governor, then to active field command by Special Order #110 to command 1st Brigade, 1st Division, XVIII Army Corps, Army of the James.

**Brigadier General Edward Winslow Hinks** (2nd United States Cavalry/19th Massachusetts Infantry). Transferred to command Point Lookout, March 1864 to April 1864. Relieved April 1864 by Special Order #110 and transferred to commanding officer, 3rd Division, XVIII Army Corps, Army of the James.

**Lieutenant Colonel Martin P. Buffam** (4th Rhode Island Infantry): Temporary command of two days for General Hinks in April, 1864.

**Colonel Alonzo Granville Draper** (14th Massachusetts Infantry/1st Massachusetts Heavy Artillery/36th United States Colored Troops): Given command of Point Lookout by Special Order# 110 April 1864. Relieved July 1864 by order to command of 2nd Brigade, 3rd Division, XVIII Army Corps, Army of the James.

**Brigadier General James Barnes**: (18th Massachusetts Infantry/1st Division, V Army Corps): Commanding Officer July 4, 1864, at Point Lookout until relieved August 1865 by general order and closure of Point Lookout.

## Appendix D

# Federal Army Units at Point Lookout

The following federal military units were posted at Point Lookout from July 1862 until its closing in August 1865. Those included in this list were posted as guards at Point Lookout for at least a month. A list reflecting all federal units that had transferred to and from Point Lookout performing duties as guards, escorts for incoming or outgoing exchanged or transferred prisoners, would prove too numerous and would not give a true figure for those who actually made up the garrison force of Point Lookout.[1]

### Cavalry

**Company A, Purnell Legion Cavalry (Maryland)**: Posted in St. Mary's County from at least January 1863 (perhaps as early as July, 1862) until July 1865.

**Smith's Independent Company, Cavalry (Maryland)**: On "special duty" at Point Lookout from late 1862 to June 1863. Arrived between October 1862 and January 1863; stationed at Point Lookout in and out of the area during this time.

**5th United States Cavalry (Companies A and D)**: A detachment was assigned to Point Lookout around June 1864 when they were part of a foraging expedition across the Potomac River into Westmoreland County, VA, on the Northern Neck. The unit was returned to the regiment in July 1864.

**2nd United States Cavalry (detached companies)**: A detachment was assigned to Point Lookout around June 1864 when they were part of a foraging expedition across the Potomac River into Westmoreland County, VA, on the Northern Neck.

**5th Massachusetts (colored) Cavalry**: June 30, 1864–March 24, 1865. Lieutenant Colonel Charles Francis Adams Jr. eventually commanded the unit while at Point Lookout.

### Infantry

**Independent Battalion, New York Infantry (Enfans Perdous "Lost Children")**: The battalion had only six companies organized and was assigned as some of the first guards at

1 Further information regarding specific units who were posted at Point Lookout can be found in regimental histories or in *War of the Rebellion: Official Records of the Union and Confederate Armies.* 128 vols. Washington, D.C.: Government Printing Office 1899. Harrisburg, Pa: Historical Times, Inc. 1985.

Hammond General Hospital under Maj. John Carter Brown from January 1, 1863, until transferred to South Carolina in February 1863.

**8th New York National Guard (New York State Militia Companies A & G. Detachment commanded by Capt. Anthony S. Woods, Company G)**: Assigned as laborers and guards to Capt. Abraham Edwards, Assistant Quartermaster at Hammond General Hospital. July 1862–August, 1862 (mustered out in September 1862 and reformed into another New York regiment.)

**85th Pennsylvania Infantry (2 companies)**: Arrived August 1862. Relieved December 2, 1862. Served as hospital guards. Detachment commanded by Capt. Nicholas Hager, Company F.

**2nd Maryland (Eastern Shore):** Commanded by Col. Robert S. Rodgers. Stationed as hospital guards attached to the "1st Separate Brigade." Departed June 1863.

**1st Regiment, Maryland Potomac Home Brigade**: Stationed at Point Lookout from early June 1863 to June 25, 1863, when the regiment was withdrawn for what would be the Gettysburg Campaign. Parts of the regiment may have been in St. Mary's County during May 1863.

**2nd New Hampshire Volunteer Infantry**: Arrived July 30, 1863, until detached and transferred to the XVIII Army Corps on April 7, 1864, to participate in the spring "Overland Campaign." Assigned to the garrison at Point Lookout on August 1, 1863.

**5th New Hampshire Volunteer Infantry**: Arrived November 14, 1863. They returned to the II Army Corps on May 27, 1864, to Yorktown, VA.

**12th New Hampshire Volunteer Infantry**: Arrived July 30, 1863, and stationed at Point Lookout until April 7, 1864, when detached and transferred from Point Lookout to join the XVIII Army Corps in Yorktown, VA, to participate in the spring, "Overland Campaign."

**4th Rhode Island Volunteer Infantry**: Arrived April 1, 1864. Detached and transferred on July 18, 1864.

**139th Ohio National Guard (100 days regiment)**: Arrived at Point Lookout May 1864 until mustered out of service August 22, 1864, from Point Lookout.

### Artillery

**Battery "F", 1st Rhode Island Light Artillery**: Stationed at Point Lookout December 23, 1863, until relieved by orders to Yorktown, VA, January 23, 1864.

**2nd Battery, Wisconsin Independent Light Artillery**: The 2nd arrived January 23, 1864 (relieved Battery "F," 1st Rhode Island Light Artillery). Transferred on July 1865.

### United States Colored Troops (U.S.C.T.)

**4th Regiment of Infantry, U.S.C.T.**: Sent to Point Lookout from Yorktown, Virginia early April 1864 until the end of April 1864 for reason of transfer to the Army of the Potomac.

**10th Regiment of Infantry, U.S.C.T.**: 5 Companies reported on or before April 30, 1865.

**20th Regiment of Infantry, U.S.C.T.**: 5 Companies reported on or before April 30, 1865.

**24th Regiment of Infantry, U.S.C.T.**: May 28, 1865–July 16, 1865. One company (Company B) remained at Point Lookout until the post was officially closed.

**28th Regiment of Infantry, U.S.C.T.**: Arrived April 6, 1865; transferred May 12, 1865.

**29th Connecticut Infantry, (Colored)**: Arrived April 18, 1865; transferred May 28, 1865.

**36th Regiment of Infantry (formerly the 2nd North Carolina), U.S.C.T.**: February 28, 1864–July 1, 1864. It was then transferred to the Army of the James.

### Veteran Reserve Corps (V.R.C.)

**10th V.R.C.**: Organized in New York City, NY, October 10, 1863. The 10th had mustered out by companies July 7, 1865–November 16, 1865. Two companies stationed at Point Lookout June 30, 1864.

**11th V.R.C.**: Organized at Elmira, NY, October 10, 1863. They were stationed at Point Lookout on April 24, 1864. They were eventually mustered out by companies between June 29 and November 1865.

**20th V.R.C.**: Organized in Baltimore, MD, January 12, 1864. Stationed at Point Lookout from May 1864 until the last company was mustered out by companies on November 1, 1865.

**34th Company, 2nd Battalion (consolidated with 20th Company, 2nd Battalion), V.R.C., formerly Company "G," 18th Veteran Reserve Corps**: Organized in Nashville, TN, August 1863. Designation changed April 25, 1864. Mustered out with the detachment at Point Lookout on June 29, 1865.

**166th Company, 2nd Battalion, V.R.C.**: Organized at Point Lookout and assigned to Hammond General Hospital from April 24, 1864; mustered out on August 24, 1865.

# Bibliography

## Primary Sources

### Archival and Manuscript Collections


Arkansas State Archives, Little Rock, AR.

Evans Atwood. Diary.

Bowditch, Charles P., War Letters. Unpublished manuscript, Aug. 7, 1864, Family Papers Massachusetts Historical Society. Boston, MA.

Camenga, Dietrich. Letter, Kathy Kleiman. Personal Collection.

Hesburgh Libraries, University of Notre Dame, Notre Dame, IN.

Read Family. Correspondence.

National Archives and Records Administration, Washington, D.C.

Colonel Henry Brewerton to Brig. Gen. Richard Delafield, January 5, 1865, Records 77 File Number 989, DeGrange Index 1864-1865.

District of St. Mary's. Press Copies of Letters and Telegrams Sent, Books 251-258. 1863-1865. Washington, D.C., n.d.

Letters, Lists of People, Prisoner Financial Records, Prisoner Lists, Vessels Boarded, 1864–1865. Vols. 376–378. Washington, D.C. n.d.

"List of Confederate Soldiers, Sailors and Civilians Who Died While Prisoners of War, Died at Point Lookout, Maryland." In *Register of Confederate Soldiers, Sailors and Civilians Who Died in Federal Prisons and Military Hospitals in the North. 1861–1865*, 530–612. Washington, D.C.: National Archives Microfilm Publications, 1972.

Records of the Office of the Chief of Engineers. Record Group 77.

Records of the Office of the Quartermaster Department. Record Group 92.

Register of Confederate Soldiers, Sailors, and Citizens Who Died in Federal Prisons and Military Hospitals in the North. Washington D.C., n.d. Microfilm. M-918 Roll-1.

U.S. War Department, U.S. Army Corps of Engineers. Annual Report for Year Ending 30th June 1865, (Fort Monroe, Fort Wool, and Field Works at Point Lookout, DeGrange Index, RG 77, b1692 (New York City, NY, 1865).

Point Lookout State Park, Point Lookout, MD.

Eleanor Ford. Letter collection.

South Carolina Historical Society, Charleston, SC.

Baker Family Papers.

Erastus Watson Everson. Papers.

South Caroliniana Library, Columbia, SC.

Flinn, J. William. Papers.

James T. Wells. Letter.

Special Collections and University Archives, University of Maryland Libraries.

Point Lookout Civil War Collection.

Thomas, James William, 1st Sgt. Co. A, 1st Maryland CSA. *The Diary of.*

(St. Mary's Historical Society collection). Cooper-Trent Lithographic Corporation.

University of Michigan William L Clements Library, Ann Arbor, MI.

Point Lookout Prison Camp, 1863–1865. Collection.

Virginia Historical Society, Richmond, VA.

James Franklin. Diary.

War Department, Office of the Commissary General of Prisoners. *Morning Report of Prisoners of War. Point Lookout, MD.* Report no. 241. 1863.

## Published Sources and Government Series

Adams, Charles Francis, Jr. *A Cycle of Adams Letters 1861–1865.* Edited by Worthington Chauncey Ford. 2 vols. Boston, MA: Houghton Mifflin, 1920.

Adams, John W. *My Experiences as Army Chaplain.* Westbrook, ME, n.d.

Allen, George H. *Forty-Six Months with the Fourth Rhode Island Volunteers, in the War of 1861 to 1865. History of Its Marches, Battles, and Camp Life.* Providence, RI: J. A. and R. A. Reid, 1887.

"Appendix I Section VI. National Cemeteries." In *Proclamations and Orders,* 595–604. Vol. 2. National Park Service, n.d.

Barnes, Joseph K., Joseph Javier Woodward, Charles Smart, George A. Otis, and D. L. Huntington, comps. *The Medical and Surgical History of the War of the Rebellion (1861–65).* 6 vols. Washington, D.C.: Government Printing Office, 1888.

Benson, Barry. *Berry Benson's Civil War Book: Memoirs of a Confederate Scout and Sharpshooter.* Edited by Susan Williams Benson. Athens, GA: University of Georgia Press, 1992.

Blakeman, A. Noel, ed. *Personal Recollections of the War of the Rebellion.* New York: G. P. Putnam's Sons, 1912.

Butler, Benjamin F. *Private and Official Correspondence of General Benjamin F. Butler: During the Period of the Civil Way.* Vol. 4. Norwood, MA: Plimpton Press, 1917.

Child, William. *Letters from a Civil War Surgeon: The Letters of Dr. William Child of the Fifth New Hampshire Volunteers*. Solon, ME.: Polar Bear, 2001.

*Deserters, Prisoners Exchanged, Received and Released, Refugees. 1863–1865*. Vols. 369–370. Point Lookout, MD, n.d..

Douglas, Henry Kyd. *I Rode with Stonewall, Being Chiefly the War Experiences of the Youngest Member of Jackson's Staff from the John Brown Raid to the Hanging of Mrs. Surratt*. Chapel Hill, NC: University of North Carolina Press, 1940.

Gibbons, Abby Hopper. *Life of Abby Hopper Gibbons: Told Chiefly through Her Correspondence*. Edited by Sarah Hopper Emerson. 2 vols. New York: J. P. Putnam's and Sons, 1897.

Hall, James E. *The Diary of a Confederate Soldier*. Edited by Ruth Woods Dayton. Lynchburg, OH. Commonwealth Book Co. 2020.

Haynes, Martin A. *A Soldier Boy's Letter to "The Girl I Left Behind Me": 1861–1864*. 1916 ed. Lakeport, NH: Self Published, n.d.

Howard, McHenry. *Recollections of a Maryland Confederate Soldier and Staff Officer under Johnston, Jackson, and Lee*. Baltimore: Williams and Wilkins Company, 1914.

Hubbs, G. Ward, ed. *Voices from Company D: Diaries by the Greensboro Guards, Fifth Alabama Infantry Regiment, Army of Northern Virginia*. Athens, GA: University of Georgia Press, 2003.

Hutt, Charles Warren. "The Diary of Charles Warren Hutt." *St. Mary's Chronicles*, May 1970. Monthly Bulletin of St. Mary's County Historical Society. Vol. 18, no.4

Johnson, Bradley. "My Ride around Baltimore in 1864." In *Southern Historical Society Papers*, edited by R. A. Brock. Vol. 30. Richmond, VA, 1902.

Keiley, A. M. *In Vinculis: Or, the Prisoner of War, Being the Experience of a Rebel in Two Federal Pens, Interspersed with Reminiscences of the Late War, Anecdotes of Southern Generals, Etc.* New York: Blelock and Company, 1866.

Kimmel, Ross M., and Michael P. Musick, comps. *I Am Busy Drawing Pictures: The Civil War Art and Letters of Private John Jacob Omenhausser*. Illustrated by John Jacob Omenhausser. Maryland State Archives, 2014.

Leon, L. *Diary of a Tar Heel Confederate Soldier*. Charlotte, NC: Stone Publishing, 1913.

Lincoln, Abraham. *Nov. 5, 1863–Sept. 12, 1864*. Vol. 7 of *Collected Works of Abraham Lincoln*. New Brunswick, NJ: Rutgers University Press, 1953.

Maryland Department of Natural Resources. *Point Lookout State Park Land Unit Plan*. Annapolis, MD, 1996.

——. Department of Public Improvements. *Master Plan of Development Point Lookout State Park St. Mary's County, Maryland*. Compiled by Rummel, Klepper, & Kahl. Baltimore: Consulting Engineers, 1966.

National Cemetery Administration, comp. *Federal Stewardship of Confederate Dead*. Washington, D.C.: U.S. Department of Veterans Affairs, 2016.

Neese, George Michael. *Three Years in the Confederate Horse Artillery: A Gunner in Chew's Battery, Stuart's Horse Artillery, Army of Northern Virginia*. San Francisco: Pickle Partners Publishing, 2014.

Peyton, George Quintus, comp. *A Civil War Record for 1864–1865*. Edited by Robert Allen Hodge. Fredericksburg, Va. 1981.

Porter, G. W. D. "Nine Months in a Northern Prison." In *April–December, 1878*, edited by Edwin L. Drake, 330–40. Vol. 1 of *The Annals of the Army of Tennessee and Early Western History*. Nashville: A. D. Hayes, 1878.

Risdon, George P. "Letters of Charles P. Risdon, Private. Company F, Twentieth Veteran Reserve Corps." *Chronicles of St. Mary's*, June 1983. Monthly Bulletin of St. Mary's County Historical Society. Volume 31, No. 6.

Shotwell, Randolph Abbott. *The Papers of Randolph Abbott Shotwell.* Edited by Rebecca Cameron and Joseph Gregoire de Roulhoc Hamilton. Vol. 1. North Carolina Historical Commission, 1929.

Spencer, Edward. "Point Lookout." *Overland Monthly and Out West Magazine*. May 1870, 411–422.

Thomas, Armstrong. "Third Book of Diary." In *Thomas Brother of Mattapany, Their Ancestry, the Manor House, Their Descendants*, 72–83. Washington, D.C.: Self Published, 1963.

United States Congress. "An Act for Enrolling and Calling out the National Forces, and for Other Purposes." In *The Statutes at Large, Treaties, and Proclamations*, edited by George P. Sanger, 763. Vol. 12. Boston: Little, Brown and Company, 1863.

United States Department of the Army. "Article IV (129–139)." In *Revised United State Army Regulations of 1861. With an Appendix Containing the Changes and Laws Affecting Army Regulations and Articles of War to June 25,1863.* Washington, D.C.: Government Printing Office, 1863.

——. "Articles 117–129." In *Revised United State Army Regulations of 1861. With an Appendix Containing the Changes and Laws Affecting Army Regulations and Articles of War to June 25,1863.* Washington, D.C.: Government Printing Office, 1863.

——. *Revised United State Army Regulations of 1861. With an Appendix Containing the Changes and Laws Affecting Army Regulations and Articles of War to June 25,1863.* Washington, D.C.: Government Printing Office, 1863.

United States. Naval War Records Office, comp. *War of the Rebellion: Official Records of the Union and Confederate Navies.* Vol. 10. Washington, D.C.: Government Printing Office, 1894.

United States War Department, *The War of the Rebellion: A Compilation of the Official Records of the Union and Confederate Armies.* 128 volumes in 3 series. Washington D.C.; United States Government Printing Office, 1899. Reprint: Historical Times. Harrisburg, Pa. 1971.

Welles, Gideon. *The Civil War Diary of Gideon Welles: Lincoln's Secretary of the Navy.* Edited by William E. Gienapp and Erica L. Gienapp. Urbana, IL: Knox College Lincoln Studies Center and the University of Illinois Press, 2014.

Wilkeson, Frank. *Turned Inside Out: Recollections of a Private Soldier in the Army of the Potomac.* Lincoln, NE: University of Nebraska Press, 1997.

Wood, Robert C., comp. *Confederate Handbook; A Compilation of Important Data and Other Interesting and Valuable Matter Relating to the War between the States, 1861–1865.* New Orleans: Graham Press, 1900.

## Newspapers

*Alexandria* [VA] *Gazette*

*Baltimore News American*

*The Daily Dispatch* [Richmond, VA]

*Daily National Republican* [Washington D.C.]

*Evening Star* [Washington D.C.]

*Hammond Gazette* [Point Lookout, MD]

*The National Republican* [Washington D.C.]

*New York Times*

*Saint Mary's Beacon* [Leonardtown, MD]

*The San Francisco Call*

*Savannah Morning News*

## Secondary Sources

Bartlett, Asa W. *History of the Twelfth Regiment New Hampshire Volunteers in the War of the Rebellion.* Concord, NH: Ira C. Evans, 1897.

Beitzell, Edwin W. *The Jesuit Missions of St. Mary's County, Maryland.* 1959.

——. *Point Lookout Prison Camp for Confederates.* Self published through St. Mary's County Historical Society, 1972.

——. "The Activities of the Freeman's Bureau in Southern Maryland. 1865–1870." *St. Mary's Chronicles* 31, no. 2 (February 1959): 282–89.

——. "Baptisms at Point Lookout." *Chronicles of St. Mary's* 28, no.2 (February 1980).

——. "Story of an Escaped Confederate (Simon Seward)." *St. Mary's Chronicles*, 28, no. 4 (April 1980), 170.

Beringer, Richard E., Herman Hattaway, Archer Jones, and William N. Still, Jr. *Why the South Lost the Civil War.* Athens, GA: University of Georgia Press, 1986.

Blanton, DeAnne, and Lauren M. Cook. *They Fought like Demons: Women Soldiers in the American Civil War.* New York: Vintage, 2003.

Blue, John. *Hanging Rock Rebel: Lt. John Blue's War in West Virginia and the Shenandoah Valley.* Edited by Daniel P. Oates. Shippensburg, PA: Burd Street Press, 1994.

Booth, Geo. W., comp. *Illustrated Souvenir Maryland Line Confederate Soldiers' Home.* Pikesville, MD: Maryland Line Home, 1894.

Boseworth, S. N. "Escaped from Point Lookout Prison." In *Confederate Veteran* 18, no. 10. Edited by S. A. Cunningham. Nashville: United Confederate Veterans, 1910.

Branigin, Elba L. *History of Johnson County Indiana.* Indianapolis, IN: B. F. Bowen, 1913.

Brockett, L. P., and Mary C. Vaughan. *Women's Work in the Civil War: A Record of Heroism, Patriotism and Patience.* Chicago: Zegler, McCurdy, and Company, 1867.

Brown, Dee Alexander. *The Galvanized Yankees.* Lincoln: University of Nebraska Press, 1985.

Bruns, James H. *Crosshairs on the Capital: Jubal Early's Raid on Washington, D.C., July 1864–Reasons, Reactions, and Results.* Havertown, PA: Casemate, 2021.

Bryant, James K., II. *The 36th Infantry United States Colored Troops in the Civil War: A History and Roster.* Jefferson, N.C.: McFarland, 2012.

Buhk, Tobin T. *True Crime in the Civil War: Cases of Murder, Treason, Counterfeiting, Massacre, Plunder, and Abuse.* Mechanicsburg, PA: Stackpole Books, 2012.

Burwell, W. R. "Forbes Lost His Rations." In *Confederate Veteran* 9, no. 12. Edited by S. A. Cunningham. Nashville: United Confederate Veterans, 1903.

Butts, Michèle Tucker. *Galvanized Yankees on the Upper Missouri: The Face of Loyalty.* Boulder: University Press of Colorado, 2003.

Carroll, Dillon J. *Invisible Wounds: Mental Illness and Civil War Soldiers.* Baton Rouge: Louisiana State Press, 2021.

Catton, Bruce. *Grant Take Command.* Boston, MA: Little, Brown and Company, 1969.

Chase, Philip Steven. *Battery F, First Regiment Rhode Island Light Artillery, in the Civil War 1861–1865.* Providence, RI: Snow and Farnham, 1892.

Coddington, Ronald S. *Faces of the Confederacy: An Album of Southern Soldiers and Their Stories.* Baltimore: Johns Hopkins University Press, 2008.

Cone, A. J. "Prison Commander at Point Lookout, M.D." In *Confederate Veteran* 20, no. 11. Edited by S. A. Cunningham. Nashville: United Confederate Veterans, 1912.

Copley, John M. *A Sketch of the Battle of Franklin, Tennessee; With Reminiscences of Camp Douglas.* Widener, AR: Southern Heritage Press, 2012.

Cross, Andrew B. "Military Prison at Point Lookout." *The War and the Christian Commission* (1865): 18–34.

Curtis, Finley P., Jr. "The Black Shadow of the Sixties." In *Confederate Veteran* 24, no. 9. Edited by S. A. Cunningham. Nashville: United Confederate Veterans, 1920.

Davis, George B. *Outlines of International Law with an Account of Its Origin and Sources and of Its Historical Development.* New York: Harper and Brothers Publishing, 1898.

De Loss Love, William. *Wisconsin in the War of the Rebellion: A History of All Regiments and Batteries.* Chicago: Church and Goodman, 1866.

De Vattel, Emmerich. "138. The Right to Weaken an Enemy by Every Justifiable Method." In *Of War*, 344–45. Vol. 3 of *The Law of Nations or the Principles of Natural Law in Four Books* (1758). Lonang Institute, 2005.

Dobak, William A. *Freedom by the Sword: The U.S. Colored Troops, 1862–1867.* Washington, D.C.: U.S. Army Center of Military History, 2011.

Doyle, W. E. "A Confederate Prisoner." In *Confederate Veteran* 34, no. 2. Edited by S. A. Cunningham. Nashville: United Confederate Veterans, 1926.

Drake, Edwin L., ed. *The Annals of the Army of Tennessee and Early Western History: Including a Chronological Summary of Battles and Engagements in the Western Armies of the Confederacy.* Vol. 1. Nashville: A.D. Haynes, 1878.

Dyer, Frederick H. *A Compendium of the War of the Rebellion.* Des Moines, IA: Dyer Publishing, 1908.

Eicher, John H., David J. Eicher, and John Y. Simon. *Civil War High Commands.* Stanford: Stanford University Press, 2001.

Elliott, James Carson. *The Southern Soldier Boy. A Thousand Shots for the Confederacy.* Raleigh, NC: Edwards and Broughton Printing Company, 1907.

Emerson, Gary. "Swallowing the Eagle: The Question of Loyalty at the Elmire Prison Camp." *The Chemung Historical Journal* 2, no. 2 (2016): 6962–6968.

Ernul, J. B. *Life of a Confederate Soldier in a Federal Prison.* Vanceboro, NC, 1908.

Figg, Royall W. *"Where Men Only Dare to Go!" or the Story of a Boy Company.* Richmond, VA: Whitten and Shepperson, 1885.

Fox, William F. *Regimental Losses in the American Civil War, 1861–1865. A Treatise on the Extent and Nature of the Mortuary Losses in the Union Regiments, with Full and Exhaustive Statistics Compiled from the Official Records on File in the State Military Bureaus and at Washington.* Albany, NY: Albany Publishing, 1889.

Goodwin, Doris Kearns. *Team of Rivals: The Political Genius of Abraham Lincoln.* New York: Simon & Schuster, 2005.

Graber, H. W. *A Terry Texas Ranger: The Life Record of H. W. Graber.* Austin, TX: State House Press, 1987.

Gray, Michael P. *The Business of Captivity: Elmira and Its Civil War Prison.* Kent, OH: Kent State University Press, 2001.

Hammett, Regina Combs. *History of St. Mary's County, Maryland 1634–1990.* R. C. Hammett, 1991.

Harman, N. F. "Forbes Lost His Rations." In *Confederate Veteran* 15, no. 9. Edited by S. A. Cunningham. Nashville: United Confederate Veterans, 1907.

Haynes, Martin A. *A History of the Second Regiment New Hampshire Volunteer Infantry, in the War of the Rebellion.* Lakeport, NH, 1996.

Heidler, David Stephen, Jeanne T. Heidler, David J. Coles, and James M. McPherson. *Encyclopedia of the American Civil War: A Political, Social, and Military History.* Santa Barbara, CA: ABC-CLIO, 2000.

Hesseltine, William B. *Civil War Prisons.* Kent, OH: Kent State University Press, 1972. (First appeared in *Civil War History* 8, no. 2, under James I. Robertson, Jr. editor).

Holland, Thomas Erskine. *The Laws of War on Land: Written and Unwritten.* London: Dalton House, 2018.

Holliday, B. T. "Vain Efforts for Avoid Prison." In *Confederate Veteran* 28, no. 10. Edited by S. A. Cunningham. Nashville: United Confederate Veterans, 1920.

Holmes, Clay W. *The Elmira Prison Camp: A History of the Military Prison at Elmira, N.Y, July 6, 1864 to July 10, 1865.* Vol. 6. Wilmington, NC: Broadfoot Publishing, 1993. First published 1889–1890 by Rhode Island Soldiers and Sailors Historical Society.

——. *The Elmira Prison Camp. Read by Clay W. Holmes of Elmira, Companion by Inheritance, February 7, 1912. Personal Recollections of the War of the Rebellion.* 4th ed. Edited by A. Noel Blakeman. Wilmington, NC: Broadfoot Publishing, 1992.

Hopkins, Luther. *From Bull Run to Appomattox.* Create Space Independent Publishing, 2012.

Huffman, James. *Ups and Downs of a Confederate Soldier.* New York: William E. Rudge's Sons, 1940.

Humphries, William S. "Escaped from Point Lookout Prison." In *Confederate Veteran* 19, no. 7. Edited by S. A. Cunningham. Nashville: United Confederate Veterans, 1911.

Izlar, William Valmore. *A Sketch of the War Record of the Edisto Rifles, 1861–1985*. Columbia, S.C.: August Kohn, 1914.

Johnson, Bradley T. "Confederate Dead in Maryland." In *Confederate Veteran* 5, no. 12. Edited by S. A. Cunningham. Nashville: United Confederate Veterans, 1897.

Johnston, David Emmons. *The Story of a Confederate Boy in the Civil War*. Portland, OR: Glass and Prudhomme, 1914.

Jones, Freeman W. "Addendum to an Escape from Point Lookout." In *War Talks of Confederate Veterans*, compiled by George S. Bernard. Petersburg, VA: Fenn and Owen Publishers, 1892.

Jones, G. W. *In Prison at Point Lookout*. Martinsville, VA: Bulletin Printing and Publishing, n.d.

Jones, T. Cole. *Captives of Liberty: Prisoners of War and the Politics of Vengeance in the American Revolution*. Philadelphia: University of Pennsylvania Press, 2020.

King, Curtis S., William Glenn Robertson, and Steven E. Clay. *Staff Ride Handbook for the Overland Campaign, Virginia, 4 May to 15 June 1864: A Study in Operational-level Command*. Fort Leavenworth, KS.: Combat Studies Institute Press, 2006.

King, John R. *My Experience in the Confederate Army and in Northern Prisons*. Clarksburg, WV: United Daughters of Confederacy, 1917.

LaBarre, Steven M. *The Fifth Massachusetts Colored Cavalry in the Civil War*. Jefferson, NC: McFarland & Company, 2016.

Lanier, Sydney. *Tiger Lilies: A Novel*. New York: Hurd and Houghton, 1867.

Levin, Kevin M. *Searching for Black Confederates: The Civil War's Most Persistent Myth*. Chapel Hill: University of North Carolina Press, 2019.

Livermore, Thomas L. *Dates and Events 1860–1866*. Boston: Houghton Mifflin, 1920.

Loehr, Charles T. "Point Lookout." In *Southern Historical Society Papers* 18. Edited by R. A. Brock. Richmond, VA, 1890.

——. "The Treatment of Prisoners." In *Southern Historical Society Papers* 18. Edited by R. A. Brock, Richmond, VA, 1890.

Longacre, Edward G. *A Regiment of Slaves: The 4th United States Colored Infantry, 1863–1866*. Lincoln: Bison Books/University of Nebraska Press, 2003.

Lord, Francis A. *Civil War Sutlers and Their Wares*. Cranbury, 1969.

Luecke, Barbara K. *Feeding the Frontier Army*. St. Paul, MN: Grenadier Publications, 2011.

Malone, Bartlett Yancey. *Whipt'em Everytime*. Edited by William Whatley Pierson, Jr and Bell Irvin Wiley. Wilmington, NC: Broadfoot Publishing, 1987.

"Marking Graves of Confederate Prisoners." In *Confederate Veteran* 51, no. 3. Edited by S. A. Cunningham. Nashville: United Confederate Veterans, 1897.

Masur, Louis P. *Lincoln's Hundred Days: The Emancipation Proclamation and the War for the Union*. Cambridge, MA: Belknap Press of Harvard University Press, 2012.

Mazoli, Nathan A. "Not the Soldiers We Need." *Army History* (Fall 2022): 38–54.

McBride, Alan J. A., Daniel A. Athanazio, Mitermayer G. Reis, and Albert I. Ko. "Leptospirosis." *Current Opinion in Infectious Diseases* 18, no. 5 (2005): 376–86.

McPherson, James. *Ordeal by Fire: The Civil War and Reconstruction*. New York: Alfred A. Knopf, 1982.

"Monument at Point Lookout, MD." In *Confederate Veteran* 19, no. 3. Edited by S. A. Cunningham. Nashville: United Confederate Veterans, 1911.

Neff, Stephen C. *Justice in Blue and Gray: A Legal History of the Civil War.* Cambridge, Mass.: Harvard University Press, 2010.

Park, Captain Robert E. "Diary of Captain Robert E. Park, of Twelfth Alabama Regiment." In *Southern Historical Society Papers* 2, compiled by Southern Historical Society and Rev. J. William Jones, 25–31. Richmond, VA: Open Court Publishing, 1876–07.

Plante, Trevor K. "The National Home for Disabled Volunteer Soldiers." *Prologue Magazine* (Spring 2004): 1.

"Reunited at Gettysburg." In *Confederate Veteran* 30, no. 12. Edited by S. A. Cunningham. Nashville: United Confederate Veterans, 1922.

Richter, Rick. *Three Cheers for the Chesapeake! History of the 4th Maryland Light Artillery Battery in the Civil War.* Schiffer Publishing, 2017.

Robertson, James I. *Tenting Tonight: The Soldier's Life.* Alexandria, VA: Time Life Education, 1984.

Rorabaugh, W. J. *The Alcoholic Republic: An American Tradition.* New York: Oxford University Press, 1979.

Sanders, Charles W. *While in the Hands of the Enemy: Military Prisons of the Civil War.* Baton Rouge: Louisiana State University Press, 2005.

Seward, Simon. "An Escape from Point Lookout." In *War Talks of Confederate Veterans.* Edited by George S. Bernard, 77–86. Petersburg, VA: Fenn and Owen, 1892.

——. "Perilous Escape from Point Lookout." In *Confederate Veteran* 19. Edited by S. A. Cunningham. Nashville: United Confederate Veterans, 1911.

Smith, Thomas West. *The Story of a Cavalry Regiment "Scott's 900" Eleventh New York Cavalry, from the St. Lawrence River to the Gulf of Mexico, 1861–1865.* Chicago: Veteran Association of the Regiment, 1897.

Spar, Ira. *Civil War Hospital Newspapers: Histories and Excerpts of Nine Union Publications.* Jefferson, NC: McFarland & Company, Inc., Publishers, 2017.

Speer, Lonnie R. *Portals to Hell: Military Prisons of the Civil War.* Mechanicsburg, PA: Stackpole Books, 1997.

Stahr, Walter. *Seward: Lincoln's Indispensable Man.* New York City: Simon & Schuster, 2012.

Stevens, John W. *Reminiscences of the Civil War: A Soldier in Hood's Texas Brigade, Army of Northern Virginia.* Middletown, DE: Old South Books, 2017. First published 1902 by Hillsboro Mirror Print.

Story-Dennis, Chandler Woodhouse, ed. *My Beloved Wife, Be Hopeful: 1864–1865 Letters from Henry: Surviving Point Lookout Civil War Prison Camp.* Virginia Beach, VA: Story Book House, 2019.

Stotz, Charles Morse. "Defense in the Wilderness." In *Drums in the Forest*, 2nd ed., by James Alfred Proctor, Historical Society of Western Pennsylvania, and Charles Morse Stotz. Pittsburgh: University of Pittsburgh Press, 2005.

Styple, William B., ed. *Writing and Fighting from the Army of Northern Virginia.* Kearny, N.J.: Belle Grove Pub., 2003.

Sword, Gerald J. "The Civil War Forts of Point Lookout Prison Camp for Confederates." *Chronicles of St. Mary's* 32, no. 6 (June 1984).

——. "Confederate Cemetery. Point Lookout." *Chronicles of St. Mary's* 27, no. 12 (December 1979).

——. "Hammond General Hospital. Point Lookout, Maryland." *Chronicles of St. Mary's* 31, no. 2 (February 1983).

——. "Sword House/Cove." *Chronicles of St. Mary's* (March 1954): 9.

——. "Where the Union Soldiers Slept. (Federal Dead at Point Lookout, Maryland)." *Chronicles of St. Mary's* 33, no. 3 (March 1985).

——. "Where the Union Soldiers Slept (Federal Dead at Point Lookout, Maryland)." *Chronicles of St. Mary's* 33, no. 2 (March 1985).

Sutton, E. H. *Civil War Stories*. Demores, GA, 1910.

Thompson, Holland. "Life in the Prisons." In *the Photographic History of The Civil War*, edited by Holland Thompson, Francis Trevelyan Miller, and Robert S. Lanier, 124–36. Vol. 7. Springfield, MA: Patriot Publishing, 1911.

Traywick, J. B. "Prison Life at Point Lookout." In *Southern Historical Society Papers* 18, edited by R. A. Brock, 431–435. Richmond: Published by the Society, 1890.

Triebe, Richard H. *Point Lookout Prison Camp and Hospital: The North's Largest Civil War Prison.* Wilmington, NC: Coastal Books, 2016.

Vattel, Emer de, Bela Kapossy, and Richard Whatmore. *The Law of Nations, Or, Principles of the Law of Nature, Applied to the Conduct and Affairs of Nations and Sovereigns, with Three Early Essays on the Origin and Nature of Natural Law and on Luxury*. Indianapolis: Liberty Fund, 2008.

Witt, John Fabian. *Lincoln's Code: The Laws of War in American History*. New York: Free Press, 2012.

## Unpublished

Bowditch, Charles P., letters to Father and Mother, July 15, and August 7, 1864, Bowditch Family Papers Massachusetts Historical Society, Boston, MA.

Hunter, Leslie Gene. "Warden for the Union: General William Hoffman (1807–1884)." PhD diss., University of Arizona, 1971.

Locke, John Franklin. John Locke Diary. Unpublished typescript, 1861. Provided to the author through his descendant Wilson Locke.

## Audiovisual

Barnes, James. *Rebel Prison Scenes Point Lookout, MD*. 1864. The Historical Archive.

Brewerton, Henry. "First and Third Sections of Rebel Prison at Point Lookout, MD." Map. 1865. Drawer 135, Sheet 21. National Archives, College Park, MD.

*Death and the Civil War*. Directed by Ken Burns. 2018. American Experience, 2018. DVD.

Everett, George. *Point Lookout, Md. View of Hammond Genl. Hospital and U.S. Genl. Deport for Prisoners of War*. Map. Baltimore: E. Sachse and Company, 1864.

Gilbert, E. E. "Point Lookout, Maryland." Map. 1866. RG 92, Entry 576, Box 57. National Archives and Record Administration, Washington, D.C.

*Hammond General Hospital*. Park Information Sign. Point Lookout, MD.

National Oceanographic. "AA Navigational Charts." Map. 2016. Series 1–7.

*Point Lookout.* Illustration. Record Group 92, Entry 576, Box 57. National Archives and Records Administration, Washington, D.C.

Quartermaster. "Drawings and Inventory List Point Lookout, MD." Map. RG 92, Entry 576, Box 57. National Archives and Records Administration, Washington, D.C.

Stewart, Charles S. "Redoubts, Point Lookout." Map. 1864. RG77. S9235. DeGrange Index. Library of Congress, Washington, D.C.

## Websites

The American Presidency Project. "Abraham Lincoln Event Timeline." The American Presidency Project. UC Santa Barbara. Accessed Apr. 3, 2025. https://www.presidency.ucsb.edu/documents abraham-lincoln-event-timeline.

——. "Proclamation 134—Granting Amnesty to Participants in the Rebellion, with Certain Exceptions." The American Presidency Project. UC Santa Barbara. Accessed Apr. 3, 2025. https://www.presidency.ucsb.edu/documents/proclamation-134-granting-amnesty-participants-the-rebellion-with-certain-exceptions.

Davids, Clifford B. "The Assassination of Abraham Lincoln and the Search for John Wilkes Booth as Written by Provost Guard John H. Matthews from Inside Point Lookout Prison, Maryland." Confessions of an Oral Historian (blog), Nov. 5, 2012. Accessed March 29, 2025. https://ashevilleoralhistoryproject.com/2012/11/05/lincoln/.

Delahanty, Ian. "Soldiers' Diaries and Letters." Essential Civil War Curriculum. Virginia Center for Civil War Studies at Virginia Tech. Accessed March 27, 2025. https://www.essentialcivilwarcurriculum.com/soldiers-diaries-and-letters.html.

"Historical Overview." Point Lookout Lighthouse. https://www.ptlookoutlighthouse.com/overview.shtml.

Johnson, Andrew. "Executive Orders—General Orders: 109." The American Presidency Project. University of California Santa Barbara. Last modified June 6, 1865. Accessed Feb. 20, 2025. https://www.presidency.ucsb.edu/documents/executive-order-general-orders-109.

——. "Proclamation 157—Declaring the Peace, Order, Tranquility, and Civil Authority Now Exists in and throughout the Whole of the United States of America." The American Presidency Project. University of California Santa Barbara. Last modified Aug. 20, 1866. Accessed Feb. 20, 2025. https://www.presidency.ucsb.edu/documents/proclamation-157-declaring-that-peace-order-tranquillity-and-civil-authority-now-exists.

——. "Proclamation 134—Granting Amnesty to Participants in the Rebellion, with Certain Exceptions." The American Presidency Project. University of California Santa Barbara. Accessed Feb. 20, 2025. https://www.presidency.ucsb.edu/documents/proclamation-134-granting-amnesty-participants-the-rebellion-with-certain-exceptions.

Lincoln, Abraham. "Proclamation 108—Amnesty and Reconstruction." The American Presidency Project. University of California Santa Barbara. Last modified Dec. 8, 1863. Accessed Apr. 4, 2025. https://www.presidency.ucsb.edu/documents/proclamation-108-amnesty-and-reconstruction.

Marsh, Alan. "POWs in American History: A Synopsis." National Park Service. Last modified 1998. https://www.nps.gov/ande/learn/historyculture/pow_synopsis.htm.

Matthews, John H. "The Assassination of Abraham Lincoln and the Search for John Wilkes Booth." Confessions of an Oral Historian. Clifford B. Davids. Last modified Nov. 12, 2012. Accessed Apr. 16, 2025. https://ashevilleoralhistoryproject.com/2012/11/05/lincoln/.

McCarley, J. Britt. "Feeding Billy Yank: Union Rations Between 1861 and 1865." U.S. Army Quartermaster Museum. Quartermaster Museum. Last modified Dec. 1988. Accessed Mar. 29, 2025. https://qmmuseum.army.mil/main.html.

Office of the Historian. "French Intervention in Mexico and the American Civil War, 1862–1867." Office of the Historian. U.S. Department of State. Accessed Feb. 20, 2025. https://history.state.gov/milestones/1861-1865/french-intervention

O'Malley, Brian Patrick. "What Killed Prisoners of War?—A Medical Investigation." Journal of the American Revolution. Last modified Sept. 21, 2020. Accessed Apr. 8, 2025. https://allthingsliberty.com/author/brian-p-omalley.

Pledger Murphy, John Joseph. "Diary of John Joseph Pledger Murphy, Written While in a Union Prison (Point Lookout, MD.) Being a Confederate Soldier—1865." Edited by Sandy Clark. Georgia American History and Genealogy. American and Genealogy Project. Last modified Oct. 23, 2024. https://ahgp.org/ga/Diary2.html.

Price, Anna. "Pirates, Privateers, and Civil War Maritime Laws." In Custodia Legis Law Librarians of Congress (blog), May 20, 2020. Accessed Apr. 3, 2025. https://blogs.loc.gov/law/2020/05/pirates-privateers-and-civil-war-maritime-laws/.

Sidler, Scott. "How To: Tell If You Have a Balloon House." The Craftsman Blog, Aug. 10, 2015. Accessed Feb. 20, 2025. *https://thecraftsmanblog.com/how-to-tell-if-you-have-a-*balloon-frame-house/.

Simmons, R. Hugh. "Discharges from Fort Delaware April 1865 through January 1866." Fort Delaware Society Going Home. Fort Delaware Society. Last modified Sept. 16, 2014. Accessed Apr. 16, 2025. https://www.fortdelaware.org/Going%20Home%20-%20The%20War%20is%20Over.htm.

——. "Fort Delaware Society Going Home: A Discharge Timeline." Fort Delaware Society. Last modified Sept. 16, 2014. Accessed July 28, 2017. https://fortdelaware.org/Going%20Home%20-%20The%20War%20is%20Over.htm.

# Index

## About the Author

Robert E. Crickenberger Jr. has been studying Point Lookout since 1978 and serves as a volunteer and living historian at Point Lookout State Park. He has authored and designed many interpretive signs, contributed to the park's tour book and museum, and spearheaded restoration efforts for Maryland's only surviving Civil War earthen fort and the prison site itself. He is the President of the Friends of Point Lookout and a Historic Weapons Safety Officer for the Maryland Park Service, earning him the prestigious title of Honorary Ranger. This is his first book.